Learning Disabilities
Best Practices for Professionals

Edited by

William N. Bender, Ph.D.
University of Georgia
Athens, Georgia

With 17 contributing authors

Andover Medical Publishers, Inc.

Boston   London   Oxford   Singapore   Sydney   Toronto   Wellington

Andover Medical Publishers is an imprint of Butterworth-Heinemann.

Library of Congress Cataloging-in-Publication Data

Learning disabilities : best practices for professionals / edited by
  William N. Bender.
    p. cm.
  Includes bibliographical references and index.
  ISBN 1-56372-058-2
  1. Learning disabilities—United States. 2. Learning disabled
children—Education—United States. I. Bender William L.
LC4705.L36 1993
371.9—dc20   92-31024
                                                       CIP

British Library Cataloguing-in-Publication Data

Learning Disabilities : Best Practices for
Professionals
  I. Bender, William N.
  616.85

  ISBN 1-56372-058-2

Butterworth-Heinemann
80 Montvale Avenue
Stoneham, MA 02180

10 9 8 7 6 5 4 3 2 1

Printed in the United States of America

Contents

PART III

INTERVENTIONS FOR LEARNING-DISABLED STUDENTS

Contributors

William N. Bender

William N. Bender, Ph.D., is an Associate Professor of Special Education at the University of Georgia. His interest areas include attention deficit disorders, behavioral/emotional aspects of learning disabilities, collaboration, and effective instructional practices for mainstreamed students. He is the author of two books and more than 35 articles in special education.

Harry L. Dangel

Harry L. Dangel is an Associate Professor of Special Education at Georgia State University. His primary research interests are decision-making processes in assessment and instruction and personnel needs assessment.

Deborah J. Huntington

Deborah J. Huntington will complete her Ph.D. in Special Education at the University of Georgia in 1994. During the past 17 years she has taught students with learning disabilities, mental retardation, and behavior disorders at all grade levels. She is the immediate past president of the Georgia CEC-Mental Retardation Subdivision and is presently serving on a committee of the national CEC-MR division and on the executive committee of the Georgia Confederation.

George W. Hynd

George W. Hynd is a Research Professor of Psychology and Special Education at the University of Georgia and a Clinical Professor of Neurology at the Medical College of Georgia. He has authored or edited 11 books in the area of child/pediatric neuropsychology and has written numerous chapters and articles focusing on issues in child neuropsychology, learning disabilities, and childhood psychopathology. He completed a Fulbright Fellowship in child neuropsychology in Finland and is now the Director of the Center for Clinical and Developmental Neuropsychology at the University of Georgia.

Annette La Greca

Annette La Greca is a Professor of Psychology and Pediatrics and the Director of Child Psychology at the University of Miami. She is currently the president of the "Section on Clinical Psychology" (American Psychological Association, Division 12, Section 1), and editor of the *Journal of Pediatric Psychology*. Her research interests focus on children's peer relationship difficulties and interventions for improving children's social interactions and peer support. These interests have been applied to special populations, such as children with learning disabilities and those with chronic illness. She is currently conducting research on the emotional correlates (i.e., anxiety, low self-esteem) of low peer status among school-age children and on the predictive utility of children's peer relationships for later psychological adjustment.

Richard M. Marshall

Richard M. Marshall, Ph.D., is an assistant professor in the Department of Educational Psychology at the University of Texas with a concentration in child neuropsychology. His research interests include the neuropsychological effects of chronic illness in children, nonverbal learning disabilities, attention deficit disorders, and brain imaging.

Margaret A. Martin

Margaret A. Martin will complete her doctorate in counseling psychology at the University of Georgia in 1993. Previously, she was Assistant Director of Counseling and Career Planning at Alma College in Alma, Michigan. She conducted personal and career individual and group counseling, as well as providing services for students with disabilities. Her current interests are providing individual and group counseling to college and university students on issues such as study skills, acquaintance rape, career counseling, and interpersonal relationships.

Phillip J. McLaughlin

Phillip J. McLaughlin, Ed.D., is an Associate Professor of Special Education at the University of Georgia. His interests are teacher training and career education for youth with mild mental retardation. He has published three books and is currently working on a new text, *Advances in Special Education and Rehabilitation*.

Terry M. McLeod

Terry M. McLeod is a Professor of Special Education at North Georgia College in Dahlonega, Georgia, where he serves as coordinator of the undergraduate

Special Education Program and teaches a variety of special education courses. Other than social skills in students with learning disabilities, his interests include learning disabilities in mathematics, learning disabilities in college students, and educational programming for the nonhandicapped "at risk" learner.

Lisa E. Monda-Amaya

Lisa E. Monda-Amaya, Ph.D., is an Assistant Professor at the University of Illinois, Urbana-Champaign. She is the coordinator of a program preparing teachers of students with mild handicaps in the role of collaborative consultation. Dr. Monda-Amaya's primary interests are in the areas of teacher education, effective instructional practices, mainstreaming, and collaborative consultation. Dr. Monda-Amaya also holds an appointment as a Center Associate at the Center for the Study of Reading.

Fran Reed

Fran Reed is an Assistant Professor of Education at Olivet Nazarene University in Kankakee, Illinois. She is currently completing a Ph.D. in special education at the University of Illinois. Areas of interest include mild disabilities, teacher training, and administration.

Kristin S. Scott

Kristin S. Scott, M.Ed., will complete her doctoral degree at the University of Georgia in 1994. Her major area of focus is children with learning disabilities. Research interests include instructional strategies, metacognitive learning strategies, and generalization aspects of instruction dealing with students with mild disabilities. Ms. Scott has authored several publications on various aspects of learning disabilities.

Sherri Strawser

Sherri Strawser, Ph.D., is currently an Assistant Professor of School Psychology in the Department of Special Education at the University of Nevada, Las Vegas. Dr. Strawser has taught in regular and special education and was a school psychologist in the public school system for 10 years. Her research and teaching interests focus on assessment and issues of adaptive behavior, severity, subtyping, and transition for individuals with learning disabilities. She is the co-author of the *Weller-Strawser Scales of Adaptive Behavior for the Learning Disabled* and has had numerous other publications in the field.

H. Lee Swanson

H. Lee Swanson is a Professor of Education at the University of California, Riverside. He received his Ph.D. from the University of California. He is also the editor of *Learning Disabilities Quarterly*. His research interests include information processing and individual differences found among children with learning disabilities, including the application of cognitive models to the understanding of performance deficits. He has published numerous books and scholarly articles in the field.

Cynthia O. Vail

Cynthia O. Vail, Ph.D., is an Assistant Professor of Special Education at the University of Georgia, where she also co-directs two early intervention personnel preparation grants at the master's and doctoral levels. She also has worked as a teacher of young children with emotional/behavioral disorders. Dr. Vail has written and coauthored numerous articles on topics such as behavior management and has made many national and regional presentations. Her current research interests include the effects of setting events on play and social interactions of preschoolers with behavior disorders.

Sharon Vaughn

Sharon Vaughn is a Professor at the University of Miami in the departments of Teaching and Learning and Psychology. She has taught youngsters with learning disabilities in the public schools. Her research interests focus on the social functioning of youngsters with learning disabilities, particularly on developing effective interventions to improve their social behavior and increase their peer acceptance. She is presently conducting a four-year investigation of general education teachers' planning and adaptations for students with special needs.

Carol Weller

Carol Weller, Ed.D., is an Associate Professor in the Department of Special Education at the University of Utah. Her research focuses on identification and assessment of differential subtypes and severities of learning-disabled individuals throughout the life cycle. Her publications and products have addressed assessment of mild, moderate, and severe learning problems; adaptive behavior or subtypes and severities of learning-disabled individuals; language disorders of young adults; and transition from school to work for employment in advanced technology industries. In addition, she administers the research, assessment, and instrument-development activities of the Center for Base Technical Education and Transition. She is the governor of the Division for Research of the Council for Exceptional Children and is also the Administrator of Research Program Information in the Office of the Vice President for Research.

Preface

THE READERS

This book is intended to assist the teacher, parent, and/or medical practitioner to understand the current thinking in the field of learning disabilities (LD), as well as current practices in that field. There are many occasions in which mainstream teachers, school administrators, guidance counselors, and/or medical personnel may need information on the best available practices for working with children with LD. For example, when parents are first informed that their child may have a learning disability, they often would like to have a quick overview of the issues and best practices in the field, in order to assist them in making informed decisions in conjunction with the members of the administrative placement team. This book is written at a level that should be appropriate for the educated parent.

Likewise, physicians may wish to obtain information concerning the current thinking on the relationship between school-based behavioral interventions for hyperactivity and medically recommended drug interventions. This text provides information for school personnel to consider in discussions of potential drug interventions.

Finally, every effort has been made in each chapter to present the "best practices" in use in the field today. For example, the information on metacognitive instructional techniques represents the most recent instructional emphasis in the field of LD.

THE PARTS OF THE BOOK

This book is divided into three parts. Each part is introduced by a brief heading that presents a set of facts giving certain parameters relative to the information in that section.

Part I describes the characteristics that are typically associated with LD. While not all students with LD demonstrate each of these characteristics, these types of difficulties are indicative of a learning disability. The first chapter discusses the medical bases of LD, while the next two chapters discuss the cognitive characteristics and social/emotional characteristics, respectively.

Part II describes the measurement of various characteristics. Chapter 4 traces various historical conceptualizations of LD, in order to show the rationale for the measurement procedures that are currently in use to identify a student with LD. The next chapter discusses classroom-based assessment, which must be used for effective instructional programming. Chapter 6 presents a discussion of the identification team meeting process, in order to facilitate understanding of the appropriate roles of the various professionals and lay people involved.

Part III presents information on the best practices currently employed in the field. The first two chapters discuss behavioral management approaches to instruction and metacognitive instruction, respectively. The next three chapters present information on several special instruction problem areas, including language instruction, social skills training, and interventions for attention problems. The last two chapters present information related to postschool endeavors of students with LD, including vocational transition strategies and college instructional strategies.

USE OF THIS TEXT

As mentioned previously, this book is intended to present the current "best practices" to several different audiences, including parents, practitioners—both in this and other fields—and researchers. The chapters in this book can be read and utilized independently or in conjunction with other chapters. For example, if the school district wishes to have a parent consider a medically based intervention for the child and the parent wants additional information on that type of intervention, the chapter on interventions for attention problems could be read in isolation. On the other hand, a physician who notes an increase in his or her interaction with school persons involving students with LD may wish to quickly read through the entire book. In either case, the information presented here can be used as a discussion starter between the various professionals and parents working with a child who has a learning disability.

THE AUTHORS

I am particularly proud of the group of authors who participated in the preparation of this book. Each of these professionals has years of experience in the field of LD, and many are well-recognized scholars in the field.

Acknowledgments

I wish to thank my wife, C. Renet Lovorn-Bender, without whose constant, vigilant assistance this book would not have reached completion. I would also like to thank Deborah Huntington for her assistance in the editorial preparation of this text.

Learning Disabilities

Characteristics of Students with Learning Disabilities

This section includes three chapters that investigate the various characteristics typically associated with learning disabilities (LD). Certain characteristics such as attention and social skills are discussed later in the book. However, the information in this section should give the reader a broad understanding of students with LD.

FACT SHEET ON CHARACTERISTICS

While easy generalizations about the characteristics of particular children with LD should be avoided, there are many cognitive and behavioral similarities among these children and adolescents. The information below is intended to present the basic characteristics associated with LD.

- Students with verbal LD tend to be male, and ratios of 3 to 1 or 4 to 1 (male to female) are not uncommon in some school classes. However, students with nonverbal LD are more rare, and those disabilities tend to be equally split between the sexes.
- Students with LD tend to have IQs in the low- to mid-90s, or slightly below the average of 100. This is because of language skills that are measured on most IQ tests.
- Postmortem studies of students with LD reveal some brain abnormalities, which may account for the learning disability.
- Students with LD tend to have problems in memory processing, which leads to difficulty in academic work. These problems are associated with strategic thinking and the ability to move awareness of a stimuli from short-term to long-term memory. These students have a long-term memory that is comparable to that of non–students with LD.
- Students with LD tend to have a lower self-concept than do non–students with LD.

- Students with LD tend to be more external in their locus of control and attributions than other students.
- Students with LD tend to exhibit behavioral abnormalities that, frequently, distinguish between students with LD and those without. These behaviors include high levels of off-task behavior in the classroom, inability to get along with peers, and high levels of impulsivity.

1

Neurological Basis
of Learning Disabilities

Richard M. Marshall
George W. Hynd

Learning disabilities (LD) have been associated with central nervous system (CNS) disturbances since Bastian (1898), Hinshelwood (1900), and Morgan (1896) first presented accounts of children with normal intellectual functioning who had problems achieving appropriate academic skills. Numerous theories have been proposed to explain the biological substrate of LD, but most have not withstood tests of scientific scrutiny. Despite the intuitive appeal of a neurobiological etiology, until recently there have been few hard data to support a direct link between CNS status and LD.

There are at least two explanations for the lack of data. First, despite the discoveries by Broca and Wernicke in the midnineteenth century, it was not until the end of that century that the first postmortem studies on patients with acquired alexia were conducted by Dejerine (Geschwind 1985). Interestingly, Morgan and Hinshelwood postulated that the anomaly causing the congenital "word blindness" they described would be in the same brain area that Dejerine had identified in acquired alexia. Unfortunately, further efforts to locate this anomaly in other patients were abandoned until Galaburda and Kemper (1979) renewed the search for localized anomalies using postmortem techniques. Simply put, the first problem in establishing a relationship between brain anomalies and LD was that, as Geschwind (1985) put it, "no one looked."

The second problem is that until recently researchers did not possess the technology to answer the questions they asked. Recent advances in electrophysiology and neuroimaging provide information about brain structure and function that had previously been inaccessible.

In the past two decades, postmortem and neuroimaging studies have provided important new information regarding possible relationships between brain structure and learning. At the same time, however, this technology is providing evidence that sites of putative anomalies may not be precisely located nor

The brain imaging research conducted at the University of Georgia and discussed in this chapter was supported by a grant from the Donald D. Hammill Foundation. This support is gratefully acknowledged.

3

uniformly situated in all persons. Before discussing the most recent contributions to the neurobiological foundations of LD, it is helpful to review how certain functional brain–behavior relationships came to be localized.

LOCALIZATION OF FUNCTION

Benton (1984) provides a succinct history of the medical literature on hemispheric dominance prior to Broca that suggests a relationship between speech disorders and left hemisphere disease. Benton's review begins with Hippocrates and focuses on the work of Morgnani in the late eighteenth century and Bouillaud and Andral in the early nineteenth century. One of the purposes of Benton's review is to "discuss possible reasons for the failure to perceive the association [between aphasic disorders and diseases of the left hemisphere]" (Benton 1984, p. 808).

Benton's history ends with Marc Dax, the French physician who first formulated the hypothesis relating left hemisphere disease to aphasia. Unfortunately, Dax never published his findings. A summary of his work was published by his son in 1865, two years after Broca presented his findings of nine patients with "aphemia" (later termed *aphasia*) at the Paris Medical Society.

It is Broca, of course, who is credited with the discovery that damage to the left frontal cortex results in expressive aphasia. Broca's area is fairly well circumscribed, and neuroanatomists generally agree that it includes the third convolution of the left hemisphere (Bogen and Bogen 1976). (See Figure 1.1.)

The second major contribution to the localization of function was made by Wernicke in 1874. He postulated that damage at the juncture of the left parietal, temporal, and occipital lobes results in receptive aphasia. Unlike Broca's area, which is well defined, the precise boundaries of Wernicke's area have been the subject of considerable controversy. Bogen and Bogen (1976) provide 17 differing descriptions of its geographic boundaries. Generally, however, it is believed to encompass the posterior third of the left superior temporal gyrus. (See Figure 1.1.)

After Broca and Wernicke, the next important step in specifying a link between brain lesions and language functions was made by the French neurologist Dejerine in 1891 and 1892. Using postmortem procedures, Dejerine demonstrated that lesions in Wernicke's area produced alexia. In fact, Dejerine was able to specify that a lesion in one region of Wernicke's area produced alexia with agraphia while lesions in another region produced alexia without agraphia.

By the end of the nineteenth century, it was established that lesions in reasonably well-defined areas of the left cerebral cortex resulted in a variety of receptive and expressive language disorders. As Dejerine had shown, alexia without agraphia involved an apparent sparing of all abilities except reading, suggesting that reading (like speech) had a specific locus in the left hemisphere.

In the late 1890s, when Morgan and Hinshelwood presented their cases of congenital word blindness, they described symptoms similar to alexia with agraphia, that is, loss of a specific language ability—in this case, reading. Furthermore, they theorized that the area of involvement in congenital word

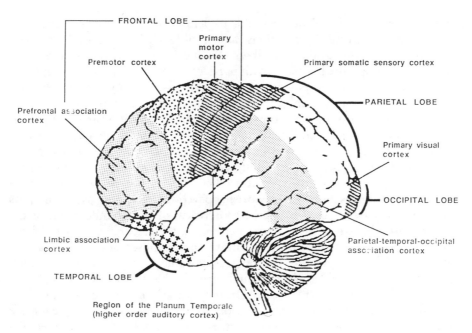

FRONTAL LOBE

Primary motor cortex

Premotor cortex

Prefrontal association cortex

Primary somatic sensory cortex

PARIETAL LOBE

Primary visual cortex

OCCIPITAL LOBE

Limbic association cortex

Parietal-temporal-occipital association cortex

TEMPORAL LOBE

Region of the Planum Temporale (higher order auditory cortex)

Figure 1.1 The brain as viewed in horizontal section. The major pathways and cortical regions thought to be involved in fluent reading are depicted. Neurolinguistic processes important in reading are also noted. (From G. W. Hynd and C. R. Hynd 1984 with permission.) It should be pointed out that this proposed neurolinguistic model may place too much emphasis on processes lateralized to the left cerebral hemisphere. Bastian (1898) argued cogently that bilateral central-posterior processes were involved in reading—an idea that has recently received some tentative support from an examination of rCBF in normal readers while they read controlled narrative text. ("Dyslexia: Neuroanatomical Neurolinguistic Perspectives," *Reading Research Quarterly, 19,* 482–498.)

blindness was the same area Dejerine had implicated in acquired alexia. This important connection between a brain anomaly and specific language disorders would not be confirmed, however, for another 83 years.

In the late nineteenth and early twentieth centuries, there was a major reaction against the localizationist position that human behaviors (speech, hand movements, walking) were located in well-defined areas of the cerebral cortex. At a theoretical level, opponents of localization argued that it was another form of phrenology. Even more damaging evidence came in 1892 (at about the time of Dejerine's postmortems) when Friedrich Goltz provided experimental evidence refuting the localizationist position. Goltz's experiment was a simple procedure, but it had profound consequences on the localizationist position. Following removal of the neocortex, major portions of the basal ganglia, and parts of the midbrain from three dogs, Goltz was able to demonstrate preservation of simple motor, orienting, and feeding functions that should have been lost had they been housed in specific cortical sites. Faced with such evidence, the localizationist position correlating specific behaviors with particular anatomical sites was replaced with the antilocalizationist position that behavior—especially complex human behavior—results from widespread interconnected neural networks.

It was into this antilocalizationist climate that the notion that congenital language disorders seemed similar in many ways to acquired language disorders was introduced. But as psychologists attempted to explain the causal mechanism of congenital language disorders (as well as disturbances in perceptual motor processing and hyperactivity-distractibility), they looked not to possible neurobiological mechanisms but to behaviorism, psychophysics, and psychoanalysis (Kolb and Whishaw 1980). Lest we be too critical of this abandonment of the study of the brain, we need to remember that these researchers did not have anatomical techniques that provided accurate, in vivo observation and measurement, and their postmortem and lesion studies sometimes produced contradictory evidence. For example, even though specific behavior changes could be linked to focal brain lesions, removal of entire brain sections did not produce consistent and predictable changes in behavior. Facing this contradictory evidence and lacking the technology for accurate measurement, psychologists and educators eschewed neurobiological explanations of learning and behavior.

MINIMAL BRAIN DAMAGE

Because of the global disruptions caused by two world wars and global depression, scientific research into the neurological correlates of developmental disorders slowed dramatically during the first half of the twentieth century. But in the 1940s interest in structural abnormalities resurfaced, this time in the United States. During the 1930s, Alfred Strauss and Kurt Werner left Nazi Germany and began work at the Wayne County Vocational School in Detroit. Before fleeing their homeland, both men had worked with Kurt Goldstein, who had studied the behavioral effects of head injuries in German soldiers who had fought in World War I. Goldstein had concluded that brain damage in adults produced a variety of cognitive and behavioral disturbances, including poor impulse control, inattention, poor perceptual motor abilities, and difficulties with reading and memory.

Similar disturbances were noted in children who had survived the worldwide encephalitis epidemic of 1916 to 1917. Survivors included large numbers of children with documented brain damage and with symptoms similar to those described by Goldstein in German soldiers. Thus, despite the general lack of enthusiasm for the classical lesion-deficit model popular in the middle nineteenth century, evidence from these two sources prompted researchers and clinicians to reconsider neurobiological explanations for their patients' cognitive and behavioral deficits. Not surprisingly, it was during this time that Orton proposed that severe reading disability (*strephosymbolia*) was due to delayed cerebral lateralization. Because they lacked the neurological substrates for language, these children were unable to perform the complex linguistic tasks of transforming printed symbols into meaningful units.

But it was the work of Werner and Strauss and, later, Strauss and Lehtinen (1947) that provided the impetus for later brain–behavior discoveries. This group made two important contributions. First, they stressed (as Goldstein had earlier) that deficits following brain injury were diffuse and produced a cluster of symptoms, including disorders in spoken language, written language, and perception and motor difficulties, hyperactivity, distractibility, and inattention. Such a view is consistent with current neurological thinking that the most common causes of brain damage in children (e.g., infections, anoxia, and malformations) result in diffuse damage (Kolb and Whishaw 1980). Second, Strauss and his colleagues provided training for a generation of teachers and researchers. Beginning with the premise that certain deficits in language, movement, and behavior were due to "minimal brain injuries" (as it was termed in the 1947 text by Strauss and Lehtinen), their students (including Kirk, Myklebust, Cruikshank, Kephart, and Frostig) took LD from its tentative nineteenth-century beginnings to the close of the twentieth century.

THE SEARCH FOR THE STRUCTURAL BASIS OF LD

The years between Dejerine's discoveries in the late eighteenth century to Galaburda's postmortem study in 1979 were not a period of complete inactivity. However, mainstream efforts to explain congenital language disorders took a different course. Having concluded that LD resulted not from damage but from dysfunction, researchers virtually abandoned their search for structural brain anomalies, focusing instead on evaluating and remediating learning deficits. For example, Samuel Orton, a neurologist, correctly theorized that the area of the brain responsible for letter reversals was the area Dejerine had identified. As Geschwind reminds us, however, though he identified the area of involvement accurately, "for some reason he thought there should be no structural disorder" (Geschwind 1985, p. 3). Rather, he attributed strephosymbolia to "incomplete establishment of cerebral dominance," and he devoted himself to the diagnosis and, especially, to the remediation of this disorder. Once he had articulated his theory implicating incomplete hemispheric specialization and the angular gyrus, Orton's efforts turned almost immediately to building more effective remediation programs for children so afflicted.

To focus on the behavior at the expense of understanding the underlying pathology was consistent with current psychological thinking. Even before Skinner, increasing numbers of psychologists and educators were embracing the science of behavior. Cruikshank—and later Kirk—emphasized remediation rather than etiology. The emphasis on remediation marks a significant change in focus. By the early 1970s, only a handful of researchers continued the search for structural disorders. The overwhelming majority had already switched, perhaps for good reason; efforts to document structural brain abnormalities had provided disappointingly little direct evidence to support their theories.

As a result, research aimed at articulating a coherent neurobiological theory waned. Examples of procedures that failed to document underlying brain abnormalities in LD are electroencephalography (EEG) and the neurological examination. Developed in 1929 by Hans Berger, brain electrical activity recorded via EEG promised to provide valuable new insights into brain function by producing "unique signatures for many abnormal and/or normal variations in mental state" (Duffy and McAnulty 1985, p. 105). But after comprehensive reviews of studies attempting to correlate EEG and LD, both Denckla (1977) and Conners (1977) concluded there were no differences in any EEG variations between control and LD subjects. In fact, raw EEG data have never conclusively been shown to be useful in identifying LD subjects, in differentiating LD and non-LD subjects, or in subtyping LD subjects.

Likewise, the pediatric neurological examination has failed to differentiate children with and without LD. This is true for the standard neurological examination conducted to rule out neurological disease and to evaluate neurodevelopmental status (Hynd and Willis 1988), as well as for the extended neurological examination (including evaluation of "soft signs") that is conducted because of the observation that children with LD have increased neurodevelopmental delays.

Results of evaluations of soft neurological signs have been inconsistent. Some argue that soft signs can be reliably assessed and that they can be used to discriminate LD and non-LD children (Morrison 1986). Others, including Denckla (1978), have adopted a more conservative approach. She distinguishes between mild and subtle classical abnormalities and developmental soft signs. The former indicate localization and "give us entrance rights . . . into the consideration of brain mechanics underlying complex behavior" (Denckla 1978, p. 241). Developmental soft signs, on the other hand, imply the "failure of some integrated brain mechanism to appear in time" (p. 243) and should not be considered direct evidence of structural involvement.

It is now generally agreed that children with LD have increased incidence of gross motor dysfunctions, dysfunctions in reflexes and motor skills, and nystagmus. However, a causal link between neurobehavioral dysfunction and LD has yet to be made.

Prior to 1978, therefore, there were few hard data to document the biological substrate of LD. Evidence for a neurological etiology was behavioral-inferential. That is, because children with LD behave as though they are brain damaged, brain areas known to subserve these behaviors are presumed to have been compromised in some way. As a result, a wide range of perceptual and cognitive-linguistic deficiencies has been proposed as explanations for difficulties in learning. These include mixed laterality, auditory and visual perceptual deficits, deficits in cross-modal integration, problems in intersensory integration, deficits in temporal order recall, deficits in attention, and deficits in phonological coding (Hynd 1989). Over the past two to three decades, attempts to provide support for these various explanations have produced an enormous literature in the field of LD. Unfortunately much of this literature is characterized by inconsistencies and differences, and we continue to be far from a consensus on the neurobiological substrates of LD.

Despite the apparent chaos, recent neuropsychological research indicates that several generalizations may be emerging (Hynd 1989). These include the following:

1. LD may be due to a congenital neurological deficit.
2. LD may involve many different perceptual and cognitive-linguistic processes.
3. The perceptual and cognitive-linguistic processes may manifest differently in subpopulations of LD.
4. There may be age by deficit interactions in subtypes of LD.

The neuropsychological perspective also provides a useful and coherent typology that can be used to evaluate the evidence provided by recent contributions from biomedical technology. LD subtypes include dyslexia and other developmental language disorders, attention deficit hyperactivity disorder (ADHD), and right hemisphere/nonverbal learning disabilities. Each subtype may involve different parts of the cortex, each seems to appear early in life, each has a protracted developmental course, and each is susceptible to developmental disturbances (Pennington 1991). The remaining three sections of this chapter are devoted to a discussion of these three LD subtypes. Each section includes explanations of the LD, the neurobiological theories associated with each LD, and recent contributions from postmortem and neuroimaging studies that support the underlying neurobiological theory.

DYSLEXIA AND DEVELOPMENTAL LANGUAGE DISORDERS

Although there are a variety of phonological and nonphonological disorders of speech and language, the focus of this section is on *dyslexia*, "a rare but definable and diagnosable form of primary reading retardation with some form of CNS dysfunction" (Harris and Hodges 1981, p. 95). It is established that 3% to 6% of school-age children have unexpected disorders of reading and spelling. These disorders are unexpected because they occur in the presence of normal intellectual functioning. Multiple genetic and environmental factors have been implicated as causes, and there is general agreement that dyslexia is etiologically heterogeneous (see Pennington 1991 for a review of genetic and environmental mechanisms).

In addition to etiology, a second area of controversy surrounding dyslexia involves speculations about its neurological underpinnings. Until the 1970s, evidence linking dyslexia to an underlying brain defect was correlational (Golden

1982; Taylor and Fletcher 1983) and inferential (Taylor 1987; Taylor and Fletcher 1983).

The Neurolinguistic Context of Brain Mechanisms Implicated in Dyslexia

Interpretations of computed tomography (CT), magnetic resonance imaging (MRI), electroencephalography (EEG), and other technological measures are made within some neurolinguistic context. One theoretical explanation, the Wernicke-Geschwind model, has its origins in Dejerine's postmortem findings of patients with alexia with and without agraphia. According to this model, visual stimuli register as neural images in the primary occipital cortex. These neural images are then projected to the area of the angular gyrus, where they are associated with other sensory and perceptual input. Linguistic-semantic comprehension is presumed to involve the left parietal-temporal cortex and the auditory association cortex. Neural images from these areas are then transmitted via intrahemispheric fibers to Broca's area (Geschwind 1979). Deviations in one or more of these areas have been related to functional language deficits. Recent research indicates that cytoarchitectonic and morphological differences in these areas may be related to LD.

Though the Wernicke-Geschwind model provides an accepted conceptual framework to explain written and spoken language disorders (Hynd and Hynd 1984), the search for presumed focal brain deficits in children with developmental disabilities is fraught with problems. In the first place, no evidence of gross brain abnormality has ever been found on neurological examination. Second, there is no validity for inferring localized deficits in children with developmental dysfunction from localized findings in acquired dyslexia. As Kinsbourne reminds us, "it cannot, however, simply be assumed that a developmental deficit will turn out to involve abnormality in the same region of brain as its acquired analogue" (Kinsbourne 1989, p. 109).

Lacking a specific neuropathology in the classical sense, researchers have focused instead on nontraumatic biological variations in brain development to explain developmental dysfunction (Duane 1989). These variations include hemispheric asymmetries, differences in electrophysiologic activity, laterality differences, cytoarchitectonic abnormalities, and differences in callosal morphology.

Hemispheric Asymmetries

Hemispheric asymmetries are evident throughout the life span. Geschwind and Levitsky (1968) performed postmortem analyses on 100 adult human brains. They reported that 68% had larger planum temporale in the left hemisphere. Larger planum temporale have also been observed during fetal development (Chi et al. 1977) and during the neonatal period (Witelson and Paillie 1973). Subsequent investigations with newborns using EEG also support these findings (Molfese and Molfese 1980). So pervasive is this observation of a larger left planum temporale that it is considered evidence that the left hemisphere subserves linguistic functions in humans.

Additional evidence of hemispheric asymmetry is provided by studies using CT scans. LeMay (1981) studied 100 right-handed males and reported that 78% had left > right occipital length, 67% had left > right occipital width, 70% had right > left frontal length, and 53% had right > left frontal width. Pieniadez and Naeser (1984) confirmed these findings using postmortem analysis. These findings are now considered consistent and reliable brain asymmetries that, like plana asymmetry, are presumed to be related to language functions in humans.

Weinberger and colleagues (1982) report that in 75% of normal brains, the right frontal region is larger than the left. Thus, we have evidence that the left planum temporale, the right frontal regions, and the left posterior regions are larger in the majority of normal human brains. (See Figure 1.2.)

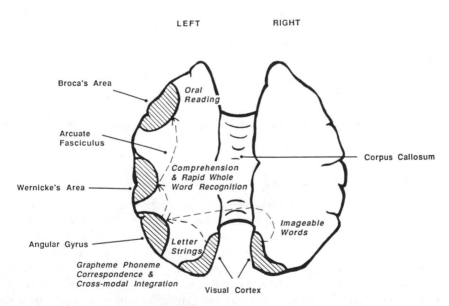

Figure 1.2 The four lobes of the left hemisphere (frontal, parietal, occipital, temporal) as well as important regions associated with each lobe. The region of the planum temporale in the left hemisphere (at the most superior, posterior aspect of the temporal lobe) is believed to be vitally important in higher-order auditory processing, including phonological coding, and in the comprehension of language. Postmortem and neuroimaging studies indicate that the planum temporale is larger on the left side in approximately two-thirds of normals. Symmetry or reversed asymmetry (L ≤ R) in this region appears much more frequently in the brains of dyslexics than in normals. (From G. W. Hynd, R. M. Marshall, and J. J. Gonzalez (1991). "Learning Disabilities and Presumed Central Nervous System Dysfunction," *Learning Disabilities Quarterly, 14,* 283–296.)

Nine neuroimaging (CT/MRI) studies have been conducted testing the hypothesis that subjects with dyslexia would show less symmetry or reversed asymmetry in brain regions known to be important to language, the planum temporale and the posterior cortex (Hynd, Marshall, and Gonzalez 1991). For example, a study by Hynd and colleagues (1990) compares MRI scans of dyslexic, ADD/H, and normal subjects. In addition to smaller left anterior width and left insular regions, subjects with dyslexia had significantly smaller left planum temporale than normal subjects. The authors also report that 70% of normal and ADD/H subjects had left > right patterns of planum asymmetry, and that 90% of dyslexic subjects had right > left patterns of planum asymmetry. The authors attribute this specific difference in planum asymmetry to "some deviation in cortico-genesis [that] preferentially affects the left planum temporale during development" (Hynd et al. 1990, p. 923).

The nine neuroimaging studies have been reviewed by Hynd and Semrud-Clikeman (1989) and by Semrud-Clikeman and colleagues (1991). The reviewers suggest three tentative conclusions. First, there is no hard evidence of a structural defect or lesion that is diagnostic of learning disabilities. The absence of a specific defect is consistent with previous research in developmental disorders (Kinsbourne 1989), and it underscores the difficulties inherent in drawing inferences from acquired to developmental disorders. Second, when careful morphological measures of these regions of interest (the planum temporale, posterior, and frontal areas) are made, less asymmetry is evident in the subjects with dyslexia than in the nondyslexic subjects. And third, when symmetry or reversed asymmetry is present in the planum temporale or the left posterior cortex, subjects may evidence significantly more neurological deficits (Hynd, Marshall, and Gonzalez 1991).

Postmortem Studies of LD

To date, there have been eight postmortem studies addressing the relationship between neurodevelopmental anomalies and specific LD. The first, by Drake (1968), was of a 12-year-old boy with severe learning and behavior problems. On autopsy, Drake found abnormal neuronal patterns in both parietal lobes as well as thinning and stretching of the corpus callosum. Unfortunately, Drake's results were largely ignored until Galaburda and Kemper (1979) presented their first postmortem report of a 19-year-old boy with dyslexia and academic failure. In this and subsequent cases, unique distributions of cortical and subcortical anomalies have been reported. These anomalies include disordered cortical layering, polymicrogyria in the left planum temporale, and focal abnormalities in the region of the planum temporale. Postmortem evidence also indicates that females with dyslexia have neurodevelopmental anomalies similar to males, including symmetries in the planum temporale and in the parieto-occipital regions. Because 25% of normal subjects also have symmetrical planum temporale, this finding alone may not have diagnostic significance; its presence, however, may represent an additional component of dyslexia (Rosen et al. 1986).

Furthermore, subsequent research by Galaburda and Eidelberg (1982) in-dicated that cytoarchitectonic anomalies are also evident in the medial geniculate nucleus and in the lateral posterior nucleus of the thalamus. Evidence of thalamic involvement is important because it suggests a link between linguistic function and the allocation of attention, a topic subsequently reported by Hynd and Semrud-Clikeman (1989) and Hynd and colleagues (in press). The importance of these postmortem studies is that they provide direct neuropathological evi-dence that neurodevelopmental factors may be associated with LD. Furthermore, these neurodevelopmental anomalies seem to develop during the third trimester of pregnancy.

Evidence from Electrophysiology

Though it was hoped that EEG recordings would reveal unique features of clinical abnormalities and/or normal variations in mental state, "EEG abnormal-ities found were too unspecific to form useful diagnostic constellations" (Duffy and McAnulty 1985). In his review of EEG studies of dyslexia, Hughes (1977) concluded that there was a high incidence of abnormal findings. In a rebuttal to Hughes, Conners (1977) pointed out significant methodological issues, including differences in EEG abnormalities and differences in subject selection criteria. Based on these and other methodological differences, Conners concluded that raw EEG data were of little value in differentiating normal readers from dyslex-ics. Conners's conclusion was recently reaffirmed by Galin (1989), who cites three methodological problems with existing research: variations in dyslexic pop-ulations, which make replication difficult; the lack of understanding of how cognitive processes are related to EEG variables; and the lack of knowledge of how normal reading occurs and what is the typical EEG pattern produced by normal readers.

Failure to find classic EEG abnormalities (e.g., epileptiform spikes and slow waves) prompted researchers to search for more subtle differences in EEG pat-terns that may distinguish normal and disabled readers. The technology used in-volves computer-enhanced analysis of EEG data; the procedures are based on the knowledge that EEG records contain so much information that human visual in-spection is not adequate to perform analyses required to distinguish subtle dif-ferences related to neurocognitive processing (Duffy et al. 1979).

Unlike EEG tracings that are recorded while the person is in a relaxed and passive state, neurocognitive assessment is performed while the person is engaged in a cognitive task. Cognitive performance produces brain electrical activity as well as muscle artifact. Computer analysis serves to interpret the former while identifying and eliminating the latter, an impossible task using visual inspection alone (Languis and Wittrock 1986).

Three methods of computer-assisted analysis of brain electrical activity have been used to measure neurocognitive functioning. One, analysis of EEG brain wave activity, involves collecting and analyzing the frequency patterns of ongoing EEG while the learner performs a cognitive task, such as reading aloud.

Of interest is the percent of each EEG frequency band (delta, theta, alpha, and beta) at selected time epochs during task performance. This technique has been useful in localizing changes in brain electrical activity during various cognitive tasks.

A second approach uses event-related potentials (ERPs). ERPs have less voltage than the four EEG frequency bands; unlike background EEG, ERPs are elicited in response to a target stimulus and they are time-locked. Researchers have associated basic cognitive processes with ERP waveforms occurring at specific intervals following the target stimulus. John (1963) classified ERPs as exogenous and endogenous. *Exogenous* responses are detected within 40 milliseconds of the stimulus. They are very stable and predictable, and their occurrence does not require the subject's active participation. *Endogenous* components occur 100 milliseconds after stimulus presentation. Their elicitation is influenced by the nature of the task and the level of attention allocated by the subject (Languis and Wittrock 1986).

ERPs are considered to be reliable indices of higher-order cognitive processes, and differences in late onset ERP (i.e., 280 ms to 400 ms) have been used to differentiate the cognitive performance of students with reading disabilities from those with normal reading ability. Holcomb and colleagues (1985, 1986) compared children with reading disability (RD), attention deficit disorder with hyperactivity (ADD/H), attention deficit disorder without hyperactivity (ADD/WO), and normal controls. The authors report that the P300 amplitude was significantly smaller and its latency was significantly longer in all clinical groups and that RD children had smaller P300 components when words (versus symbols) were used as stimulus items. Similar results are reported by Harter and colleagues (1988). They report that RD subjects had smaller amplitude at P240 over the left hemisphere and a larger P500 over the right central and the right occipital regions. They also note that subjects with RD and ADD produced distinctive ERP waveforms.

Stelmack and colleagues (1988) used visual ERP elicited during a recognition memory task to compare normal and disabled readers. Normal readers had larger N400 amplitude, interpreted as evidence of semantic evaluation. No significant P300 differences between RD and normal readers were found, suggesting that attentional deficits may not be involved in recognition memory performance (Stelmack et al. 1988).

Because of its relationship to attentional processing and to the evaluation of the stimulus, P300 has been the most frequently used waveform in the study of neurocognitive processes. Cognitively, P300 seems to involve updating of memory, and it is thought to be generated by the hippocampus and other brain structures involved in memory (Languis and Wittrock 1986).

Numerous investigations analyzing P300 waveforms in children and adults with dyslexia have been reported in the past decade. Duffy, Denckla, Bartels, and Sandini (1980) and Duffy, Denckla, Bartels, Sandini, and Kiessling (1980) compared dyslexic and normal control subjects and reported significant differences in P300 in the medial frontal lobes, the left lateral frontal lobes, the left midtemporal lobe, and the posterior quadrants of each hemisphere. Simmons and colleagues (1985) report reductions in P300 amplitude from the left temporoparietal regions, the same area that Galaburda and associates (1985) noted had neuronal ectopias on postmortem analyses of four dyslexic brains. Subsequent research supports bilateral amplitude reduction (Naylor 1987) and more pronounced reduction of amplitude in the left central regions (Harter et al. 1988).

The third method used in evaluating neurocognitive functioning is the probe ERP technique. This procedure utilizes the advantages of both spontaneous EEG and ERP. In probe ERP, task-irrelevant auditory and visual stimuli are presented to subjects while they are engaged in cognitive processing tasks. The assumption underlying probe ERP is that "a brain region is less responsive to the probe stimulus when that region is engaged in the primary concurrent task" (Languis and Wittrock 1986, p. 223). The N100 waveform seems to be particularly sensitive to the subject's attentional allocation to the cognitive task. Brain electrical activity mapping (BEAM) takes advantage of this phenomenon by comparing brain activity at specific locations in subjects with and without dyslexia. Increases (signifying cortical attenuation) and decreases (signifying cortical activation) in alpha activity in specific brain areas "are shown to be 80% to 90% successful in classifying subjects as dyslexic or normal" (Languis and Wittrock 1986, p. 224). Duffy, Denckla, Bartels, and Sandini (1980) compared dyslexic and normal readers. The authors report "aberrant physiology" in the dyslexics in bifrontal areas, the left temporal area, and the left posterior quadrant. In addition, dyslexics had generally increased alpha activity. This was interpreted by the authors to represent a relative reduction of cortical activity in severely disabled readers.

Since the 1970s, an accumulation of evidence from various sources (postmortems, electrophysiology, and neuroimaging) suggests that the left hemisphere is specialized for language processing in humans and that specific brain regions may be involved in learning disabilities. Results of studies using these techniques to compare normal and disabled readers indicate that anomalies in well-defined areas of the cortex are related to specific language disorders, including dyslexia.

NONVERBAL LEARNING DISABILITIES

There is a second group of children who have adequate verbal acquisition but who have deficits in arithmetic achievement, social perception, and visual-spatial skills. Gerstmann (1940) first described this cluster of symptoms in a group of adults with deficits in right hemispheric functions, including deficits in calculations, spelling, finger agnosia, and left/right discrimination. Noting the same cluster of symptoms in children, Kinsbourne and Warrington (1963) argued that a developmental Gerstmann's syndrome also existed. Johnson and Myklebust (1967) first used the term "nonverbal learning disabilities" to describe children with deficits in concept development, social perception, interpersonal relationships, and increased rates of distractibility and disinhibition.

With prevalence rates ranging from 0.1% to 1% (Rourke 1989), non-verbal learning disabilities (NVLD) are thought to occur far less than dyslexia and other verbal learning disabilities. Moreover, males and females appear to be equally affected. Whereas the male to female ratio in verbal LD may be as high as 4:1 (Smith 1991), the ratio in NVLD appears to be 1:1 (Rourke 1989). Increased rates of NVLD among females may reflect the higher rates of NVLD associated with female inherited disorders, particularly Turner's syndrome and Fragile X. NVLD have also been associated with Asperger's syndrome, Williams's syndrome, AIDS, the leukodystrophies, and cerebral palsy; Turner's and Fragile X, however, are the only generic etiologies that have been identified (Pennington 1991).

In addition to those with an inherited risk, Rourke lists five other groups of children who are at increased risk for NVLD: (1) those who have suffered moderate to severe head injury, (2) those with inadequately treated hydrocephalus, (3) those on large doses of radiation therapy, (4) those with congenital absence of the corpus callosum, and (5) those with right hemisphere tissue removal (Rourke 1989). Each of these involves the brain's white matter, and Rourke proposed that brain anomalies associated with NVLD are associated with white matter disease and destruction. In fact, Rourke (1987) considers white matter the "common pathway" of NVLD.

Brain Mechanisms Underlying NVLD

To date, there are three classification systems utilized by researchers investigating NVLD. The systems, however, have more similarities than differences. Rourke and Finlayson (1978) coined the term "nonverbal perceptual-organization-output-disabled" (NPOOD) to describe children with average to above average reading and spelling ability, but with arithmetic and visual-spatial deficits, the inability to shift previously learned operations to new situations, psychomotor impairment, and differences in interpreting social cues, such as gestures and facial expressions. Denckla (1978) also considers NVLD a distinct subtype of LD. Consistent with other researchers, she was able to identify a group of children with deficits in arithmetic, visual-spatial skills, and social-perceptual skills. She attributes these deficits to right hemisphere dysfunction, based on her findings that these children had left-sided motor weakness.

Voeller (1986) also documented left-sided neurological deficits in students with right hemisphere dysfunction. Besides the typical symptoms associated with NVLD, children with right hemisphere deficits were found to have increased incidence of ADD and motor impersistence (Voeller 1986; Voeller and Heilman 1988). Direct evidence documenting structural or functional differences in children with NVLD is sparse, however. Voeller (1986) used CT scans, EEG, and neuropsychological assessment to evaluate her subjects. Sixty-nine percent had significant Performance > Verbal discrepancies on the Wechsler Intelligence Scale for Children-Revised. Fifty-three percent met the *Diagnostic and Statistical Manual of Mental Disorders, Third Edition (DSM, III)* (APA 1980) criteria for

ADD/H and 40% met criteria for ADD/WO. In addition, 73% had abnormal CT scans, including large right parietal lesions (13%); focal atrophy (13%); dilated right lateral ventricle (20%); and larger than normal right/left asymmetry (27%). Four of 15 subjects (26%) also has abnormal EEG activity in the right hemisphere.

Evidence of Right Hemisphere Dysfunction and NVLD

Most of the evidence linking right hemisphere dysfunction with NVLD is from behavioral studies of adults with right hemisphere damage. Semrud-Clikeman and Hynd (1990) have reviewed these studies, and they conclude that these investigations support the hypothesis that right hemisphere lesions produce cognitive deficits similar to those reported in children with NVLD, namely, deficits in attention, arithmetic, and spatial orientation, as well as in increased rates of depression.

Besides behavioral data, other evidence for hemisphere specialization has been documented via electrical stimulation mapping (Penfield and Roberts 1959), commissurotomy (Sperry 1982), split-brain research using the Wada Carotid Amytal Test (Wada and Rasmussen 1960), dichotic listening (Kimura 1961), and postmortem analysis of adults (Geschwind and Levitsky 1968), children (Wada et al. 1975), and infants (Witelson and Paillie 1973).

Each of these methodologies reveals a consistent pattern of right hemisphere cerebral specialization. As with left hemisphere specialization for language, right hemisphere specialization for certain cognitive functions is well established. Such specialization appears early in development and does not change significantly after 3 years of age. Despite the recent advances from biomedical research, however, direct evidence establishing a relationship between specific brain structures and NVLD is lacking.

There is evidence from both clinical and laboratory studies implicating the right hemisphere in ADHD. Evidence for right hemisphere control of attention is also available from studies using neuropsychological tests. Voeller (1986) used neurological, behavioral, and neuropsychological techniques to identify children with right hemisphere dysfunction. Fourteen of 15 (93%) of those identified with right hemisphere dysfunction also met the *DSM III* criteria of ADD. As reported earlier, 8 of 15 were diagnosed as ADD/H and 6 of 15 were diagnosed as ADD/WO.

ATTENTION DEFICIT HYPERACTIVITY DISORDER

The cluster of symptoms associated with ADHD have been associated with LD since the two were first subsumed in the diagnosis of "minimal brain injuries" (Strauss and Lehtinen 1947) and later in "minimal brain dysfunction" (MBD) (Clements 1966). In the mid 1960s, learning disorders and attention problems were dissociated; parents and educators shifted their focus to learning problems and adopted the term "LD" to describe children with unexpected difficulties in academic achievement. Meanwhile, psychiatrists and psychologists continued to focus on the behavioral triad of inattention, impulsivity, and hyperactivity. As a result of this conceptual schism, the definition of LD that was adopted for use in P.L. 94-142 reflected parents' and educators' concerns with learning, whereas psychologists and psychiatrists developed the classification for attention deficit disorder used in the *DSM III* (APA 1980).

Despite this separation, LD and ADHD are known to co-occur at higher than expected rates. Shaywitz and Shaywitz (1988), for example, report that 33% of their subjects with dyslexia also had ADHD. The exact nature of the relationship between ADHD and dyslexia has not been delineated. Whether one is causal or whether they just co-exist remains a matter of much theoretical speculation.

Recent contributions from split-brain research (Ellenberg and Sperry 1980; Sperry 1982) and from cognitive psychology (Posner 1988; Posner et al. 1988) suggest that attention is not a unitary construct, and that cortical and subcortical structures in conjunction with specific cerebral hemispheres work in unison to process the various components of attention system.

Evidence for lateralized localization of function comes from various sources. Heilman and Van Den Abell (1980) report decreases in right hemisphere EEG alpha rhythms, indicating that the right hemisphere is dominant for attention. Adults with right hemisphere disturbances have been shown to have hemispatial neglect (Vallar and Perani 1986), decreased vigilance and attention (Mesulem 1981), and motor impersistence (Kertesz et al. 1985). Voeller and Heilman (1988) report similar findings in children.

In their review of the neurobiological mechanisms underlying ADD/H, Zametkin and Rapoport (1987) point out that existing data suggest that various neurotransmitters and neuroanatomical regions are involved in ADD/H. More recently, Hynd, Hern, and colleagues (1991) listed 18 neuroanatomical hypotheses implicating the septal region, the reticular activating system, the frontal lobes, and hemispheric localization in ADHD. Such disparate findings underscore the complexities involved in specifying the neurobiological substrates of ADHD.

Although numerous abnormalities have been identified via neurochemical studies, no specific neurotransmitters, neuromodulators, nor neuroanatomical substrates have been identified (Zametkin and Rapoport 1990). Pharmacological studies will continue to test responses to dopaminergic and noradrenergic agents used alone and in combination.

But it is the advances in our ability to image the brain in vivo that are providing the most valuable information about the neuroanatomical substrates of ADHD. These procedures include regional cerebral blood flow (rCBF), CT/MRI, and single photon emission computed tomography (SPECT).

Initial studies using CT found no abnormalities (Shaywitz et al. 1983) in ADD/H nor in MR (Moeschler et al. 1981). Such unequivocal or insignificant findings are now considered secondary to methodological problems involving subject selection and to technical inadequacies of early CT scanners. More recent investigations are providing useful information.

Lou and colleagues (1984) used CT to chart the cerebral distribution of a radioactive trace element. Their first study revealed that children with ADHD had lower metabolism in the caudate nucleus, a subcortical structure associated with motor regulation. Moreover, metabolic activity increased with the administration of methylphenidate. In a follow-up study, Lou and associates (1989) were able to replicate their initial findings and to specify that the right striatum (which provides subcortical to frontal projections) was metabolically deficient. The authors theorized that children with caudate-striatal hypometabolism have different inhibitory responses to environmental stimuli, resulting in diminished ability to attend selectively.

These findings are consistent with those of Zametkin and colleagues (1990), who used positron emission tomography (PET) scans to study regional cerebral glucose metabolism in a group of adults with residual ADHD. They reported that global and regional glucose metabolism were reduced in their hyperactive patients. Although 30 of 60 specific brain regions were significantly different, the authors reported that the greatest areas of suppression were in the premotor and superior prefrontal regions.

Prefrontal and frontal lobe involvement in attention is consistent with data from various sources of more than a decade. In his review of this literature, Mattes (1980) offered the opinion that the frontal lobes anterior and medial to the prefrontal motor cortex were dysfunctional in children with ADD. Behavioral evidence supporting his conclusion is provided in studies by Dykman and colleagues (1971) and by Gaultieri and Hicks (1985). Additional, though limited, support is also provided by Chelune and associates (1986), who report that children with ADHD performed less well than normal controls on the Wisconsin Card Sort Test (WCST). The WCST requires concept learning and memory and is believed to reflect frontal lobe integrity (Hynd, Hern, et al. 1991).

Although few in number, CT/MRI and postmortem studies provide the best evidence of morphological differences in subjects with ADHD. In their review of neuroimaging studies, Hynd, Hern, and colleagues (1991) concluded that deviations in normal patterns of neuronal migration during the fifth to seventh months of gestation may be implicated in morphological alterations typically reported in subjects with ADHD, including smaller right anterior width and frontal and prefrontal changes.

CONCLUSION

The evidence for structural and functional changes in the brains of children with LD is sometimes inconclusive and inconsistent. Nevertheless, a rapid accumulation of evidence from diverse sources suggests that certain conclusions are emerging. First, educators and psychologists need no longer fear that they are relying too heavily on the medical model when they seek a neurological explanation for a student's learning or attention problems. In fact, CNS disturbance is explicitly mentioned in the definition of LD from the National Joint Committee on Learning Disabilities (NJCLD) (1987).

To be sure, not all learning problems are due to brain anomalies. Information-processing problems, maturational lags, cognitive styles, adverse environmental circumstances, and sociocultural differences also compromise children's learning potential. It is time for physiologic causes, including underlying brain anomalies, to join this list.

There is one caveat, however. First, most neurologists, including pediatric neurologists, have not been trained to evaluate the neurobiological causes of learning and attention problems. Unless they have a specific interest or training in this area, their most important contribution continues to be in assessing neurologic status and in ruling out neurological disease and dysfunction. Likewise, most PET and CT scanners and MRI machines are used to search for disease and physical disorders. Generally, it is only at research centers with research protocols dedicated to the study and application of these technologies to learning and behavior where evaluations of the neurobiological causes of learning and attention problems can be conducted.

Second, current neurobiological theory may be where Denckla (1978) said MBD research was a decade ago. In trying to convince her colleagues to look at the brain when trying to understand MBD, she wrote, "It is my position, therefore, that we look for MBD as an archaeologist might look for an ancient city under the rubble and ruins of the surface. Again, we are looking for correlates (multivariate, not univariate), risk factors, uncompensated-for imbalances ('Caution: brain factors at work')" (Denckla 1978, p. 232). Denckla's message is still appropriate. Brain factors are still at work, and technology is making it possible for us to view the "ancient city" as never before.

Third, there is a striking commonality among diverse sources of evidence. Postmortems, MRI, rCBF, computerized EEG, and neuropsychology provide amazingly similar information regarding brain anomalies and LD. Such evidence, though not conclusive, cannot be ignored. Underlying brain function is not just intuitively or theoretically appealing. Differences in brain structure and function in LD and non-LD children are well documented. Furthermore, the correlations between brain structure and function and learning and attention problems have been clearly established. We can no longer speak of *whether* there is a relationship between brain anomalies and cognitive processing—only of what the relationship is, and how it manifests itself in various subtypes of learning disorders.

Fourth, a major contribution of increasing knowledge of brain–behavior relationships has important implications for instruction, particularly remediation. In a sobering message to professionals, Ferry (1981, 1986) reminds us that, despite our best efforts, children with cerebral palsy (CP) are not going to grow new neurons. We are going to have to maximize the skills these children possess and to compensate for those that are missing. To continue therapy at the expense of assisting children to compensate for their deficits is to perform a disservice. Ferry's reminder seems appropriate to the field of LD at the present time. Children with LD, like children with CP, are not going to grow new neurons, nor are they going to change the structure or function of their brains. They can, however, learn to function despite their difficulties. Remediation programs have traditionally had dismal records of accomplishment. Children with dyslexia become adults with dyslexia; children with ADHD become adults with the residual deficits associated with ADHD. Given what we know of the brain's role in both, it is time for those charged with the care of children to provide them with the skills they need to manage their circumstances as early as possible.

REFERENCES

American Psychiatric Association (APA). (1980). *Diagnostic and statistical manual of mental disorders: DSM III* (3rd ed.). Washington, DC: APA.

Bastian, H. C. (1898). *Aphasia and other speech defects.* London: Lewis.

Benton, A. (1984). Hemispheric dominance before Broca. *Neuropsychologia, 22,* 807–811.

Bogen, J. E., & Bogen, G. M. (1976). Wernicke's region—where is it? *Annals of the New York Academy of Sciences, 280,* 834–843.

Chelune, G. J., Ferguson, W., Koon, R., & Dickey, T. (1986). Frontal lobe disinhibition in attention deficit disorder. *Child Psychiatry and Human Development, 16,* 221–232.

Chi, J. G., Dooling, E. C., & Gieles, F. H. (1977). Left-right asymmetries of the temporal speech areas of the human fetus. *Archives of Neurology, 34,* 346–348.

Clements, S. D. (1966). *Minimal brain dysfunction in children* (NIDB Monograph No. 3). Public Health Service Publication (No. 1415). Washington, DC: U.S. Department of Health, Education, and Welfare.

Conners, C. K. (1977). Critical review of "electroencephalographic and neurophysiological studies of dyslexia." In A. L. Benton & D. Pearl (Eds.), *Dyslexia: An appraisal of current knowledge* (pp. 251–261). New York: Oxford University Press.

Denckla, M. B. (1977). Critical review of "electroencephalographic and neurophysiological studies of dyslexia." In A. L. Benton & D. Pearl (Eds.), *Dyslexia: An appraisal of current knowledge* (pp. 241–249). New York: Oxford University Press.

Denckla, M. B. (1978). Minimal brain dysfunction. In J. S. Chall & A. F. Mirsky (Eds.), *Education and the brain* (pp. 223–268). Chicago: National Society for the Study of Education.

Denckla, M. B. (1983). The neuropsychology of social-emotional learning disabilities. *Archives of Neurology, 40,* 461–462.

Drake, W. E. (1968). Clinical and pathological findings in a child with a developmental learning disability. *Journal of Learning Disabilities, 1,* 9–25.

Duane, D. D. (1988). Neurobiological correlates of learning disorders. *Journal of the American Academy of Child and Adolescent Psychiatry, 28,* 314–318.

Duffy, F. H., Burchfiel, J. L., & Lombroso, C. T. (1979). Brain electrical activity mapping (BEAM): A method for extending the clinical utility of EEG and evoked potential data. *Annals of Neurology, 5,* 309–321.

Duffy, F. H., Denckla, M. B., Bartels, P. H., and Sandini, G. (1980). Dyslexia: Regional differences in brain electrical activity by topographic mapping. *Annals of Neurology, 7,* 412–420.

Duffy, F. H., Denckla, M. B., Bartels, P. H., Sandini, G., and Kiessling, L. S. (1980). Dyslexia: Automated diagnosis by computerized classification of brain electrical activity. *Annals of Neurology, 7,* 421–428.

Duffy, F. H., and McAnulty, G. B. (1985). Brain electrical activity mapping (BEAM): The search for physiological signature of dyslexia. In F. H. Duffy & N. Geschwind (Eds.), *Dyslexia: A neuroscientific approach to clinical evaluation.* Boston: Little, Brown.

Dykman, R. A., Ackerman, P. T., Clements, S. D., & Peters, J. E. (1971). Specific learning disabilities: An attentional deficit syndrome. In H. R. Myklebust (Ed.), *Progress in learning disabilities.* (vol. 2). Orlando, FL: Grune & Stratton.

Ellenberg, L., & Sperry, R. W. (1980). Lateralized division of attention in the commissurotimized and intact brain. *Neuropsychologia, 18,* 411–418.

Ferry, P. C. (1981). On growing new neurons: Are early intervention programs effective? *Pediatrics, 67,* 38–41.

Ferry, P. C. (1986). Infant stimulation programs: A neurological shell game? *Archives of Neurology, 43,* 281–282.

Galaburda, A. M., & Eidelberg, D. (1982). Symmetry and asymmetry in the human posterior thalamus: II. Thalamic lesions in a case of developmental dyslexia. *Archives of Neurology, 39,* 333–336.

Galaburda, A. M., & Kemper, T. L. (1979). Cytoarchitectonic abnormalities in developmental dyslexia: A case study. *Annals of Neurology, 6,* 94–100.

Galaburda, A. M., Sherman, G. F., Rosen, G. D., Aboitz, F., & Geschwind, N. (1985). Developmental dyslexia: Four consecutive cases with cortical anomalies. *Annals of Neurology, 18,* 222–233.

Galin, D. (1989). EEG studies in dyslexia. In D. J. Bakker & H. van der Vlugt (Eds.), *Learning disabilities: Vol. 1. Neuropsychological correlates and treatment.* Amsterdam: Swets & Zeitlinger.

Gaultieri, C. T., & Hicks, R. E. (1985). Neuropharmacology of methylphenidate and neural substrate for childhood hyperactivity. *Psychiatric Clinics of North America, 8,* 875–892.

Gerstmann, J. (1940). Syndrome of finger agnosia, disorientation for right and left, agraphia and acalculia. *Archives of Neurology and Psychiatry, 44,* 389–408.

Geschwind, N. (1979). Specialization of the human brain. *Scientific American, 241,* 180–199.

Geschwind, N. (1985). The biology of dyslexia: The after-dinner speech. In D. B. Gray & J. F. Kavanagh (Eds.), *Behavioral measures of dyslexia* (pp. 1–19). Parkton, MD: York Press.

Geschwind, N., & Levitsky, W. (1968). Human brain: Left-right asymmetries in temporal speech region. *Science, 161,* 186–187.

Golden, G. S. (1982). Neurobiological correlates of learning disabilities. *Annals of Neurology, 12,* 409–418.

Harris, T. L., & Hodges, R. W. (Eds.). (1981). *A dictionary of reading and related terms.* Newark, DE: International Reading Association.

Harter, M. R., Diering, S., & Wood, F. B. (1988). Separate brain potential characteristics in children with reading disability and attention deficit disorder: Relevance-independent effects. *Brain and Cognition, 7,* 54–86.

Heilman, K. M., & Van Den Abell, T. (1980). Right hemisphere dominance for attention: The mechanism underlying hemispheric asymmetries of inattention (neglect). *Neurology, 30,* 327–330.

Hinshelwood, J. (1900). Congenital word blindness. *Lancet, 1,* 1506–1508.

Holcomb, P. J., Ackerman, P. T., & Dykman, R. A. (1985). Cognitive event-related potentials in children with attention and reading deficits. *Psychophysiology, 22,* 656–667.

Holcomb, P. J., Ackerman, P. T., & Dykman, R. A. (1986). Auditory event-related potentials in attention and reading disabled boys. *International Journal of Psychophysiology, 3,* 263–273.

Hughes, J. R. (1977). Electroencephalographic and neurophysiological studies in dyslexia. In A. L. Benton & D. Pearl (Eds.), *Dyslexia: An appraisal of current knowledge* (pp. 205–240). New York: Oxford University Press.

Hynd, G. W. (1989). Learning disabilities and neuropsychological correlates: Relationship to neurobiological theory. In D. J. Bakker & H. van der Vlugt (Eds.), *Learning disabil-*

ities: Vol. 1. Neuropsychological correlates and treatment (pp. 123–147). Amsterdam: Swets & Zeitlinger.

Hynd, G. W., Hern, K. L., Voeller, K. K., & Marshall, R. M. (1991). Neurobiological basis of attention-deficit hyperactivity disorder (ADHD). *School Psychology Review, 20,* 174–186.

Hynd, G. W., & Hynd, C. R. (1984). Dyslexia: Neuroanatomical/neurolinguistic perspectives. *Reading Research Quarterly, 19,* 482–498.

Hynd, G. W., Marshall, R. M., & Gonzalez, J. J. (1991). Learning disabilities and presumed central nervous system dysfunction. *Learning Disability Quarterly, 14,* 283–296.

Hynd, G. W., Marshall, R. M., & Semrud-Clikeman, M. (in press). Developmental dyslexia, neurolinguistic theory, and deviations in brain morphology. *Reading and Writing.*

Hynd, G. W., & Semrud-Clikeman, M. (1989). Dyslexia and brain morphology. *Psychological Bulletin, 106,* 447–482.

Hynd, G. W., Semrud-Clikeman, M., Lorys, A. R., Novey, E. S., & Eliopulos, D. (1990). Brain morphology in developmental dyslexia and attention deficit disorder/hyperactivity. *Archives of Neurology, 47,* 919–926.

Hynd, G. W., & Willis, W. G. (1988). *Pediatric neuropsychology.* Boston: Allyn and Bacon.

John, E. R. (1963). Neural mechanisms of decision making. In W. S. Fields & W. Abbott (Eds.), *Information storage and neural control.* Springfield, IL: Thomas.

Johnson, D. J., & Myklebust, H. R. (1967). *Learning disabilities: Educational principles and practices.* New York: Grune & Stratton.

Kertesz, A., Nicholson, I., Cancelliere, A., Kassa, K., and Black, S. E. (1985). Motor impersistence: A right hemisphere syndrome. *Neurology, 35,* 662–666.

Kimura, D. (1961). Cerebral dominance and the perception of verbal stimuli. *Canadian Journal of Psychology, 15,* 166–171.

Kinsbourne, M. (1989). Neuroanatomy of dyslexia. In D. J. Bakker and H. van der Vlugt (Eds.), *Learning disabilities: Vol. 1. Neuropsychological correlates and treatment* (pp. 105–122). Amsterdam: Swets & Zeitlinger.

Kinsbourne, M., & Warrington, E. K. (1963). The developmental Gerstmann syndrome. *Archives of Neurology, 8,* 490–501.

Kolb, B., & Whishaw, I. Q. (1980). *Fundamentals of human neuropsychology.* San Francisco: Freeman.

Lou, H. C., Henriksen, L., & Bruhn, P. (1984). Focal cerebral hypoperfusion in children with dysphasia and/or attention deficit disorder. *Archives of Neurology, 41,* 825–829.

Lou, H. C., Henriksen, L., Bruhn, P., Borner, H., & Nielsen, J. B. (1989). Striatal dysfunction in attention deficit and hyperkinetic disorder. *Archives of Neurology, 46,* 48–52.

Languis, M., & Wittrock, M. C. (1986). Integrating neuropsychological and cognitive research: A perspective for bridging brain–behavior relationships. In J. E. Obrzut & G. W. Hynd (Eds.), *Child neuropsychology: Vol. 1. Theory and research.* Orlando, FL: Academic Press.

LeMay, M. (1981). Are there radiological changes in the brains of individuals with dyslexia? *Bulletin of the Orton Society, 31,* 135–141.

Mattes, J. A. (1980). The role of frontal lobe dysfunction in childhood hyperkinesis. *Comprehensive Psychiatry, 21,* 358–369.

Mesulem, M. M. (1981). A cortical network for directed attention and unilateral neglect. *Annals of Neurology, 10,* 309–325.

Moeschler, J. B., Bennett, F. C., & Cromwell, L. D. (1981). Use of the CT scan in the medical evaluation of the mentally retarded child. *Journal of Pediatrics, 98,* 63–65.

Molfese, D. L., & Molfese, V. J. (1980). Cortical responses of preterm infants to phonetic and non-phonetic speech stimuli. *Developmental Psychology, 16,* 574–581.

Morgan, W. P. (1896). A case of congenital word-blindness. *British Medical Journal, 2,* 1378.

Morrison, D. C. (1986). Neurobehavioral dysfunction and learning disabilities in children. In S. J. Cecci (Ed.), *Handbook of cognitive, social, and neuropsychological aspects of learning disabilities* (pp. 475–491). Hillsdale, NJ: Erlbaum.

National Joint Committee on Learning Disabilities. (1987). Learning disabilities: Issues on definition. A position paper. *Journal of Learning Disabilities, 20,* 107–108.

Naylor, H. (1987). *Event-related potentials and behavioral assessment: A 20 year follow-up of adults who were diagnosed as RD in childhood.* Unpublished doctoral dissertation, University of North Carolina at Greensboro.

Penfield, W., & Roberts, L. (1959). *Speech and brain mechanisms.* Princeton, NJ: Princeton University.

Pennington, B. F. (1991). *Diagnosing learning disorders.* New York: Guilford.

Pieniadez, J. M., & Naeser, M. A. (1984). Computed tomographic scan cerebral asymmetries and morphological brain asymmetries. *Archives of Neurology, 41,* 403–409.

Posner, M. I. (1988). Structures and functions of selective attention. In T. Boll and B. Bryant (Eds.), *Clinical neuropsychology and brain function: Research, measurement, and practice* (pp. 173–202). Washington, DC: American Psychological Association.

Posner, M. I., Petersen, S. E., Fox, P. T., & Raichle, M. E. (1988). Localization of cognitive operations in the human brain. *Science, 240,* 1627–1631.

Rosen, G. D., Sherman, G. F., & Galaburda, A. M. (1986). Biological interactions in dyslexia. In J. E. Obrzut & G. W. Hynd (Eds.), *Child neuropsychology: Vol. I. Theory and research* (pp. 155–173). Orlando, FL: Academic Press.

Rourke, B. P. (1987). Syndrome of nonverbal learning disabilities: The final common pathway of white-matter disease/dysfunction? *The Clinical Neuropsychologist, 1,* 209–234.

Rourke, B. P. (1989). *Nonverbal learning disabilities: The syndrome and the model.* New York: Guilford.

Rourke, B. P., & Finlayson, M. A. J. (1978). Neuropsychological significance of variations in patterns of academic performance: Verbal and visual spatial abilities. *Journal of Abnormal Child Psychology, 6,* 121–133.

Semrud-Clikeman, M., & Hynd, G. W. (1990). Right hemisphere dysfunction in nonverbal learning disabilities: Social, academic, and adaptive functioning in adults and children. *Psychological Bulletin, 107,* 196–209.

Semrud-Clikeman, M., Hynd, G. W., Novey, E. S., & Eliopulos, D. (1991). Dyslexia and brain morphology: Relationships between neuroanatomical variations and neurolinguistic tasks. *Learning and Individual Differences, 3,* 225–242.

Shaywitz, B. A., Shaywitz, S. E., Byrne, T., Cohen, D. J., & Rothman, S. (1983). Attention deficit disorder: Quantitative analysis of CT. *Neurology, 33,* 1500–1503.

Shaywitz, S., & Shaywitz, B. (1988). Attention deficit disorder: Current perspectives. In J. Kavanagh & T. Truss, Jr. (Eds.), *Learning disabilities: Proceedings of the national conference* (pp. 369–498). Parkton, MD: York Press.

Smith, C. D. (1991). *Learning disabilities: The interaction of learner, task, and setting* (2nd ed.). Boston: Allyn and Bacon.

Simmons, J., Languis, M. L., & Drake, M. (1985). *Neurocognitive event-related potential assessment of dyslexic and normal college students.* Paper presented at the American Psychological Association, Los Angeles.

Sperry, R. (1982). Some effects of disconnecting the cerebral hemispheres. *Science, 217,* 1223–1226.

Stelmack, R. M., Saxe, B. J., Noldy-Cullum, N., Campbell, K. B., & Armitage, R. (1988). Recognition memory for words and event-related potentials: A comparison of normal and disabled readers. *Journal of Clinical and Experimental Neuropsychology, 10,* 185–200.

Strauss, A., & Lehtinen, L. (1947). *Psychopathology and education of the brain-injured child* (vol. 1). New York: Grune & Stratton.

Taylor, H. G. (1987). The meaning and value of soft signs in the behavioral sciences. In D. E. Tupper (Ed.), *Soft neurological signs* (pp. 297–335). New York: Grune & Stratton.

Taylor, H. G., & Fletcher, J. M. (1983). Biological foundations of "specific developmental disorders": Methods, findings, and future directions. *Journal of Clinical Child Psychology, 12,* 46–65.

Vallar, G., & Perani, D. (1986). The anatomy of unilateral neglect after right-hemisphere stroke lesions. A clinical CT-scan correlation study in man. *Neuropsychologica, 24,* 609–622.

Voeller, K. K. (1986). Right hemisphere deficit syndrome in children. *American Journal of Psychiatry, 143,* 1004–1009.

Voeller, K. K., & Heilman, K. M. (1988, September). *Motor impersistence in children with attention deficit hyperactivity disorder. Evidence for right hemisphere dysfunction.* Paper presented at the 17th annual meeting of the Child Neurology Society, Halifax, Nova Scotia.

Wada, J. A., Clarke, R., & Hamm, A. (1975). Cerebral hemispheric asymmetry in humans: Cortical speech zones in 100 adults and 100 infant brains. *Archives of Neurology, 32,* 239–246.

Wada, J. A., & Rasmussen, T. (1960). Intracarotid injection of sodium amytal for the lateralization of cerebral speech dominance: Experimental and clinical observations. *Journal of Neurosurgery, 17,* 266–282.

Weinberger, D. R., Luchins, D. J., Morihisa, J., & Wyatt, R. J. (1982). Asymmetrical volumes of the right and left frontal and occipital regions of the human brain. *Neurology, 11,* 97–100.

Witelson, S. F., & Paillie, W. (1973). Left hemisphere specialization for language in the newborn. *Brain, 96,* 641–646.

Zametkin, A. J., Nordahl, T. E., Gross, M., King, C., Semple, W. E., Rumsey, J. & Hamburger, S. (1990). Cerebral glucose metabolism in adults with hyperactivity of childhood onset. *New England Journal of Medicine, 323,* 1361–1366.

Zametkin, A. J., & Rapoport, J. L. (1987). Neurobiology of attention deficit disorder with hyperactivity: Where have we come in 50 years? *Journal of the American Academy of Child and Adolescent Psychiatry, 26,* 676–686.

2

Cognitive Abilities

H. Lee Swanson

The purpose of this chapter is to provide an overview of the cognitive characteristics of students with learning disabilities (LD). Because children with and without LD have been differentiated on a multitude of cognitive measures, the present chapter will focus on those processes that are amenable to instruction. The chapter will also outline some educational principles to enhance children's cognitive abilities.

Helping students with LD to become better cognitive processors of information is clearly an important educational goal. This goal is based upon several studies suggesting that the cognitive processes used by students with LD do not appear to exhaust—or even tap—their intellectual capability (e.g., Bos and Anders 1990; Borkowski et al. 1989; Palincsar and Brown 1984; Swanson 1990). For example, their lack of academic and social interaction success in the classroom seems to be based on skills that are modifiable or teachable, such as their ability to shift from one cognitive strategy to another, to abandon inappropriate strategies, to process information with one strategy and then select another, or to consider several processing approaches in rapid succession in order to arrive at a correct solution to a problem. The objective of this chapter is to provide an educational foundation for understanding the learning-disabled student's cognitive abilities.

COGNITIVE CHARACTERISTICS

Several studies made within the last few years support the notion that children with LD have trouble accessing and coordinating a number of cognitive activities. The research in this area can be summarized as follows: Children with LD experience difficulty with such self-regulating mechanisms as checking, planning, monitoring, testing, revising, and evaluating during an attempt to learn or solve problems (e.g., Bauer and Emhert 1984; Bos and Anders 1990; Brown and Palincsar 1988; Dallego and Moely 1980; Palincsar and Brown 1984; Pressley et al. 1987; Pressley, Symons, et al. 1989; Wong 1982; Wong and Jones 1982). In

This chapter draws liberally from several other writings (Swanson 1991b; Swanson 1985; Swanson and Ransby [in press]), and the reader is referred to these sources for more extensive information.

addition, these children suffer from deficits in such mental operations as logically organizing and coordinating incoming information that requires carrying out mental operations (e.g., Swanson 1982, 1983a). Such children perform poorly on a variety of tasks that require the use of general control processes of strategies for solution (e.g., see Wong [1991] for a review). Under some conditions, well-designed strategy training improves performance (e.g., Gelzheiser 1984; Gelzheiser et al. 1987), while at other times some general cognitive constraints prevent the effective use of control processes (Baker et al. 1987; Swanson 1989; see Cooney and Swanson 1987 for a review). However, when metacognitive training includes instruction related to self-evaluation and enhancing attributions related to effective strategy use, training attempts are successful (e.g., Borkowski et al. 1989; Palincsar and Brown 1984; Dallego and Moeley 1980; Scruggs et al. 1987; Scruggs and Mastropieri 1989; Spear and Sternberg 1987; Swanson and Rathgeber 1986; Torgesen et al. 1979; Wong et al. 1977).

The implication from these findings is that the previous research, which has primarily focused on certain isolated cognitive processing deficits (e.g., attention, short-term memory), must now incorporate findings that suggest that children with LD also suffer from higher-order processing problems involving processes that monitor the whole cognitive system (e.g., Swanson 1987b; Torgesen et al. 1988). No doubt it is possible that isolated or specific cognitive processing deficiencies influence higher-order cognitive problems. It can also be argued, however, that a learning disability may be related to the efficient regulation or *coordination* of mental processes that are not related to a specific type of processing deficiency (see Swanson 1988 for a related discussion). It is not the intent of the previous comments to suggest that the domain-specific or process-specific models of LD be abandoned, but rather that they be put into perspective. While the notion of specificity is a critical assumption in the field of learning disabilities (Stanovich 1986, 1988), this orientation has generated many competing hypotheses. Further, even if a specific deficit is isolated, the problem is pervasive over time in its influence on cognition and the acquisition of knowledge. Without denying a specific etiology of LD, there are both theoretical and practical benefits to focusing on the higher-order processing difficulties of children with learning disabilities. Before outlining some educational principles related to enhancing these students' processing of information, it is important to focus on some of the specific cognitive processes that influence high-order functioning.

INFORMATION PROCESSING

The present review draws heavily from the information-processing literature, since this is the most influential model in cognitive psychology to date (see Anderson 1990 for a review). The central assumptions of the information-processing model are (1) A number of operations and processing stages occur between a stimulus and a response, (2) the stimulus presentation initiates a sequence of stages, (3) each stage operates on the information available to it, (4) these operations transform the information in some manner, and (5) this new information is the input to the succeeding stage. In sum, the information-processing approach focuses on how input is transformed, reduced, elaborated, stored, retrieved, and used.

One popular means of explaining the cognitive performance of students with LD is to draw upon fundamental constructs that are inherent in most models of information processing (e.g., see Brainerd and Reyna 1991; Ceci 1986; Kolligan and Sternberg 1987; Kyllonen and Christal 1990; Pennington et al. 1990; Torgesen 1991; Siegel and Ryan 1989; Swanson 1991a). Three constructs are fundamental: (1) a constraint or *structural* component, akin to the hardware of a computer, which defines the parameters within which information can be processed at a particular stage (e.g., sensory storage, short-term memory, working memory, long-term memory); (2) a *strategy* component, akin to the software of a computer system, which describes the operations of the various stages; and (3) an *executive* component, by which learners' activities (e.g., strategies) are overseen and monitored. These constructs are represented in Figure 2.1.

In terms of definition, *sensory memory* refers to the initial representation of information that is available for processing for a maximum of 3 to 5 sec. *Short-term memory* processes information between 3 and 7 sec and is primarily concerned with storage, via rehearsal processes. *Working memory* focuses on the storage of information and also on the active interpretation of newly presented information. *Long-term memory* is a permanent storage with unlimited capacity. The *executive component* monitors and coordinates the functioning of the entire system (see Baddeley 1986 for a review). Some of this monitoring may be automatic, with little awareness on the individual's part, whereas other types of monitoring require effortful and conscious processing. Let us briefly review the research in each area as it applies to cognitive abilities of students with LD.

Sensory Memory

As shown in Figure 2.1, basic environmental information (e.g., visual, auditory) is assumed first to enter the appropriate sensory register. A common paradigm to assess the processing of sensory information is recognition. The subject is asked to determine whether information that was present briefly (e.g., for a millisecond) had occurred. The task may be simply to answer "yes" or "no" to individual items or may require selecting among a set of items. Common dependent measures in this research are correct detection and response time.

Information in this initial store is thought to include a mental representation of the physical stimulus. For example, the mental representation of a visual stimulus usually includes an image or icon. If an array of letters is presented tachistoscopically and the child is then asked to write out those letters after a 30-sec delay between instructions, the child can reproduce about six or seven letters from the images represented in the sensory register. The mental representations may vary between subjects within and across stimulus presentations. For example, students who are presented a letter of the alphabet may produce a photographic trace that decays quickly, or they may physically scan the letter and

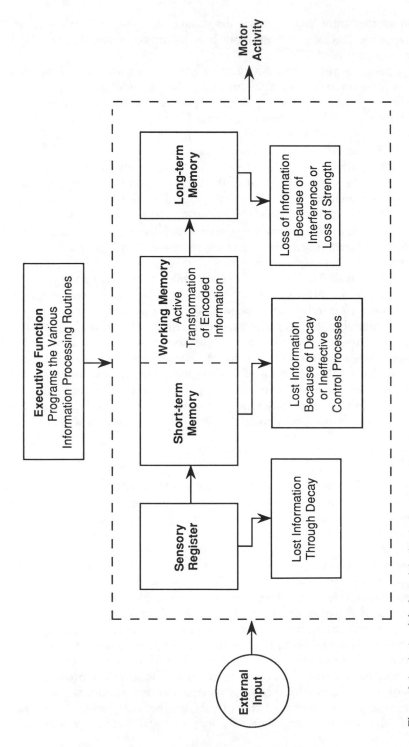

Figure 2.1 A simplified model of information processing.

transfer the information into an auditory (e.g., echo or sound)-linguistic (meaning) representation. Information that is presented visually may also be recorded into other modalities (e.g., auditory). The transfer of visual information to an auditory-linguistic store is made at the individual's discretion.

In general, research on the sensory register of children with LD suggests that the sensory register is intact. For example, Elbert (1984) provides evidence that students with and without LD are comparable at the encoding stage of word recognition, but that children with LD require more time to conduct a memory search (also see Mazer et al. 1983; Manis 1985). Additional evidence that children with and without LD are comparable at the recognition stage of information processing is provided by Lehman and Brady (1982). These researchers found that reading-disabled and normal readers were comparable in their ability to encode word information (e.g., indicating whether a word was heard or seen and information concerning a word's category). However, reading-disabled children relied on smaller subword components in the decoding process than did normal readers.

Many accounts of poor recognition of information by students with LD have been attributed to attention deficits (e.g., see Hallahan and Reeve 1980 for review). However, this conclusion is in question (Bauer 1979b; Samuels 1987a, 1987b; Swanson 1981, 1983a). For example, McIntyre and colleagues (1978) reported a lower than normal span of apprehension in students identified as LD. Mazer and associates (1983) attribute the lower span of apprehension to a slower rate of information pickup from the sensory store. Despite the common assumption of differences in attention to visual and auditory stimulus between children with and without LD, Bauer (1979b) argues that the attentional resources of children with LD are adequate for performance on a variety of memory tasks. In other words, the differences are not great enough to account for the differences in memory performance. For example, children with and without LD are comparable in their ability to recall orally presented sets of three letters or three words within 4 sec after presentation (Bauer 1979b). Similarly, these groups are comparable in their ability to recognize letters and geometric shapes after a brief visual presentation when recognition is less than 300 micro-sec after stimulus offset (Morrison et al. 1977). In view of these findings, it does not appear that retrieval of information from sensory storage is a major factor in the cognitive processing deficits exhibited by students with LD (also see Jorm 1983 for a review).

Short-Term Memory

From the sensory register, information is transferred into the limited-capacity short-term memory. Information lost in this memory is assumed to decay or disappear, but actual time of decay is longer than time available in the sensory register. Exact rate of decay of information cannot be estimated because this component is controlled by the subject. Short-term memory retains information in auditory-verbal-linguistic representations. Using the example of a child recalling letters, the child may subvocally rehearse a letter by voicing the letter.

Given that students with LD differ on measures of short-term memory, what cognitive processing deficits underlie such differences? In general, variations in short-term memory performance of students with LD have been attributed to processes such as rehearsal and the meaningfulness of the material (Torgesen 1988; Torgesen et al. 1991). A crucial factor in memory performance of students with LD is their ability to encode units or sequence the items so that they can be recoded into smaller units (Torgesen et al. 1991). Other factors that affect capacity include: (1) information load, (2) similarity of items, (3) number of items processed during subsequent activities, and (4) passage of time (Bauer 1979b; Gelzheiser 1984; Shankwieler et al. 1979; Siegel and Ryan 1988; Swanson 1983c, 1984b; Worden et al. 1982). The exact nature of problems with the capacity of short-term memory is somewhat obscure in students with LD (see Cooney and Swanson 1987 for a review). Research results have been unclear as to whether the limitation is one of processing capacity, storage capacity, or some interaction between the two.

Control processes in short-term memory include a choice as to which information to scan and a choice of what and how to rehearse. *Rehearsal* refers to the conscious repetition of information, either subvocally or orally, to recall information at a later date. Learning a telephone number or street address illustrates the primary purpose of rehearsal. Additional control processes also involve organization (ordering, classifying, or tagging information to facilitate retrieval) and mediation (comparing new items with items already in memory).

Organizational strategies in which students with LD are deficient include (Pressley et al. 1989; Gelzheiser et al. 1987; Scruggs and Mastropieri 1989; Scruggs et al. 1987; Swanson and Rathgeber 1986; Swanson, Cooney, and Overholser 1989; Wong et al. 1977):

1. *Chunking:* Grouping items so that each one brings to mind a complete series of items (e.g., grouping words into a sentence)
2. *Clustering:* Organizing items into categories (e.g., animal, furniture)
3. *Mnemonics:* Idiosyncratic methods for organizing materials)
4. *Coding:* Varying the qualitative form of information (e.g., using images rather than verbal labels, substituting pictures for words)

Mediation of information in students with LD may be facilitated by:

1. Making use of preexisting associations, eliminating the necessity for new ones
2. Utilizing instructions, either verbal or usual (asking the child to imagine) to aid in retrieval and organization
3. Cuing at recall by using verbal and imaginary information to facilitate mediation

A number of important studies have provided a foundation for much of the current processing research. For example, concerning research on short-term memory control processes, Torgesen and Goldman (1977) studied lip movements of children during a memorization task. Children with LD were found to exhibit fewer lip movements than the non-LD students. To the extent that these lip movements reflect the quantity of rehearsal, these data support a rehearsal-deficiency hypothesis. Haines and Torgesen (1979) and others (e.g., Dawson et al. 1980; Koorland and Wolking 1982) also report that incentives can be used to increase the amount of rehearsal and, thus, recall. Bauer and Emhert (1984) suggest that one difference between nonhandicapped students and students with LD is in the quality of the rehearsal rather than the quantity of rehearsal, per se.

Another major source of difficulty that students with LD experience during their attempts to memorize material has been highlighted by Gelzheiser and colleagues (1983). These authors recorded a brief statement made by a student with LD following an attempt to retain a passage containing four paragraphs about diamonds. The student reported that she could identify major themes of the story but could not categorize the various pieces of information under these major items. She was able to abstract the essence of the story but was unable to use this as a framework to organize the retention of the specific passage. Swanson (1983b) found that students with LD rarely reported the use of an organizational strategy when they were required to rehearse several items. He reasoned that, because these students were capable of rehearsal, the problem was not a deficiency in rehearsal but instead was a failure to perform elaborative processing of each word. *Elaborative processing* was defined as processing that goes beyond the initial level of analysis to include more sophisticated features of the words and ultimately the comparison of these features with others in the list (also see Swanson 1989).

Another major source of difficulty related to short-term memory processing is LD students' inefficient use of phonological codes (sound units). Torgesen (1988) conducted studies on a small group of subjects who performed in the retarded range of verbatim recall on sequences of verbal information. His analysis of those students' performance deficits suggest that they are due to coding errors and represent the phonological features of language. He suggests that the students' short-term memory problems relate to the acquisition of fluent word identification and word analysis skills. Additional support for the notion of phonological coding errors comes from studies suggesting that good and poor readers differ in the extent to which they recall similar- and dissimilar-sounding names (Shankwieler et al. 1979). An interaction is usually found in which poor readers perform better on "rhyming-word and similar letter-sounding tasks" because they have poor access to a phonological code (e.g., Shankwieler et al. 1979; Siegel and Linder 1984)—that is, good readers recall more information for words or letters that have distinct sounds (e.g., *mat* vs. *book*, *A* vs. *F*) than words or letters that sound alike (*mat* vs. *cat*, *B* vs. *D*). In contrast, poor readers are more comparable in their recall of similar and dissimilar words or sounds than skilled readers. This finding suggests that good readers are disrupted when words or sounds are alike because they process information in terms of sound (phonological) units (see, however, Hall et al. 1983). In contrast, poor readers are not efficient in processing information into sound units (phonological codes) and therefore are not disrupted in performance if words or letter sound alike (see Johnson et al. 1987).

In summary, the poor short-term memory of students with LD has been related to problems in rehearsal, organization, elaborative processing, and phonological coding; that is, studies suggest that those students suffer short-term memory difficulties and these problems manifest themselves in terms of how information is strategically processed (e.g., rehearsal) and how information is mentally represented (e.g., phonological codes).

Working Memory

Working memory is viewed as a dynamic and active system because it simultaneously focuses on both processing and storage demands, whereas short-term memory primarily focuses on the storage of information and is considered a more passive system (Baddeley 1986; Daneman and Carpenter 1980). Thus, short-term memory is partly understood as a component of a limited capacity system from accumulating and holding segments of information in order (e.g., speech or orthographic units) as they arrive during a listening or reading task. Material in short-term memory is retained if it is rehearsed. In contrast, working memory is concerned with the interpretation and integrating of information with previously stored information (see Siegel and Ryan 1989; Swanson 1991a; Swanson, Cochran, and Ewars 1990 for application to learning disabilities).

How does the formulation of working memory help us understand memory problems of students with LD better than the concept of short-term store? First, it suggests that verbal rehearsal plays a smaller role in learning and memory (Baddeley 1986), an important point because some studies do show that performance deficits of these students are not related to rehearsal, per se (e.g., see Swanson 1983b,c). For example, previous studies of short-term memory operations of students with LD—such as rehearsal (Bauer 1979b)—have not explained how constraints in long-term memory contribute to academic performance; that is, they have not shown how word knowledge, associations, and attentional capacity contribute to some of the problems we see occurring in short-term memory tasks. Furthermore, measures (e.g., digit span) commonly used in assessing differences in many studies between nonhandicapped students and students with LD are weakly correlated with academic ability (Daneman and Carpenter 1980, 1983), suggesting that such short-term tasks may not capture the essence of academic performance, namely the combination of processing and long-term memory storage functions. Second, the idea of a working memory system is useful because it is viewed as an active memory system directed by a central executive (to be discussed) and the resources stored in long-term memory (Baddeley 1986).

A recent study (Swanson, Cochran, and Ewars 1989) sought to determine the *extent* to which less skilled readers suffer from working memory deficiencies.

A sentence span task (Daneman and Carpenter 1980) was used to measure the efficiency of storage and processing operations combined. The task requires recalling the last word of several sentences as well as answering a comprehension question about a sentence. Materials for the sentence span task were unrelated declarative sentences, 7 to 10 words in length, arranged into sets of two, three, four, or five. Examples of the sentences for recalling the last word in a series of three sentences for words are

1. We waited in line for a *ticket.*
2. Sally thinks we should give the bird its *food.*
3. My mother said she would write a *letter.*

To ensure that children comprehended the sentences (i.e., processed their meaning) and did not merely treat the task as one of short-term memory, they were required to answer a question after each group of sentences was presented. For the three-sentence set, for example, they were asked "Where did we wait?" The results of this study suggest that working memory of students with LD is inferior to that of non-LD readers. Thus, studies that suggest that memory deficiencies among students with LD are localized to a short-term storage system must be reevaluated within the context of a model that incorporates the operations of working memory.

Long-Term Memory

The amount of information, as well as the form of information, transferred to long-term memory is primarily a function of control processes (e.g., rehearsal). Long-term memory is a permanent storage of information of unlimited capacity. How information is stored is determined by the uses of links, associations, and general organizational plans. Information stored in long-term memory is primarily semantic. Forgetting occurs because of item decay (loss of information) or interference.

In comparison to the volume of research on short-term memory processes, research on long-term memory of students with LD is sparse; however, the available research provides considerable support for the assertion that storage and retrieval problems are primary sources of individual differences in long-term memory performance (e.g., Brainerd et al. 1987; Swanson 1987c for review). Numerous studies have also shown that students with LD are less skilled than non-handicapped peers in the use of rehearsal strategies used to store information in long-term memory (Bauer 1979a,b; Tarver et al. 1976; Torgesen and Goldman 1977). The main source of support for the assertion of rehearsal deficits in students with LD is the diminished primacy effect (i.e., better recall of items at the beginning of a list over the middle items of the list) of the serial position curve (Bauer 1979a). Primacy performance is a measure of the accessibility of items placed in long-term storage. Thus, the primacy effect is thought to reflect greater rehearsal of those items at the beginning of the list.

In terms of retrieving information from long-term memory, students with LD can use organized strategies for selecting retrieval cues (Wong 1982) and different word attributes (e.g., graphophonic, syntactic, semantic) to guide retrieval (Blumenthal 1980); however, they appear to select less efficient strategies, conduct a less exhaustive search for retrieval cues, and lack self-checking skills in the selection of retrieval cues (Wong 1982). Swanson (1984b, 1987c) also provides evidence suggesting that long-term memory deficits may arise from failure to integrate visual and verbal memory traces of visually presented stimuli at the time of storage or retrieval. His findings suggest that semantic memory limitations contribute to these children's failure to integrate verbal and visual codes. Ceci and colleagues (1980) present data that suggest there are separate pathways for auditory and visual inputs to the semantic memory system and that students with LD may have an impairment in one or both of these pathways. They studied students with visual and auditory impairments and found that the recall deficit arises in both storage and retrieval. When only one modality is impaired, the long-term memory deficit is hypothesized to arise at the time of storage. Furthermore, semantic orienting tasks were found to ameliorate the recall deficits of the students with single modality impairments but not those with impairments in both visual and verbal modalities (Ceci et al. 1980, experiment 2).

Other investigators (for a review see Worden 1986) have suggested that long-term memory of students with LD is intact, but the strategies necessary to gain access to this information are impaired. This notion has been challenged (Baker et al. 1987), and evidence suggests that these students' long-term memory for tasks that require semantic processing is clearly deficient when compared with that of nondisabled peers (Swanson 1986). Moreover, some experimental evidence suggests that students with LD may have problems in the structural component of information processing (e.g., Baker et al. 1987; Cohen 1981; Swanson 1987c; Torgesen and Houck 1980). Specifically, Torgesen and Houck (1980) in a seminal study completed a series of eight experiments in which subgroups of students with and without disabilities were compared on a digit span task (see Torgesen et al. 1991 for replication studies). Treatment variations among the eight experimental conditions included manipulations of rehearsal, incentives, and related mnemonic activities. Not all subjects with disabilities benefited from strategy intervention, suggesting that structural or capacity difficulties may exist in some students with LD (also see Swanson 1984b, 1986, 1989).

Taken as a whole, the results reviewed here suggest that the cognitive processes involved in entering a memory trace into the long-term store may account for weaknesses in long-term recall of students with LD. Additional research to discover methods for remediating these deficits is certainly warranted.

Executive Function

An executive function is a cognitive activity that determines the order in which processes will be performed. In other words, it is the organization directive for various memory strategies. The executive function does not perform the searching task or organize and sort out material; instead, it directs the various mental activities to a goal.

Neisser (1967) sums up some important points related to executive processing:

1. Retrieval of information consists of many programmed searches simultaneously and independently (parallel search or multiple search).
2. Control of parallel and sequential processes is directed by the executive routine.
3. Executive function and search processes are learned and based on earlier processing, the implication being that:
   a. Individuals learn to organize and retrieve.
   b. There are individual styles of organization.
4. Failure to recall is failure to access, the implication being that there is a misguided search strategy.

Measures of executive processing usually include dual processing tasks (e.g., see Swanson 1990) that vary the processing load (difficulty of material) and type of processing required (verbal, nonverbal). Although executive functioning has been researched with respect to its importance and application to memory of students with mental retardation (Belmont et al. 1982; Campione et al. 1985), its application to the field of LD is just emerging (Borkowski et al. 1989; Brown and Palincsar 1988; Pressley et al. 1989; Swanson 1989). A focus on executive processing is an important area of research because planning activities prior to solving a problem, monitoring behavior in action, reorganizing strategies, and evaluating the outcomes of any strategic action have characterized the functioning of students with LD in a number of academic domains (e.g., Bos and Anders 1990; Palinscar and Brown, 1984). Strategy deficits in these learners have been noted in terms of failing to monitor cognitive progress or to notice important task differences in learning tasks (for a review see Pressley et al. 1989). The focus of research has been to determine whether or not LD students can review their own cognitive strategies, select and reject them appropriately, and persist in searching for the most suitable task strategies at various stages of performance (Palinscar and Brown 1984; Pressley et al. 1987). Support for possible problems in executive functioning of students with LD can be found in studies where such students have difficulty checking, planning, and monitoring control processes (e.g., Bos and Anders 1990; Gelzheiser et al. 1983; Wong 1982; Wong and Jones 1982; Palincsar and Brown 1984). This type of research focuses on how decisions or strategies are prioritized, the kinds of decisions that these students make at a specific point in implementing strategy, and how they make decisions related to an unresolved processing stage (e.g., cannot understand the essence of the passage).

Interactive Nature of LD Problems

Overall, current research suggests that children with LD experience problems with a number of information-processing components. Most of the research has focused on short-term memory, and problems in short-term memory may very likely influence processes related to working memory, long-term memory, and executive processes. As yet, research has not identified the independent effects and contributions of various memory components on the overall cognitive functioning of students with LD. Thus, it is best to view their cognitive difficulties as reflecting interactive problems between and among various memory-processing components. One means for addressing these "interactive problems" is to focus on instruction that facilitates the coordination of multiple processes. Such instruction will be reviewed in the remainder of the chapter.

APPLICATIONS OF COGNITIVE RESEARCH TO PRACTICE
Strategy Deficit Model

Based on the previous review, it is clear that a number of researchers in the field of LD have converged on the notion that the ability to access knowledge of a student with LD remains inert, unless the student is explicitly prompted to use certain cognitive strategies (e.g., see Swanson 1984a, 1990 for review). For example, students with LD may be taught to (1) organize lists of pictures and words in common categories, (2) rehearse the category names during learning, and (3) use the name and retrieval cues at the time of the test (e.g., see Cooney and Swanson 1987 for a review). The data suggest that when children with LD are explicitly encouraged to use such strategies on some tasks, their performance improves and thus the discrepancy between the general intellectual ability and contextually related deficits is lessened.

Based on these findings, learning-disabled students are viewed as having poor strategies for approaching the complex requirements of academic tasks and thus as being unable to meet their academic potential. Students with LD are further described as inefficient learners—those who either lack certain strategies or choose inappropriate strategies and/or generally fail to engage in self-monitoring behavior. A concept theoretically important to cognitive instruction is related to access. *Access* refers to the notion that the information necessary for successful task performance resides within the child. Some children are not able to access information flexibility; that is, a particular behavior is limited to a constrained set of circumstances (Campione et al. 1985). In addition, some learning-disabled children are *not* "aware" of their own cognitive processes and/or have difficulty consciously describing and discussing their own cognitive activities that allow them to access information (see Wong 1991).

Conceptualizing in Terms of Strategy Deficiencies

There are five advantages in conceptualizing the cognitive abilities of students with LD in terms of strategy deficiencies.

1. *Focus on the modifiable.* Differences between ability groups are conceptualized in terms of cognitive processes that are susceptible to instruction, rather than fundamental or general differences in ability. Thus, rather than focusing

on isolated elementary memory-processing deficiencies, the types of questions that are addressed by strategy research are more educationally relevant. For example, a focus is placed on what students with LD can do without strategy instruction, what they can do with strategy instruction, strategies to modify existing strategy instruction, and strategies to modify existing classroom materials to improve instruction.

2. *Rule creation and rule following.* Cognition involves planned activities, and a focus on strategies allows one to search for underlying "plans" that influence behavior.

3. *Differential operations.* The strategy-deficiency conceptualization incorporates the notion that environmental factors might be seen to operate differentially on the students' declarative and procedural knowledge. That is, certain strategies might be seen to operate differentially on students with different declarative and procedural knowledge. There is a small, but significant, body of research suggesting that when explicit information-processing models are used to study task performance, it is possible to demonstrate aptitude by strategy interactions. Thus, the efficacy of a strategy for learning depends upon a person's pattern of cognitive abilities.

4. *Students' participation.* This conceptualization allows for children to be actively involved in the instruction. That is, students can participate in the analysis of which cognitive strategies work best for them.

5. *Allowing theorizing.* This conceptualization allows for theorizing and instructional development. For example, materials can be developed to maximize strategy use based on the principles of effective cognitive instruction.

Effective cognitive instruction must entail: (1) information about a number of strategies, (2) how to control and implement those procedures, and (3) how to gain recognition of the importance of effort and personal causality in producing successful performance. Further, any of these components taught in isolation is likely to have diminished value in the classroom context. Considering these important components of cognitive instruction, let us now briefly outline some major principles that must be considered if cognitive instruction is to be successful.

Principles of Cognitive Instruction
Strategies Serve Different Purposes
One analysis of the cognitive strategy research suggests there is no single best strategy for students with LD within or across particular domains (Swanson 1989). As can be seen in a number of studies, research is in pursuit of the best strategy to teach students with disabilities (see Cooney and Swanson 1987 for a review). A number of studies, for example, have looked at enhancing these children's performance through the use of advanced organizers, skimming, questioning, taking notes, summarizing, and so on. Apart from the fact that students with LD have been exposed to various types of strategies, the question of which strategies are the most effective is not answered. We know that in some situations,

such as remembering facts, the key word approach (see Chapter 8) appears to be more effective than direct instruction models (Scruggs et al. 1987), but, of course, the rank ordering of different strategies changes in reference to the different types of learning outcomes expected. For example, certain strategies are better suited to enhancing students' understanding of what they previously read, while other strategies are better suited to enhancing students' memory of words or facts. The point is that there are a number of ways that different strategies can effect different cognitive outcomes.

Law of Parsimony

Cognitive instruction must operate on the law of parsimony. There are a number of "multiple-component packages" of cognitive instruction that have been suggested for improving learning-disabled children's functioning. These packages have usually encompassed some of the following: skimming, imagining, drawing, elaborating, paraphrasing, using mnemonics, accessing prior knowledge, reviewing, orienting to critical features, and so on.

No doubt there are some positive aspects to these strategy packages. They are an advance over some of the studies that one sees in the LD literature that focus on rather simple or "quick fix" strategies (e.g., rehearsal or categorization to improve performance). These programs promote skills in a specific domain and have a certain metacognitive embellishment about them. The best of these programs involve (1) teaching a few strategies well rather than superficially, (2) teaching students to monitor their performance, (3) teaching students when and where to use the strategy in order to enhance generalization, (4) teaching strategies as a integrated part of an existing curriculum, and (5) teaching with a great deal of supervised student feedback and practice.

The problems with such packages, however, at least in terms of instructional intervention, is that little is known about which components best predict student performance, nor do they readily permit one to determine why the strategy worked. The multiple-component approaches that are found in many strategy-intervention studies must be carefully contrasted with a component-analysis approach that involves the systematic combination of instructional components known to have an additive effect on performance. Good strategies are composed of the sufficient and necessary processes for accomplishing their intended goal, consuming as few intellectual processes as necessary to do so (Pressley et al. 1987).

Similar Strategy Used

Good strategies for non-LD students are not necessarily good strategies for students with LD. Strategies that enhance access to procedural and/or declarative knowledge for non-LD students will not, in some cases, be well suited for the child with LD. For example, in a study by Swanson and Cooney (1987), it was discovered that students who do well in math benefited from strategies that enhanced the access of procedural knowledge, whereas children poor in mathematics benefited by strategies that enhanced declarative knowledge. To further illustrate, Wong and Jones (1982) trained adolescents with and without LD in a self-questioning strategy to monitor reading comprehension. Results indicated that although the strategy training benefited the adolescents with learning disabilities, it actually *lowered* the performance of non–learning-disabled adolescents. This concept is also illustrated in a study by Dansereau and colleagues (1979) in which college students were presented a networking strategy for transforming text material into nodes and links. Control subjects, who were not taught the strategy, showed typical positive correlation between their grade-point average (GPA) and achievement; for the experimental subjects, the GPA and achievement scores were negatively correlated. Not only were the cognitive instructions ineffective; they were actually damaging to the high-GPA subjects.

To illustrate this point further, Swanson (1989) presented learning-disabled, mentally retarded, gifted, and average achieving students a series of tasks that involved base and elaborative sentences. Their task was to recall words embedded in a sentence. The results of the first study suggested that children with LD differ from the other groups in their ability to benefit from elaboration. It was assumed that the elaboration requirement placed excessive demands on these children's central processing strategies when compared to the other ability groups. This finding was qualified in the next study and suggested that encoding difficulty must be taken into consideration when determining strategy effects, but the results suggest that children with disabilities may require additional strategies to make their performance comparable to their cohorts'. In another study (Swanson, Cooney, and Overholser 1989), college students with LD were asked to recall words in a sentence under semantic and imagery instructional conditions. The results, contrary to the extant literature, suggested that those readers were better able to remember words in a sentence during instructional conditions that induced semantic processing. In contrast, nondisabled readers favored imagery processing over semantic processing conditions. In sum, these results suggest that strategies that are effective for non–learning-disabled students may in fact be less effective for students with LD.

Processing Differences Persist

The use of effective strategies does not necessarily eliminate processing differences. It is recommended that if children with LD are presented a strategy that allows for the efficient processing of information, then improvement in performance is due to the fact that the strategies are affecting the same processes as with nondisabled students (e.g., Torgesen et al. 1979). This assumption has emanated primarily from studies that have imposed organization on seemingly unorganized material. For example, there is considerable evidence that readers with LD do not initially take advantage of the organizational features of material (e.g., Dallego and Moely 1980). Some studies (e.g., Torgesen et al. 1979) suggest that when those children are instructed to organize information into semantic or related categories, their performance is comparable to that of nondisabled students. However, the notion that readers with LD process the organizational features of information in the same fashion as nondisabled students is questionable (Swanson 1988). For example, Swanson and Rathgeber (1986) found in categorization tasks that readers with LD can retrieve information without interrelating superordinate, subordinate, and coordinate classes of information as the nondisabled children do. Thus, children with LD can learn to process information in an organizational sense without knowing the meaning of the material. The point is that just because these children are sensitized to internal structure of material via some strategy (e.g., by cognitive strategies that require the sorting of material), it does not mean they will make use of the material as intended by the instructional strategy.

To further illustrate this problem, let us consider a pilot study completed in an LD classroom (Swanson et al. 1987). Two adolescents with LD who had serious memory and reading comprehension problems were given two tasks. One task required remembering critical details of various stories read daily from a newspaper column. The second task, which assessed any possible generalization of training effect from the primary task, required the retrieval of critical information on a social studies assignment. Intervention on the primary task required the child to use a visual mnemonic strategy to organize main ideas and to link the main ideas in terms of an outline. Mental processes were assessed by asking the children to report verbally the "ways" they were remembering the information. Student responses during task performance were tape recorded and the verbal protocols were coded and categorized in terms of the information-processing strategies used. The results suggested that the students were using a number of strategies (e.g., rehearsal) to sustain and/or direct their prose recall. A majority of these strategies emerged over training sessions and, in many cases, were sustaining the imagery of visual mnemonics.

Comparable Strategy Usage
Comparable performance does not mean comparable strategies. While the previous principle suggests that different processes may be activated *during* intervention that are not necessarily the intent of the instructional intervention, it is also likely that students with disabilities use different strategies on tasks in which they seem to have little difficulty and it is likely that these tasks will be overlooked by the teacher for possible intervention. It is commonly assumed that although children with LD have isolated processing deficits and require general learning strategies to compensate for these deficits, they process information comparably to their normal counterparts on tasks they have little trouble with. Yet, several authors suggest that there are a number of alternative ways of achieving successful performance, and there is some indirect evidence that students with disabilities may use qualitatively different mental operations (Shankwieler et al. 1979) and processing routes (e.g., Swanson 1986) when compared to their nondisabled counterparts. For example, a recent study (Swanson

1988) suggests that those children may use qualitatively different processes on tasks that are easy for them.

Strategy/Knowledge Base Match

Strategies must be considered in relation to a student's knowledge base and capacity. There must be a match between strategy and learner characteristics. One important variable that has been overlooked in the LD intervention literature is the notion of processing constraints (Swanson, 1984b,c, 1987a,c; Swanson, Cochran, and Ewers 1989). Most LD strategy research, either implicitly or explicitly, has considered cognitive capacity to be a confounding variable and has made very little attempt to measure its influence. Swanson (1984b) conducted three experiments related to performance on a word recall task among learning-disabled students and found that recall is related to cognitive effort, or the mental input a limited-capacity system expends to produce a response. He found that readers with LD were inferior in their recall of materials that made high effort demands when compared to nondisabled readers. Further, it was found that skilled readers accessed more usable information from semantic memory for enhancing recall than readers with LD. In a subsequent study (Swanson 1986), he found that children with LD were inferior in the quality and internal coherence of information stored in semantic memory as well as the means by which it is accessed. The implication of this finding is also noted in the study (Swanson 1989) discussed earlier comparing learning-disabled, mentally retarded, gifted, and normal achieving students' use of elaborative encoding strategies. The results suggested that slow learning, normal, and gifted children improved in performance using elaborative strategies when compared to nonelaborative strategies. In contrast, children with LD were less positively influenced by elaborative strategies, possibly due to excessive demands placed on central processing capacity.

Performance Differences Persist

Comparable strategy use may not eliminate performance differences. In a *production deficiency* view of learning disabilities, it is commonly assumed that, without instruction, students with LD are less likely to produce strategies than are their normal counterparts. Several studies have indicated that residual differences remain between ability groups even when ability groups are instructed/or prevented from strategy use (Gelzheiser 1984; Wong et al. 1977). For example, in a study by Gelzheiser and colleagues (1987), children with and without LD were compared on their ability to use organizational strategies. After instruction in organizational strategies, the groups were compared on ability to recall information on a posttest. The results indicated that children with disabilities were comparable in strategy use to nondisabled children but were deficient in overall performance. In another study, Swanson (1983c) found that the recall of students with LD did not improve from baseline level when trained with rehearsal strategies. They recalled less than normally achieving peers, although the groups were comparable in the various types of strategy use. The results basically support the notion that groups of children with different learning histories may continue to learn differently, even when the groups are equated in terms of strategy use. Thus, while a learning disability may include difficulties in learning to use a strategy, some students with LD will require intervention to equate performance differences with their counterparts.

Strategies Do Not Necessarily Develop

Strategies taught do not necessarily become transformed into expert strategies. One mechanism that promotes expert performance is related to strategy transformation (e.g., Chi et al. 1988). It often appears that children who become experts at certain tasks have learned simple strategies and through practice have discovered ways to modify them into more efficient and powerful procedures. In particular, proficient learners use higher-order rules to eliminate unnecessary or redundant steps in order to hold increasing amounts of information. Children with LD, in contrast, may learn most of the skills related to performing an academic task and perform appropriately on that task by carefully and systematically following prescribed rules or strategies. Although these children can be taught strategies, recent evidence suggests that the difference between children with and without LD is that the latter have modified such strategies to become more efficient (Swanson and Cooney 1985). It is plausible that children with LD remain novices because they fail to transform simple strategies into more efficient forms (see Swanson and Cooney 1985).

SUMMARY

In summary, I have briefly characterized research on the cognitive problems of students with LD. What we know about these individuals' cognitive abilities is somewhat paralleled by what we know about their information-processing ability. The chapter stresses the importance of cognitive operations, or mechanisms that facilitate the acquisition of information, in understanding LD. Within this framework, students with LD, as well as their normal achieving counterparts, are perceived as learning through various intervening stages of cognition. At present, research on poor academic performance of students with LD is best conceptualized as an interaction among their deficient cognitive processes and a multitude of external variables (instruction, context, etc.). This chapter also suggests that there are some principles of cognitive instruction that have educational application to learning disabilities. These principles relate to the purposes of strategies, using as few processes as necessary, individual differences in strategy use and performance, learner constraints, and the transfer of strategies into more efficient processes.

REFERENCES

Anderson, J. (1990). *Cognitive psychology and its implications*. New York: Freeman.
Baddeley, A. D. (1986). *Working memory*. London: Oxford University Press.
Baker, J. G., Ceci, S. J., & Hermann, N. D. (1987). Semantic structure and processing: Im-

plications for the learning disabled child. In H. L. Swanson (Ed.), *Memory and learning disabilities* (pp. 83–110). Greenwich, CT: JAI Press.

Bauer, R. H. (1979a). Memory, acquisition, and category clustering in learning disabled children. *Journal of Experimental Child Psychology, 27,* 365–383.

Bauer, R. H. (1979b). Memory processes in children with learning disabilities: Evidence for deficient rehearsal. *Journal of Experimental Child Psychology, 24,* 415–430.

Bauer, R. H., & Embert, J. (1984). Information processing in reading-disabled and non-disabled children. *Journal of Experimental Child Psychology, 37,* 271–281.

Belmont, J. M., Butterfield, E. C., & Ferretti, R. P. (1982). To secure transfer of training instruct self-management skills. In D. K. Detterman & R. J. Sternberg (Eds.), *How and how much can intelligence be increased.* Norwood, NJ: Ablex.

Blumenthal, S. H. (1980). A study of the relationship between speed of retrieval of verbal information and patterns of oral reading errors. *Journal of Learning Disabilities, 3,* 568–570.

Borkowski, J. G., Estrada, M., Milstead, M., & Hale, C. A. (1989). General problem-solving skills: Relations between metacognition and strategic processing. *Learning Disability Quarterly, 12,* 57–70.

Bos, C., & Anders, P. L. (1990). Toward an interactive model: Teaching test-based concepts to learning disabled students. In H. L. Swanson & B. K. Keogh (Eds.), *Learning disabilities: Theoretical and research issues* (pp. 247–261). Hillsdale, NJ: Erlbaum.

Brainerd, C. J., Kingman, J., & Howe, M. L. (1987). Long-term memory development and learning disability: Storage and retrieval loci of disabled/nondisabled differences. In S. Ceci (Ed.), *Handbook on cognitive social, and neurological aspects of learning disabilities.* Hillsdale, NJ: Erlbaum.

Brainerd, C. J., & Reyna, V. F. (1991). Acquisition and forgetting processes in normal and learning-disabled children: A disintegration/reintegration theory. In J. Obrzut and G. W. Hynd (Eds.), *Neuropsychological foundations of learning disabilities* (pp. 147–175). New York: Academic Press.

Brown, A. L., & Palinscar, A. S. (1988). Reciprocal teaching of comprehension strategies: A natural history of one program for enhancing learning. In J. Borkowski & J. P. Das (Eds.), *Intelligence and cognition in special children: Comparative studies of giftedness, mental retardation, and learning disabilities.* New York: Ablex.

Campione, J. C., Brown, A. L., Ferrara, F. A., Jones, R. S., & Steinberg, E. (1985). Breakdown in flexible use of information: Intelligence related differences in transfer following equivalent learning performances. *Intelligence, 9,* 297–315.

Ceci, S. J. (1986). Developmental study of learning disabilities and memory. *Journal of Experimental Child Psychology, 38,* 352–371.

Ceci, S. J., Ringstrom, M. D., &, Lea, S. E. G. (1980). Coding characteristics of normal and learning-disabled 10 year olds: Evidence for dual pathways to the cognitive system. *Journal of Experimental Psychology: Human Learning & Memory, 6,* 785–796.

Chi, M. T. H., Glaser, R., & Farr, M. (1988). *The nature of expertise.* Hillsdale, NJ: Erlbaum.

Cohen, R. L. (1981). Short-term memory deficits in reading disabled children in the absence of opportunity for rehearsal strategies. *Intelligence, 5,* 69–76.

Cooney, J. B., & Swanson, H. L. (1987). Overview of research on learning disabled children's memory development. In H. L. Swanson (Ed.), *Memory and learning disabilities* (pp. 2–40). Greenwich, CT: JAI Press.

Dallego, M. P., & Moely, B. E. (1980). Free recall in boys of normal and poor reading levels as a function of task manipulation. *Journal of Experimental Child Psychology, 30,* 62–78.

Daneman, M., & Carpenter, P. A. (1980). Individual differences in working memory and reading. *Journal of Verbal Learning Verbal Behavior, 19,* 450–466.

Daneman, M., & Carpenter, P. A. (1983). Individual differences in integrating information between and within sentences. *Journal of Experimental Psychology: Learning, Memory & Cognition, 9,* 561–575.

Dansereau, D. F., McDonald, B. A., Collins, D. W., Garland, J., Holley, C. D., Diehoff, G., & Evans, S. H. (1979). Evaluation of a teaching strategy system. In H. F. O'Neil & C. D. Spielberger (Eds.), *Cognitive and affective learning strategies* (pp. 3–43). New York: Academic Press.

Dawson, M. H., Hallahan, D. P., Reeve, R. E., & Ball, D. W. (1980). The effect of reinforcement and verbal rehearsal on selective attention in learning-disabled children. *Journal of Abnormal Child Psychology, 8,* 133–144.

Dempster, F. N., & Cooney, J. B. (1987). Individual differences in digit span, susceptibility to proactive interference, and aptitude/achievement test scores. *Intelligence, 6,* 399–416.

Elbert, J. C. (1984). Short-term memory encoding and memory search in the word recognition of learning-disabled children. *Journal of Learning Disabilities, 17,* 342–345.

Gelzheiser, L. (1984). Generalization from categorical memory tasks to prose by learning disabled adolescents. *Journal of Educational Psychology, 76,* 1128–1138.

Gelzheiser, L. M., Cort, R., & Shephard, M. J. (1987). Is minimal strategy instruction sufficient for learning disabled students. *Learning Disability Quarterly, 10,* 267–275.

Gelzheiser, L. M., Solar, R. A., Shephard, M. J., & Wozniak, R. H. (1983). Teaching learning disabled children to memorize: Rationale for plans and practice. *Journal of Learning Disabilities, 16,* 421–425.

Haines, D., & Torgesen, J. K. (1979). The effects of incentives on short-term memory and rehearsal in reading disabled children. *Learning Disability Quarterly, 2,* 18–55.

Hall, J., Wilson, K., Humphreys, M., Tinzmann, M., & Bowyer, P. (1983). Phonemic-similarity effects in good vs poor readers. *Memory & Cognition, 11,* 520–527.

Hallahan, D. P., & Reeve, R. (1980). Selective attention and distractibility. In B. Keogh (Ed.), Advances in special education (pp. 141–182). Greenwich, CT: JAI Press.

Johnson, R. S., Rugg, M., & Scott, T. (1987). Phonological similarity effects, memory span and developmental reading disorders. *British Journal of Psychology, 78,* 205–211.

Jorm, A. F. (1983). Specific reading retardation and work memory: A review. *British Journal of Psychology, 74,* 311–342.

Kolligian, J., & Sternberg, R. J. (1987). Intelligence, information processing, and specific learning disabilities: A triarchic synthesis. *Journal of Learning Disabilities, 20,* 8–17.

Koorland, M. A., & Wolking, W. D. (1982). Effect of reinforcement on modality of stimulus control in learning. *Learning Disability Quarterly, 5,* 264–273.

Kyllonen, P. C., & Christal, R. E. (1990). Reasoning ability is (little more than) working-memory capacity?! *Intelligence, 14,* 389–433.

Lehman, E. B., & Brady, K. M. (1982). Presentation modality and taxonomic category as encoding dimensions from good and poor readers. *Journal of Learning Disabilities, 15,* 103–105.

Lorsbach, T. C., & Worman, L. J. (1989). The development of explicit and implicit forms of memory in learning disabled children. *Contemporary Educational Psychology, 14,* 67–76.

Manis, F. R. (1985). Acquisition of word identification skills in normal and disabled readers. *Journal of Educational Psychology, 27,* 28-90.

Mazer, S. R., McIntyre, C. W., Murray, M. E., Till, R. E., & Blackwell, S. L. (1983). Visual persistence and information pick-up in learning disabled children. *Journal of Learning Disabilities, 16,* 221–225.

McIntyre, C. W., Murray, M. E., Coronin, C. M., & Blackwell, S. L. (1978). Span of apprehension in learning disabled boys. *Journal of Learning Disabilities, 11,* 13–20.

Morrison, F. J., Giordani, B., & Nagy, J. (1977). Reading disability: An information processing analysis. *Science, 196,* 77–79.

Morrison, S. R., & Siegel, L. S. (1991). Arithmetic disability: Theoretical considerations and empirical evidence for this subtype. In L. Feagans, E. Short, & L. Meltzer (Eds.), *Subtypes of learning disabilities: Theoretical perspectives and research* (pp. 189–209). Hillsdale, NJ: Erlbaum.

Neisser, U. (1967). *Cognitive psychology.* New York: Appleton-Century-Crofts.

Palinscar, A. S., & Brown, A. L. (1984). Reciprocal teaching of comprehension-fostering and monitoring activities. *Cognition and Instruction, 1,* 117–175.

Paris, S. G., Cross, D. R., & Lipson, M. Y. (1984). Informed strategies for learning: A program to improve children's reading awareness and comprehension. *Journal of Educational Psychology, 76,* 1239–1252.

Pennington, B. F., Van Orden, G. C., Smith, S. D., Green, P. A., & Haith, M. M. (1990). Phonological processing skills and deficits in adult dyslexic. *Child Development, 61,* 1753–1778.

Pressley, M., Johnson, C. J., & Symons, S. (1987). Elaborating to learn and learning to elaborate. *Journal of Learning Disabilities, 20,* 76–91.

Pressley, M., Scruggs, T. E., & Mastropieri, M. A. (1989). Memory strategy research in learning disabilities: Present and future directions. *Learning Disabilities Research, 4,* 68–77.

Pressley, M., Symons, S., Snyder, B. L., & Cariglia-Bull, T. (1989). Strategy instruction research is coming of age. *Learning Disability Quarterly, 12,* 36–54.

Samuels, S. J. (1987a). Information processing and reading. *Journal of Learning Disabilities, 20,* 18–22.

Samuels, S. J. (1987b). Why is it difficult to characterize the underlying cognitive deficits in special education populations. *Exceptional Children, 54,* 60–62.

Scruggs, T. E., & Mastropieri, M. A. (1989). Mnemonic instruction of LD students: A field-based evaluation. *Learning Disability Quarterly, 12,* 119–125.

Scruggs, T. E., Mastropieri, M. A., Levin, J. R., & Gaffney, J. S. (1987). Facilitating the acquisition of science facts in learning disabled students. *American Educational Research Journal, 22,* 575–586.

Shankwieler, D., Liberman, I. Y., Mark, S. L., Fowler, L. A., & Fischer, F. W. (1979). The speech code and learning to read. *Journal of Experimental Psychology: Human Learning & Memory, 5,* 531–545.

Siegel, L., & Linder, B. A. (1984). Short-term memory processing in children with reading and arithmetic learning disabilities. *Developmental Psychology, 20,* 200–207.

Siegel, L. S., & Ryan, E. B. (1988). Development of grammatical-sensitivity, phonological, and short-term memory skills in normally achieving and learning disabled children. *Developmental Psychology, 24,* 28–37.

Siegel, L. S., & Ryan, E. B. (1989). The development of working memory in normally achieving and subtypes of learning disabled children. *Child Development, 60,* 973–980.

Spear, L. C., & Sternberg, R. J. (1987). An information-processing framework for understanding reading disability. In S. Ceci (Ed.), *Handbook of cognitive, social and neuropsychological aspects of learning disabilities* (pp. 3–32). Hillsdale, NJ: Erlbaum.

Stanovich, K. E. (1986). Matthew effects in reading: Some consequences of individual differences in the acquisition of literacy. *Reading Research Quarterly, 21,* 360–407.

Stanovich, K. E. (1987). Introduction. *Merrill-Palmer Quarterly, 33,* 253–254.

Stanovich, K. E. (1988). Explaining the differences between the dyslexic and the garden-variety poor reader: The phonological core variable–difference model. *Journal of Learning Disabilities, 21,* 590–605.

Swanson, H. L. (1981). Vigilance deficit in learning disabled children: A signal detection analysis. *Journal of Child Psychology and Psychiatry, 22,* 393–399.

Swanson, H. L. (1982). Conceptual processes as a function of age and enforced attention in learning disabled children: Evidence for deficient rule learning. *Contemporary Educational Psychology, 7,* 152–160.

Swanson, H. L. (1983a). A developmental study of vigilance in learning disabled and non-disabled children. *Journal of Abnormal Child Psychology, 11,* 415–429.

Swanson, H. L. (1983b). Relations among metamemory, rehearsal activity and word recall in learning disabled and nondisabled readers. *British Journal of Educational Psychology, 53,* 186–194.

Swanson, H. L. (1983c). A study of nonstrategic linguistic coding on visual recall of learning disabled and normal readers. *Journal of Learning Disabilities, 16,* 209–216.

Swanson, H. L. (1984a). Does theory guide teaching practice? *Remedial and Special Education, 5,* 7–16.

Swanson, H. L. (1984b). Effects of cognitive effort and word distinctiveness on learning disabled and nondisabled readers' recall. *Journal of Educational Psychology, 76,* 894–908.

Swanson, H. L. (1984c). Semantic and visual memory codes in learning disabled readers. *Journal of Experimental Child Psychology, 37,* 124–140.

Swanson, H. L. (1985). Assessing learning disabled children's intellectual performance: An information processing perspective. In K. Gadow (Ed.), *Advances in learning and behavioral disabilities* (vol. 4) (pp. 225–272). Greenwich, CT: JAI Press.

Swanson, H. L. (1986). Do semantic memory deficiencies underlie disabled readers' encoding processes? *Journal of Experimental Child Psychology, 41,* 461–488.

Swanson, H. L. (1987a). The combining of multiple hemispheric resources in learning disabled and skilled readers' recall of words: A test of three information processing models. *Brain & Cognition, 6,* 41–54.

Swanson, H. L. (1987b). Information processing theory and learning disabilities: An overview. *Journal of Learning Disabilities, 20,* 3–7.

Swanson, H. L. (1987c). Verbal coding deficits in the recall of pictorial information in learning disabled readers: The influence of a lexical system. *American Educational Research Journal, 24,* 143–170.

Swanson, H. L. (1988). Learning disabled children's problem solving: Identifying mental processes underlying intelligent performances. *Intelligence, 12,* 261–278.

Swanson, H. L. (1989). Central processing strategy differences in gifted, average, learning disabled and mentally retarded children. *Journal of Experimental Child Psychology, 47,* 370–397.

Swanson, H. L. (1990). Intelligence and learning disabilities. In H. L. Swanson & B. K. Keogh (Eds.), Learning disabilities and research issues (pp. 97–113). Hillsdale, NJ: Erlbaum.

Swanson, H. L. (1991a). A subgroup analysis of learning-disabled and skilled readers' working memory: In search of a model of reading comprehension. In L. Feagans, E. Short, and L. Meltzer (Eds.), *Subtypes of learning disabilities: Theoretical perspectives and research* (pp. 209–228). Hillsdale, NJ: Erlbaum.

Swanson, H. L. (1991b). Learning disabilities, distinctive encoding, and hemispheric resources: An information processing perspective. In J. Obrzut and G. W. Hynd (Eds.), *Neuropsychological foundations of learning disabilities* (pp. 147–175). New York: Academic Press.

Swanson, H. L., Cochran, K., & Ewers, C. (1989). Working memory and reading disabilities. *Journal of Abnormal Child Psychology, 17,* 745–756.

Swanson, H. L., Cochran, K. F., & Ewers, C. A. (1990). Can learning disabilities be determined from working memory performance. *Journal of Learning Disabilities, 23,* 59–67.

Swanson, H. L., & Cooney, J. (1985). Strategy transformations in learning disabled children. *Learning Disability Quarterly, 8,* 221–231.

Swanson, H. L., Cooney, J. D., & Overholser, J. D. (1989). The effects of self-generated visual mnemonics on adult learning disabled readers' word recall. *Learning Disabilities Research, 4,* 26–35.

Swanson, H. L., Kozleski, E., & Stegic, P. (1987). Effects of cognitive training on disabled readers' prose recall: Do cognitive processes change during intervention. *Psychology in the Schools, 24,* 378–384.

Swanson, H. L., & Ransby, M. (in press). The study of cognitive processes in learning disabled students. In S. Vaughn & C. Bos (Eds.), *Research issues in learning disabilities: Theory, methodology, assessment, and ethics.* New York: Springer-Verlag.

Swanson, H. L., & Rathgeber, A. (1986). The effects of organizational dimensions on learning disabled readers' recall. *Journal of Educational Research, 79,* 155–162.

Tarver, S. G., Hallahan, D. P., Kauffman, J. M., & Ball, D. W. (1976). Verbal rehearsal and selective attention in children with learning disabilities: A developmental lag. *Journal of Experimental Child Psychology, 22,* 375–385.

Torgesen, J. K. (1978). Memorization process in reading-disabled children. *Journal of Educational Psychology, 69,* 571–578.

Torgesen, J. K. (1988). Studies of children with learning disabilities who perform poorly on memory span tasks. *Journal of Learning Disabilities, 21,* 605–612.

Torgesen, J. K. (1991). Subtypes as prototypes: Extended studies of rationally defined extreme groups. In L. Feagans, E. Short, & L. Meltzer (Eds.), *Subtypes of learning disabilities: Theoretical perspectives and research* (pp. 229–247). Hillsdale, NJ: Erlbaum.

Torgesen, J. K., Bowen, C., & Ivey, C. (1978). Task structure vs. modality of the visual-oral digit span test. *Journal of Educational Psychology, 70,* 451–456.

Torgesen, J. K., & Goldman, T. (1977). Rehearsal and short term memory in second grade reading disabled children. *Child Development, 48,* 56–61.

Torgesen, J. K., & Houck, D. G. (1980). Processing deficiencies of learning disabled children who perform poorly on the digit span task. *Journal of Educational Psychology, 72,* 141–160.

Torgesen, J. K., Murphy, H. A., & Ivey, C. (1979). The effects of an orienting task on the memory performance of reading disabled children. *Journal of Learning Disabilities, 12,* 396–402.

Torgesen, J. K., Rashotte, C. A., & Greenstein, J. (1988). Language comprehension in learning disabled children who perform poorly on memory span tests. *Journal of Educational Psychology, 80,* 480–487.

Torgesen, J. K., Rashotte, J., Greenstein, J., & Portes, P. (1991). Further studies of learning disabled children with severe performance problems on the digit span test. *Learning Disabilities: Research & Practice, 6,* 134–145.

Wong, B. Y. L. (1982). Strategic behaviors in selecting retrieval cues in gifted, normal achieving and learning disabled children. *Journal of Learning Disabilities, 15,* 33–37.

Wong, B. Y. L. (1991). Assessment of metacognitive research in learning disabilities: Theory, research and practice. In H. L. Swanson (Ed.), *Handbook on the assessment of learning disabilities: Theory, research and practice* (pp. 265–284). Austin, TX: Pro-Ed.

Wong, B. Y. L., & Jones, W. (1982). Increasing metacomprehension in learning-disabled and normally-achieving students through self-questioning training. *Learning Disability Quarterly, 5,* 228–240.

Wong, B. Y. L., Wong, R., & Foth, D. (1977). Recall and clustering of verbal materials among normal and poor readers. *Bulletin of the Psychonomic Society, 10,* 375–378.

Worden, P. E. (1986). Comprehension and memory for prose in the learning disabled. In S. J. Ceci (Ed.), *Handbook of cognitive, social and neuropsychological aspects of learning disabilities* (vol. 1) (pp. 241–262). Hillsdale, NJ: Erlbaum.

Worden, P. E., & Nakamura, G. V. (1983). Story comprehension and recall in learning-disabled vs. normal college students. *Journal of Educational Psychology, 74,* 633–639.

Worden, P. E., Malmgren, P., & Gabourie, P. (1982). Memory for stories in learning disabled adults. *Journal of Learning Disabilities, 15,* 145–152.

3

Social/Behavioral Characteristics

Terry M. McLeod

Evidence shows that many students with learning disabilities (LD) experience behavioral abnormalities and social skill deficits. Social and behavioral characteristics are important because of the effect they have on the child's relationships with parents and teachers, on the child's academic progress in school, and on the child's social adjustment as an adult (Bryan and Bryan 1986).

This chapter is a review of the literature regarding the social and behavioral characteristics of children with LD. Topics covered include behavioral characteristics, self-concept, locus of control, adaptive behavior, social skills, and parents', teachers', and peers' perceptions of students with LD.

BEHAVIORAL CHARACTERISTICS

Although students with LD may possess average to above average intelligence, they often exhibit social skill deficits that are manifested in a variety of behaviors. Children with LD are often described as exhibiting lack of judgment, difficulties in perceiving how others feel, problems in socializing and making friends, problems in establishing family relationships, social disabilities in the school setting, poor self-concept, and problems in adaptive behavior (Lerner 1989). When asked to assign behavioral characteristics to students with LD, teachers use terms such as "aggressive," "hyperactive," "possessing a short attention span," "withdrawn," "possessing no sense of responsibility or self-discipline," "disruptive," "disinterested," "angry," "hostile," "attention seeking," and "having a poor attitude toward school." The same teachers rated students with LD as more academically competent but more troublesome than mentally retarded students (Keogh et al. 1974). It is important to understand that there is no certainty as to which, if any, behavioral characteristic(s) a given child with LD will exhibit. Some children present an array of the aforementioned traits, others only one or two, and still others present no social/behavioral deficits at all. Equally important is the indication that, rather than being specific to children with LD, these traits may be present with equal frequency in children exhibiting mild mental retardation or behavioral disorders (Gresham et al. 1987). Hence, extreme caution should be taken before concluding that the presence of a particular behavior, or array of behaviors, indicates the presence of a learning disability.

SELF-CONCEPT
Effect on School Performance

It is quite common to find students with LD being described as having low self-concept or negative self-perception. Such statements seem logical in light of the number and variety of difficulties experienced by these students (Grolnick and Ryan 1990). Concern for self-concept in students with LD is based not only on the viewpoint that self-concept affects general mental health and happiness of the child but also on the realization that self-concept has a direct effect on classroom behavior and students' attitude toward academic material (Cooley and Ayers 1988). The effect of self-concept on achievement was clearly demonstrated in Kershner's (1990) study of self-concept and IQ as predictors of remedial success in children with LD. Data from this study indicated that self-concept predicted patterns of successful achievement in spelling, arithmetic, and written language. IQ, on the other hand, was found to have no effect on students' ability to profit from remedial activities.

Causes of Negative Self-Concept

Potential causes of negative self-concept in students with LD are neither unique nor surprising. They include academic failure and negative feedback at school (Sabatino 1982); the negative effects of labeling, including the potential for self-fulfilling prophecy (Good 1982; Rosenthal and Jacobsen 1968); and the potential social stigma and interruption of classroom activities inherent in pulling students out of the regular classroom to attend special education classes (Biklen and Zollers 1986; Reynolds and Wang 1983).

It should be noted, however, that some studies discount the negative effects of pullout programs. Studies have shown that students with LD have more positive self-concepts when they spend some time in a resource program (Coleman 1983; Rogers et al. 1978). Battle and Blowers (1982) found that the self-concepts of students placed in special education classes actually improved after the students were removed from the regular classroom. It is entirely possible that placement in a resource setting, where academic tasks are designed specifically for the individual student and success is more common than in the regular classroom, has the effect of raising the self-concepts of students with LD.

Global and Academic Self-Concept

Studies of self-concept in students with LD can be divided into two categories. One category includes studies that examine a global self-concept; the other examines particular aspects of self-concept and most often includes academic or cognitive self-concept. Any examination of studies addressing self-concept in students with LD should begin with a determination of the category in which the study fits (Cooley and Ayers 1988).

Studies that examine self-concept from a global point of view utilize general measures of self-concept such as the Coopersmith (Coopersmith 1981) inventory or the Piers-Harris (Piers 1984) scale. While it can be argued that it is rare for a person to have consistent negative feelings about every aspect of self, studies examining global self-concept in students with LD have generally supported the hypothesis that these students have lower global self-concepts than do normally achieving students (Bingham 1980; Bryan and Pearl 1979; Larsen et al. 1973; Margalit and Zak 1984). It should be noted, however, that Silverman and Zigmond (1983) found no such differences in a study that included a population of adolescents with LD.

Findings in studies examining specific components of self-concept reveal that the academic self-concepts of students with LD are consistently lower than those of normally achieving students (Bryan 1986; Chapman and Boersma 1979; Hiebert et al. 1982; Priel and Leshem 1990). However, when measures of self-worth, as opposed to academic self-concept, are used, students with LD score about the same as their normally achieving peers (Lincoln and Chazan 1979; Pearl et al. 1983; Tollefson et al. 1982; Priel and Hunter 1990; Winne et al. 1982). Thus, these studies indicate that students with LD have a rather realistic concept of their academic abilities and yet are able to maintain a level of self-worth that is no lower than that of normally achieving students.

Studies have also been conducted in which both a global self-concept and an academic self-concept were considered. The findings in these studies have been mixed. Battle (1979) and Rogers and Saklofske (1985) found that both global and academic self-concept measures differentiated between students with LD and normally achieving students. Other studies indicate that only academic self-concept measures differentiated between the two groups (Carrol et al. 1984; Winne et al. 1982).

Cooley and Ayers (1988) suggest that a reason for the inconsistent results in these studies may lie in the fact that global measures of self-concept have included in them a small proportion of academic self-concept questions. In their study of global and academic self-concept, Cooley and Ayers (1988) found a difference in global self-concept between students with LD and normally achieving students. Further statistical analysis indicated that the difference was due largely to the academic component within the global self-concept measure being utilized. Removal of the academic component resulted in these differences disappearing. The authors concluded that in some studies the small number of academic items is enough to cause the instruments to differentiate among groups and in other studies the effect is not strong enough to differentiate among groups.

Another dimension was added to the issue of self-concept and LD in a study by Grolnick and Ryan (1990). The authors compared the general, cognitive, and academic self-concepts of students with LD, normally achieving students, and low achieving students. As before, there was a significant difference between students with LD and normally achieving students in academic and cognitive self-concept, with the students with LD having the lower scores. However, there was no significant difference between students with LD and the low achieving group. Additionally, no group differences were found in general self-concept. These results bring to light the question of whether low academic self-concept is a discrete characteristic of students with LD or whether such self-concept deficits exist in all students experiencing academic difficulty. Further research is needed in this area.

The results of these studies indicate consistent findings of academic self-concept deficits in students with LD. Findings of general self-concept deficits are less consistent and more open to conjecture. The data suggest that the most effective methods for raising the self-concept of students with LD will be those that increase students' academic self-concept (Cooley and Ayers 1988).

LOCUS OF CONTROL
Developmental Theory and Characteristics

Locus of control, also referred to as *attribution,* is a concept that refers to how people perceive control factors in specific events in their lives. Individuals who attribute success or failure on a certain task to their own skills, ability, and behavior are said to have an internal locus of control. Individuals who believe that outcomes are based on luck, fate, or the behavior of others are said to have an external locus of control.

Lewis and Lawrence-Patterson (1989), in their review of literature, found support for developmental theory indicating that internality in nondisabled children increases with age. Lawrence and Winschel (1975) hypothesize that locus of control in nondisabled children is external for both success and failure at the age of 4 or 5. By age 6 to 7, locus of control for success becomes internalized, and by age 10 to 11, locus of control for both success and failure is internalized.

The importance of locus of control, as it applies to the education of children, lies in the effect that it has on children's attitudes toward school-related tasks. Children who possess an internal locus of control are found to exhibit high levels of perseverance on difficult tasks; to delay gratification; and to seek, retain, and reproduce information (Stipek and Weisz 1981; Dweck 1975). Conversely, children who possess an external locus of control generally feel that they have little impact on the outcome of tasks and that task difficulty, luck, or fate control their successes and failures. These children respond to difficult tasks with withdrawn behavior, lowered task completion, and negative self-concept (Dweck and Repucci 1973). Children who exhibit these traits are often described as exhibiting "learned helplessness" and may be unable to complete difficult or challenging tasks even when equipped with the skills and abilities to do so (Bryan 1986). Some studies have found traits of learned helplessness to be common in students with LD (Pearl et al. 1980; Stipek and Hoffman 1980). Developing an understanding of locus of control as it relates to students with LD is critical in that it may enable practitioners to develop more effective intervention strategies (Bender 1987).

Learning Disabilities and Locus of Control

Studies addressing locus of control in students with LD have had mixed findings. Several studies indicate that students with LD exhibit a significantly higher external locus of control than do their normally achieving peers (Chapman and Boersma 1979; Fincham and Barling 1978; Lewis and Lawrence-Patterson 1989; Rogers and Saklofske 1985; Tarnowski and Nay 1989). Other studies indicate that students with LD are also less likely to interpret success as an indicator of ability and more likely to interpret failure as an indicator of a lack of ability (Aponik and Dembo 1983; Bryan and Pearl 1979; Butkowsky and Willows 1980; Friedman and Medway 1987; Keogh et al. 1972; Palmer et al. 1982; Pearl et al. 1980; Pearl et al. 1983). However, other studies fail to demonstrate such traits (Cooley and Ayers 1988; Tollefson et al. 1982).

Cooley and Ayers (1988) did find a significant correlation between school-related self-concept and the attributions of students with LD. Children with low school-related self-concept were also more likely to exhibit external locus of control with reference to school success and failure. This pattern of behavior often leads to lack of motivation with reference to school-related tasks.

Although Friedman and Medway (1987) were able to demonstrate that students with LD exhibited an external locus of control with reference to school success and failure, they were not able to identify tendencies toward learned helplessness. These findings conflict with other studies in which students with LD demonstrated lower expectation for success than did their normally achieving peers (Pearl et al. 1980; Stipek and Hoffman 1980).

The mixed findings in studies examining the locus of control of students with LD make it difficult to draw firm conclusions regarding this issue. There are some indications that self-concept and locus of control are correlated. It remains to be seen whether that relationship is cause–effect or circular (Cooley and Ayers 1988). Indications are that positive results can be achieved by addressing students' academic self-concept (Cooley and Ayers 1988) and through attribution retraining (Bryan 1986).

ADAPTIVE BEHAVIOR
Definition

Initially defined as "the effectiveness or degree with which individuals meet the standards of personal independence and social responsibility expected for age and cultural group" (Grossman 1983, p. 1), *adaptive behavior* is a concept that was first applied in the identification of persons exhibiting mental retardation. In mental retardation, intellectual performance must be significantly below average and there must be one or more significant deficits in adaptive behavior. Adaptive behavior measures designed with the purpose of identifying mental retardation typically rely on information provided by teachers and/or parents and look at performance in nonschool environments that require personal care; communication; and social, civic, and vocational skills.

Weller and her coworkers provide a theoretical formulation of adaptive behavior problems in students with LD that differs from the concept of adaptive behavior just described (Weller 1980; Weller and Strawser 1981). They defined adaptive behavior as a set of behaviors including on-task behavior, use of language in social situations, participation in effective social relationships, and social coping in the learning environment (Weller 1980; Weller and Strawser 1981). It is important to note that whereas the Grossman definition of adaptive behavior refers to nonschool environments, the Weller and Strawser formulation views the behaviors as necessary for adaptation to the public school classroom. Adaptive behavior differs from problem- or task-related behavior because it refers to those aspects of the child's behavior that are adaptive to the demands of the classroom (Bender and Golden 1989).

Learning Disabilities and Adaptive Behavior

Research with students with LD has begun to identify deficits in adaptive behavior in mainstream and special education classes as a major associated problem (Bender 1986a; Weller and Strawser 1987; Weller et al. 1985). Research with adolescents has also noted deficits in behaviors that lead to success in academic situations (Bender 1985b; Epstein et al. 1985). McKinney and colleagues (1982) compared the task-oriented behaviors of matched pairs of learning-disabled and non–learning-disabled students. Results indicated that the learning-disabled children demonstrated less task-oriented behavior and more nonconstructive off-task behavior than did the non–learning-disabled children. Also, the learning-disabled children were rated as less extroverted, less creative, and less curious than non–learning-disabled children. This array of behaviors was more extensive than the unitary high levels of off-task behavior demonstrated in earlier studies (Bryan 1974; Richey and McKinney 1978).

Weller (1980) discusses a consolidated perspective in which the academic deficits and measures of ability typically used to identify students with LD are supplemented with an evaluation of adaptive behavior. It is suggested that only when adaptive behavior information is available can a discrimination between mild/moderate and moderate/severe LD be made. Thus, according to Weller, while eligibility for LD programs may be based on academic and intellectual assessment, placement in specific types of LD programs should be based, to some degree, on consideration of adaptive behavior.

Similarly, in their topical review of the adaptive behavior of students with LD, McKinney and Feagans (1983) conclude that students with LD have been shown to exhibit relatively stable patterns of classroom behavior that distinguish them from normally achieving students and contribute to difficulties in school learning. They feel that the findings have applied relevance for both diagnostic practice and intervention techniques and that adaptive classroom behavior is extremely important in the understanding and definition of LD.

Although many comparisons have indicated task-oriented problems and other specific types of problems among students with LD (Bender 1985a; McKinney and Feagans 1983, 1984), Bender and Golden (1988) conducted one of the few studies that directly compared learning-disabled and non–learning-disabled groups on adaptive behavior. Using the construct and the instrument prepared by Weller and Strawser (1981), 54 learning-disabled students were compared with 54 non–learning-disabled students by using mainstream teachers' ratings of the behaviors of the two groups. Results indicated that the learning-disabled students were rated as demonstrating less adaptive behavior than the non–learning-disabled group on each subscale, including social coping, relationships, pragmatic language, and production. The learning-disabled group was also rated higher on three of the five subscales of problem behavior. Hence, behavioral problems among mainstreamed students with LD go beyond task-oriented behaviors and are broader than may originally have been thought.

Correlates of Adaptive Behavior

Given the previously cited information, the issue becomes one of documenting the correlates of the adaptive behavior problems in an attempt to suggest potential relationships that may have an impact on adaptive behavior. Bender (1986a, 1987b) found that certain personality factors such as temperament and self-concept may impact on the classroom behavior of students with LD. Cardell and Parmar (1988) investigated the temperament characteristics of children with LD by comparing responses of their teachers on the Temperament Assessment Battery (Martin 1984) to those of teachers of normally achieving students. The teachers of students with LD consistently evidenced perceptions in the negative direction, as compared to teachers of normally achieving students. It was hypothesized that teachers' perceptions of temperament may affect their perception of the child with LD. This raises the possibility that interventions designed to affect self-concept or other personality measures may also have a positive impact on the adaptive behavior of mainstreamed students with LD. These findings were confirmed in a study conducted by Bender and Golden (1989) in which teachers rated the adaptive behavior, classroom behavior, and self-concept of mainstreamed and self-contained students with LD. The results of the study support the suggestion that learning-disabled students' failure may be related to dysfunctional behavioral adaptations to the learning environment, rather than to academic failure exclusively (Bender and Golden 1988; McKinney and Feagans 1983). In light of these findings, there is a need for similar research employing multiple measures of adaptive behavior, for research specific to mainstreamed students with LD, and for research on adaptive behavior in specific subtypes of LD. Additionally, research is needed to determine whether intervention paradigms that attempt to change self-concept and problem behaviors in the classroom lead to improvement in the overall adaptive behavior of students with LD (Bender and Golden 1989).

SOCIAL SKILLS
Social Skills Deficits as a Primary Learning Disability

Few would deny that the acquisition of social skills is of major importance if one expects to become a contributing member of society. To this end, much attention has been focused on the social skills of children with LD, resulting in unprecedented growth in social skills research (Gresham 1988). The effect of the emergence of social skill deficits as a major topic is demonstrated by the Interagency Committee on Learning Disabilities' (ICLD) proposal of a modified definition of LD that includes social skills deficits as a primary learning disability (Gresham and Elliott 1989; ICLD 1987). While there exists a lack of agreement as to whether lack of social skills should be considered a primary learning disability (Forness and Kavale 1991), research in this area continues to proliferate.

In their critique of the ICLD's social skills proposal, Forness and Kavale (1991) reviewed five hypotheses about the causal nature of social skill deficits in students with LD.

The hypotheses are:

1. Social skill deficits result from the same neurologic dysfunction that is presumed to cause the academic aspect of the students' learning disability.
2. Social skill deficits are secondary deficits that develop out of and as a result of the students' academic difficulty. Presumably, the academic problems inherent in LD lead to negative consequences that prevent the development of social skills.
3. Social learning theory indicates that students with LD fail to learn and perform social skills due to lack of environmental opportunity and reinforcement.
4. The stress of parenting a handicapped child may lead to dysfunctional family situations that precipitate social skill deficits in the child.
5. The occurrence of social skill deficits in students with LD may be the result of comorbidity, or overlap, between LD and other conditions such as hyperactivity and depression.

There is no clear, concise evidence supporting any one of these hypotheses over the others. Additionally, it should be recognized that this listing is quite preliminary and not exhaustive. The possibility exists that additional underlying causal factors remain to be discovered (Forness and Kavale 1991).

Impact of Social Skill Deficits

Research indicates that social skill deficits are common in students with LD and that these deficits have a negative effect on learning-disabled students' relationships with both peers and teachers, as well as on their ability to function in the regular classroom environment (McConaughy 1986; McConaughy and Ritter 1986; Pearl 1987; Pearl et al. 1986; Ritter 1989; Stilliadis and Weiner 1989). Social skill deficits also appear to have a major impact on learning-disabled students' decisions as to whether to complete or drop out of school (Seidel and Vaughn 1991). In a study designed to investigate the extent to which learning-disabled students who drop out of school differ from learning-disabled high school completers on self-perceptions of social alienation from classmates and teachers, it was found that learning-disabled students who dropped out reported significantly stronger perceptions of social alienation from both their teachers and classmates than did students with LD that completed high school (Seidel and Vaughn 1991). As a result of such findings, various intervention techniques targeting social skill deficits have been devised and employed in efforts to make students with LD more socially capable (Blackbourn 1989; Hazel et al. 1982; LaGreca and Mesibov 1979, 1981; Vaughn 1985; Vaughn et al. 1988; Vaughn et al. 1991).

Two things that the majority of the previously mentioned intervention studies have in common is that they usually involve elementary-age children and they address the relationship between students with LD and their peers. Although studies exist that indicate that adolescents with LD exhibit social skill deficits (Bryan et al. 1989; McConaughy 1986; McConaughy and Ritter 1986; Ritter 1989), there is presently a paucity of research relating these deficits to the mainstream classroom performance of adolescents with LD. With the notable exception of a study by Salend and Salend (1986) in which mainstream and special education teachers specified social skill competencies necessary for successful performance in regular classrooms in secondary schools, little has been done to examine the degree to which secondary age students with LD understand what social skills are important in order to be successful in the mainstream. A major result of the Salend and Salend study is the categorization of social skills into three functions that are necessary for effective functioning in the secondary-level mainstream classroom. These functions include exhibiting appropriate work habits, respecting others and their property, and following school rules. The authors feel that their study might provide the groundwork for identifying specific target behaviors and intervention strategies that might prove helpful in eliminating social skill deficits in adolescents with LD (Salend and Salend 1986).

Directions for Research

Given that the majority of research in the area of social skill deficits has occurred in the last seven to eight years (Gresham and Elliott 1989), a great deal remains to be explored. One such issue involves determining whether social skill deficits are specific only to students with LD or whether such deficits are common to an array of students including, but not limited to, those with mild mental retardation and behavioral disorders. Research indicates the latter may be a more accurate assessment (Gresham et al. 1987). Other issues involve the validation of instruments for assessing social skill deficits and validation of intervention methodology for treatment of social skill deficits in students with LD (Forness and Kavale 1991).

PERCEPTIONS OF PARENTS, TEACHERS, AND PEERS
Parental Perceptions

As in the case of any handicapping condition, the diagnosis of learning disability in a child is likely to precipitate a variety of stresses and concerns for the parents of that child. Parents of children with LD often hold attitudes toward their children that differ from those held by parents of nondisabled children, and those attitudes affect aspects of the child's life that are extremely important. The attitude of the family toward a child with a learning disability affects not only the success of educational programs but also the child's self-concept and motivation (McLoughlin 1985).

Parents of children with LD tend to hold rather negative attitudes toward the academic abilities of their children. These parents hold lower academic expectations for their children than do parents of nonhandicapped children, even in areas in which the child performs competently (Chapman and Boersma 1979). Additionally, mothers of children with LD tend to view their children's successes in much the same way their children do, linking success more to luck and less to ability than do mothers of nondisabled children (Pearl and Bryan 1982; Hiebert et al. 1982). In a comparison of parent-child perceptions of LD, it was found that parents exhibited significantly more negative perceptions of their learning-disabled children's academic and problem-solving abilities than did their children (McLoughlin et al. 1987).

Negative parental perceptions tend to extend into the social domain as well. Studies show that parents of children with LD perceive their children as being less persistent, more impulsive, and less considerate than nondisabled children (Owen et al. 1977; Strag 1972). Parents also hold a lower estimation of their children's self-esteem and social skills than do their children (Coleman 1984; McLoughlin et al. 1987).

These data indicate that, as previously stated, parents tend to hold rather negative perceptions of their learning-disabled children's academic and social abilities. Of interest is the indication that parents' perceptions of their children's LD were more negative than the children's self-perceptions. While some of the difference may be attributed to negative attitude brought on by parental fear, stress, and concern, indications are that much of the difference may be attributed to inaccurate or unrealistic perceptions on the part of children with LD. It appears that deficiencies in a variety of areas, including self-esteem, organizational skills, and social relationships, persist into the adolescence and adulthood of individuals with LD (Association of Children and Adults with Learning Disabilities 1982).

These findings indicate that in order to prevent misunderstanding and inaccurate perceptions, it is of great importance that parents and their learning-disabled children establish effective avenues of communication. Additionally, indications are that the need for support for both parents and children may extend through, and well beyond, the school-age years. Teachers, counselors, parent organizations, and family counselors can be sources of information and assistance in such cases (McLoughlin et al. 1987).

Teacher Perceptions

Teachers' perceptions of children with LD parallel those of parents. In one of the earliest studies of teachers' perceptions, it was found that children with LD were perceived as less cooperative, less attentive, less able to organize themselves, less able to cope with new situations, less socially acceptable to others, less accepting of responsibility, and less tactful than their normally achieving peers (Bryan and McGrady 1972). Later studies, utilizing a variety of rating scales, revealed teachers to perceive children with LD as showing more problem behaviors (Cullinan et al. 1981), engaging in appropriate social skills less often (Bursuck 1989), being less persistent and showing less task initiative (Palmer et al. 1982; Perlmutter et al. 1983), and being more distractible and more introverted (Perlmutter et al. 1983) than nondisabled children. Additionally, teachers perceive students with LD as less desirable to have in the classroom (Garrett and Crump 1980).

In an effort to determine the impact of temperament on academic status, Keogh (1983) found that three factors describe temperament in children: task orientation (the ability to stay with a task through completion), personal-social flexibility (adaptability in social situations), and reactivity (tendency to overreact or become annoyed, upset, or argumentative). Studies show that teachers rate children with LD as less task oriented and more reactive than their nondisabled peers (Bryan and Bryan 1986; Bender 1985b). Teachers seem to be particularly aware of behaviors that express apparent disproportionate responses (reactivity) to environmental stimuli (Bender 1987a).

Students with LD tend to be held in low esteem by teachers. This can lead to feelings of rejection and social alienation. Such feelings may ultimately cause the student to drop out of school (Seidel and Vaughn 1991). Efforts should be made to prevent such occurrences through formal efforts such as social skill instruction (Vaughn 1985) and through informal efforts such as ensuring that students with LD have every opportunity to participate in the social and extracurricular activities available in the child's school and community (Seidel and Vaughn 1991).

Peer Perceptions

Most studies addressing the peer status of children with LD utilize a sociogram measuring peer standing within a group of children. The two types of sociometric procedures most commonly used are nomination procedures and rating scale procedures (Weiner 1987).

Nomination procedures involve requesting that children name members of their group (class, grade, school, etc.) who possess certain characteristics or meet certain criteria. Nomination sociograms can be either positive or negative. Positive nomination sociograms require children to name others they like, thus measuring peer acceptance. Negative nomination sociograms require children to name those they dislike, thus measuring peer rejection. It should be understood, however, that acceptance and rejection are not poles on a common continuum. Many children who receive few positive nominations also receive few negative nominations and are considered to be isolates or neglected (Asher and Renshaw 1981).

Rating scale procedures require that the child rate every member of the peer group on a continuum with negative and positive ratings at each pole. These measures normally involve a 3- or 5-point scale. Because sex bias is often a factor in children's ratings of peers, many investigators choose to calculate scores based on same-sex ratings only (Weiner 1987). Both the nomination and rating scale methods of measuring peer status are considered reliable and have good concurrent and predictive validity (Weiner 1987).

In 1974, Bryan conducted a study of peer reactions to students with LD in 62 third-, fourth-, and sixth-grade classrooms. Because peer popularity and peer rejection are not always correlated, the sociometric test consisted of items designed to measure a child's popularity and rejection by others. Results showed that when a child with LD was compared at random to any other classmate, the child with LD was significantly less popular and significantly more rejected by peers than were normally functioning children. The results were the same when peer assessments of the same children were made one year later to assess the stability of peer status (Bryan 1976), as were those of Scranton and Ryckman (1979) using the same measure as Bryan with first- through third-grade students. A number of subsequent studies found that children with LD were held in lower esteem by their peers than were their normally functioning peers (Bruininks 1978; Garrett and Crump 1980; Horowitz 1981; Siperstein et al. 1978; Siperstein and Goding 1983; Sheare 1978). Additionally, Weiner (1987), in her review of the literature, found indications that girls with LD may have more serious peer status problems than boys with LD, that fewer children with LD were positively rated and more children with LD were negatively rated by their peers, and that teachers' and students' ratings of students with LD are positively correlated.

This is not to say that all students with LD experience rejection by their peers. Siperstein and Goding (1983) found that while the majority of learning-disabled students in their study were unpopular with their peers, 5% of the students with LD were selected by 70% of their classmates as students they liked best. Additionally, while Perlmutter and colleagues (1983) found that tenth-graders generally liked their nondisabled classmates better than their classmates with LD, 6 of the 28 students with LD were ranked in the top 25% in terms of popularity. The fact remains that, although there are exceptions, students with LD are held in relatively low esteem by many, if not all, of their peers.

SUMMARY

This chapter reviewed the social and behavioral characteristics of children with LD. It was found that children with LD exhibit a wide range of negative behavioral characteristics, but that these characteristics are not necessarily exclusive to the learning-disabled population. The same characteristics may also be found in children who are mentally retarded or behaviorally disordered. Studies examining self-concept in children with LD indicate that these children generally have lower self-esteem than that of normally achieving children. Further examination indicates that this low self-esteem seems to be limited to academic ability and does not necessarily carry over into general self-concept. Studies of locus of control generally indicate that children with LD generally possess an external locus of control for success and an internal locus of control for failure. Thus, they tend to credit their successes to the efforts of others, or to external conditions, and their failures to their own lack of ability.

Research in the area of adaptive behavior indicates that children with LD exhibit deficits in behaviors that lead to success in academic situations. These students' academic failures may be related to dysfunctional behavioral adaptations to the learning environment rather than to academic failure exclusively. Additionally, research indicates that children with LD exhibit an array of social skill deficits that interfere with their everyday functioning.

Finally, these factors combine to cause parents, teachers, and peers to hold rather negative views of children with LD. Indications are that these views not only affect the children's ability to function in school, but that they also affect the individuals as they move into adulthood. In light of the continuing strong evidence that children with LD experience behavioral and social skill deficits, it is important that research be conducted to identify which children are likely to experience such problems and what methods of treatment are most effective in minimizing or eliminating the problems.

REFERENCES

Aponik, D. A., & Dembo M. H. (1983). LD and normal adolescents' attributions of success and failure at different levels of task difficulty. *Learning Disability Quarterly, 6,* 31–39.

Asher, S. R., & Renshaw, P. D. (1981). Children without friends: Social knowledge and social-skill training. In S. R. Asher & J. M. Gottman (Eds.), *The development of children's friendships* (pp. 273–296). Cambridge: Cambridge University Press.

Association of Children and Adults with Learning Disabilities. (1982). ACLD vocational committee completes survey on LD adults. ACLD Newsbriefs, No. 145, pp. 1, 5, 20–23.

Battle, J. (1979). Self-esteem of students in regular and special classes. *Psychological Reports, 44,* 212–214.

Battle, J., & Blowers, T. (1982). A longitudinal comparative study of the self-esteem of students in regular and special education classes. *Journal of Learning Disabilities, 15,* 100–102.

Bender, W. N. (1985a). Differences between learning disabled and non-learning disabled children in temperament and behavior. *Learning Disability Quarterly, 8,* 11–18.

Bender, W. N. (1985b). Differentiated diagnosis based on the task-related behavior of learning disabled and low achieving adolescents. *Learning Disability Quarterly, 8,* 261–266.

Bender, W. N. (1986a). Teachability and behavior of learning disabled children. *Psychological Reports, 59,* 471–476.

Bender, W. N. (1986b). Teachability and personality of learning disabled children: Predictions of teachers' perceptions from personality variables. *Learning Disability Research, 2,* 4–9.

Bender, W. N. (1987a). Correlates of classroom behavior problems among learning disabled and non-disabled children in mainstream classes. *Learning Disability Quarterly, 10,* 317–324.

Bender, W. N. (1987b). Secondary personality and behavioral problems in adolescents with learning disabilities. *Journal of Learning Disabilities, 20,* 280–285.

Bender, W. N., & Golden, L. B. (1988). Comparison of adaptive behavior of learning disabled and non-learning disabled children. *Learning Disability Quarterly, 11*, 55–61.

Bender, W. N., & Golden, L. B. (1989). Prediction of adaptive behavior of learning disabled students in self-contained and resource classes. *Learning Disabilities Research, 5*(1), 45–50.

Biklen, D., & Zollers, N. (1986). The focus of advocacy in the LD field. *Journal of Learning Disabilities, 19*, 579–586.

Bingham, A. (1980). Career attitudes among boys with and without specific learning disabilities. *Exceptional Children, 44*, 341–342.

Blackbourn, J. M. (1989). Acquisition and generalization of social skills in elementary-aged children with learning disabilities. *Journal of Learning Disabilities, 22*, 28–34.

Bruininks, V. L. (1978). Actual and perceived peer status of learning disabled students in mainstream programs. *Journal of Special Education, 12*, 51–58.

Bryan, T. (1974). Peer popularity of learning disabled children. *Journal of Learning Disabilities, 7*, 621–625.

Bryan, T. (1976). Peer popularity of learning disabled children: A replication. *Journal of Learning Disabilities, 9*, 307–311.

Bryan, T. (1986). Self-concept and attributions of the learning disabled. *Learning Disabilities Focus, 1*(2), 82–89.

Bryan, T., & Bryan, J. H. (1986). *Understanding learning disabilities* (3rd ed.). Palo Alto, CA: Mayfield.

Bryan, T., & McGrady, H. J. (1972). Use of a teacher rating scale. *Journal of Learning Disabilities, 5*, 199–206.

Bryan, T., & Pearl, J. H. (1979). Self-concepts and locus of control of learning disabled children. *Journal of Clinical Child Psychology, 8*, 223–226.

Bryan, T., Pearl, R., & Fallon, P. (1989). Conformity to peer pressure by students with learning disabilities: A replication. *Journal of Learning Disabilities, 22*, 458–459.

Bryan, T. S. (1974). An observational analysis of classroom behaviors of children with learning disabilities. *Journal of Learning Disabilities, 7*, 26–34.

Bursuck, W. (1989). A comparison of students with learning disabilities to low achieving and higher achieving students on three dimensions of social competence. *Journal of Learning Disabilities, 22*, 188–194.

Butkowsky, I. S., & Willows, D. M. (1980). Cognitive motivational characteristics of children varying in reading ability: Evidence of learned helplessness in poor readers. *Journal of Educational Psychology, 72*, 408–422.

Cardell, C. D., & Parmar, R. S. (1988). Teacher perceptions of temperament characteristics of children classified as learning disabled. *Journal of Learning Disabilities, 21*, 497–502.

Carrol, J. L., Friederich, D., & Hundt, J. (1984). Academic self-concept and teachers' perceptions of normal, mentally retarded and learning disabled elementary students. *Psychology in the Schools, 21*, 343–348.

Chapman, J. W., & Boersma, F. J. (1979). Academic self-concept in learning disabled children: A study with the Student's Perception of Ability Scale. *Psychology in the Schools, 16*, 201–206.

Coleman, J. M. (1983). Handicapped labels and instructional segregation: Influences on children's self-concepts versus the perception of others. *Learning Disability Quarterly, 6*, 3–11.

Coleman, J. M. (1984). Mothers' predictions of the self-concept of their normal or learning disabled children. *Journal of Learning Disabilities, 17*, 214–217.

Cooley, E. J., & Ayers, R. R. (1988). Self-concept and success-failure attributions of non-handicapped students and students with learning disabilities. *Journal of Learning Disabilities, 21*, 174–178.

Coopersmith, S. (1981). *Coopersmith self-esteem inventory*. Palo Alto, CA: Consulting Psychologists Press.

Cullinan, D., Epstein, M. H., & Lloyd, J. W. (1981). School behavior problems of learning disabled and normal girls and boys. *Learning Disability Quarterly, 4,* 163–169.

Dweck, C. S. (1975). The role of expectations and attributions in the alleviation of learned helplessness. *Journal of Personality and Social Psychology, 31,* 674–685.

Dweck, D. W., & Repucci, N. D. (1973). Learned helplessness and reinforcement responsibility in children. *Journal of Personality and Social Psychology, 25,* 109–116.

Epstein, M. H., Bursuck, W., & Cullinan, D. (1985). Patterns of behavior problems among the learning disabled: Boys aged 12–18, girls aged 6–11, and girls aged 12–18. *Learning Disability Quarterly, 8,* 123–129.

Fincham, F. A., & Barling, J. (1978). Locus of control and generosity in learning disabled, normal achieving and gifted children. *Child Development, 49,* 530–533.

Forness, S. R., & Kavale, K. A. (1991). Social skill deficits as primary learning disabilities: a note on problems with the ICLD diagnostic criteria. *Learning Disabilities Research and Practice, 6,* 44–49.

Friedman, D. E., & Medway, F. J. (1987). Effects of varying performance sets and outcome on the expectations, attributions, and persistence of boys with learning disabilities. *Journal of Learning Disabilities, 20,* 312–316.

Garrett, M. K., & Crump, W. D. (1980). Peer acceptance, teacher references, and self-appraisal of social status among learning disabled students. *Learning Disability Quarterly, 3,* 42–48.

Good, T. L. (1982). How teachers' expectations affect results. *American Education, 18,* 25–32.

Gresham, F. M. (1988). Social competence and motivational characteristics of learning disabled students. In M. Wang, M. Reynolds, & H. Walberg (Eds.), *The handbook of special education: Research and practice* (pp. 283–302). Oxford, England: Pergamon Press.

Gresham, F. M., & Elliot, S. N. (1989). Social skill deficits as a primary learning disability. *Journal of Learning Disabilities, 22,* 120–124.

Gresham, F. M., Elliott, S. N., & Black, F. L. (1987). Teacher-rated skills of mainstreamed mildly handicapped and nonhandicapped children. *School Psychology Review, 16,* 78–88.

Grolnick, W. S., & Ryan, R. M. (1990). Self-perceptions, motivation, and adjustment in children with learning disabilities: A multiple group comparison study. *Journal of Learning Disabilities, 23,* 177–184.

Grossman, H. J. (Ed.). (1983). *Classification in mental retardation* (rev.). Washington, DC: American Association on Mental Deficiency.

Hazel, J. S., Schumaker, J. B., Sherman, J. A., & Sheldon J. (1982). Application of a group training program in social skills and problem solving skills to learning disabled and non-learning disabled youth. *Learning Disability Quarterly, 5,* 398–408.

Hiebert, B., Wong, B., & Hunter, M. (1982). Affective influences on learning disabled adolescents. *Learning Disability Quarterly, 5,* 334–343.

Horowitz, E. C. (1981). Popularity, decentering ability, and role-taking skills in learning disabled and normal children. *Learning Disability Quarterly, 4,* 23–30.

Interagency Committee on Learning Disabilities. (1987). *Learning disabilities: A report to the U.S. Congress.* Bethesda, MD: National Institutes of Health.

Keogh, B. K. (1983). Individual differences in temperament: A contribution to the personal, social, and educational competence of learning disabled children. In J. D. McKinney & L. Feagans (Eds.), *Current topics in learning disabilities.* Norwood, NJ: Ablex.

Keogh, B. K., Cahill, C. W., & MacMillan, D. L. (1972). Perception of interruption by educationally handicapped children. *American Journal of Mental Deficiency, 77,* 107–108.

Keogh, B. K., Tchir, C., & Windeguth-Behn, A. (1974). Teachers' perceptions of educationally high-risk children. *Journal of Learning Disabilities, 7,* 367–374.

Kershner, J. R. (1990). Self-concept and IQ as predictors of remedial success in children with learning disabilities. *Journal of Learning Disabilities, 23,* 368–374.

LaGreca, A. M., & Mesibov, G. B. (1979). Social skills intervention with learning disabled children: Selecting skills and implementing training. *Journal of Clinical Child Psychology, 8,* 234–241.

LaGreca, A. M., & Mesibov, G. B. (1981). Facilitating interpersonal functioning with peers in learning disabled children. *Journal of Learning Disabilities, 14,* 197–199.

Larsen, S. C., Parker, R., & Jorjorian, S. (1973). Differences in self-concept of normal and learning disabled children. *Perceptual and Motor Skills, 37,* 510.

Lawrence, E., & Winschel, J. (1975). Locus of control: Implications for special education. *Exceptional Children, 41,* 483–490.

Lerner, J. (1989). *Learning disabilities* (5th ed.). Boston: Houghton Mifflin.

Lewis, S. K., & Lawrence-Patterson, E. (1989). Locus of control of children with learning disabilities and perceived locus of control by significant others. *Journal of Learning Disabilities, 22,* 255–257.

Lincoln, A., & Chazan, S. (1979). Perceived competence and intrinsic motivation in learning disability children. *Journal of Clinical Child Psychology, 8,* 213–216.

Margalit, M., & Zak, I. (1984). Anxiety and self-concept of learning disabled children. *Journal of Learning Disabilities, 17,* 537–539.

Martin, R. (1984). *The temperament assessment battery: Interim manual.* Athens, GA: Developmental Metrics.

McConaughy, S. H. (1986). Social competence and behavioral problems of learning disabled boys aged 12–16. *Journal of Learning Disabilities, 19,* 101–106.

McConaughy, S. H., & Ritter, D. R. (1986). Social competence and behavioral problems of learning disabled boys aged 6–11 years. *Journal of Learning Disabilities, 29,* 39–45.

McKinney, J. D., & Feagans, L. (1983). Adaptive classroom behavior of learning disabled children. *Journal of Learning Disabilities, 17,* 360–367.

McKinney, J. D., & Feagans, L. (1984). Academic and behavioral characteristics of learning disabled children and average achievers: Longitudinal studies. *Learning Disability Quarterly, 7,* 251–264.

McKinney, J. D., McClure, S., & Feagans, L. (1982). Classroom behavior of learning disabled children. *Learning Disability Quarterly, 5,* 42–52.

McLoughlin, J. A. (1985). The families of children with disabilities. In W. H. Berdine & A. E. Blackhurst (Eds.), *An introduction to special education* (2nd ed.) (pp. 617–659). Boston: Little, Brown.

McLoughlin, J. A., Clark, F. L., Mauck, A. R., & Petrosko, J. (1987). A comparison of parent-child perceptions of student learning disabilities. *Journal of Learning Disabilities, 20,* 357–360.

Owen, R. W., Adams, P. A., Forrest, T., Stolz, L. M., & Fisher, S. (1977). Learning disorders in children: Sibling studies. *Monographs of the Society for Research in Child Development, 36,* No. 144.

Palmer, D. J., Drummond, F., Tollison, P., & Zinkgraff, S. (1982). An attributional investigation of performance outcomes for learning-disabled and normal-achieving pupils. *Journal of Special Education, 16,* 207–219.

Pearl, R. (1987). Social cognitive factors in learning disabled children's social problems. In S. J. Ceci (Ed.), *Handbook of cognitive, social, and neuropsychological aspects of learning disabilities.* Hillsdale, NJ: Erlbaum.

Pearl, R., & Bryan, T. (1982). Mothers' attributions for their learning disabled child's successes and failures. *Learning Disability Quarterly, 5,* 53–57.

Pearl, R., Bryan, T., & Donahue, M. (1980). Learning disabled children's attributions for success and failure. *Learning Disability Quarterly, 3,* 3–9.

Pearl, R., Bryan, T., & Herzog, A. (1983). Learning disabled and nondisabled children's strategy analysis under conditions of high and low success. *Learning Disability Quarterly, 6,* 67–74.

Pearl, R., Bryan, T., & Werner, M. (1983). *Learning disabled children's self-esteem and desire for approval.* Paper presented at the International Conference on the Association for Children and Adults with Learning Disabilities, Chicago.

Pearl, R., Donahue, M., & Bryan, T. (1986). Social relations of learning disabled children. In J. K. Torgesen & B. Y. L. Wong (Eds.), *Psychological and educational perspectives on learning disabilities.* Orlando, FL: Academic Press.

Perlmutter, B., Crocker, J., Cordray, D., & Garstecki, D. (1983). Sociometric status and related personality characteristics of mainstreamed learning disabled adolescents. *Learning Disability Quarterly, 6,* 20–30.

Piers, E. (1984). *Piers-Harris children's self-concept scale* (rev. ed.). Los Angeles: Western Psychological Services.

Priel, B., & Leshem, T. (1990). Self-perceptions of first- and second-grade children with learning disabilities. *Journal of Learning Disabilities, 23,* 637–642.

Reynolds, M., & Wang, M. (1983). Restructuring "special" school programs: A position paper. *Policy Studies Review, 2,* 189–212.

Richey, D. D., & McKinney, J. D. (1978). Classroom behavioral styles of learning disabled boys. *Journal of Learning Disabilities, 11,* 279–282.

Ritter, D. R. (1989). Social competence and problem behavior of adolescent girls with learning disabilities. *Journal of Learning Disabilities, 22,* 460–461.

Rogers, C. M., Smith, M. D., & Coleman, J. M. (1978). Social comparison in the classroom: The relationship between academic achievement and self-concept. *Journal of Education Psychology, 70,* 50–57.

Rogers, H., & Saklofske, D. H. (1985). Self-concept, locus of control and performance expectations of learning disabled children. *Journal of Learning Disabilities, 18,* 273–278.

Rosenthal, R., & Jacobson, L. (1968). *Pygmalion in the classroom: Teacher expectations and pupils' intellectual development.* New York: Holt, Rinehart, & Winston.

Sabatino, D. A. (1982). Research on motivation of learning disabled populations. In K. D. Gadow and I. Bialer (Eds.), *Advances in learning and behavioral disabilities* (vol. 1) (pp. 75–116). Greenwich, CT: JAI Press.

Salend, S. J., & Salend, S. M. (1986). Competencies for mainstreaming secondary level learning disabled students. *Journal of Learning Disabilities, 19,* 460–461.

Scranton, T. R., & Ryckman, D. B. (1979). Sociometric status of learning disabled children in an integrative program. *Journal of Learning Disabilities, 6,* 402–407.

Seidel, J. F., & Vaughn, S. (1991). Social alienation and the learning disabled school dropout. *Learning Disabilities Research and Practice, 6,* 152–157.

Sheare, J. B. (1978). The impact of resource programs upon the self concept of peer acceptance of learning disabled children. *Psychology in the Schools, 15,* 406–411.

Silverman, R., & Zigmond, N. (1983). Self-concept in learning disabled adolescents. *Journal of Learning Disabilities, 16,* 478–482.

Siperstein, G., Bopp, M. J., & Bak, J. J. (1978). Social status of learning disabled children. *Journal of Learning Disabilities, 11,* 98–102.

Siperstein, G., & Goding, M. J. (1983). Social integration of learning disabled children in regular classrooms. *Advances in Learning and Behavioral Disabilities, 2,* 227–263.

Stilliadis, K., & Weiner, J. (1989). Relationship between social and peer status in children with learning disabilities. *Journal of Learning Disabilities, 22,* 624–629.

Stipek, D. J., & Hoffman, J. M. (1980). Children's achievement-related expectancies as a function of academic performance histories and sex. *Journal of Educational Psychology, 72,* 861–865.

Stipek, D. J., & Weisz, J. R. (1981). Perceived personal control and academic achievement. *Review of Educational Research, 51,* 101–137.

Strag, G. A. (1972). Comparative behavioral ratings of parents with severe mentally retarded, special learning disability, and normal children. *Journal of Learning Disabilities, 5,* 631–635.

Tarnowski, K. J., & Nay, S. M. (1989). Locus of control in children with learning disabilities and hyperactivity: A subgroup analysis. *Journal of Learning Disabilities, 22,* 381–383.

Tollefson, N., Tracy, D., Johnson, E., Buenning, M., Farmer, A., & Barke, C. (1982). Attribution patterns of learning disabled adolescents. *Learning Disability Quarterly, 5,* 14–20.

Vaughn, S. (1985). Why teach social skills to learning disabled students? *Journal of Learning Disabilities, 18,* 588–590.

Vaughn, S., Lancelotta, G. X., & Minnis, S. (1988). Social strategy training and peer involvement: Increasing peer acceptance of a female, LD student. *Learning Disabilities Focus, 4,* 32–37.

Vaughn, S., McIntosh, R., & Spencer-Rowe, J. (1991). Peer rejection is a stubborn thing: Increasing peer acceptance of rejected students with learning disabilities. *Learning Disabilities Research and Practice, 6,* 83–88.

Weiner, J. (1987). Peer status of learning disabled children and adolescents: A review of the literature. *Learning Disabilities Research, 2,* 62–79.

Weller, C. (1980). Discrepancy and severity in the learning disabled: A consolidated perspective. *Learning Disability Quarterly, 3,* 84–90.

Weller, C., & Strawser, S. (1981). *Weller-Strawser scales of adaptive behavior for the learning disabled.* Novato, CA: Academic Therapy.

Weller, C., & Strawser, S. (1987). Adaptive behavior of subtypes of learning disabled individuals. *Journal of Special Education, 21,* 101–115.

Weller, C., Strawser, S., & Buchanan, M. (1985). Adaptive behavior: Designator of a continuum of severity of learning disabled individuals. *Journal of Learning Disabilities, 18,* 199–204.

Winne, P. H., Woodlands, M. J., & Wong, B. Y. L. (1982). Comparability of self-concept among learning disabled, normal and gifted students. *Journal of Learning Disabilities, 15,* 470–475.

PART II

Assessment of Students with Learning Disabilities

In many ways the traditional distinction between assessment (testing) on the one hand and instruction (teaching) on the other has become less dramatic in education generally. While many different types of assessments are utilized with students with LD, those assessments that are based on frequent measurement of actual curriculum and behavioral skills seem to be receiving the most research interest. With this general trend in mind, the following three chapters present a wide array of information on assessment, both norm-based and curriculum-based. Also, information on efficient team meeting processes is presented.

FACT SHEET ON ASSESSMENT

With the trend toward more classroom-based assessment and curriculum-based assessment, there is still frequent use of assessments that compare a child with a learning disability to a "norm group." Thus, the following generalizations may seem somewhat contradictory, but the reader is encouraged to explore these assessment practices in the following chapters.

- Eligibility decisions, which document the existence of a learning disability, typically depend on the documentation of a discrepancy between ability (as measured by an IQ test) and achievement.
- Most state definitions of LD reflect this concern for ability-achievement discrepancy.
- The most common discrepancy models utilized today are standard score discrepancy models or models based on standard score discrepancy that also consider regression to the mean—thus referred to as *regression models*.
- A thorough assessment will include assessment in numerous domains of development, including, at a minimum, assessment of cognitive ability, achievement in various areas, and socioemotional and behavioral

functioning. Some consideration of assessment of the learning environments into which the child may be placed should also be included.

- Numerous problems have been highlighted in the overdependence on norm-based assessment devices such as IQ and achievement tests, and many researchers have called for less use of such measures and more use of curriculum-based assessment measures.
- Error analysis on a student's daily work can be an effective form of assessment to pinpoint specific academic problems that require additional work.
- Criterion-referenced tests compare a child's performance with a list of stated objectives or performance goals for that child. These tests are usually much more useful in planning a child's educational program than are norm-based measures.
- Direct observation and anecdotal records of teachers are also useful in planning the educational activities for a child with LD.
- The determination of eligibility and the preparation of an individualized educational plan for a child are responsibilities that rest with a team of professionals and the child's parents. School psychologists, general education teachers, special education teachers, the school principal, and the child may also serve on the team to discuss the child's educational goals.
- Medical specialists may be asked to sit in on this team meeting. Physicians who prescribe drug interventions for children with LD would be expected to inquire about the child's changes in behavior that may be attributed to the intervention.
- A list of questions that can be used to guide the team's deliberations is included.

4

Assessment and Identification Practices

Sherri Strawser

The story is told of the blind men who found an elephant and did not know what it was. "It is like a tree," said one, who had flung his arms around the elephant's leg. "No! It is like a rope," said another, who had caught hold of the elephant's tail. "It is more like a fan," said the third. He was feeling the shape of the elephant's ear. "No, no, you are all wrong; it is something with no beginning and no end," said the fourth, who was walking around the animal, feeling its sides.

The blind men in the fable could very well have been given the task of assessing learning disabilities (LD) instead of an elephant. *Assessment* has been defined as "a *goal-directed problem-solving process* that uses various measures within a theoretical framework" (Swanson 1991, p. 4). In the fable, we do not know whether the blind men had a specified goal for their assessment activities, but we can be certain that they were not working within a theoretical framework that provided an operational definition of *elephant*. Unfortunately, the theoretical framework of *elephant* is much less complex than *learning disability*. When presented with an entity that is defined in the federal legislation as

> a disorder in one or more of the basic psychological processes involved in understanding or in using language, spoken or written, which may manifest itself in an imperfect ability to listen, think, speak, read, write, spell, or to do mathematical calculations. The term includes such conditions as perceptual handicaps, brain injury, minimal brain dysfunction, dyslexia, and developmental aphasia. The term does not include children who have learning problems which are primarily the result of visual, hearing, or motor handicaps, or mental retardation, or emotional disturbance, or of environmental, cultural, or economic disadvantage. (U.S. Office of Education 1977, p. 65083)

It is possible for persons with functional sensory capabilities and their eyes wide open to identify a myriad of individuals with difficulties as learning-disabled. Often, this is what happens. Learning disabilities is a disorder that subsumes a vast

71

range of problems and is associated with a wide variety of characteristics. Yet, almost daily, one can find a newspaper article, magazine spread, or television talk-show interview that takes the blind-men approach to LD. The entire program or article may be devoted to a single facet of LD, or the terms used in the report may be *dyslexia* or *minimal brain dysfunction* rather than *learning disability*. This is confusing because it suggests that a "best" approach to LD exists or that individuals with dyslexia or MBD are in some way different from those with LD but are not being served in educational programs.

DEFINITIONS OF STUDENTS WITH LEARNING DISABILITIES

Among professionals in the field, LD is recognized as a diverse, heterogeneous disorder that can affect many different parts of an individual's life (e.g., academic success, motor or perceptual functioning, social adaptation, etc.). Yet, we also have used the blind-men approach with much of the research intended to clarify the definition of LD and identify assessment strategies and effective interventions for individuals with LD. In line with guidelines for sound research methodology, research studies have been done on selected portions of the heterogeneous population. The error in this approach is not in the investigation of a subset of the whole, but in the attempt, like the blind men, to apply the findings or characteristics of the subset to the whole regardless of the theoretical framework that guided the investigation.

This state of affairs has not come about because the researchers or practitioners in LD are any less capable, professional, or holistic in their methodology than other scholars; it has arisen from the very nature of the disability. Learning disabilities continues to be a disorder without a comprehensive theory (Weller 1987) or a unitary definition that is accepted by professionals, governmental agencies, and individuals affected with and by LD. It is a disorder that has been called the "victim of its own history" (Kavale and Forness 1985, p. 39) because the various theoretical perspectives for LD (Swanson 1991), as well as the terms used to describe it, have been both derived from and complicated by its varied roots and development. In order to understand assessment practices for LD, it is necessary to present a history of the terms and definitions that have been used and their influences on assessment and identification practices.

The Damage Phase

The disorder now called LD emerged from medical investigations in a number of related yet different disciplines. In the 1800s, researchers studied the basics of neurological functioning (Wiederholt 1974). Some studies focused on spoken language disorders in adults with localized brain injury. These pioneering investigations in cerebral localization of mental functions and differentiation of speech functions provided basic models for research in normal language development, as well as disorders of language known as *aphasia* (Smith 1991).

Other research was done on disorders of perception and written language. The term *congenital word blindness* was used in the early 1900s to describe children with normal vision and cognitive ability whose inability to read was similar to that of adults who had lost the ability to read as a result of brain damage (Hinshelwood 1917).

In the early phase, investigators were interested in the relationship of research in brain damage and the learning problems of children. These investigations reflected a theoretical framework that focused on neurological and perceptual functions and had a major influence on initial definitions and related assessment strategies for LD (Lovitt 1989). This damage theme was inspired by the work of Goldstein (1939), who found that World War I soldiers with head wounds exhibited difficulties such as hyperactive, distractible, or explosive behavior; perseveration (continuation of a behavior once it has begun); perceptual disorders; and conceptual or organizational disorders. Although Goldstein's work was done with adults, it influenced several individuals who were working with children. Similar patterns of behaviors were observed in brain-injured mentally retarded children (Werner and Strauss 1940), as well as in intellectually normal, non–brain-injured children (Cruickshank et al. 1957; Strauss and Kephart 1955). Research conducted by these individuals contributed to the early definition used to describe children with the disorder now referred to as LD.

> In 1947, Strauss and Lehtinen defined a *brain-injured* child as a child who before, during, or after birth has received an injury to, or suffered an infection of, the brain. As a result of such organic impairment, defects of the neuromotor system may be present or absent; however, such a child may show disturbances in perception, thinking, and emotional behavior, either separately or in combination. These disturbances can be demonstrated by specific tests. These disturbances prevent or impede a normal learning process. Special educational methods have been devised to remedy these specific handicaps. (p. 4)

This definition suggested a cause for the problems manifested by a group of children with difficulties in learning, provided criteria for assessment, predicted problems for the child in the learning process, and promised remedy of the disability, although the conclusions were all somewhat vague. Originally, Strauss and Lehtinen (1947) established seven criteria for assessment of the brain-injured child. Three biological criteria evaluated evidence of mental retardation, nervous system damage, and subtle neurological difficulties. The remaining criteria were referred to as the "behavioral" criteria and included perceptual problems, perseveration, conceptual or thinking disorders, and behavioral difficulties similar to those described by Goldstein (1939). Several years later, the biological criteria were omitted from the identification process (Strauss and Kephart 1955), which made the term *brain injury* even more of a misnomer. Although the definition gained acceptance, *brain injury* was viewed as undesirable because it implied a permanent condition, was assessed using nonmedical criteria, and did not lead to the development of effective instructional methods (Mercer 1987).

The controversy over the term led Stevens and Birch (1957) to propose the term "Strauss syndrome" to describe children with learning problems that were presumed to be a result of some type of damage to the brain. This syndrome was defined by the presence of several or all of the following characteristics: erratic and inappropriate behavior, poor behavioral organization, distractibility, persistent perception problems, hyperactivity, awkwardness, and poor motor performance. With this term and its identification criteria, the presumed cause for learning and performance problems of children shifted from physiological damage, which was frequently difficult to prove, to a symptom complex that was behavioral in nature and readily assessed. In addition, the term extended the notion that an identifiable syndrome, which was related to brain functions, could be responsible for learning problems that were less than severe in nature and only suggestive of a milder form of brain disturbance (Kavale and Forness 1985).

The Dysfunction Phase

In the next phase, LD were related to problems of brain function rather than damage. One model emphasized the dominance of one hemisphere over the other and the multisensory nature of language and reading (Orton 1937). Proponents of this model studied children of normal intelligence and attributed language and reading disabilities (called *dyslexia*) to neurological impairment. Both assessment and instructional techniques utilized a multisensory approach to evaluate the reception and expression of information through visual, auditory, tactile (touch), and kinesthetic (motion) sensory modes (Fernald 1943).

Other models emerged from research into language functions and the specific processes (e.g., reception, discrimination, memory, expression) that were thought to form the groundwork for normal language development (Johnson and Myklebust 1967; Kirk et al. 1968). These investigations represented the move from a primarily visual-perceptual-motor premise for learning disorders to an auditory-verbal framework for reading and writing that came to be known as the *specific abilities model*. It postulated that there are certain abilities that are required for adequate language development and that dysfunctions of these abilities can be identified, measured, and remediated (Mercer 1987).

Samuel Kirk, one of the most influential individuals associated with this model, is credited with making the term *learning disability* widely known. He defined it as:

> a retardation, disorder, or delayed development in one or more of the processes of speech, language, reading, writing, arithmetic, or other school subjects resulting from a psychological handicap caused by a possible cerebral dysfunction and/or emotional or behavioral disturbances. It is not the result of mental retardation, sensory deprivation, or cultural and instructional factors. (Kirk 1962, p. 263).

This definition was very different from those in vogue in the early 1960s because it included problems in language and language-based academic subjects and emotional factors as possible causes but excluded problems that were caused by other disabling conditions or extrapersonal factors. In this phase, assessment targeted the student's processing strengths and weaknesses presumed to underlie language and academic problems (Smith 1991). The *Illinois Test of Psycholinguistic Abilities* (ITPA) (Kirk et al. 1968) was based on this model and widely used for this purpose.

In the period from the early 1940s to the mid-1960s, approximately 40 different terms were being used to describe individuals whose learning and/or behavioral patterns were neither normal nor fit known disabilities (Smith 1991). Although *learning disabilities* had been used by some, many professionals continued to support a medical orientation and use the term *minimal brain dysfunction (MBD)* to refer to the same set of learning problems described by other terms. To clarify the situation, a national task force was named to study the issues surrounding terminology and the symptomatology related to a presumed neurological condition that affected academic and behavioral functioning but not overall intellectual abilities (Kavale and Forness 1985). Clements's (1966) Task Force I reported MBD to apply to:

> children of near average, average, or above average general intelligence with certain learning or behavioral disabilities ranging from mild to severe, which are associated with deviations of function of the central nervous system. These deviations may manifest themselves by various combinations of impairment in perception, conceptualization, language, memory, and control of attention, impulse, or motor function. The aberrations may arise from genetic variations, biochemical irregularities, perinatal brain insults, or other illnesses or injuries sustained during the years which are critical for the development and maturation of the central nervous system or from unknown causes. . . . During the school years, a variety of learning disabilities is the most prominent manifestation of the condition which can be designated by this term. (pp. 9–10)

The characteristics of MBD were listed, in descending order of frequency, as: hyperactivity, perceptual-motor impairments, emotional lability (i.e., wide swings in mood not associated to the situation), coordination deficits, attention disorders, impulsivity, memory and thinking disorders, specific learning disabilities, speech and hearing disorders, and equivocal neurological signs and EEG irregularities (Clements 1966). These characteristics could have been viewed as a guide for the assessment of MBD, but they were not presented as being required in any specific number or pattern for diagnosis.

The MBD definition was the first proposed at a national level and came to be synonymous with LD. It is still used by some individuals, especially in the medical field, although it was not widely accepted by educators. *Minimal brain dysfunction* connotes a medical etiology that usually was unsubstantiated, and the use of "minimal" was questioned because cerebral aberrations serious enough to cause learning and behavioral difficulties were thought to be more than minimal (Bryan and Bryan 1986). Further, educators believed it to be of little use in planning instructional strategies or programs (Mercer 1987).

The Discrepancy Phase

For almost 30 years, the field has been in the discrepancy phase, for several reasons. The concept that students with LD can be identified by a discrepancy between their intellectual capacity and their academic achievement or performance has had a major influence on definition and assessment practices in the field. In some states there is "discrepancy" between the definition of LD adopted and the criteria for identification (Mercer et al. 1990), and there continues to be discrepancy within the field with regard to theoretical and identification issues, assessment practices, and effective instructional strategies for individuals with LD.

The idea of aptitude–achievement discrepancy was introduced by Barbara Bateman, who proposed that LD were defined by

> an educationally significant discrepancy between . . . estimated intellectual potential and actual level of performance related to basic disorders in the learning process, which may or may not be accompanied by demonstrable central nervous dysfunction, and which are not secondary to generalized mental retardation, educational or cultural deprivation, severe emotional disturbance, or sensory loss. (Bateman 1965, p. 220):

In addition to popularizing the discrepancy notion, her definition emphasized children and excluded learning disorders that were the result of other causes, but it was rather vague with regard to etiology and the achievement areas that could be affected.

A few years later, the U.S. Office of Education (USOE) Bureau of Education for the Handicapped was given the responsibility for funding special education services for students with LD (Mercer 1987) and needed a definition appropriate for educational purposes. The National Advisory Committee on Handicapped Children (NACHC) was created to study the issues surrounding all definitions that were being used to refer to the same disability and to develop a definition that was acceptable to educators. The result was:

> Children with special learning disabilities exhibit a disorder in one or more of the basic psychological processes involved in understanding or in using spoken or written language. These may be manifested in disorders of listening, thinking, talking, reading, writing, spelling, or arithmetic. They include conditions which have been referred to as perceptual handicaps, brain injury, minimal brain dysfunction, dyslexia, developmental aphasia, etc. They do not include

learning problems which are due primarily to visual, hearing, or motor handicaps, to mental retardation, emotional disturbance, or to environmental disadvantage. (NACHC 1968, p. 34)

Although the ideas of Kirk (1962) and Bateman (1965) were reflected, the discrepancy identifier was not included. With this definition, however, LD was recognized as a category of special education; it paved the way for the development of programs and funding patterns several years later.

In 1977, LD was included as a fundable disability in federal law for the first time. The definition that was included in Public Law 94-142 (USOE 1977) was the one that appeared at the beginning of this chapter. This definition was essentially identical to the one produced by the NACHC in 1968. Despite several attempts to improve upon the definitive parameters of LD in the intervening years (Kass and Myklebust 1969; McIntosh and Dunn 1973, Wepman et al. 1975), the conflicting nature of the data on LD characteristics led the legislators to accept a definition for economic and administrative purposes that still allowed for the accommodation of the myriad of differing theoretical philosophies and treatment practices that existed (Senf 1977).

To clarify eligibility for LD programs, additional regulations were produced (USOE 1977). They specified that children may be classified as having a specific learning disability if their achievement is not commensurate with their age and ability levels, when provided with appropriate learning experiences. The severe discrepancy between achievement and intellectual ability could occur in any one or more of the following areas: oral expression, listening comprehension, written expression, basic reading skills, reading comprehension, mathematics calculation, or mathematics reasoning. Like several previous definitions (Bateman 1965; Kirk 1962; NACHC 1968), the regulations excluded individuals with an ability–achievement discrepancy that was *primarily* the result of other handicapping conditions or environmental, economic, or cultural disadvantage (USOE 1977).

Although the regulations were intended to simplify the identification process (USOE 1977), they may have added to the confusion because of omissions and inconsistencies with the definition (Hammill 1990). A discrepancy clause was not included in the definition but appeared in the identification regulations without criteria for the modifier "severe." The reverse was true for "basic psychological processes" and problems in spelling. Finally, the word "children" was used in the regulations, but there was no implication in the definition that LD did not occur in adulthood.

The Definition du Jour Phase

Following P. L. 94-192, there have been a number of attempts to remedy the difficulties of previous definitions or address changes in the knowledge base of LD that have occurred in recent years. Since Kirk's (1962) definition, 11 have been proposed that differ on the (1) means by which underachievement is verified; (2) cause; (3) existence in adults; (4) inclusion of problems in oral language, conceptual skills, and socioemotional skills as LD; (5) specification of included academic problems; and (6) coexistence with other disabilities such as mental retardation or emotional disturbance (Hammill 1990). As a means to reduce the confusion created by numerous definitions or classification criteria, some researchers have not drafted new definitions but have called for consistent reporting of "marker variables" of individuals being studied (Keogh et al. 1982) and the investigation of well-defined subgroups of LD and the assessment and intervention practices specific to each (Adelman and Taylor 1986; Weller and Strawser 1987).

Although Hammill (1990) said that "consensus is near" (p. 82), research by Mercer and colleagues (1990) revealed that considerable unconformity still is present in the definition and operational criteria used for LD. Several years after P.L. 94-142 was passed, 22 of 50 states used the USOE (1977) definition, 14 used the definition with some variation, 12 used a different definition, and 2 did not use a definition of LD (Mercer et al. 1985). Five years later, 20 states were found to use the USOE (1977) definition verbatim, 9 use it with minor modifications, 20 use a different definition, and 2 use no definition. The discrepancy component was included by 88% of the states and, although most components of the federal definition continue to be used by a majority of states, many differences exist among identification procedures. Table 4.1 presents the data from the Mercer and colleagues (1990) survey.

DISCREPANCY MODELS

The requirement of "severe discrepancy between achievement and intellectual ability" (USOE 1977, p. 65083) appeared straightforward but has been operationalized by a number of different models. Each model is based on procedures or formulas of varying sophistication and has differing levels of appeal to individuals concerned with LD (Chalfant 1984; Cone and Wilson 1981; Mather and Healy 1990), as described in the following:

1. Grade level deviation, or the "Pat's achievement is two years below grade level" models.
2. Expectancy formula, or the "Based on Pat's IQ, Pat should be achieving at this grade level" models.
3. Standard score comparison or the "I've had introductory statistics so I converted all Pat's scores to comparable scales. According to the table in the district manual, there is a significant discrepancy between Pat's ability and achievement" models.
4. Regression equation, or the "I only had introductory statistics so I can't explain it, but when I entered Pat's test scores into the computer program it said the discrepancy was enough for a learning disability" models.
5. Clinical judgment, or the "I believe there is a significant discrepancy between Pat's ability and achievement" models.

Grade Level Deviation Models

Grade level deviation models are based on the comparison of individuals' achievement scores with their current grade placement. The models have used either a constant amount (expressed in years or percent) below current grade level or a graduated amount of deviation from grade level (Cone and Wilson 1981). As the names indicate, the constant level models use a fixed number of years' (e.g., one or two years) deficit as an indicator of severe discrepancy, but the graduated deviation models increase the number of years of deficit as grade placement increases. For example, the child in elementary school may be one-half to one year below grade level to qualify for services, but the senior high school student must be at least two to three years behind before being considered.

Grade level deviation models are the easiest to calculate and explain, but they are fraught with conceptual problems and measurement error. The child must attend school (and fail) for several years before such a discrepancy can be identified. These models use grade equivalent (GE) scores that express performance in grades and tenths of a grade (e.g., 4.5). Although this type of score seems to indicate the individual's overall functioning level, it only means that the individual got as many items correct as the *average* student at that grade level (Reynolds 1985; Salvia and Ysseldyke 1991). The individual's actual range of successes and failures on test items could cover many grade levels. Further, the amount of performance that is necessary to advance one grade level is not the same for all grades or subjects. Thus, it is more debilitating to be a grade or two behind in the primary grades or have a disability in some subjects (Chalfant 1984). For example, a three-year deficit in reading has a greater effect on one's overall performance in school (including social studies, language arts, science, etc.) than the same deficit in math, and less overall effect for a student in grade 12 than in grade 5. Finally, this approach does not include considerations for differences in potential or capacity for achievement. It only evaluates underachievement from the current grade placement and has been found to overidentify individuals who are slow learners (i.e., achieving several years below grade level while working to capacity) and underidentify those with high levels of ability who may be achieving several years behind their capacity but score only slightly below grade level (Chalfant 1984; Cone and Wilson 1981; Smith 1991).

Expectancy Formula Models

Expectancy formulas first were used to predict reading levels and later were modified to evaluate expected achievement in other academic areas (Smith 1991). These models identify discrepancy by (1) estimating the performance that could be expected from individuals based on intellectual ability, provided by IQ or mental age (MA) score and/or years in school; and (2) calculating the difference between expected and actual achievement to arrive at the level of discrepancy. The following section presents several of the most commonly used expectancy formulas.

Table 4.1 Components included in each state definition and/or criteria

Components	AL	AK	AZ	AR	CA	CO	CT	DE	DC	FL	GA	HI	ID	IL	IN	IA	KS
Definition Type																	
1977 only		D	D	D								D	D				
1977 with variation														D			
Different	D				D	D	D	D	D	D	D						
No definition used															D	D	D
Intelligence																	
Average or above	C	-									D				C	C	
Above mental retardation criteria							C			C						C	C
Not stated	D	B	B	B	B	B	D	B	B	D	C	B	B	D	D	D	D
Process																	
Process disorder	D	D	D	B	B	D	B	B	D	B	B	D	D	D	B	D	D
Language disorder	B	D	B	B	B	B	B	B	B	B	B	B	B	D	B	D	D
Academic																	
Reading	B	D	B	B	B	B	D	B	B	B	B	B	B	D	B	D	B
Writing	B	D	B	B	B	B	D	B	B	B	B	B	B	D	B	D	B
Spelling	D	D	D	D	B	B	D	D		B	D	D	D	D	D		
Arithmetic	B	D	B	B	B	B	D	B	B	B	B	B	B	D	B	D	B
Exclusion–Primary																	
Visual impairment	C	D	B	D		B	B	B	B	B	B	B	B	D	B	B	B
Auditory impairment	C	D	B	D		B	B	B	B	B	B	B	B	D	B	B	B
Motor impairment	C	D	B	D			B	B	B	B	B	B	B	D	B	B	B
Mental retardation	C	D	B	D	B	B	B	B	B	B	B	B	B	D	B	B	B
Emotional disturbance	C	D	B		B	C	C	B	B	B	B	B	B	D	B	B	B
Environmental disadvantage	C	D	B	D	B	C	C	B	B	D	B	B	B	D	B	B	B
Neurological Impairment																	
Included		D	D	D				D			D	D	D	D			

	KY	LA	ME	MD	MA	MI	MN	MS	MO	MT	NE	NV	NH	NJ	NM	NY	NC
Discrepancy																	
Included	B	C	C	B	B	C	B	C	C	B	C	C	C	C	C	B	B
Operationalization of Discrepancy																	
Standard scores	C				C		C	C	C	C	C				C	C	C
Standard deviation	C				C		C	C	C	C	C				C	C	C
Regression formula				C													
WISC-R verbal v. performance					C												
40–50% or more discrepancy						C											
Grade-level discrepancy												C					
No statement about operationalization			C						C				C				
Components	KY	LA	ME	MD	MA	MI	MN	MS	MO	MT	NE	NV	NH	NJ	NM	NY	NC
Definition Type																	
1977 only	D							D	D	D	D						
1977 with variation		D	D										D				
Different					D	D	D					D		D	D	D	D
No definition used				D													
Intelligence																	
Average or above											C				B		
Above mental retardation																	
Not stated	B	B	B	B	B	B	B	B	B	B		B	B	B		D	B
Process																	
Process disorder	D	D	D	D	D	D	D	D	B	D	D	B	D	B	D	D	B
Language disorder	B	B	B	B	B	B	B	B	B	B	B	C	B	C	C	D	B
Academic																	
Reading	B	B	B	B	B	B	B	B	B	B	B	C	B	C	B	D	B
Writing	B	B	B	B	B	B	B	B	B	B	B	C	B	C	B	D	B
Spelling	D	D	D	B	D	D		D	D	D	D	D	D	C	B	D	
Arithmetic	B	B	B	B	B	B	B	B	B	B	B	C	B	C	B	D	B

Continued

Table 4.1 Components included in each state definition and/or criteria (*continued*)

Components	KY	LA	ME	MD	MA	MI	MN	MS	MO	MT	NE	NV	NH	NJ	NM	NY	NC
Exclusion-Primary																	
Visual impairment	B	B	C	B		B	B	B	B	B	B	B	B	D	B	D	B
Auditory impairment	B	B	C	B		B	B	B	B	B	B	B	B	D	B	D	B
Motor impairment	B	B	C	B		B	B	B	B	B	B	B	B	D	B	D	B
Mental retardation	B	B	C	B		B	B	B	B	B	B	B	B	D	B	D	B
Emotional disturbance	B	B	C	B		B	B	B	B	B	B	B	B	D	B	D	B
Environmental disadvantage	B	B	C	B		B	B	B	B	B	B	B	B	D	B	D	B
Neurological Impairment																	
Included		D		D		D		D	D	D	D		D	B	D	D	
Discrepancy																	
Included	C	C	C	C		C	B	C	C	C	C	B	C		C	D	B
Operationalization of Discrepancy																	
Standard scores			C	C			C				C				C		C
Standard deviation		C	C	C				C	C		C						C
Regression formula				C			C	C	C	C							
WISC-R verbal v. performance																	
40–50% or more discrepancy																D	
Grade-level discrepancy																	
No statement about operationalization	C					C						C	C				

Components	ND	OH	OK	OR	PA	RI	SC	SD	TN	TX	UT	VT	VA	WV	WI	WY
Definition Type																
1977 only	D	D	D			D	D				D		D			
1977 with variation				D								D		D		
Different					D				D	D					D	D
No definition used								D								
Intelligence																
Average or above					D						C			C	C	
Above mental retardation criteria									C		C		D	B		C
Not stated	B	B	B	B		B	B	D	D	D		B	C	D		B

Process										
Process disorder	D	D	D	D	D	D	D	B	D	D
Language disorder	B	B	B	B	B	B	B	B	B	B
Academic										
Reading	B	B	B	B	B	B	B	B	B	B
Writing	B	B	B	B	B	B	B	B	B	B
Spelling	D	D	D	D	D	D	D	D	B	B
Arithmetic	B	B	B	B	B	B	B	B	B	B
Exclusion-Primary										
Visual impairment	B	B	B	B	B	B	C	B	C	D
Auditory impairment	B	B	B	B	B	B	C	B	C	D
Motor impairment	B	B	B	B	B	B	C	B	C	D
Mental retardation	B	B	B	B	B	B	C	B	C	D
Emotional disturbance	B	B	B	B	B	B	C	B	C	D
Environmental disadvantage	B	B	B	B	B	B	C	B	C	D
Neurological Impairment										
Included	D	D	D	B	D	D	D	D	D	D
Discrepancy										
Included	C	C	C	C	C	C	B	C	B	C
Operationalization of Discrepancy										
Standard scores	C	C	C	C		C	C		C	C
Standard deviation	C	C		C		C	C		C	C
Regression formula	C			C	C	C	C		C	C
WISC-R verbal v. performance										
40–50% or more discrepancy										C
Grade-level discrepancy										C
No statement about operationalization		C		C		C				C

Key: D = Component included only in state definition; C = Component included only in state identification criteria; B = Component included in both state definition *and* criteria.

Johnson and Myklebust (1967) proposed that a learning quotient (LQ) could be used to express the degree of acquired learning relative to the potential for learning as a ratio of achievement to MA. Consideration was given to physiological maturity, or chronological age (CA), and school experience for students under 12 years of age. Formulas were used to determine expectancy age (EA) and LQ, and an LQ under 90 was seen as indicative of a learning disorder:

$$EA = \frac{\text{Mental Age} + \text{Life Age} + \text{Grade Age}}{3}$$

$$LQ = \frac{AA}{EA} \times 100$$

Life Age = CA as indicator of physiological maturity
Grade Age = present grade level + 5.2 years (average school entrance age)
AA (Achievement Age) = student's grade level achievement scores + 5.2 years

The Bond and Tinker (1973) formula also based expectancy on a combination of age and intelligence, with the reasoning that a student who has spent more years in school can be expected to have acquired more skills than one who has been in school less time.

$$\text{Reading Grade Expectancy} = \text{Years in School} \times \frac{IQ}{100} + 1.0$$

Years in School = years completed, beginning with first grade
1.0 = beginning of grade one

The method by Harris (1970) proposed a greater weighing for intellectual ability than for age.

$$\text{Expectancy Age} = \frac{2\,MA + CA}{3}$$

A modification of this method was suggested by the USOE (1976) to document severe discrepancy in the classification of LD and was widely adopted by states in the years following passage of P.L. 94-142 (Cone and Wilson 1981).

$$\text{Severe Discrepancy Level (SDL)} = CA\left(\frac{IQ}{300} + .17\right) - 2.5$$

These methods appeared to offer an advantage over the grade level deviation models, but they have major limitations. There was considerable variance in the students who were identified by each one (Algozzine et al. 1979), importance was placed on variables that may have been inappropriate predictors of achievement for students with LD (e.g., age and IQ test scores), and all methods were considered statistically unsound (Cone and Wilson 1981; Danielson and Bauer 1978; McLeod 1979). These methods use grade equivalent (GE) or age equivalent (AE) scores in formulas that add to their mathematical weaknesses because GE and AE scores are measured on a rank order scale and cannot be subjected to the arithmetic required for formulas (Reynolds 1985; Salvia and Ysseldyke 1991). The rank tells if one performance is better than another, but without indication of how much better because the units are not equal along the scale. For example, the distance between the noses of the horses finishing first and second in a race is not the same as the distance between the horses finishing fourth and fifth. In educational terms, a GE of 4.0 on a reading test does not represent reading ability that is twice as good as a GE of 2.0 because the achievement related to one grade level is not equal along the scale from Kindergarten to 12th grade (Salvia and Ysseldyke 1991).

Standard Score Comparison Models

To avoid problems presented by GEs, some discrepancy models use standard scores that convert test scores to a scale with equal units and known measures of average and variability (Chalfant 1984). Basic standard score models involve obtaining standard score values for IQ and achievement and comparing the differences between the scores to those required by state guidelines for a significant discrepancy (Cone and Wilson 1981). These procedures are quite simple to follow because most IQ and achievement tests provide standard scores and tables of required differences often are printed in state or district manuals. The weaknesses of standard score comparison models include their lack of consideration for differences in technical characteristics of the tests used, little agreement on the level required for a severe discrepancy (Mercer et al. 1990), and their tendency to misclassify children as learning-disabled depending on their IQ score (Kavale 1987).

Regression Equation Models

The previous models assume that IQ scores can predict academic success, but IQ has been found to be as accurate a predictor of reading achievement as a flip of the coin and even less so when IQs are higher or lower than average (Smith 1991). The term *regression toward the mean* is used to describe this phenomenon, in which scores on an achievement measure move closer (or regress) to the average when scores on an intelligence measure are higher or lower than average. Therefore, students whose IQs are above the mean tend to get achievement scores that are lower than expected, and students with below average IQs obtain scores higher than expected (Cone and Wilson 1981). The regression phenomenon is the likely culprit in the cases where students are missed as learning-disabled or misdiagnosed as learning-disabled.

Discrepancy models that use regression equations attempt to control for this type of error (Evans 1990). Regression is a statistically superior method of determining if a real discrepancy exists; however, accurate results depend on the technical quality and reliability of the tests used (Reynolds 1985). Computer hackers use the term GIGO for this notion, which stands for "garbage in, garbage out." If the scores entered in the equation come from unreliable tests, using a statistically sound equation does not make up for the inadequacy of the scores. Regression models have been called "state-of-the-art in determining a severe discrepancy" (Reynolds 1985, p. 47), but they have other limitations. For example, it is difficult to express some diagnostic factors in numerical terms (Evans 1990), many tests do not meet the technical standards to be used (Cone and Wilson 1981), and there is considerable difference among tests in the way the same skill is measured (Willson 1987).

The mathematics of regression equations are beyond the scope of this chapter and are usually calculated by computer after the diagnostician enters the test scores. Although this process is user-friendly, it reveals another limitation of these models. Training programs for most school personnel rarely include enough courses in statistics to cover regression. Therefore, teachers and diagnosticians may have little understanding of the workings and limitations of the regression method. They must trust the output of a computer program for the discrepancy determination, and they may not have the background to interpret or question the results. When one part of the identification process (i.e., discrepancy) is quantified in an unknown and nearly magical way, it can take prominence over other criteria or even come to be considered the definitive factor exclusive to the identification of LD (Kavale 1987).

Clinical Judgment Model

Clinical judgment may be the means used by the assessment team to establish discrepancy when the component is not specifically operationalized (Mercer et al. 1990) or when individuals are identified outside the standard educational system (e.g., adults). This model may conjure up examples that make it seem risky (i.e., the individual who is perceived as average in one family might be considered "slow" in another). However, reliance on quick statistical formulas that provide "cut-off" levels has tended to negate the fact that educational personnel *can* be quite accurate in their judgments (Gerber and Semmel 1984; Mastropieri 1987; Weller et al. 1990). Clinical judgments must not be made capriciously but must be based on a sound theoretical perspective and guided by the evaluation of specific responses to task demands in a variety of environments and the individual's ability to profit from instructional efforts (Feuerstein 1979; McLeskey and Waldron 1991; Scruggs 1987).

It is ironic that the ability–achievement discrepancy notion that was viewed as a means to increase objectivity in the definition and identification morass and reduce the numbers of students served as learning-disabled (Mather and Healy 1990) may have added to the differences that prevail within the field. As in the blind men and elephant metaphor, research results from samples identified by one discrepancy model and definition may not generalize to individuals identified under a different model or definition. As a result, the field remains in the discrepancy phase, in that one can find research to support as well as refute most assessment practices or instructional methods used with LD. For that reason, the assessment practices that are discussed in the remainder of this chapter are based on general guidelines. Specific procedures associated with different state practices or theoretical paradigms must be considered when applying this information to one's own situation.

RECOMMENDED PRACTICES IN THE ASSESSMENT OF LEARNING DISABILITIES

It is common for special education teachers or diagnosticians to be asked by general education teachers, parents, administrators, and others: "What is the learning disability test?" or "Would you test this student for learning disabilities?" These questions suggest two important misconceptions about LD assessment. First, people may believe that LD can be diagnosed by giving a special test; and, second, the manner in which diagnosticians "look for" LD is somehow different from identifying other disorders.

In addition to the mandate that a learning disability cannot be identified by a single assessment instrument or person (USOE 1977), the basic diagnostic process is the same regardless of the disability. The diagnosis of any disability is not an event but rather is a goal-oriented process that is guided by a series of questions posed at each stage. To answer the questions, members of the multidisciplinary team obtain data from a variety of procedures and tests. At several stages in the process, the same tests might be used for students who may be retarded, emotionally disturbed, learning disabled, or "normal." It is not the use of a special test, but the *results* obtained at each stage in the process that lead to the identification of a learning disability, a different disability, or no disability. The assessment of LD requires the use of a variety of tests and techniques; however, the tests are the "*tools* that may be used in a process—not the process itself" (Gearheart and Gearheart 1990, p. 4). The following sections describe each stage in the process in terms of the leading questions, goal, responsible personnel, and procedures.

Stage 1: Screening or Prereferral

The process begins with awareness of a problem. Typical questions at this stage might be: Is there a problem in learning or performance? What might be causing the problem? What can be done to deal with the problem? Is specialized testing necessary? Too often, the answers are: Yes . . . a learning disability . . . refer the individual to special education . . . of course. These answers may be wrong. Achievement is influenced by many factors, and failure to achieve cannot automatically be attributed to a learning disability.

Goal

Learning "problems" may result from any number of causes, including poor nutrition, medical problems, lack of motivation, excessive absences, cultural differences, poor teaching, or a learning disability. At this stage, assessment is used to verify that a problem exists, specify the nature of the problem (Salvia and Ysseldyke 1991), and attempt to solve it in the regular educational environment. To do so, we first must examine the characteristics of the learning environment and the adaptation of the individual to that environment.

Personnel

Because awareness of a problem most often originates from the classroom teacher or parent, the personnel responsible for assessment at this stage usually are not special educators. Many states require the general education teacher to gather information from the parent and implement classroom-based assessments and strategies in order to identify and resolve problems before referring a student for evaluation. District instructional specialists, special education personnel, or teacher-support teams can assist the teacher with problem clarification and academic or behavioral interventions, such as those described elsewhere in this book, but the classroom teacher has primary responsibility for these activities.

It is very important that the student's general education teacher is not excluded at this stage. The classroom teacher is a valuable member of the multidisciplinary team and is crucial to the overall educational program for students with LD. When a referral is made to special education, the "ownership" of the problem and the "problem child" can be transferred to some other professional or set of professionals (e.g., the special education teacher, the speech and language pathologist, the school psychologist). As a practitioner, the author sometimes was told, "*Your* student is in trouble again on the playground," or asked, "Do you know that *your* boy has not turned in any work for a week?" This language conveys the notion that when students are referred to special education, they no longer "belong" to the general education teacher, regardless of the percentage of time spent in the regular classroom. Because the majority of students with LD continue to receive instruction in the mainstream, it is critical that the classroom teacher does not abrogate responsibility for the student if a problem is perceived.

Procedures

Assessment cannot be focused on an individual as the source of the problem until all other sources of poor academic performance are explored and eliminated. Before making assumptions about LD as the cause of a problem, one must consider the classroom environment, the curriculum that is being used, the fit between the student's skills and the curriculum requirements, the means through which instruction is delivered, and the ways performance is rewarded (Smith 1991; Salvia and Ysseldyke 1991; Taylor et al. 1988; Strawser 1989). An important feature of the environment is the language of the classroom, in terms of the grammatical complexity and vocabulary necessary to grasp what is going on and what is required to keep up. Some students may experience problems processing the information or responding to tasks because of the level of language used in the classroom environment rather than an internal disability (Gruenewald and Pollack 1984). For example, a freshman physics major in a doctoral-level quantum mechanics class may not have a specific disability in learning but can appear (and feel) disabled because of the language of the specific classroom.

The next step is to evaluate the student's environmental and educational history, medical status, and visual and auditory acuity. Students who move frequently or miss a lot of school might be having difficulties because of a lack of continuous instruction, or students may experience problems related to the language they speak at home and differences in cultural or ethnic expectations. Alternative services such as Chapter I or bilingual education may be appropriate to meet the needs of the student and should be explored before referring the student to special education (Bos et al. 1984–1985). If the problem seems related to sensory difficulties that are correctable, strategies to obtain glasses or for preferential seating or alternate means for work completion must be pursued before going further. If a sensory problem is severe enough to be classified as a visual, hearing, or motor disability, the student is referred to the multidisciplinary team and the appropriate medical personnel for specialized evaluation.

In most districts, curriculum specialists or special educators are available to consult with the teacher and help develop classroom-based assessments to evaluate the environmental factors; pinpoint the student's strengths and weaknesses across language, academic, social skill, and functional adaptation areas; and develop accommodations or interventions to solve the problem in the mainstream classroom. If such strategies fail to solve the problem, the referral for specialized assessment has been validated in that attempts to meet the student's individual needs have been made and documented (Bos et al. 1984–1985) and the requirement of most states to exclude environmental causes of academic problems has been met (Mercer et al. 1990). In addition, results of the clinical assessments and interventions are used to specify difficulties to be evaluated further (Gearheart and Gearheart 1990; Weller et al. 1990) and to suggest future goals and objectives for the student, regardless of the outcome of the assessment process.

Stage 2: Identification of the Disability

The questions that guide the next stage are: Can the verified problem be identified as a disability? Is the disability a learning disability?

Goal

At this stage the focus of assessment is to discover whether the problem is related to a disability and to differentiate between LD and other disabilities. The majority of definitions exclude other disabilities from being primary causes of LD (Mercer et al. 1990), so assessment at this stage must provide the team the data to differentiate between individuals who meet the identification guidelines of other disabilities (e.g., mental retardation or emotional/behavioral disorder) from those who meet the guidelines for LD. Formal assessment procedures that provide comparisons among students are used for this purpose.

Formal assessment usually employs individually administered tests that have been standardized, in that they consist of a set of tasks given with uniform directions and compare performance to an identified standard (Swanson and Watson 1989). The tests that are known as *norm-referenced* compare scores with the average performance (*norm*) of a clearly defined and representative group of individuals (Sattler 1990). Typically, norm-referenced instruments are used for identification purposes because they (1) provide information about the referred individual relative to peers, and (2) have the mathematical adequacy to be used in the complex calculations that are part of the identification and eligibility criteria of the majority of states.

Personnel

At this point in the process, knowledge of the range of disabilities and the assessment requirements for each is necessary. The team personnel who assume responsibility for most of the assessment at this stage are special educators, educational diagnosticians, school psychologists, and other related personnel (e.g., speech and language pathologists).

Procedures

The initial step is to notify the student's parent(s) or guardian(s) of the intent to conduct an individualized evaluation, to specify the areas to be assessed, and to request written permission for the evaluation. When consent is received, the assessment activities focus on gathering information about the student's functioning in the domains of intelligence, socioemotional behavior, and achievement.

Intellectual domain   Traditionally, intelligence has been thought of as a mental ability factor that explains and predicts an individual's capacity to learn and perform. Intelligence tests sample skills in a number of areas (e.g., verbal reasoning, numerical facility, perceptual speed, memory) and compare the score to the average for the test taker's age. The result is called the individual's cognitive ability, intelligence quotient (IQ), potential, or aptitude (Gearheart and Gearheart 1990) and has often been considered a rather fixed entity. Recent concepts of intelligence have broadened to include models based on the examination of an individual's information-processing abilities across multiple facets of intelligence. These models emphasize the strategies and processes an individual uses to solve problems and adapt to the environment, rather than the amount of knowledge an individual has acquired (Feuerstein 1979; Sternberg 1985).

Table 4.2 lists a few of the tests that are used to assess the domain of intelligence. Each test has undergone procedures to standardize the scoring, establish test consistency, and validate that the instrument measures intelligence. A review of the list, however, reveals the wide variety of skills and behaviors that are sampled by different intelligence tests. On the surface, the disparity among tests seems confusing. One could ask why so many tests are necessary or which one is the "best" intelligence test. Although several of the tests are the most frequently used, there are intelligence tests that can be used with individuals who have language difficulties, motor limitations, or other problems that might

Table 4.2 Standardized instruments: Intelligence domain

Test	Ages	Score	Domains/Subtests
Wechsler Intelligence Scale for Children-Revised (WISC-R) (1974)	6-0 to 16-6	Full Scale IQ	Verbal IQ; Performance IQ
Wechsler Preschool and Primary Scale of Intelligence-Revised (WPPSI-R) (1989)	3-0 to 7-3	Full Scale IQ	Verbal IQ; Performance IQ
Wechsler Adult Intelligence Scale-Revised (WAIS-R) (1981)	16 to 74	Full Scale IQ	Verbal IQ; Performance IQ
Stanford-Binet Intelligence Scale: Fourth Edition (SB:FE) (1986)	2-6 to 23-11	Composite, Standard Age Score (SAS)	Verbal Reasoning, Abstract/Visual Reasoning, Quantitative Reasoning, Short-term Memory
Kaufman Assessment Battery for Children (K-ABC) (1983)	2-6 to 12-5	Mental Processing, Composite score	Sequential Processing Scale, Simultaneous Processing Scale
Woodcock-Johnson Psych-educational Battery (1977)	3-0 to 80+	Broad Cognitive Ability score	Reading, Mathematics, Written Language, and Knowledge Aptitude
Woodcock-Johnson Psych-educational Battery, Revised (WJ-R) (1989)	2-0 to 90+	Broad Cognitive Ability score	Oral Language, Reading, Mathematics, Written Language, Knowledge Aptitude; 8 additional processing scales
Detroit Tests of Learning Aptitude (DTLA-2) (1985)	6 through 18	General Intelligence Quotient	Linguistic, Cognitive, Attentional, and Motoric domains
Differential Ability Scales (DAS)	2-6 to 17	Cognitive Ability score	Speed of information processing; verbal, nonverbal, quantitative reasoning; spatial imagery; perceptual matching; memory
Hiskey-Nebraska Test of Learning Aptitude (HNTLA) (1966)	3 to 16	Deviation Learning Quotient	12 subtests of verbal labeling, categorization, concept formation, and rehearsal (no verbal direction or responses required)

interfere with their ability to perform the types of tasks on other tests. The choice of the appropriate instrument for the referred individual is made on the basis of (1) the theoretical framework with which the multidisciplinary team is functioning and (2) the information from the classroom-based assessments and interventions.

The result at this point allows the team to differentiate between LD and mental retardation as a possible cause of the learning problem. Although the definitions and identification criteria of many states do not explicitly state an IQ range for LD, most exclude mental retardation as a primary cause of the learning problems (Mercer et al. 1990). This implies that the results of intelligence testing must be within the average range or, at the very least, above that indicative of mental retardation.

Socioemotional and behavioral domain Assessment in this domain allows the team members to evaluate whether the learning problem is the primary result of an emotion- or attention-based disorder that necessitates a distinctly different type of assessment and intervention. Although the term "learning disabilities" suggests problems that are limited to learning, early assessment models relied on behavioral indicators of LD (e.g., immature, hyperactive, distractible, impulsive) that continue to influence identification, as evidenced by current definitions of LD that either (1) include problems in social skills or self-esteem as manifestations of LD (Association for Children with Learning Disabilities 1986; Interagency Committee on Learning Disabilities Definition 1987), (2) state that LD can co-exist with secondary social and emotional disturbances (NJCLD 1988 cited in Hammill 1990), or (3) exclude the identification of LD for individuals exhibiting emotional disturbance (USOE 1977).

The decision made at this point concerns the relationship of observed behaviors or set of affective characteristics to the learning problem. This is one of the most complex decisions in the entire process, for several reasons. First, it may be difficult to distinguish whether social problems are the primary cause or a secondary effect of failure to learn. It is difficult to achieve if one is experiencing emotional troubles; it is quite common for any individual to act out or stop trying if his or her efforts result in failure. Second, research has shown that several subgroups within the diagnostic category of LD possess affective and adaptive behavior characteristics that are readily observed and easily misinterpreted as primary problems (Lahey et al. 1978; McKinney and Speece 1986; Strawser and Weller 1985). Finally, if the origin of a learning problem is not clear, it is much easier to accept a diagnosis of learning-disabled than one of emotionally disturbed or behaviorally disordered. The label "LD" has become almost socially acceptable and does not engender the concerns by teachers or parents that may be associated with other identifications. This is supported by research findings that students with behavior disorders are often misclassified as learning-disabled (Bender and Golden 1990; Speece et al. 1985; Weller and Strawser 1987).

There are a number of assessment devices based on teachers' ratings that are used to assist in the measurement of the socioemotional/behavioral domain.

The most commonly used are presented in Table 4.3. Further, some instructional programs aimed at improvement of behavior and/or social skills also include assessment devices that may be used to assess students with LD.

Achievement domain Achievement assessment is the most common form of assessment in the educational system when one considers informal classroom tests, daily or weekly evaluations of subject material, annual evaluations of all students in the district, as well as the individually administered tests that are a part of the LD assessment process. Although the majority of assessment instruments used on a daily or yearly basis in the educational system are administered in groups, the assessment of achievement for LD identification requires the student to be tested in the areas of suspected disability with an individually administered, technically adequate instrument (Reynolds 1985). There are many tests available for this purpose; some assess achievement across multiple areas (e.g., reading, mathematics, written expression, spelling), and others test a wide range of subskills within one achievement area. Although most notions of achievement are limited to reading, writing, and arithmetic, individuals who manifest problems in listening comprehension and oral expression also can be classified as having a learning disability (USOE 1977). In this case the measurement of "achievement" takes the form of individualized assessment of language and communication skills. In Table 4.4, several of the most commonly used tests of achievement or performance are listed.

Stage 3: Eligibility decisions

The question posed at this point is: If the problem is identifiable as a learning disability, is the individual eligible for services in special education? It may seem redundant to question whether an individual can or should receive services if that individual has a learning disability. In fact, this question is not redundant at all. Diagnosis or identification is not synonymous with eligibility. Meeting the identification characteristics for a learning disability is not enough; the problem also must be of sufficient severity to warrant the type or intensity of instruction provided by special education services.

Goal
At this stage the multidisciplinary team determines whether the specific eligibility criteria required for placement in special education services have been met. As previously discussed, LD eligibility criteria vary with regard to the type of problem, presence of discrepancy, and level of academic failure required for an individual to receive services (Mercer et al. 1990). Therefore, an individual may exhibit many of the diagnostic characteristics associated with LD but not be eligible for services under state guidelines. This is a difficult concept to grasp, so the following scenario may be helpful. Think of yourself as a person with a learning disability standing at the Four Corners—a well-known point in the Southwest at which four states intersect. As you box-step through the different states,

Table 4.3 Standardized instruments: Behavioral domain

Test	Ages	Domains/Subtests
Behavior Evaluation Scale-2 (BES-2) (McCarney and Leigh 1990)	Grades K–12	Learning problems, interpersonal difficulties, inappropriate behaviors, unhappiness, depression. T.
Behavior Rating Profile (Brown and Hammill 1983)	Grades 1–12	Home, school peers. S-Pa-T-Pe.
Burks' Behavior Rating Scales (Burks 1977)	Grades 1–9	Self-blame, dependency, withdrawal, anxiety, social conformity, sense of identity, impulse control, attention, physical fears/symptoms. T.
Coopersmith Self Esteem Inventories (Coopersmith 1981)	Elem. grades	Self-perception in social, academic, & personal contexts. S.
Revised Behavior Problem Checklist (BPC) (Quay and Peterson 1987)	Grades K–12	Personality disorders, inadequacy-immaturity, socialized delinquency, conduct disorders. T.
Social Skills Rating System (Elliott 1989)	3–18	Social skills, problem behaviors, & academic competence. S-Pa-T.
Walker Problem Behavior Identification Checklist (Walker 1983)	Pre-K–6	Acting out, withdrawal, distractibility, disturbed peer relations, immaturity. T.
Weller-Strawser Adaptive Behavior Scale (Weller and Strawser 1981)	K–12	Task orientation, social coping, pragmatic language. T.

Forms available: S = self, Pa = Parent, T = teacher, Pe = peers.

you do not change, but you may or may not qualify to receive LD services in the state where you happen to be standing because the eligibility criteria for Arizona, New Mexico, Colorado, and Utah are quite different.

Personnel
At this point the special educator, educational diagnostician, school psychologist, or another member of the multidisciplinary team as specified by state regulations leads the activities because he or she is the member of the team who has been trained in the discrepancy model or guidelines used to determine eligibility in the state. However, the evaluation of eligibility is a team process, and no single member makes the final decision.

Procedures
The activities at this stage do not involve administering further assessment instruments but, rather, evaluating the results obtained on the previous instruments and strategies. To accomplish this, the team applies the specific eligibility criteria or compliance guidelines for the state. Typically, the guidelines require the team to:

1. Examine the prereferral information and the results of the intellectual and socioemotional evaluations to ensure that the problem is not primarily the result of factors or other disabilities excluded by state definition.
2. Ensure that achievement in the areas of suspected disability was measured with acceptable instruments.
3. Compare the individual's ability and achievement scores using the discrepancy model or procedures required by the state.
4. Evaluate whether the discrepancy result corresponds to the state's minimum requirements for placement in a program for LD.
5. Summarize the data at a meeting, which the parents may attend, and prepare a written report.

Although some consider ability–achievement discrepancy to be the deciding factor in the classification process, discrepancy is not the only indicator of a learning disability and is not exclusive to LD (Kavale 1987; Reynolds 1985). As evident from Step 4, the presence of a discrepancy is not a guarantee of placement in an LD program. The problem may be serious enough to create difficulties for the student and initiate a referral but not be at the level required for learning disability services. In such cases the student is said to "not qualify" for special education and remains in the regular educational program.

When the individual is not eligible for placement, the outcome can seem frustrating for all involved because the student does not receive special services and the teacher already may have tried to deal with the problem in the regular classroom environment. Perhaps this frustration and the desire to help all students who are not achieving satisfactorily have led to the classification of students who have academic problems related to slowed learning ability or troublesome

Table 4.4 Standardized instruments: Achievement domain

Test	Grade/Age	Areas/Subtests
Wide Range Achievement Test-Revised (WRAT-R) (1984)	Level I: 5-0 to 11-11; Level II: 12-0 to 74-11	Reading (word recognition), Spelling, Arithmetic
Peabody Individual Achievement Test-Revised (PIAT-R) (1989)	5 through adult	Mathematics, reading recognition, reading comprehension, spelling, written expression, general information
Test of Academic Progress (1988)	Grades K–12	Mathematics, reading, spelling
Kaufman Test of Educational Achievement (KTEA) (1985)	Grades 1–12	Reading decoding, reading comprehension, mathematics applications, spelling
Kaufman Assessment Battery for Children-The Achievement Scale (K-ABC) (1983)	2-6 to 12-5	Expressive Vocabulary, Faces and Places, Arithmetic, Riddles, Reading/Decoding, Reading/Understanding
Woodcock-Johnson Psycho-educational Battery Part II-Tests of Achievement (1977)	3-0 to 80+	Reading, mathematics, written language, knowledge (science, social studies, humanities) clusters
Woodcock-Johnson Psycho-educational Battery, Revised (WJ-R) WJ-R Tests of Achievement (1989)	2-0 to 90+	Reading, mathematics, written language, knowledge, and skills clusters

Test	Grade/Age Range	Content Areas
Woodcock Reading Mastery Tests-Revised (WRMT-R) Forms G and H (1987)	K through college	Word Identification, Word Attack, Word Comprehension, Passage Comprehension, Visual-Auditory Learning, Letter Identification
KeyMath Diagnostic Arithmetic Test-Revised (KM-R) (1988)	Grades K–9	Basic Concepts (numeration, rational numbers, geometry), Operations (addition, subtraction, multiplication, division, mental computation), Applications (measurement, time and money, estimation, interpreting data, problem solving)
Test of Adolescent Language-2 (1987)	Grades 6–12	Listening, speaking, reading, writing, spoken and written language, vocabulary, grammar, expressive and receptive language
Test of Language Competence-Expanded Edition (TLC-Expanded) (1988)	Level 1: 5 to 9 Level 2: 9 to 19	Scores in expressing and interpreting intents, screening composite, and expanded composite; subtests: ambiguous sentences, listening comprehension, oral expression, figurative language
The Test of Language Development-Intermediate (TOLD-2) (1988)	8-6 through 13	Sentence combining, vocabulary, word ordering, grammatic comprehension, and malapropisms
Test of Written Language-2 (TOWL-2) (1988)	Grades 2–12	Thematic maturity, word usage, style, spelling, vocabulary, handwriting

behaviors but do not meet the discrepancy requirements and other identification guidelines for LD (McLeskey and Waldron 1991; Strawser and Weller 1985; Ysseldyke et al. 1983). This need not be the case. The information collected by this point in the process can be used to generate recommendations for classroom interventions or groupings that can help the teacher address the problem in the regular setting.

Stage 4: Instructional Programming Decisions

The questions that guide this stage are: Once the problem has been identified as a learning disability, what kind of learning disability is it? What services and instruction should the student receive?

The assessment process does not end with the determination of eligibility. Individuals with very different types of problems can be classified as learning-disabled, but if all could benefit from a single type of program or instruction, there would be no need to refer them to special education. Therefore, once an individual has been classified as having a learning disability, the team must distinguish among the unique subgroups within the diagnostic category of LD. By this point, raising the issue of heterogeneity may seem to be the epitome of redundancy: however, assessment to differentiate among the subgroups that constitute the learning-disabled population is an efficient way to formulate the specific programming and instructional recommendations that are the essence of special education.

Assessment procedures that are appropriate for classification contribute little to the development of the individual educational plan (IEP) for instructional objectives, strategies, materials, and evaluation procedures, and they do not identify the subgroup of LD to which the student belongs. For these purposes, data from additional diagnostic and informal assessments are necessary to ascertain the appropriate environment for instruction and the educational and vocational needs of the individual.

Goal
The goal at this step is to identify the specific characteristics of the individual that relate to program grouping and instructional decisions.

Personnel
As in Stage 1, assessment is a team effort. Contributions from the special education teacher, diagnostician, regular classroom teacher, parent, and related services personnel all provide information that is applicable to the goal.

Procedures
The activities to accomplish the goal at this stage can be viewed from two perspectives. The first perspective focuses on assessing the individual student in numerous areas to identify specific skill strengths and deficits and select appro-

priate instructional delivery procedures. This perspective utilizes and extends many of the classroom-based assessment techniques that provide data for previous stages in the process and that are detailed in Chapter 7.

In the second perspective the subgroup of the individual directs further assessment for instruction. Early studies established subgroups on the basis of a single academic or behavioral factor such as reading, language, or classroom behavior (see Hooper and Willis 1989). Recently, researchers have identified learning-disabled subgroups on the basis of a range of academic, classroom behavior, and adaptive behavior variables that affect educational success (Bender and Golden 1990; Strawser and Weller 1985; Weller and Strawser 1987). These studies found diverse learning-disabled subgroup clusters that presented differing assessment, programming, and instructional needs. Such studies demonstrated the need to generate educational or vocational recommendations on the basis of subgroup characteristics.

To provide a practical means to assess subgroup membership, Weller and her associates (1990) developed descriptive vignettes that teachers or diagnosticians can use to identify the individual's subgroup and determine follow-up assessment and intervention needs. When these data are combined with the adaptive behavior profile from the *Weller-Strawser Scales Adaptive Behavior for the Learning Disabled* (Weller and Strawser 1981), the team can select remedial techniques to maximize instructional time and determine the need for or extent of further assessment.

It is important to note that although the two perspectives take different direction to assessment at this stage, the goal is the same. The subgroup approach is relatively new; thus, many of the theoretical frameworks that guide training programs in education and psychology may have only recently addressed it.

CONCLUSION

The ambiguity of the definition and identification criteria for LD and the "soft" term (as opposed to mentally retarded or emotionally disturbed) has prompted some to call LD a "sociologic sponge" (Senf 1987, p. 87) that has the flexibility to absorb individuals with all kinds of problems. This view is supported by the fact that from 2% to over 20% of the school-aged population are identified as learning-disabled (Silver 1988). The ongoing difficulties associated with definition and assessment practices have even prompted some to argue that "the learning disabilities category has outlived its usefulness" because the operational criteria used for LD do not produce a unique group of students (Algozzine 1985, p. 72).

From a broader perspective, it is critical to remember that the category called "learning disabilities" is very new. In our era of fast foods and quick fixes, we may forget that it took centuries for medicine to progress from diagnosing disorders by assessing the balance of elements (i.e., fire, air, earth, water) or "humors" in the body. So, although it may be as difficult to provide the assessment criteria for the definitive "LD Person" as it is for the definitive "Normal Person," individuals with a learning disability and those who live with them urge us to continue to try.

REFERENCES

Adelman, H. S., & Taylor, L. (1986). The problems of definition and differentiation and the need for a classification schema. *Journal of Learning Disabilities, 19*, 514–520.

Algozzine, B. (1985). Low achiever differentiation: Where's the beef? *Exceptional Children, 52*, 72–75.

Algozzine, B., Forgnone, C., Mercer, C., & Trifiletti, J. (1979). Toward defining discrepancies for specific learning disabilities: An analysis and alternatives. *Learning Disability Quarterly, 2*(4), 25–31.

Association for Children with Learning Disabilities. (1986). ACLD description: Specific learning disabilities. *ACLD Newsbriefs, 158*, 1–3.

Bateman, B. (1965). An educator's view of a diagnostic approach to learning disorders. In J. Hellmuth (Ed.), *Learning disorders* (vol. 1) (pp. 219–239). Seattle, WA: Special Child Publications.

Bender, W. N., & Golden, L. B. (1990). Subtypes of students with learning disabilities as derived from cognitive, academic, behavioral, and self-concept measures. *Learning Disability Quarterly, 13*, 183–194.

Bos, C. S., Weller, C., & Vaughn, S. R. (1984–1985). At the crossroads: Issues in assessment of the learning disabled. *Diagnostique, 10*, 98–114.

Bond, G. L., & Tinker, M. A. (1973). *Reading difficulties, their diagnosis and corrections* (3rd ed.). New York: Appleton-Century-Crofts.

Bryan, T. H., & Bryan, J. H. (1986). *Understanding learning disabilities* (3rd ed.). Palo Alto, CA: Mayfield.

Chalfant, J. C. (1984). *Identifying learning disabled students: Guidelines for decision making.* (Contract No. 300-83-1-0187). Washington, DC: U.S. Department of Education, Office of Special Education Programs.

Clements, S. D. (1966). *Minimal brain dysfunction in children. Terminology and identification* (NINDS Monograph No. 3, U.S. Public Health Service Publication No. 1415). Washington, DC: U.S. Department of Health, Education, and Welfare.

Cone, T. E., & Wilson, L. R. (1981). Quantifying a severe discrepancy: A critical analysis. *Learning Disability Quarterly, 4*, 359–371.

Cruickshank, W. M., Bice, H. V., & Wallen, N. E. (1957). *Perception and cerebral palsy.* Syracuse, NY: Syracuse University Press.

Danielson, L. C., & Bauer, J. N. (1978). A formula-based classification of learning disabled children: An examination of the issues. *Journal of Learning Disabilities, 11*, 163–176.

Evans, L. D. (1990). A conceptual overview of the regression discrepancy model for evaluating severe discrepancy between IQ and achievement scores. *Journal of Learning Disabilities, 23*(7), 406–412.

Fernald, G. M. (1943). *Remedial techniques in basic school subjects.* New York: McGraw-Hill.

Feuerstein, R. (1979). *The dynamic assessment of retarded performers: The learning potential assessment device, theory, instruments, and techniques.* Baltimore, MD: University Park Press.

Gearheart, C., & Gearheart, B. (1990). *Introduction to special education assessment: Principles and practices.* Denver, CO: Love.

Gerber, M. M., & Semmel, M. I. (1984). Teacher as imperfect test: Reconceptualizing the referral process. *Educational Psychologist, 19*, 137–148.

Goldstein, K. (1939). *The organism.* New York: American Book Company.

Gruenewald, L., & Pollack, S. (1984). *Language interaction in teaching and learning.* Baltimore, MD: University Park Press.

Hammill, D. O. (1990). On defining learning disabilities: An emerging consensus. *Journal of Learning Disabilities, 23*(2), 74–84.

Harris, A. (1970). *How to increase reading ability: A guide to developmental and remedial methods* (5th ed.). New York: McKay.

Hinshelwood, J. (1917). *Congenital word blindness.* London: Lewis.

Hooper, S. R., & Willis, S. R. (1989). *Learning disability subtyping: Neuropsychological foundations, conceptual models, and issues in clinical differentiation.* New York: Springer-Verlag.

Interagency Committee on Learning Disabilities. (1987). *Learning disabilities: A report to the U.S. Congress.* Bethesda, MD: National Institutes of Health.

Johnson, D. J., & Myklebust, H. R. (1967). *Learning disabilities: Educational principles and practices.* New York: Grune & Stratton.

Kass, C., & Myklebust, H. (1969). Learning disability: An educational definition. *Journal of Learning Disabilities, 2,* 377–379.

Kavale, K. A. (1987). Theoretical issues surrounding severe discrepancy. *Learning Disabilities Research, 3*(1), 12–20.

Kavale, K. A., & Forness, S. R. (1985). *The science of learning disabilities.* San Diego, CA: College-Hill Press.

Keogh, B., Major-Kingsley, S., Omori-Gordon, H., & Reid, H. P. (1982). *A system of marker variables for the field of learning disabilities.* Syracuse, NY: Syracuse University Press.

Kirk, S. A. (1962). *Educating exceptional children.* Boston: Houghton Mifflin.

Kirk, S. A., McCarthy, J. J., & Kirk, W. D. (1968). *Illinois test of psycholinguistic abilities* (rev. ed.). Urbana: University of Illinois Press.

Lahey, B. B., Stempniak, M., Robinson, E. J., & Tyroler, M. J. (1978). Hyperactivity and learning disabilities as independent dimensions of child behavior problems. *Journal of Abnormal Psychology, 87,* 333–340.

Lovitt, T. C. (1989). *Introduction to learning disabilities.* Boston: Allyn and Bacon.

Mastropieri, M. A. (1987). Statistical and psychometric issues surrounding severe discrepancy: A discussion. *Learning Disabilities Research, 3*(1), 29–31.

Mather, N., & Healy, W. C. (1990). Deposing aptitude–achievement discrepancy as the imperial criterion for learning disabilities. *Learning Disabilities: A Multidisciplinary Journal. 1*(2), 40–48.

McIntosh, D., & Dunn, L. (1973). Children with major specific learning disabilities. In L. Dunn (Ed.), *Exceptional children in the schools: Special education in transition* (2nd ed.). New York: Holt, Rinehart & Winston.

McKinney, J. D., & Speece, D. L. (1986). Academic consequences and longitudinal stability of behavioral subtypes of learning disabled children. *Journal of Educational Psychology, 78,* 365–372.

McLeod, J. (1979). Educational underachievement: Toward a defensible psychometric definition. *Journal of Learning Disabilities, 12,* 322–330.

McLeskey, J., & Waldron, N. L. (1991). Identifying students with learning disabilities: The effect of implementing statewide guidelines. *Journal of Learning Disabilities, 24,* 501–506.

Mercer, C. D. (1987). *Students with learning disabilities* (3rd ed.) Columbus, OH: Merrill.

Mercer, C. D., Hughes, C., & Mercer, A. R. (1985). Learning disabilities definitions used by state education departments. *Learning Disability Quarterly, 8,* 45–55.

Mercer, C. D., King-Sears, P., & Mercer, A. R. (1990). Learning disabilities definitions and criteria used by state education departments. *Learning Disabilities Quarterly, 13,* 141–152.

National Advisory Committee on Handicapped Children. (1968). *First annual report, special education for handicapped children.* Washington, DC: U.S. Department of Health, Education, and Welfare.

Orton, S. T. (1937). *Reading, writing, and speech problems in children.* New York: Norton.

Reynolds, C. R. (1985). Measuring the aptitude–achievement discrepancy in learning disability diagnosis. *Remedial and Special Education, 6*(5), 37–55.

Salvia, J., & Ysseldyke, J. E. (1991). *Assessment* (5th ed.). Boston: Houghton Mifflin.

Sattler, J. M. (1990). *Assessment of children* (3rd ed.). San Diego, CA: Sattler.

Scruggs, T. E. (1987). Theoretical issues surrounding severe discrepancy: A discussion. *Learning Disabilities Research, 3*(1), 21–23.

Senf, G. M. (1977). A perspective of the definition of LD. *Journal of Learning Disabilities, 10*(9), 8–10.

Senf, G. M. (1987). Learning disabilities as sociologic sponge: Wiping up life's spills. In S. Vaughn & C. Bos (Eds.), *Research in learning disabilities: Issues and future directions* (pp. 87–96). Boston: College-Hill Press.

Silver, L. B. (1988). A review of the federal government's Interagency Committee of Learning Disabilities report to the U.S. Congress. *Learning Disabilities Focus, 3,* 73–80.

Smith, C. R. (1991). *Learning disabilities: The interaction of learner, task, and setting* (2nd ed.). Boston: Allyn and Bacon.

Speece, D. L., McKinney, J. D., & Appelbaum, M. I. (1985). Classification and validation of behavioral subtypes of learning disabled children. *Journal of Educational Psychology, 77,* 67–77.

Sternberg, R. J. (1985). *Beyond IQ: A triarchic theory of human intelligence.* New York: Cambridge University Press.

Stevens, G. D., & Birch, J. W. (1957). A proposal for clarification of the terminology used to describe brain-injured children. *Exceptional Children, 23,* 346–349.

Strauss, A. A., & Kephart, N. C. (1955). *Psychopathology and education of the brain-injured child: Vol. 2. Progress in theory and clinic.* New York: Grune & Stratton.

Strauss, A. A., & Lehtinen, L. (1947). *Psychopathology and education of the brain-injured child.* New York: Grune & Stratton.

Strawser, S. (1989). Programming, attitudes, and policies impacting the employment opportunities of underserved students: Creation of a new "Nation at Risk?" In D. Wandry (Ed.), *Base technical education: An alternative for underserved populations* (pp. 5–9). Salt Lake City, UT: Center for Base Technical Education and Transition.

Strawser, S., & Weller, C. (1985). Use of adaptive behavior and discrepancy criteria to determine learning disabilities severity subtypes. *Journal of Learning Disabilities, 18,* 205–212.

Swanson, H. L. (1991). Introduction: Issues in the assessment of learning disabilities. In H. L. Swanson (Ed.), *Handbook on the assessment of learning disabilities: Theory, research, and practice* (pp. 1–19). Austin, TX: Pro-Ed.

Swanson, H. L., & Watson, B. L. (1989). *Educational and psychological assessment of exceptional children: Theories, strategies, and applications* (2nd ed.). Columbus, OH: Merrill.

Taylor, R. L., Willits, P. P., & Richards, S. B. (1988). Curriculum-based assessment: Considerations and concerns. *Diagnostique, 14,* 14–21.

Tucker, R. W. (1985). Curriculum-based assessment: An introduction. *Exceptional Children, 52,* 199–204.

U.S. Office of Education. (1976). Education of handicapped children: Assistance to states: Proposed rulemaking. *Federal Register, 41,* 52404–52407.

U.S. Office of Education. (1977). Assistance to states for education of handicapped children: Procedures for evaluating specific learning disabilities. *Federal Register, 42,* 65082–65085.

Weller, C. (1987). A multifaceted hierarchical theory of learning disabilities. In S. Vaughn & C. Bos (Eds.), *Research in learning disabilities: Issues and future directions* (pp. 35–46). Boston: College-Hill Press.

Weller, C., & Strawser, S. (1981). *Weller-Strawser scales of adaptive behavior for the learning disabled*. Novato, CA: Academic Therapy Publications.

Weller, C., & Strawser, S. (1987). Adaptive behavior of subtypes of learning disabled individuals. *Journal of Special Education, 21*(1), 101–115.

Weller, C., Strawser, S., Callahan, J. S., Pugh, L. A., & Watanabe, A. K. (1990). Assessment of subtypes of learning disabilities: A practical approach to diagnosis and intervention. *Special Services in the Schools, 6*(1/2), 99–120.

Wepman, J. M., Cruickshank, W. M., Deutsch, C. P., Morency, A., & Strother, C. R. (1975). Learning disabilities. In N. Hobbs (Ed.), *Issues in the classification of children* (vol. 1) (pp. 300–317). San Francisco: Jossey-Bass.

Werner, H., & Strauss, A. A. (1940). Causal factors in low performance. *American Journal of Mental Deficiency, 45,* 213–218.

Wiederholt, J. L. (1974). Historical perspectives on the education of the learning disabled. In L. Mann & D. Sabatino (Eds.), *The second review of special education* (pp. 103–152). Philadelphia: JSE Press.

Willson, V. L. (1987). Statistical and psychometric issues surrounding severe discrepancy. *Learning Disabilities Research, 3*(1), 24–28.

Ysseldyke, J., Algozzine, B., & Epps, S. (1983). A logical and empirical analysis of current practice in classifying students as handicapped. *Exceptional Children, 50,* 160–166.

5

Informal Assessment in the Classroom

Lisa E. Monda-Amaya
Fran Reed

Assessment has become an integral part of the educational process. *Educational assessment* is defined as the process of collecting data for the purpose of specifying and verifying problems and for making instructional decisions about students (Salvia and Ysseldyke 1991). Data collected affect decisions regarding referral and placement, instructional planning and adaptation, and pupil progress monitoring and evaluation. In special education, assessment practices are governed by legal mandates and should be guided by ethical principles. This chapter addresses issues concerning assessment practices and provides an overview of informal assessment methods that can be used to maximize instructional effectiveness.

Assessment devices can be classified into two categories: formal and informal measures. Traditionally, assessment practices have been characterized by formal assessment measures that use specific procedures in the administration, scoring, and interpretation of the tests (McLoughlin and Lewis 1990). They are administered with the intent of profiling a student's strengths and weaknesses (Ysseldyke and Christenson 1987). Formal assessment measures are generally norm-referenced or standardized, designed to compare student performance with that of a reference group.

THE NEED FOR INFORMAL ASSESSMENT

Although formal assessment has been part of the educational process for many years, much controversy has arisen over its use. Throughout the 1970s and 1980s, significant legislation and litigation had a direct impact on assessment practices in special education. Requirements were made that measurement devices used in the identification of and placement of students into special programs be technically adequate and culturally fair. Researchers and practitioners questioned the validity and reliability of formal assessment measures, particularly their relevance to instructional planning and implementation (Castiglione 1981; Duran 1989; Gable et al. 1991; Galagan 1985; Jenkins and Pany 1978; Valencia and Pearson 1988; Ysseldyke and Christenson 1987). Further, there was an increasing demand for assessment data that would be valuable in guiding instructional decisions and would provide for accountability and documentation of student progress within the curriculum (Deno and Mirkin 1980).

In the field of learning disabilities, problems inherent in the referral and placement process as well as issues in defining the population and selecting appropriate assessment instruments to identifying students (based on components of the various definitions) have led to serious concerns. The adequacy of norm groups used in the standardization of formal assessment instruments has been questioned (Castiglione 1981; Fuchs et al. 1987; Goldman 1990), particularly when these instruments are administered to students from culturally and linguistically diverse backgrounds (Ortiz and Wilkinson 1991). Also, the use of formal assessment data in making instructional decisions has been challenged. Each of these concerns is addressed in this chapter.

Difficulty reaching consensus on a standard definition of learning disability has been an issue for some time (Hammill 1990; Silver 1988; see also Chapter 4). Some of this controversy surrounds the use of processing components and discrepancy scores in defining the population. In most states the definition of LD is based on the determination of the existence of a processing deficit. The concept of process disorders underlying LD has been described as an unproductive conceptual model (Algozzine and Ysseldyke 1983) in that there is a lack of empirical support that programs based on this model increase student achievement (Arter and Jenkins 1977; Hammill and Larsen 1974). Further, the reliability and validity of formal assessment instruments used to detect these deficits have also been questioned.

The use of discrepancy scores in identifying students with learning disabilities also has presented problems (Clarizio and Phillips 1986; Hammill 1990). In many definitions, it has been proposed that formulas be used to determine discrepancies between academic achievement and intellectual functioning. Hammill (1990) notes that objections have been raised regarding the mathematical soundness of the formulas and the psychometric adequacy of the scores that are used in the equation.

Another area of controversy has been the system for identification and placement of children in special education (Galagan 1985). Decisions for placement in special education are based primarily on results of formal assessment instruments. Statistics indicate that 92% of the students referred for evaluation are assessed and 72% are eventually placed in special education (Algozzine et al. 1981, cited in Ysseldyke and Algozzine 1983). West and Idol (1990) note that "approximately 5% of all the nation's students are assessed each year under special education, and these assessment services account for 12 cents of each dollar spent for special education, about $2 billion per year or $1,273 per assessment" (p. 22).

Further, the dependence on psychoeducational assessment for identification purposes has led to mislabeling (Humphries and Wilson 1986; Ysseldyke and Algozzine 1983); overidentification (Bursuck and Lessen 1987); and, for some students, permanent placement in special education with little movement back into the mainstream (Bursuck and Lessen 1987). Standardized tests have not been found to be reliable in distinguishing students with LD from their nondisabled peers (Ysseldyke, Algozzine, and Epps 1982) or from those students identified as low achievers (Jenkins et al. 1988; Seigel 1989a, 1989b; Ysseldyke, Algozzine, et al. 1982). Often students who are mislabeled or overidentified come from culturally and linguistically diverse backgrounds (Reschly 1988). For that reason, there has been an increasing awareness of issues regarding fairness in the use of formal assessment with these students (Duran 1989; Figueroa 1989; Fuchs et al. 1987; Ortiz and Wilkinson 1991; Seigel 1989a; Ysseldyke and Regan 1980). Many researchers suggest that the nondiscriminatory assessment component of P.L. 94-142 can best be approximated by using alternatives to norm-referenced tests (Ortiz and Wilkinson 1991; Ysseldyke and Regan 1980).

Issues regarding the technical adequacy of formal assessment instruments—particularly validity and reliability—for students with special needs have also been raised. For example, Fuchs and colleagues (1987) found that very few of the formal assessment instruments most frequently used with special-needs populations included individuals with disabilities or those from culturally and linguistically diverse backgrounds in the standardization sample. They stated that, if the standardization sample did not include individuals representing the populations upon whom a test was to be used, then eligibility, placement, and instructional decisions could not be made based on the results obtained from those tests.

Of particular interest to classroom teachers is the curricular and instructional validity of formal assessment instruments. Formal assessment scores have been found to provide little information for developing instructional programs, writing goals and objectives, and assisting in the decision-making process (Algozzine and Ysseldyke 1982, cited in Ysseldyke and Christenson 1987; Castiglione 1981; Duran 1989; Gable et al. 1991; Galagan 1985; Jenkins and Pany 1978; Valencia and Pearson 1988). Diagnostic reports that summarize student performance data on formal assessment measures are rarely used in program planning and implementation (Fuchs et al. 1987; Pyl 1989). Research has shown that teachers tend to base instructional decisions on unsystematic forms of informal assessment data (Potter and Mirkin 1982, cited in Wesson et al. 1984).

Currently there is an increasing movement to integrate students with handicaps into the general education setting and to decrease student classification into the various categories of disability. Stainback and Stainback (1990) discuss the concept of inclusive schooling in which all students in the mainstream are provided with "appropriate educational programs that are challenging yet geared to their capabilities and needs as well as any support and assistance that they and/or their teachers may need to be successful in the mainstream" (p. 3). An inclusive school enables all students to have successful learning experiences in the mainstream, including students with handicaps, those at risk for school failure, and those from culturally and linguistically diverse backgrounds. Formal assessment has been found to be of little value in this environment because it assists in perpetuating a dual system of education (Galagan 1985) and provides little information for planning and implementing instruction that can accommodate diversity. In light of this current philosophical emphasis, there is a trend away from formal assessment and toward more direct, curriculum-based measures of student performance.

EFFECTIVE INSTRUCTION

The concept of inclusion has become an important consideration in providing appropriate education to students with special needs. In creating successful learning environments for the inclusion of all students, teachers should consider a variety of factors related to student outcome (see Bursuck and Lessen 1987; Evans et al. 1989; Heiss 1977; Ysseldyke and Christenson 1987) and examine the interaction among these factors. These factors include student characteristics such as behavior, motivation, and learning rate or style; environmental factors such as the learning environment itself, the academic focus, or the class rules; and instructional factors such as allocated time, teacher expectations, and monitoring and evaluation procedures (Ysseldyke and Christenson 1987).

While formal assessment devices provide the teacher with an isolated picture of student performance on a particular skill assessed in a very specific way, additional student, environmental, and instructional factors cannot be addressed. Standardization procedures often prohibit variations in administration, scoring, and interpretation to accommodate these factors. Therefore, all necessary components in planning and implementing effective instruction cannot be considered. For this reason, alternatives to formal assessment should be selected.

One important variable in designing effective instruction that is directly related to student achievement is the degree to which teachers actively monitor student progress and evaluate student performance (Christenson et al. 1989). To maximize instructional effectiveness, assessment procedures should be used on an ongoing basis, thereby reflecting small increments of change (Fuchs et al. 1988). When formal assessment measures are the basis for evaluating student performance, problems arise because of the frequency by which they can be administered. These measures are often administered only once or twice a year, and little systematic monitoring occurs in the interim. Jenkins and Pany (1978) found that student achievement in a particular curriculum area may not be truly reflected in achievement test scores, and they assert that standardized achievement tests are not sensitive to curricular differences and academic gains.

Monitoring of student progress toward goals established in the individual educational plan (IEP) is required by law (Deno, Mirkin and Chiang 1982; Fuchs 1986; Fuchs et al. 1989; Shinn et al. 1989) and requires instruments that can be used on an ongoing basis and are sensitive to changes in performance, instruction, or administrative arrangement (Deno, Mirkin and Chiang 1982). Continuous monitoring systems are used to evaluate pupil progress toward IEP goals and objectives, evaluate the effectiveness of pupil programs, and modify and adapt those programs as needed. "Frequent and systematic monitoring of students' progress helps students, parents, teachers, administrators, and policy-makers identify strengths and weaknesses in learning and instruction" (U.S. Department of Education, 1986, p. 43).

Ongoing monitoring using informal assessment devices has been found to be critical to the design of effective instruction (Deno, Marston and Mirkin 1982; Jenkins and Pany 1978) and has been linked to increased academic learning time (Wesson et al. 1988) and increased student achievement (Fuchs 1986; Fuchs and Fuchs 1986; Fuchs et al. 1988; Shinn et al. 1989; Wesson et al. 1988). Fuchs and Fuchs (1986) conducted a meta-analysis that examined research focusing on the effectiveness of ongoing assessment. They found that when ongoing monitoring is used, student achievement can be expected to increase from the 50th percentile to the 75th percentile.

Teacher behavior also is affected when systematic monitoring procedures are used. These procedures provide teachers with greater awareness of student performance (Fuchs et al. 1988), increase teacher effectiveness (Deno, Marsten, and Mirkin 1982; Fuchs 1986; Fuchs et al. 1990) and enhance pedagogical behavior (Fuchs et al. 1988). Teachers who do not monitor pupil progress tend to be less specific in describing IEP goals, maintain rather than revise goals when needed, and overrate student performance (Fuchs et al. 1989).

Informal assessment provides the means for systematically collecting student performance data that are instructionally relevant; it is critical to the development of effective instructional programs. Through informal assessment procedures, teachers can directly monitor student behavior as well as evaluate the instruction provided and the learning environment. This monitoring and evaluation can be done frequently and are directly related to what is taught. There are various types of informal assessment measures that can be used for these purposes. Galagan (1985) proposed that there is little justification for the continued use of psychometric measures whose effectiveness in meeting the needs of students has been so validly questioned.

INFORMAL ASSESSMENT

Informal assessment devices are procedures without rigid administration, scoring, and interpretation rules (McLoughlin and Lewis 1990). Through informal assessment, student performance is evaluated in the existing curriculum or the natural environment with instructionally relevant instruments. These instruments provide information about current levels of performance, aid in the selection of goals and objectives, point to the need for instructional modification, document student progress, and suggest directions for further assessment. Further, informal assessment instruments do not simply consider student behavior on a specific task; they also enable the teacher to examine additional factors that might affect student performance.

There are many types of informal assessment devices that can be used to measure characteristics of the student, the learning environment, and the success of various aspects of the instructional program. One type of informal assessment is curriculum-based assessment, which is the process of determining instructional needs by directly assessing specific curriculum skills (Choate et al. 1992). Curriculum-based assessment can include such techniques as curriculum-based measurement, response and error analysis conducted on student work samples, academic probes, task analysis, and teacher-made tests. Criterion-referenced tests represent another type of informal assessment measure. Through observation, a third form of informal assessment, data can be collected through a direct observation format, anecdotal records, or ecobehavioral assessment. Informal assessment data can also be collected through the use of interviews, checklists, and questionnaires. Each of these assessment methods is described in the remainder of the chapter.

Curriculum-based Assessment

Current demands placed on teachers to provide effective instruction to all students within the context of the curriculum indicate that teachers must be actively involved in ongoing evaluation of student performance. Teachers who are active decision makers and who consistently monitor pupil progress in all curricular areas create an environment that fosters student success. This section describes the role of curriculum-based assessment (CBA) in instructional decision making.

The term "curriculum-based assessment" can be used to describe a variety of assessment techniques that measure student achievement in the curriculum (Bursuck and Lessen 1987; Gickling 1981; Tucker 1987). It is defined as "any approach that uses direct observation and recording of a student's performance in a local school curriculum as a basis for gathering information to make instructional decisions" (Deno 1987, p. 41). The goal of CBA is to eliminate the "instructional mismatch" between the curriculum and the skills of the student (Gickling and Thompson 1985). When students are placed appropriately in the curriculum and instructional adaptations are made as needed, learning is enhanced.

Elements of CBA have existed in education for years (Tucker 1985), but the concept itself originated with the work of Eaton and Lovitt (Blankenship and Lilly 1981), who recommended that placement in a reading curriculum be dependent upon a student's daily performance in oral reading. Gickling and associates pioneered the current movement of tieing the assessment directly to the curricula (Shinn 1989) and are credited with first using the term "curriculum-based assessment" (Tucker 1985).

Advantages of Curriculum-based Assessment

Curriculum-based assessment has been found to be useful at all levels of the assessment process from initial screening to program evaluation. For the purpose of screening and referral, CBA provides systematic observational data concerning student performance, measures the degree of deviance from peer performance, and provides information for instructional intervention that would either legitimize or correct the need for the referral. When making referrals, general educators using CBA measures are able to specify skill deficits (Blankenship and Lilly 1981). "In short, CBA would cure the palpable illegalities presently afflicting the subjective referral systems operating nationwide" (Galagan 1985, p. 291).

Traditionally, formal assessment measures have been used in determining eligibility for special services. As previously mentioned, much controversy has been generated concerning the use of these measures. Curriculum-based measurement (CBM), which is one type of CBA, has been found to be an effective tool for identifying students with special needs (Deno 1985; Galagan 1985; Germann and Tindal 1985; Jenkins et al. 1979; Marston and Magnusson 1985; Marston et al. 1984). It provides information that is directly related to the curriculum, demonstrates reliability in consistently identifying the same students in need of instructional assistance, and is time- and cost-efficient (Shinn and Marston 1985). It is advantageous to use curriculum-based measures to make eligibility decisions because focus is directed away from defining an area of exceptionality and detecting failure within the child and toward identifying instructional deficits that can be addressed in the classroom curriculum.

The essential measure of success for a student is progress in the local curriculum (Tucker 1985). One of the greatest advantages to using CBA devices is that the focus of assessment is on academic and task-related skills; therefore, assessment results are meaningful to the provision of instruction (Bursuck and Lessen 1987). Once the student has been identified as being in need of special services, CBA devices should be used on a regular basis in all curricular settings. Data obtained through these measures are useful in making instructional decisions, writing IEPs, measuring progress toward objectives, providing information about program effectiveness, and documenting the effectiveness of instructional strategies (Shinn and Marston 1985). Goals and objectives developed using CBA data (1) are more applicable in the classroom, (2) lessen the gap between curriculum and instruction, (3) avoid compartmentalization of information, (4) allow for greater flexibility and sequencing of material, and (5) allow students to view the match between instruction and testing (Fuchs and Deno 1991; Idol et al. 1986).

Curriculum-based procedures can be used in any subject area and, with repeated use over time, are sensitive to even the smallest changes in student progress toward a goal. For this reason they are useful for measuring ongoing student progress (Deno 1985; Marston and Magnusson 1985; Salvia and Hughes 1990). Teachers can use CBA data to assess performance levels and make on-the-spot decisions regarding instructional modification or adaptation.

Finally, in light of the current emphasis to meet the needs of all students in the general education setting, CBA measures assist in fostering a collaborative environment between teachers, support personnel, parents, and administrators. By using CBA, educators can work together to understand student characteristics and instructional and environmental factors that are necessary to develop effective instructional programs for all students.

Types of Curriculum-based Assessment

Fuchs and Deno (1991) outline two major areas into which most forms of CBA can be categorized—specific subskill mastery measurement and general outcome measurement. The distinctive features of the two models are described in Table 5.1. In using specific subskill mastery measurement, teachers break down a task or behavior into specific subskills that are written as short-term objectives. Criterion-referenced test items are devised that effectively assess those objectives within the local curriculum. Most CBA systems belong to the mastery measurement model.

The CBM techniques developed in the past decade by Deno and colleagues (Deno 1985; Fuchs 1986; Shinn 1989) are a form of CBA that reflect the general outcome measurement model, which was developed to "overcome the shortcomings" of specific subskill mastery measurement (Fuchs and Deno 1991, p. 489). General outcome measurement systems were developed that could be used efficiently, ensured reliability and validity, provided assessment information that helps teachers plan better instructional programs, and could be used to answer questions about the effectiveness of programs in producing overall student growth (Fuchs and Deno 1991). Fuchs and Deno (1991) describe this model as being specific and prescriptive in its approach and having procedures that remain constant over time. These features are similar to the elements of more traditional paradigms of assessment. The primary area of departure from the more traditional models is in the application of social validity measures, repeated performance sampling, and direct observation of a variety of curriculum skills over the entire year.

Curriculum-based Measurement.

Curriculum-based measurement (CBM) is a form of CBA in which "teachers specify long term academic goals, conduct ongoing assessments that monitor student progress toward that goal, evaluate the adequacy of student progress and the instructional plan, and develop instructional changes that increase the probability of goal attainment" (Fuchs et al. 1990, p. 42). Fuchs and Deno (1991) state that CBM is a general outcome measurement that can be viewed as an effective "bridge" between traditional psychometric models of assessment and current observational assessment strategies in that it takes the notion of standardized measurement and applies concepts of social validity (direct observation, peer sampling, graphic display of data, etc.). Curriculum-based measurement has been found to positively affect student achievement and provide teachers with greater awareness of student needs (Wesson et al. 1986) and to be successful with a variety of subject matter (see Fuchs 1987; Fuchs et al. 1991; Potter and Wamre 1990) and in a variety of settings (Bean and Lane 1990). Table 5.2 provides samples of objectives and measurement strategies in the areas of reading, spelling, and mathematics.

Table 5.1 Comparison of specific subskill mastery and general outcome measurement

Specific Subskill Mastery CBA	*General Outcome Measurement* CBM
Focus:	
Mastery measurement of specific curriculum subskills	Prescriptive procedures. Assessment of global learning outcomes.
Key Elements:	
1. *Hierarchies:*	
Skill Hierarchy—Teachers determine skill hierarchies that prescribe a sequence for instruction and measurement.	Instructional Hierarchies— Teachers specify general domains focusing on the broader desired outcome of the curriculum.
2. *Retention & Generalization:*	
A. Does not automatically assess retention and generalization of related skills.	A. Automatically assessed— Samples broad domains that represent past and future instructional targets.
B. Assessment results present constricted instructional focus that may limit maintenance and transfer of skills (cannot address cognitive skill development).	B. Enables monitoring for maintenance and transfer of skills.
3. *Instruction and Measurement:*	
A. Measures short-term objectives.	A. Measures long-term curricular goal performance.
B. Instruction validity is strong.	B. Less sensitive to acquisition of specific skills currently taught.
C. Measurement framework is limited.	C. Content and criterion validity are strong.
4. *Measurement Shifts:*	
Shift in measurement each time skill is mastered.	Can monitor progress throughout the year without shift in measurement device.
5. *Test Construction:*	
A. Reliance on teacher-made, criterion-referenced tests.	A. Standardized, prescriptive.
B. Unknown technical characteristics.	B. Documented validity and reliability.

(Adapted from "Paradigmatic Distinction Between Instructionally Relevant Measurement Models." by L. S. Fuchs and S. L. Deno, 1991, *Exceptional Children, 57,* 488–500.)

Table 5.2 Sample of curriculum-based measurement procedures in three subject areas

	Behavioral Objective	Administration	Scoring and Evaluation
Reading	Given 300 word passages from the third-grade reading series, Monica will read correctly 85 words per minute with no more than 3 errors per minute.	Monica is handed one 300-word passage and is asked to read it aloud. Mr. Scott times the reading and marks Monica's errors on an instructor's copy of the passage.	Mr. Scott may calculate Monica's reading fluency (words correct per minute) and accuracy (errors per minute). Upon charting her progress, Mr. Scott may examine performance to determine which reading group is best for Monica.
Mathematics	Given addition problems from the 6th-grade math text, Allen will calculate these problems at a rate of 15 problems correct per minute with no more than 2 errors per minute.	Allen is handed a test form with 30 addition problems that are representative of the various forms of addition found throughout the text. Ms. Jones will time Allen's performance.	Ms. Jones may calculate Allen's fluency (problems correct per minu te) and accuracy (errors per minute) in problem solving. She might also choose to conduct an error analysis to determine the types of errors made by the student. Allen's performance data will provide information on appropriate instructional levels in addition.
Spelling	Given 20 words from the 5th-grade spelling text, Laura will spell 6 words correctly in 1 minute.	Twenty spelling words are dictated to Laura by Ms. Jordan at a rate of at least one word every 10 seconds. Laura will immediately spell each word into a tape recorder.	Ms. Jordan can examine Laura's performance in terms of words spelled correctly and calculate spelling fluency (number of words spelled correctly per minute) and accuracy (number of errors per minute). Evaluation of Laura's performance data and the types of errors she has made provides information for adapting instruction to meet her needs.

Deno and Fuchs (1987) suggest that in designing and constructing a CBM device, there are 10 steps that should be taken. A summary of the steps and examples they describe is provided in Table 5.3.

Once the teacher completes the initial steps in designing and constructing the device, pupil performance is directly measured. Fuchs (1987) suggests that the data base should be evaluated using either a goal-oriented strategy or an experimental approach. The goal-oriented strategy would enable teachers to examine both how quickly the student must progress to reach a goal and how quickly the student is actually progressing under the current instructional program. The experimental approach involves systematic modification of the student's instructional program using alternative interventions. Further discussion of these strategies is provided in Fuchs (1987) and Deno (1986). Teachers should evaluate the data and make decisions regarding (1) the appropriateness of the goals and objectives, revising them as necessary; (2) the adequacy of student growth and whether modification of instruction is necessary; and (3) the efficacy of different interventions so that effective instruction components are continually developed (Fuchs et al. 1991).

One of the biggest problems with CBM is that teachers consider the process time-consuming (Wesson 1987). Wesson (1987) suggests a number of techniques for increasing the efficiency of CBM in the areas of organization, preparation of materials, administration of the assessment measures, scoring, and using the data. Mechanical devices (e.g., computer) and teaching the student to score and graph the results (Wesson et al. 1986) have also been suggested as means for increasing efficiency.

Response and Error Analysis

Another type of CBA is analysis of student work samples through response and error analysis. Analyzing student work samples supplies the teacher with valuable information for instructional planning and modification and assists in determining a student's strengths and weaknesses. Teachers can examine either permanent products such as student journals (Gausted and Messemheimer-Young 1991; McKillip and Stanic 1988), class assignments, projects, tests, or homework assignments; or evaluate oral responses to questions or problems. Work sample analysis can be conducted in any subject (for examples, see Deno et al. [1982], and Parker et al. [1991]).

In a recent study of the use of CBM in the area of spelling, Fuchs and colleagues (1991) found that teachers who used CBM procedures effected greater gains in spelling achievement with students with LD than teachers who did not use CBM procedures. Further, teachers who used a skills-analysis approach (information on correct and incorrect words and types of errors) in conjunction with CBM produced greater gains, could better identify phonetic errors, and were better able to specify skills for instruction than either a CBM without skills analysis group or a control group.

Table 5.3 Constructing a curriculum-based measurement device

Behavior	Example
1. Select a behavior to be measured.	Reading aloud from text.
2. Select a basic measurement strategy.	Performance measurement is selected to evaluate the student's performance on the reading of passages at a designated level of difficulty. The goal is to improve overall performance on the material.
3. Select a score, a difficulty level, and the size of the measurement domain.	a. The score selected is the number of correctly and incorrectly read words. b. The difficulty level is the level of text (low, medium, or high range) selected for measurement. A level of text is selected that is in the student's mid-range of difficulty. c. A mid-size measurement domain is selected, which would consist of one level within a particular reading series.
4. Determine the frequency of administration and the duration of measurement device.	a. Measurement will take place twice a week. b. The duration of measurement will be 60 seconds.
5. Select a criterion of mastery or goal.	90 words correct with no more than 4 errors (a 90% accuracy criterion).
6. Select a procedure for generating test samples.	Randomly select passages representative of goal (each passage is assigned a number: numbers are randomly drawn).
7. Select administration and scoring procedures.	Design administration and scoring procedures that will be used consistently across testing occasions.
8. Complete a goal and objective form.	a. Goal: In 16 weeks, when presented with stories for 1-minute timed readings, from the Level 6 reading book, (student name) will read aloud 90 words per minute, with no more than 4 errors. b. Objective: During each successive week, when presented with a random selection for 1 minute from the level 6 reading series, (student name) will read aloud at an average increase of 4 words per week with no increase in errors.
9. Design a measurement system form.	Design a form that includes the following information: a) behavior, b) frequency, c) duration of test, d) difficulty level, e) size of domain, and f) administration and scoring procedures.
10. Determine how to use the data that will be collected.	Graphing the data, displaying data points and goal. Evaluate daily performance using rule decisions. Determine and implement instructional change based on performance data.

(Adapted by S. L. Deno and L. S. Fuchs, 1987, "Developing Curriculum-based Measurement Systems for Data-based Special Education Problem Solving," *Focus on Exceptional Children, 19*(8), 1–16.)

One distinct advantage of using data produced by student work samples is that the information provided reflects students' daily performance in the curriculum. Further, the data collection process is straightforward and not very time-consuming. Teachers can collect samples of student work on a regular basis. Once work samples have been collected, response and error analysis can be conducted (McLoughlin and Lewis 1990).

In conducting a response analysis, the teacher evaluates both correct and incorrect responses by focusing on such variables as frequency, duration, rate, and percentage (McLoughlin and Lewis 1990). Response analysis data can be collected, charted, and evaluated on a daily basis and allow the teacher to examine all aspects of student performance on a task.

One example of response analysis would be to determine the fluency and accuracy rates of responses. Moving students to fluency at a task is considered essential to generalization and application of knowledge. Increases in fluency or oral reading, for example, have been linked to increases in comprehension (Samuels 1979).

Oral reading fluency is expressed as the number of words read correctly per minute and is determined using the following equation:

$$\frac{\text{Number of words read correctly}}{\text{Total reading time in seconds}} \times 60$$

Accuracy is defined as the number of errors per minute and is determined by using the following equation:

$$\frac{\text{Number of errors}}{\text{Total reading time in seconds}} \times 60$$

These equations can be used to determine fluency in all subject areas. As fluency increases, teachers should look for a corresponding decrease in errors.

Tindal and Parker (1989) provide another example of response analysis in the area of written expression. They suggest that a teacher can examine production variables (e.g., total number of words, number of words spelled correctly, number of words in the correct sequence) and production-independent variables (e.g., percentage of words spelled correctly, percentage of words in the correct sequence, and average number of words in correct sequence) in evaluating student performance. A teacher might also choose to conduct a response analysis on variables such as frequency of sentence type regarding both form (fragmented, simple, compound, complex) and function (declarative, interrogative, imperative, exclamatory), the vocabulary used (noting the words not previously used in a writing sample), and quality of ideation (i.e., relevance, originality, and logical progression) (Minner et al. 1989).

Table 5.4 provides an example of a basic format for use in conducting a response analysis in the area of mathematics. The data collected on correct and incorrect responses can be charted for use in the design and evaluation of instructional programs.

Table 5.4 Sample response analysis sheet: Mathematics
1. Activity: Addition worksheet
2. Types of Items Presented: 24 problems
3. Total Time for Student to Complete the Activity: 6 minutes, 10 seconds
4. Number/Percent of Items Correct: 13 items/ 54%
5. Number/Percent of Items Incorrect: 11items/ 46%
6. Fluency: $\dfrac{\text{Number of items answered correctly}}{\text{Total time in seconds}} \times 60$

$$\frac{13}{370} \times 60 = 2.11 \text{ problems correct per minute}$$

7. Accuracy: $\dfrac{\text{Number of errors}}{\text{Total time in seconds}} \times 60$

$$\frac{11}{370} \times 60 = 1.78 \text{ errors per minute}$$

Error analysis is a set of procedures used to categorize a student's errors so that teaching decisions can be made based on performance within the school curriculum (Grimes 1981). Errors are considered to be an important part of the learning process (Grimes 1981), and analysis of errors is a critical component of CBA (Gable et al. 1991). Although closely associated with response analysis, this type of analysis focuses specifically on the types of errors executed.

In error analysis, errors are classified into three categories of responses: random errors, errors in concept formation, and errors in unlearned concepts (Grimes 1981). Given the types of errors a student has made, instruction will vary. If random errors are displayed, the teacher may assume that the student is capable of answering correctly but is providing incorrect responses (possibly due to carelessness). Errors in concept formation indicate areas in which additional instruction and practice are needed to develop a basic understanding of the concept. Students displaying errors due to lack of knowledge should receive initial instruction focused at the acquisition stage of learning.

Students with LD have been found to display a substantially greater number of error responses in certain academic subjects than their nonhandicapped peers (see Adams 1990; Thomas et al. 1987). Therefore, an important aspect of instructional planning and implementation is an evaluation of error responses to ensure that the level and type of instruction being provided are appropriate.

In the area of reading, common miscues include substitutions, omission, insertions, reversals, and syntactically and semantically unacceptable responses (Adams 1990). Teachers can examine a sample of oral reading to determine levels of fluency and, at the same time, conduct a miscue analysis to evaluate student responses.

Thomas and colleagues (1987) describe errors in writing expository text, including redundancies (sentences that fail to provide new information), early termination (ending before an idea is complete), irrelevancies (listing tangentially related material), and mechanical errors (grammatical errors). They found that while successful students exhibit "knowledge-telling strategies" in writing expository text, students with LD often have difficulty in this area. The knowledge-telling strategy includes exhibiting goal-oriented planning, internal contextual constraints, and interconnectedness and revising work. Error and response analyses could be conducted to determine whether students were utilizing the strategies that could make them successful in this area.

In spelling, teachers should be able to recognize and classify a variety of different types of errors. In conducting an analysis, teachers could look for errors that involve vowel teams, vowel + *r*, doubling omissions, suffixes, vowel + *n*, dual consonants, final *e*, and blends (Fuchs et al. 1990).

Seven clusters of errors have been identified in the area of mathematics (Enright 1985) that can be analyzed to determine frequency of occurrence. The types of errors that teachers can look for include:

1. Problems in regrouping possibly indicate that the student has difficulty understanding the concept of place value.
2. Process substitution errors occur when the student makes changes in the process of the computation.
3. Omissions are made when the student leaves out a step or part of an answer.
4. Errors of directionality indicate that the computation was performed correctly, but the steps were conducted in the wrong sequence.
5. Errors of placement are incidents of numbers or answers being written in the wrong place.
6. Errors may also occur in which the student performs the wrong operation as a result of inattention to the computation sign.
7. Errors may occur due to a lack of basic understanding of concepts or a failure to acquire the necessary prerequisite skills.

Academic Probes

Academic probes are timed samples of academic behaviors. Probes are excellent methods for keeping ongoing records of student performance (Bursuck and Lessen 1987) and are constructed to assess acquisition, fluency, and maintenance on specific objectives. They can be administered frequently and in brief sessions and require little investment of teacher and student time (Salvia and Hughes 1990).

McLoughlin and Lewis (1990) suggest that probes should be used to examine the relationship between the instructional task and the student's ability. Based on the data collected, program modifications can be made that are related either to the instructional strategies used to teach the task or to task characteristics. In this case, performance is assessed under the standard conditions, instructional adaptations are made, and performance is once again assessed, but under the modified conditions (McLoughlin and Lewis 1990).

In designing a probe, questions or problems are created for a specific objective and developed into a quick assessment device (see Table 5.5).

It is important to note that since fluency or rate measures are obtained, more problems should be provided in the assessment than the student can complete in the time allotted (Salvia and Hughes 1990). Once the probe has been administered, the scores are calculated and can be charted. Student performance is then evaluated and instructional modifications are made as needed.

Task Analysis

Task analysis serves both as a diagnostic tool and as a basis for establishing an instructional sequence (Moyer and Dardig 1978). It is described as the process of identifying, breaking down, and sequencing subcomponents of a target behavior and subsequently evaluating student progress toward the attainment of those subcomponent skills (Magg 1989; Moyer and Dardig 1978). Rusch and colleagues (1988) note that task analyses can be used to (1) identify prerequisite skills, (2) sequence skills from simple to complex, and (3) select and organize tasks to enhance generalization. A task analysis can be developed for academic (Magg 1989; Rusch et al. 1988), social (Howell 1985; Rusch et al. 1988), and vocational skills (Rusch et al. 1988).

In designing and administering task assessment, the teacher must pinpoint a target behavior or task and write a terminal objective. The teacher then must isolate the behavior selected and analyze it, breaking it down into teachable subtasks described in measurable terms. To assist in identifying essential subtasks, the teacher may choose to do one of the following: (1) watch a master perform the task (either teacher or a student), (2) work backwards from the terminal objective, (3) use brainstorming (components are written down initially without regard for sequence and later ordered), or (4) alter the conditions in the terminal objective (Moyer and Dardig 1978).

Once the essential subtasks have been determined, an assessment tool is developed containing questions at each level of the subtask. The assessment measure is administered, and student performance data are evaluated for use in planning and implementing instruction. Based on the results of this assessment, teachers can determine the student's entry level at a particular skill or decide where breakdowns may be occurring in the instructional plan. The task analysis can then be used to determine subsequent skills that must be taught and can provide an ongoing record of student progress toward mastery of the objective.

Teacher-made Tests

Teacher-made tests are advantageous in that they are developed from the curriculum and can be used flexibly to meet a teacher's specific needs (Salvia and Hughes 1990). Teachers know how the subject matter was taught and can devise an instrument that more accurately reflects student knowledge. The design of teacher-made tests can range from very simple tasks such as asking a

Table 5.5 Sample timed probe: Basic multiplication facts

2 × 4	4 × 6	5 × 3	9 × 2	6 × 2	3 × 4
4 × 4	2 × 5	9 × 3	3 × 2	0 × 4	5 × 4
8 × 2	7 × 3	5 × 2	4 × 1	9 × 4	3 × 3
8 × 3	4 × 9	2 × 0	4 × 8	1 × 3	2 × 7
1 × 2	7 × 4	2 × 2	3 × 6	0 × 3	9 × 4
8 × 4	6 × 3	5 × 1	4 × 9	5 × 4	2 × 3
9 × 3	4 × 0	7 × 2	4 × 8	8 × 3	7 × 2

student to recite the alphabet, to devising written quizzes to assess text knowledge. For example, Valencia and Pearson (1988) suggest a number of variations in format for assessing reading comprehension skills that include multiple-choice formats, student-generated questions, and open-ended questions. They also suggest that teachers can assess prior knowledge of a topic by asking the student to rate the likelihood that an idea or event may occur or by using semantic maps.

Teacher-made tests are often criterion-referenced so that mastery of skills is dependent upon meeting preset criteria. As with any criterion-referenced test, reliability and validity are often questioned, but teacher-made assessment devices such as probes have been found to be reliable in assessing student achievement (Deno, Mirkin and Chiang 1982; Fuchs 1986; Marston et al. 1984). One of the problems associated with teacher-made tests is that they may lack precision (Salvia and Hughes 1990).

Criterion-Referenced Tests

Criterion-referenced tests (CRTs) are another form of informal assessment. They are defined as measurement devices that assess skill mastery and compare student performance to curricular standards (McLoughlin and Lewis 1990). They differ from norm-referenced instruments in that they focus on mastery of specific skills as performance is compared to preset criteria. CRTs can be either commercially developed or teacher-made materials. As a teacher-made test, CRTs are more specific to the current curriculum focus in the instructional program. Test items on commercially available CRTs are closely linked to a general instructional curriculum and assist the teacher in determining goals and objectives.

There are a number of advantages to using CRTs over norm-referenced tests (Tindal and Marston 1990). First, CRTs describe the tasks that students can perform successfully. Second, CRTs focus on a limited set of tasks that are specific to the curriculum, rather than assessing a broad range of skills in an academic area. Also, CRTs measure mastery by using a specific set of criteria. Finally, scores obtained reflect small increases in student performance that often are not detected in norm-referenced tests.

A variety of commercially available CRTs (e.g., the Brigance Inventories and the Enright Inventory of Basic Arithmetic Skills) are described in Taylor (1989). In developing CRTs in the classroom, teachers should identify instructional goals, perform a task analysis to specify objectives to be mastered, develop test items that assess each objective, and determine the criteria of acceptable performance (Taylor 1989).

Some of the problems with CRTs have to do with questions of validity and reliability (Rusch et al. 1988; Salvia and Hughes 1990). Unlike norm-referenced tests, content validity is not an issue because the objectives to be measured are carefully selected from the curriculum. Although commercially available materials may not be a precise match to the curriculum, they are a preferred choice over norm-referenced tests in planning instruction. Validity and reliability issues for commercial materials should be addressed in the test manual, and evidence of normative data should be present.

Observation

Naturalistic observation is defined as the process of observing and recording behaviors in a naturalistic environment (Magg 1989). Use of this method allows for a broader look at behavior as well as factors affecting behavior. Some of the advantages to using naturalistic observation (Bailey and Wolery 1989) include

1. It can be used easily.
2. Observation and analysis can be conducted of multiple skill domains.
3. It provides a context for observing a child's preferred learning strategies.

Factors that often jeopardize the validity and reliability of naturalistic observation include (Johnson and Bolstad 1973; Odom and Schuster 1986) such elements as observer bias, observer agreement and accuracy, subject awareness of being observed, and generalization of observer agreement. Three types of naturalistic observation are direct observation, anecdotal reports/records, and eco-behavioral assessment.

Direct Observation

Direct observation, one type of naturalistic observation, has been found to be an objective, trustworthy, and valid means for assessing behavior (Odom and Karnes 1988). It enables teachers to collect ongoing, quantifiable information (Odom and Karnes 1988) concerning the specific behaviors that have been defined in advance of data collection. Direct observation provides teachers with a means to (1) detect student problems early (Taylor 1989), (2) validate information from other measurement strategies, (3) directly collect information concerning student performance in a variety of situations, (4) extend assessment activities to obtain additional information, (5) identify relationships between environmental stimuli and classroom behavior, and (6) evaluate instructional interventions (Bailey and Wolery 1989).

Direct observation is advantageous in that the information can be gathered immediately, with relative ease (Koorland et al. 1988) and is directly relevant to program planning. In order to be effective, direct observation must be implemented in a systematic, objective manner (Taylor 1989). Basic procedures to be followed in designing a direct observation assessment include (Bailey and Wolery 1989):

1. Identify and define relevant dimensions or a target behavior to be observed,
2. Select a data collection system and design data sheets,
3. Select appropriate times and situations for observation,
4. Check accuracy of data collected,
5. Use data results for decision making.

Use of systematic decision rules for data analysis and decision making enables students to achieve a greater number of goals and objectives and improve overall performance (Utley et al. 1987).

Direct observation requires skill in designing effective systems, analyzing observed information, and determining when a skill may be better assessed using direct testing techniques (Bailey and Wolery 1989). Martin and Pear (1983) noted several problems associated with using direct observation techniques. Observational reports may be vague, subjective, or incomplete, and data collection sheets or procedures may be poorly designed and ineffectively used. Some behaviors may be difficult to observe due to environmental conditions or distractions. Also, observers may be poorly trained or unmotivated. Finally, this technique may present a narrow view of the behavior.

Direct observation of student performance remains one of the most widely used assessment techniques (Taylor 1989). Adequate instruction and training in direct observation techniques provide teachers with one of the most valuable informal assessment tools. Direct observation can be an effective complement to more formal assessment systems.

Anecdotal Reports/Records

Anecdotal reports are used to describe a student's typical performance in a particular learning situation or environment (Alberto and Troutman 1982; Borg and Gall 1989). By using anecdotal reporting, an observer can examine behaviors performed by the student, the conditions under which the behaviors are observed, and the factors that contribute to the behaviors (Bailey and Wolery 1989). These reports are designed to examine and describe the context and overall behavior of the student (Bailey and Wolery 1989), as opposed to using predefined target behavior (Alberto and Troutman 1982).

Teachers using anecdotal records observe students in their natural environment, recording the behaviors of a target student and examining antecedents and consequences to those behaviors. Reports should be factual records of students' behavior and their interaction with the environment and should be written clearly, concisely, and descriptively (Bailey and Wolery 1989). An accumulation of anecdotal reports can be a rich source of information concerning students that may not be captured through other sources of data collection.

There are many benefits to using anecdotal reports. They provide open-ended, nonrestricted observations of students' performance, yet there is very little need for specialized training of observers. Another advantage is that unexpected incidents can be captured and recorded as they occur.

Care should be taken to ensure that the observer is objective and that the reports are written without bias or interpretation (Borg and Gall 1989). One problem associated with anecdotal reporting is that the observer may be emotionally involved with the situation (Borg and Gall 1989) and have difficulty remaining objective. Another disadvantage is that anecdotal reporting may depend to some extent on the memory of the observer and that reliable witnesses may not be available to verify the information reported. Also, observers may focus on some aspects of performance and neglect other important elements. Finally, information of this nature is hard to code or analyze and therefore may be difficult to interpret and assess as to reliability.

Alberto and Troutman (1982) suggest the following guidelines for writing anecdotal records. The teacher should:

1. Write down the setting as it is initially seen, the individuals in the setting, their relationships, and the activity occurring before beginning the observation (e.g., lunch, free play).
2. Include a description of everything the target student says and does.
3. Include a description of everything said and done to the target student and by whom.
4. Clearly differentiate fact (what is actually occurring) from impressions or interpretations.
5. Provide some temporal indications of the duration of particular responses or interactions.

Ecobehavioral Assessment

The setting in which instruction occurs greatly influences student performance. Without information concerning the physical and social structure of the environment, an analysis of student performance cannot be complete (Greenwood and Carta 1987). Since instructional outcomes depend upon factors that go beyond student characteristics and instructional tasks (Ysseldyke and Christenson 1987), evaluating the instructional learning environment is critical for making effective instructional planning decisions (Bender 1988; Reynolds 1900; Ysseldyke and Christenson 1987). *Ecobehavioral assessment* is an observational method designed to assess both the student's performance and ecological factors such as teacher behavior, material utilized, and the setting in which the lesson is conducted, all of which may be considered elements of the total instructional program (Chadsey-Rusch 1985; Odom and Karnes 1988; Rush et al. 1988). Greenwood and Carta (1987) provide a more detailed description of the procedures for conducting ecobehavioral assessment.

Ecobehavioral assessment rejects the concept that instruction is uniform for all students in that it allows the teacher to examine how instruction occurs, how it evolves over time, and how students respond to the interaction of instructional and environmental events (Greenwood and Carta 1987; Rusch et al. 1988). It is a valid and reliable method for improving knowledge about the interaction of teaching and learning and improving communication among individuals (Rusch et al. 1988), and it provides benefits of utility and precision over other existing assessment methods (Greenwood and Carta 1987).

As with any observational method, care must be taken to avoid observing contrived situations or planned contexts (Rusch et al. 1988). Additional threats to assessment accuracy (Rusch et al. 1988) include variation in administration standards, low interobserver agreement, observer drift, observer bias, and the potential complexity of coding systems. Since the observer is primarily interested in studying the variation, intensity, and frequency of the student's performance in varied environments (Chadsey-Rusch 1985; Greenwood and Carta 1987), care must be taken to minimize interruptions or interference with the natural course of events (Chadsey-Rusch 1985).

When combined with other assessment methodologies, ecobehavioral assessment can assist in determining the elements of the instructional program that are responsible for producing program effects (Carta et al. 1987). It is an effective technique that allows quantification of several instructional dimensions across time.

Interviews, Questionnaires, and Checklists

Other forms of informal assessment include interviews, questionnaires, and checklists. Interviews and questionnaires are effective informal data collection procedures (Cryan 1986; Evans et al. 1989; Magg 1989; McKillip and Stanic 1988) that provide an opportunity for the teacher to ask questions and obtain reactions that assist in determining areas of further assessment (Tindal and Marston 1990). The interview allows for face-to-face interaction and can either be structured (psychometric) or partially structured (exploratory method) (see Cryan [1986]). One of the problems associated with the interview method is the level of time commitment (Cryan 1986). An interview can be a lengthy process. Other problems may include the interviewer's bias or interpretation of the information obtained, failure to ask questions that satisfy the purpose of the interview, failure to allow appropriate response time, failure to obtain trust and confidence of the respondent, and failure to report and categorize responses properly.

In situations where face-to-face interactions are not feasible, written responses can be obtained through questionnaires. Questionnaires can be developed to elicit specific information from the respondents through a structured, multiple choice or true false format, or through less structured open-ended questions (McLoughlin and Lewis 1990).

Checklists, on the other hand, contain lists of descriptive statements of traits, characteristics, behaviors, interests, skills, or knowledge concepts (Cryan 1986). The respondent is asked to verify whether the descriptive statements are representative of the student behaviors. Checklists take less time to administer than interviews and can be used to assess a greater number of students (Cryan 1986). Disadvantages to using checklists are that they are often difficult to develop, they require thorough knowledge of the task, and they may be affected by bias toward students (Cryan 1986). Another disadvantage is that checklists are often dependent upon the respondent's reading ability (Cryan 1986).

SUMMARY

In this chapter a number of issues have been raised regarding the use of standardized assessment practices for the identification and placement of students into special education and for the design of instruction programs. Overall, there has been general discontentment concerning the effectiveness of traditional assessment measures for these purposes. Consistently, problems arise regarding cost-effectiveness, technical adequacy, identification and placement procedures, and the practicality of results obtained from standardized assessment devices. The use of standardized assessment devices has resulted in a test-to-instruction gap, in which there is very little relationship between the standardized assessment measures and the curricular demands teachers place on students in the classroom.

Informal assessment, an alternative to formal assessment practices, can provide general information for the purpose of identification, placement, instructional planning and modification, and program evaluation. As a practical tool in the classroom, informal assessment instruments provide information about current levels of performance, aid in the selection of goals and objectives, point to the need for instructional modification, document student progress, and suggest directions for further assessment. Most importantly, informal assessment devices enable the teacher to examine all factors related to students' success in school. Various types of informal assessment procedures were discussed in this chapter.

One type of informal assessment is CBA. Curriculum-based assessment is a method for gathering information on student performance within a prescribed curriculum. It can include such devices as CBM, response and error analysis of student work samples, academic probes, task analysis, and teacher-made tests. Curriculum-based assessment procedures are direct, succinct techniques that draw test material from the student's curriculum, can be repeated across time thus providing a continuous measure of student performance, and tie assessment information directly to instructional decisions. The goal of CBA is to effectively match instruction and student performance to maximize opportunities for learning.

Essentially, CBA enables teachers to monitor progress toward goals and objectives, evaluate program effectiveness, adjust instructional programs, formulate instructional improvements, and improve the scope and usefulness of educational decisions. It has the advantage of being consistent with legal mandates (e.g., P.L. 94–142) that require that assessment procedures be technically adequate, culturally fair, procedurally safe (i.e., follow due process), and used to guide instructional decisions (i.e., individual IEP process). Finally, CBA fosters collaboration and communication among teachers, administrators, and parents.

Criterion-referenced tests, whether commercially available or teacher-made, represent another type of informal assessment measure. These measurement devices differ from norm-referenced tests in that they focus on skill mastery and compare student performance to prespecified standards. Although commercially available materials may not be a precise representation of the existing curriculum, they are preferred to formal assessment measures in assisting with program design and evaluation.

Naturalistic observation, a third form of informal assessment, enables teachers to examine behaviors, as well as factors affecting those behaviors. Observational data can be collected through a direct observation format, anecdotal records, or ecobehavioral assessment. Direct observation is the process of systematically collecting information on target behaviors. Anecdotal records are factual records of the students' behavior and their interaction with the environment. Teachers using this form of informal assessment can examine antecedents and consequences to a behavior in a natural environment. Ecobehavioral assessment is a method for considering all elements of the instructional program. Data collected through this type of observation system enable teachers to examine instructional practices, environmental characteristics, and student behaviors, for a more comprehensive view of student performance.

Finally, informal assessment data also can be collected through the use of interviews, checklists, and questionnaires. These procedures can provide additional data on student performance that may not be readily available to the classroom teacher through direct observation or assessment. These data may be provided by anyone in direct contact with the student, such as parents, school staff, or support personnel.

Overall, the majority of the assumptions underlying informal assessment represent "good practice" in education. Choate and colleagues (1992) summarize the advantages of using CBA. These advantages can be applied to the various forms of informal assessment in that they:

1. Assist in determining what to teach by identifying those skills that the student has and those skills that have not yet been mastered
2. Provide direct and frequent samples of student performance within the curriculum and can be used on an ongoing basis
3. Facilitate evaluation of student progress, program effectiveness, and educational research
4. In the case of CBM, have been found to be both valid and reliable measures of student performance
5. Lead to increases in student achievement
6. Can be used to help make referral decisions
7. Comply with the requirements of P.L. 94–142 for assessing students suspected as having a disability (In this regard, informal assessment procedures provide a better legal and practical foundation than traditional assessment procedures.)

REFERENCES

Adams, A. (1990). The oral reading errors of readers with LD: Variations produced within the instructional and frustrational ranges. *Remedial and Special Education, 12*(1), 48–55, 62.

Alberto, P. A., & Troutman, A. C. (1982). *Applied behavioral analysis for teachers: Influencing student performance.* Columbus, OH: Merrill.

Algozzine, B., & Ysseldyke, J. (1982). *Critical issues in special and remedial education.* Boston: Houghton Mifflin.

Algozzine, B., & Ysseldyke, J. (1983). Learning disabilities as a subset of school failure: The oversophistication of a concept. *Exceptional Children, 50*, 242–246.

Arter, J. A., & Jenkins, J. R. (1977). Examining the benefits and prevalence of modality considerations in special education. *Journal of Special Education, 11*, 281–298.

Bailey, D. B. Jr., & Wolery, M. (1989). *Assessing infants and preschoolers with handicaps.* Columbus, OH: Merrill.

Bean, R. M., & Lane, S. (1990). Implementing curriculum-based measures of reading in an adult literacy program. *Remedial and Special Education, 11*(5), 39–46.

Bender, W. N. (1988). The other side of placement decisions: Assessment for the mainstream learning environment. *Remedial and Special Education, 9*(5), 28–33.

Blankenship, C., & Lilly, M. S. (1981). *Mainstreaming students with learning and behavior problems: Techniques for the classroom teacher.* New York: Holt, Rinehart & Winston.

Borg, W. R., & Gall, M. D. (1989). *Educational research: An introduction* (5th ed.). New York: Longman.

Bursuck, W. D., & Lessen, E. (1987). A classroom-based method of assessing students with learning disabilities. *Learning Disabilities Focus, 3*(1), 17–29.

Carta, J. J., Greenwood, C. R., & Robison, S. L. (1987). Application of an ecobehavioral approach to the evaluation of early intervention programs. In R. J. Prinz (Ed.), *Advances in behavioral assessment of children and families,* (vol. 3). JAI Press.

Castiglione, S. S. (1981). Assessment of the learning disabled with regard to cognitive functioning and cognitive complexity. *Journal of Learning Disabilities, 14,* 74–80.

Chadsey-Rusch, J, (1985). Community integration and mental retardation: The ecobehavioral approach to service provision and assessment. In R. H. Bruininks & C. K. Larkin (Eds.), *Living and learning in the least restrictive environment.* Baltimore, MD: Brookes.

Choate, J. S., Enright, B. E., Miller, L. J., Poteet, J. A., & Rakes, T. A. (1992). *Curriculum-based assessment and programming* (2nd ed.). Boston: Allyn and Bacon.

Christenson, S. L., Ysseldyke, J. E., & Thurlow, M. L. (1989). Critical instructional factors for students with mild handicaps: An integrative review. *Remedial and Special Education, 10*(5), 21–31.

Clarizio, J. F., & Phillips, S. E. (1986). The use of standard scores in diagnosing learning disabilities: A critique. *Psychology in the Schools, 23,* 380–387.

Cryan, J. R. (1986). Evaluation: Plague or promise. *Childhood Education, 62*(5), 344–356.

Deno, S. L. (1985). Curriculum-based measurement: The emerging alternative. *Exceptional Children, 52*(3), 219–232.

Deno, S. L. (1986). Formative evaluation of individual programs: A new role for school psychologists. *School Psychology Review, 15,* 358–374.

Deno, S. L. (1987). Curriculum-based measurement. *Teaching Exceptional Children, 20*(1), 40–41.

Deno, S. L., & Fuchs, L. S. (1987). Developing curriculum-based measurement systems for data-based special education problem solving. *Focus on Exceptional Children, 19*(8), 1–16.

Deno, S. L., & Mirkin, P. K. (1980). Data based IEP development: An approach to substantive compliance. *Teaching Exceptional Children, 12*(3), 92–97.

Deno, S. L., Marston, D., & Mirkin, P. (1982). Valid measurement procedures for continuous evaluation of written expression. *Exceptional Children, 48,* 368–371.

Deno, S. L., Mirkin, P. K., & Chiang, B. (1982). Identifying valid measures of reading. *Exeptional Children, 49,* 36–45.

Duran, R. P. (1989). Assessment and instruction of at-risk Hispanic students. *Exceptional Children, 56,* 154–158.

Enright, B. E. (1985). *ENRIGHT computation series (Books A-D).* N. Billeria, MA: Curriculum Associates.

Evans, S. S., Evans, W. H., & Gable, R. A. (1989). An ecological survey of student behavior. *Teaching Exceptional Children, 21*(4), 12–15.

Figueroa, R. A. (1989). Psychological testing of linguistic minority students: Knowledge gaps and regulations. *Exceptional Children, 56,* 145–152.

Fuchs, L. S. (1986). Monitoring progress among mildly handicapped pupils: Review of current practice and research. *Remedial and Special Education, 7* (5), 5–12.

Fuchs, L. S. (1987). Program development. *Teaching Exceptional Children, 20*(1), 42–44.

Fuchs, L. S., Allinder, R. M., Hamlett, C. L., & Fuchs, D. (1990). An analysis of spelling curricula and teachers skills in identifying error types. *Remedial and Special Education, 11*(1), 42–53.

Fuchs, L. S., & Deno, S. L. (1991). Paradigmatic distinction between instructionally relevant measurement models. *Exceptional Children, 57,* 488–500.

Fuchs, L. S., & Fuchs, D. (1986). The effects of systematic formative evaluation: A meta-analysis. *Exceptional Children, 53,* 199–208.

Fuchs, D., Fuchs, L. S., Benowitz, S., & Barringer, K. (1987). Norm-referenced tests: Are they valid for use with handicapped students? *Exceptional Children, 54,* 263–271.

Fuchs, L. S., Fuchs, D., Hamlett, C. L., & Allinder, R. M. (1991). The contribution of skills analysis to curriculum-based measurement in spelling. *Exceptional Children, 57,* 443–452.

Fuchs, L. S., Fuchs, D., & Maxwell, L. (1988). The validity of informal reading comprehension measures. *Remedial and Special Education, 9*(2), 20–28.

Fuchs, L. S., Fuchs, D., & Stecker, P. M. (1989). Effects of curriculum-based measurement on teachers' instructional planning. *Journal of Learning Disabilities, 22*(1), 51–59.

Gable, R. A., Enright, B. E., & Hendrickson, J. M. (1991). Curriculum-based assessment and instruction in arithmetic. *Teaching Exceptional Children, 24*(1), 6–9.

Galagan, J. E. (1985). Psychoeducational testing: Turn out the lights, the party's over. *Exceptional Children, 52,* 288–299.

Gausted, M. G., & Messenheimer-Young, T. (1991). Dialogue journals of students with LD. *Teaching Exceptional Children, 23*(3), 28–32.

Germann, G., & Tindal, G. (1985). An application of curriculum-based assessment: The use of direct and repeated measurement. *Exceptional Children, 52,* 244–265.

Gickling, E. E. (1981). Curriculum-based assessment. In J. A. Tucker (Ed.), *Non-test-based assessment: A training module.* Minneapolis: National School Psychology Inservice Training Network, University of Minnesota.

Gickling, E. E., & Thompson, V. P. (1985). A personal view of curriculum-based assessment. *Exceptional Children, 52,* 205–218.

Goldman, L. (1990). Qualitative assessment. *The Counseling Psychologist, 18*(2), 205–213.

Greenwood, C. R., & Carta, J. J. (1987). An ecobehavioral interaction analysis of instruction within special education. *Focus on Exceptional Children, 19*(9), 1–12.

Grimes, L. (1981). Error analysis and error correction procedures. *Teaching Exceptional Children, 14*(1), 17–21.

Hammill, D. D., (1990). On defining learning disabilities: An emerging consensus. *Journal of Learning Disabilities, 23,* 74–84.

Hammill, D. D., & Larsen, S. (1974). The effectiveness of psycholinguistic training. *Exceptional Children, 41,* 5–15.

Heiss, W. (1977). Relating educational assessment to instructional planning. *Focus on Exceptional Children, 9*(1), 1–12.

Howell, K. W. (1985). A task-analytical approach to social behavior. *Remedial and Special Education, 6*(2), 24–30.

Humphries, T. W., & Wilson, A. K. (1986). An instructional based model for assessing LD. *Canadian Journal of Special Education, 2*(1), 55–66.

Idol, L., Nevin, A., & Paolucci-Whitcomb, P. (1986). *Models of curriculum-based assessment.* Rockville, MD: Aspen.

Jenkins, J. R., Deno, S. L., & Mirkin, P. K. (1979). Measuring pupil progress toward the least restrictive environment. *Learning Disabilities Quarterly, 2,* 81–92.

Jenkins, J., & Pany, D. (1978). Standardized achievement tests: How useful for special education? *Exceptional Children, 44,* 448–453.

Jenkins, J. R., Pious, C. G., & Peterson, D. L. (1988). Categorical programs for remedial and handicapped students: Issues of validity. *Exceptional Children, 55,* 147–158.

Johnson, S. M., & Bolstad, O. D. (1973). Methodological issues in naturalistic observation: Some problems and solutions for field research. In L. A. Hamerlynck, L. C. Handy, & E. J. Mesh (Eds.), *Behavioral change: Methodology, concepts, and practice* (pp. 7–67). Champaign, IL: Research Press.

Koorland, M. A., Monda, L. E., & Vail, C. D. (1988). Recording behavior with ease. *Teaching Exceptional Children, 21*(1), 59–61.

Magg, J. W. (1989). Assessment in social skills training: Methodological and conceptual issues for research and practice. *Remedial and Special Education, 4*(10), 6–17.

Marston, D., & Magnusson, D. (1985). Implementing curriculum-based measurement in special and regular education settings. *Exceptional Children, 52,* 266–276.

Marston, D., Tindal, G., & Deno, S. L. (1984). Eligibility for LD services: A direct and repeated measurement approach. *Exceptional Children, 50,* 554–555.

Martin, G., & Pear, J. (1983). *Behavior modification: What it is and how to do it* (2nd ed.). Englewood Cliffs, NJ: Prentice-Hall.

McKillip, W. D., & Stanic, G. M. A. (1988). Assessing for learning. *Arithmetic Teacher, 35*(6), 37–38, 52.

McLoughlin, J. A., & Lewis, R. B. (1990). *Assessing special students* (3rd ed.). New York: Macmillan International.

Minner, S., Prater, G., Sullivan, C., & Givaltney, W. (1989). Informal assessment of written expression. *Teaching Exceptional Children, 21*(2), 76–79.

Moyer, J. R., & Dardig, J. C. (1978). Practical task analysis for special educators. *Teaching Exceptional Children, 11*(1), 16–18.

Odom, S. L., & Karnes, M. B. (1988). *Early intervention for infants and children with handicaps: An empirical base.* Baltimore, MD: Brookes.

Odom, S. L., & Schuster, S. K. (1986). Naturalistic inquiry and the assessment of young handicapped children and their families. *Topics in Early Childhood Special Education, 6*(2), 68–82.

Ortiz, A. A., & Wilkinson, C. Y. (1991). Assessment and intervention model for the bilingual exceptional student (aim for the best). *Teacher Education and Special Education, 14,* 35–42.

Parker, R. I., Tindal, G., & Hasbrouck, J. (1991). Progress monitoring with objective measures of writing performance for students with mild disabilities. *Exceptional Children, 58,* 61–73.

Potter, M. L. & Wamre, H. M. (1990). Curriculum-based measurement and developmental reading models: Opportunities for cross validation. *Exceptional Children, 57,* 16–25.

Pyl, S. J. (1989). Diagnostic reports as bases for decisions on teaching. *Teaching and Teacher Education, 5*(1), 69–79.

Reschley, D. (1988). Minority MMR overrepresentation: Legal issues, research findings, and reform trends. In M. C. Wang, M. C. Reynolds, & H. J. Walberg (Eds.), *Handbook of special education research and practice* (vol. 2). New York: Pergamon Press.

Reynolds, M. C. (1990). Educating teachers for special education students. In W. R. Houston (Ed.), *Handbook of research on teachers education* (pp. 423–426). New York: Macmillan.

Rusch, F. R., Rose, T., & Greenwood, C. R. (1988). *Introduction to behavior analysis in special education.* Englewood Cliffs, NJ: Prentice-Hall.

Samuels, S. J. (1979). The method of repeated reading. *The Reading Teacher, 32,* 403–408.

Silver, C. B. (1988). A review of the federal government's Interagency Committee on Learning Disabilities report to the U.S. Congress. *Learning Disabilities Focus, 3*(2), 73–80.

Salvia, J., & Hughes, C. (1990). *Curriculum-based assessment: Testing what is taught.* New York: Macmillan.

Salvia, J., & Ysseldyke, J. E. (1991). *Assessment* (5th ed.). Boston: Houghton Mifflin.

Shinn, M. R. (Ed.). (1989). *Curriculum-based measurement: Assessing special children.* The Guilford School Practitioner Series. New York: Guilford Press.

Shinn, M. R., Gleason, M. M., & Tindal, G. (1989). Varying the difficulty of testing materials: Implications for curriculum-based measurement. *Journal of Special Education, 23*(2), 223–233.

Shinn, M., & Marston, D. (1985). Differentiating mildly handicapped, low-achieving, and regular education students: A curriculum-based approach. *Remedial and Special Education, 6*(2), 31–38.

Siegel, L. S. (1989a). IQ is irrelevant to the definition of LD. *Journal of Learning Disabilities, 22,* 469–478.

Siegel, L. S. (1989b). Why we do not need intelligence test scores in the definition and analysis of learning disabilities. *Journal of Learning Disabilities, 22,* 514–518.

Stainback, W., & Stainback S. (1990). *Support networks for inclusive schooling: Interdependent integrated education.* Baltimore, MD: Brookes.

Taylor, R. L. (1989). *Assessment of exceptional students: Educational and psychological procedures.* Englewood Cliffs, NJ: Prentice-Hall.

Thomas, C. C. Englert, C. S., & Gregg, S. (1987). An analysis of errors and strategies in the expository writing of LD students. *Remedial and Special Education, 8*(1), 21–30.

Tindal, G. A., & Marston, D. B. (1990). *Classroom-based assessment: Evaluating instructional outcomes.* Columbus, OH: Merrill.

Tindal, G., & Parker, R. (1989). Development of written retell as a curriculum based measure in secondary programs. In S. Rosenfield & M. R. Shinn, Miniseries on Curriculum-Based Assessment, *School Psychology Review, 18*(3), 297–370.

Tucker, J. (1985). Curriculum-based assessment: An introduction. *Exceptional Children, 52,* 199–204.

Tucker, J. (1987). Curriculum-based assessment is no fad. *The Collaborative Educator, 1*(4), 4, 10.

U. S. Department of Education. (1986). *What works: Research about teaching and learning.* Washington, DC: GPO.

Utley, B., Zigmond, N., & Strain, P. S. (1987). How various forms of data affect teacher analysis of student performance. *Exceptional Children, 53,* 411–422.

Valencia, S. W., & Pearson, P. D. (1988). Principles of classroom comprehension assessment. *Remedial and Special Education, 9*(1), 26–35.

Wesson, C. L. (1987). Increasing efficiency. *Teaching Exceptional Children, 20*(1), 46–47.

Wesson, C., Deno, S., Mirkin, P., Maruyama, G., Skiba, R., King, R., & Sevcik, B. (1988). A causal analysis of the relationships among ongoing curriculum-based measurement and evaluation, the structure of instruction and student achievement. *Journal of Special Education, 22*(3), 330–343.

Wesson, C., Fuchs, L., Tindal, G., Mirkin, P., & Deno, S. L. (1986). Facilitating the efficiency of on-going curriculum-based measurement. *Teacher Education and Special Education, 9,* 166–172.

Wesson, C., Skiba, R., Sevcik, B., King, R. P., & Deno, S. (1984). The effects of technically adequate instructional data on achievement. *Remedial and Special Education, 5*(5), 17–22.

West, J. F., & Idol, L. (1990). Collaborative consultation in the education of mildly handicapped and at-risk students. *Remedial and Special Education, 11*(1), 22–31.

Ysseldyke, J. E., & Algozzine, B. (1983). LD or not LD: That's not the question! *Annual Review of Learning Disabilities, 1,* 26–28.

Ysseldyke, J. E., Algozzine, B., & Epps, S. (1982). *Logical and empirical analysis of current practices in classifying students as handicapped.* Minneapolis, MN: Institute for Research on Learning Disabilities.

Ysseldyke, J. E., Algozzine, B., Shinn, M., & McGue, M. (1982). *Similarities and differences between underachievers and students labeled learning disabled: Identical twins with different mothers.* Minneapolis, MN: Institute for Research on Learning Disabilities.

Ysseldyke, J. E., & Christenson, S. L. (1987). Evaluating students' instructional environments. *Remedial and Special Education, 8*(3), 17–24.

Ysseldyke, J. E., & Regan, R. R. (1980). Nondiscriminatory assessment: A formative model. *Exceptional Children, 46,* 465–466.

6

Eligibility and Placement
Team Meetings

Harry L. Dangel

A chapter on eligibility and placement teams might appropriately be subtitled "The Process of Cooperative Decision Making." The emphasis on collaborative efforts in this chapter to determine eligibility and place students with learning disabilities (LD) is in striking contrast to traditional eligibility and placement procedures where one person can make a placement decision alone.

Unfortunately, some team meetings are more often directive than collaborative. A teacher of students with LD, when asked about how the multidisciplinary eligibility team decided on whether a student was eligible for LD services, remarked, "The school psychologist tells us if the student qualifies, and then we all sign the eligibility report" (Dangel 1988).

With a team process the regular educator, along with the school psychologist or specialist in LD, has a primary role in gathering information about the referred student, deciding on eligibility, and developing and implementing the individual educational plan (IEP). (Idol et al. 1987). Also, the decision-making process is dynamic rather than didactic, and so the work of the multidisciplinary eligibility team, which determines whether a student qualifies for LD services, and the placement team, which determines the most appropriate services for the student, becomes interactive. This chapter examines methods to improve how the eligibility team arrives at the decision of whether a student qualifies for LD services and then how the placement team determines what services to provide.

Eligibility and placement are separate functions carried out by multidisciplinary teams. The multidisciplinary eligibility team is mandated in federal rules and regulations to determine the eligibility of a student for services in LD (*Federal Register* 1977). Once eligibility has been established, the placement team determines the nature of the services to be provided. Because both teams have many of the same members and their roles are interrelated, the distinction between them frequently becomes blurred.

CRITICISMS OF MULTIDISCIPLINARY TEAMS

The work of multidisciplinary eligibility teams has been criticized for not making appropriate decisions. In fact, some believe that in the past, team

135

decision-making for determining LD eligibility has been accurate only about half the time (Algozzine and Ysseldyke 1981). Researchers have found, for example, that teachers of students with LD frequently did not understand the criteria used for identifying a student as learning-disabled (Thurlow et al. 1984); that, due to misinterpretation and incorrect procedures, psychologists did not consistently make appropriate decisions when evaluating discrepancy scores alone (Ross 1990); and that the sole use of discrepancy formulas did not objectively identify students with learning disabilities (Forness et al. 1983; Ysseldyke et al. 1983).

Even more importantly for the focus of this chapter, there is also ample evidence of wide variations in the judgment of the members of multidisciplinary eligibility teams who decide whether students with school problems should be labeled learning-disabled (Dangel and Ensminger 1988). When case studies of school-identified learning-disabled and non–learning-disabled students were evaluated by school psychologists and special education teachers, the raters were barely more accurate than chance in identifying the learning-disabled versus non–learning-disabled students (Epps et al. 1982; Epps et al. 1984). Under certain eligibility conditions, university students without an educational or psychology background were more accurate than school psychologist and special education teachers in identifying students as learning-disabled (Epps et al. 1984).

After the eligibility team has completed its work, the assessment information that has been gathered to determine eligibility for LD services is seldom useful when teachers plan the instructional program (Thurlow and Ysseldyke 1982), and even after the IEP was developed by the placement team, teachers seldom refer to its contents in implementing a student's instructional program (Pugach 1982).

Several factors have been cited as inhibiting the decision-making process of multidisciplinary teams. These include lack of training for team members in group decision making and in the interpersonal skills needed to work as a group, the use of different specialized jargon by various team members (Brey et al. 1981; Moore et al. 1989), and the emphasis of team members on standardized test results while ignoring the more relevant classroom-based information (Algozzine and Ysseldyke 1986).

THE MULTIDISCIPLINARY TEAM PARTICIPANTS

The federal guidelines for LD specify that the multidisciplinary evaluation team that determines the eligibility of a student referred for possible service consists of a school psychologist, a general educator, and a person trained in LD, along with other relevant personnel (*Federal Register* 1977). The team frequently includes other professionals from education and medicine who have expertise and information about a student's problems, although large, poorly structured teams are not effective decision makers (Barton 1983).

The General Educator

The concern within the field of LD to put less emphasis on standardized screening and diagnostic efforts and focus more on classroom-based information that has been systematically collected by the student's teacher makes the role of the regular class teacher especially important (Algozzine and Ysseldyke 1986). Also, LD, more than any other area of special education, is viewed within the context of mastering the regular curriculum. Because of this, the regular educator is part of the eligibility team in order to provide perspective on how a particular child's performance compares to that of other students in mainstream classes. There are several forms in which the regular educator can present relevant information to the eligibility team:

1. Describing the student's classroom performance compared to others in the class (e.g., "Is about 24th of 26 students in mastering the basic computational facts for third grade").
2. Providing an objective description of classroom performance (e.g., "Averages 68% accuracy on two-digit subtraction problems that require regrouping")
3. Reporting on the historical pattern of the student's achievement recorded in the permanent record (e.g., "Got As and Bs in mathematics every year prior to this one")

Also, the regular educator contributes critical information about the modifications that have been attempted and the impact of these modifications on the student's class performance. Ideally, these modifications have been part of a systematic attempt by a school-based, prereferral team to evaluate the impact of changing and individualizing the instructional program for the student, or have been the attempts of an individual regular educator to meet the student's needs. A curriculum-based assessment (CBA) procedure offers an effective means of continuously tracking the impact of instructional modifications on a student's performance (Fuchs et al. 1989). A specialist in LD may assist the regular class teacher in monitoring changes by setting up CBA programs to assess, for example, the number of correct words read per minute in the basal in order to evaluate changes in a student's achievement due to instructional modifications. In spite of the important role to be played by regular educators, there is evidence that they have been less active participants than psychologists and special educators in team meetings and their involvement has been limited to presenting data rather than proposing any action (Ysseldyke et al. 1982).

The School Psychologist

The school psychologist plays three important functions on the multidisciplinary team. As the expert on standardized assessment, the school psychologist provides an objective analysis of the existence of a severe discrepancy between ability and achievement in one of the seven academic areas that might qualify a student for LD services. The psychologist, as a trained observer of behaviors, also provides information about how the student obtained the score; for example, the level of persistence, frustration tolerance, strategies used to approach a task, and response patterns. Finally, the psychologist can frequently detect the nature of a possible learning disability by recognizing intraindividual patterns that are reflected in scores and in how the student obtained those scores. It is frequently the psychologist, based on observations of many students responding to the same items across time, who detects problems with organization skills, memory, or attention.

The Specialist in Learning Disabilities

The specialist in LD, typically a teacher certified in LD, a diagnostician, or a supervisor, provides the bridge between the classroom-based assessment of the regular educator and the formal testing of the psychologist. The specialist in LD typically does an in-depth evaluation of the student's achievement and observes the student in the mainstream class. The specialist in LD is often especially helpful in confirming the links between classroom academic achievement problems and the results of standardized tests (e.g., difficulty comprehending cause-and-effect relations in the reading text and difficulty on sequencing skills assessed by the Picture Arrangement subtest of the WISC-R).

Parents and Students

Although P.L. 94-142 specifies that parents must be involved in planning the special education program for their child, the level of their participation with multidisciplinary teams has been limited. Although parents are viewed by professionals prior to placement meetings as playing a critical role in developing an instructional plan, after the team meeting, professionals give lower ratings to parents' actual contributions (Gilliam and Coleman 1981). Parents' involvement in the eligibility process has been to provide information about their child's medical and educational history, and, while their participation in developing and implementing the IEP has much more potential for cooperation with the multidisciplinary team, their actual participation has been primarily in giving information and consent to programming decisions make by the professionals (Vaughn et al. 1988).

The contribution of parents can be increased by providing them with adequate notice of the meeting time and place, an opportunity to review their child's educational records with a knowledgeable professional prior to the meeting, an agenda for the meeting that contains a list of persons who will be attending, information on their rights regarding the assessment and planning process, and a list of materials that might be helpful to bring (Shea and Bauer 1991). A checklist of possible questions they might be asked, questions they may want to ask of others, and follow-up activities for after the meeting may also be helpful (Kroth

1985). Talking with other parents whose children are served in the LD program and observing in classrooms that serve learning-disabled students may be helpful and reassuring.

The parents and other team members may want to consider having the student attend the IEP meeting. Including the student is beneficial if the parents and teachers are in agreement that the child understands the purpose of the meeting and how he or she might contribute, understands what is being discussed and can communicate his or her interests, and would not be upset by any disagreements that might occur at the meeting (Gillespie and Turnbull 1983).

Other School Personnel

Another important specialist is the speech-language pathologist (SLP). Because language disorders are so prevalent among students with LD (Lerner 1988), the SLP is often needed to evaluate achievement in oral expression and listening comprehension when establishing whether a severe discrepancy exists between ability and achievement. The SLP also helps in identifying possible underlying language-based problems in other achievement areas (e.g., word retrieval problems that might affect reading skills or sequencing difficulty that might impair comprehension). Not only should the SLP be involved in planning the IEP for a student whose learning disability involves language-based factors, but the SLP's services should be integrated into the team's educational program, rather than being a segregated pull-out program.

The school counselor or social worker can help to provide documentation to the team about the extent to which achievement discrepancies might be related to any emotional problems or to cultural or economic differences rather than primarily due to a learning disability.

Medical Specialists

It is sometimes the pediatrician or family physician who notices developmental delays or language disorders that may be the first signs of a learning disability in young children. On the other hand, parents often turn to physicians with questions about a child's problems at home or school. About three-quarters of pediatricians surveyed reported being familiar with P. L. 94–142 and having worked with the special education programs in local schools (Lerner and Cohen 1981). Only 38%, however, had participated on a multidisciplinary team in the schools. A close working relationship among a child's physician, parents, and teachers is especially important when managing stimulant drug therapy. Physicians need information from teachers about what effects they observe during the school day so that the type and dosage of medication can be monitored and adjusted as needed.

Eligibility for LD services requires that the student's learning problems are not primarily caused by any visual or auditory problems. If a student referred for assessment does not successfully pass the school's vision and hearing screening, then a follow-up examination is needed from a specialist who can evaluate the impact of the sensory problem on learning.

COMMUNICATION SKILLS
FOR DECISION MAKING

Effective team decision making depends not only on professional competence in assessment, planning, and instruction but also on the ability to effectively share and receive information with other professionals and parents (Idol et al. 1987; Moore et al. 1989; Morsink et al. 1991). Although many professionals express concern about the negative impact of poor communication skills on the group decision-making process, there is usually little done to improve these skills (Moore et al. 1989). Suggestions for improving the quality of communication in team decision making include:

1. Allow time to establish purpose and rapport at the beginning of a meeting. This is especially important if parents are involved in the meeting.
2. Recognize individual differences in backgrounds and expertise among team members (Idol et al. 1987).
3. Adjust listening skills to match the requirements of a situation, that is, active listening (attentive, questioning, confirming, sharing) or passive listening (attentive and encouraging without intervening) (Gordon 1970).
4. Provide feedback to others through paraphrasing and clarifying (Morsink et al. 1991).
5. Use appropriate confrontational skills, such as sharing points of view, avoiding the use of "I" statements, and cooperatively searching for solutions, when disagreements arise (Idol et al. 1987).
6. Use the appropriate forms of verbal communication used to share information: descriptive for objective information, inferential for summarizing information developed through multiple observations, and evaluative for making judgments about what the observations mean within the framework of schools and classrooms (Shea and Bauer 1991).
7. Avoid the use of technical jargon by describing behavior, tasks, and activities in lay terms (Moore et al. 1989).
8. Pull themes together by summarizing information (Morsink et al. 1991).

Effective communication with parents requires special attention and skill. As previously mentioned, time should be allotted to establish rapport with the parents prior to the meeting, especially in those instances in which the parents are likely to be uncomfortable in dealing with the school and members of the placement team due to cultural differences or previous negative experiences with the educational system. Communication will be most effective when parents perceive team members as genuinely concerned and interested in working cooperatively with them in their child's best interest (Shea and Bauer 1991).

GUIDELINES FOR TEAM MEETINGS

Evidence of lack of effective decision-making by multidisciplinary teams has given rise to proposals to improve the team's effectiveness by structuring the meeting for its specific purposes (Hendrickson et al. 1988; McLoughlin and Lewis 1986; Ysseldyke 1983).

1. The team meeting should be scheduled for a specific time and should be a reasonable length.
2. A chairperson or liaison consultant is designated to direct the meeting. The chairperson introduces each team member and states the role each is to play.
3. The chairperson explicitly states the purpose of the meeting and identifies and briefly reviews the rules and regulations that are applicable. Eligibility regulations would be reviewed for eligibility team meetings and IEP procedures and placement options reviewed for placement team meetings.
4. The chairperson then describes the format for the meeting. One approach to structuring eligibility and placement discussions is to use a structured decision rule system. Such a system includes (Liberty and Haring 1990):
   a. Definition of the problem
   b. Gathering information about the nature of the problem
   c. Identifying alternative solutions
   d. Choosing among alternatives
   e. Implementing the plan
   f. Evaluating the results
5. Each team member then personally reports the results of his or her assessments. For eligibility meetings, this would include formal and informal test results, classroom and work sample information, and home and medical information. The results of monitoring the student's response to instructional modifications in regular classes is especially important here. For placement team meetings, current levels of performance and parents (and student) expectations would be presented.
6. Information is effectively presented by:
   a. Using an overhead projector so that all participants have a visual picture of the data
   b. Giving a summary of the relevant results while making available a detailed written report for the student's records and for documentation of the team's work
   c. Using a common scale to graphically display and compare test results
   d. Using examples of test items and work samples that compare the student's performance to classmates'

7. A discussion of the results would follow the formal presentation. During this time, eligibility team participants would compare and contrast results, looking for patterns or inconsistencies in the data. The decision regarding eligibility is best made by the members of the multidisciplinary eligibility team, and the discussion should remain focused within the framework of the criteria for eligibility. The placement team's discussion would be within the context of what services are needed.

CLINICAL DECISION MAKING FOR ELIGIBILITY

The eligibility team operates most effectively in deciding whether a student qualifies for LD services whenever:

1. A severe discrepancy alone does not justify eligibility of LD services (Reynolds 1984–1985)
2. Eligibility decisions include an interactive discussion of the student's classroom performance that validates the results of formal assessment (Algozzine and Ysseldyke 1986)
3. Information used to make eligibility decisions is also relevant for making placement and programming decisions (Algozzine and Ysseldyke 1986)

The model in Table 6.1 might be used as the framework to assist multidisciplinary teams to structure their interactions when making decisions about eligibility for LD services.

The team decision-making process becomes critical once the objective prerequisites of eligibility for LD placement have been established; that is, a severe discrepancy exists between ability and achievement in listening comprehension, oral expression, written expression, basic reading skills, mathematics calculation, and mathematics reasoning and factors such as mental retardation and visual and hearing problems have been eliminated. The decision points in Table 6.1 require interaction among the eligibility team members and are designed to examine the extent to which the student's achievement problems can be accommodated within the regular class.

The questions related to each decision point are not to be answered in a lock-step fashion but are overlapping and related to one another. The general flow of the decision points is from those interventions that typically can occur in general education classrooms (questions 1–3), to interventions that include more radical modifications in the regular class (often with special education consultative support—questions 4–6), to those interventions (questions 7–10) that are typically reserved for special education services.

Question 1: To what extent is the ability–achievement discrepancy due to a *lack of opportunity* to learn? The regular educator might present information about attendance patterns, number of different schools attended, and other evi-

Table 6.1 Decision points for instructional modifications

Questions	Information	Source
Are the student's achievement problems due to problems with:		
1. Opportunities to Learn?	Attendance, moves, preschool opportunities	Permanent record Parents
2. Achievement Patterns?	Level of classwork, past achievement, peers' achievement	Permanent records Regular educator Work samples
3. Quantitative Modifications?	Effects of time, level, repetition, pacing, and academic learning time	Regular educator Prereferral team Work samples
4. Motivation/Management?	Effort, interest, time on task, response to contingencies	Regular educator Prereferral team Work samples Observation
5. Classroom Coping Skills?	Task transitions, group vs. individual, structure needs	Regular Educator Prereferral team Work samples Observation
6. Individualized Instruction?	Modeling, cueing, feedback, cooperative learning	Regular educator Prereferral team Work samples Observation
7. Alternative Approaches?	Remedial instruction, strategies	LD specialist Psychologist
8. Alternative Programs?	Alternative curricula, e.g., synthetic phonics	LD specialist Psychologist
9. Foundation Programs?	Need for language, physical therapy	LD specialist SLP, PT
10. Alternative Goals?	Need for vocational, functional curriculum	Regular educator Parent Student

dence of the student having a reasonable exposure to schooling experiences (e.g., preschool programs or summer schools). Has the student been retained in a previous grade? If a student has been retained and has had multiple opportunities to learn skills and content at a particular grade level and is still not successful, the student might be considered more at risk. The more evidence there is that opportunities for learning were available and appropriate for the student without commensurate achievement, the greater the probability that the severe discrepancy is due to a learning disability. Much of this information is available in the student's school records.

Question 2: What are the *patterns of the student's achievement?* First, does the student's classroom performance match the scores on the standardized achievement tests? If not, what is the best indicator of the student's level of achievement—test scores or classroom performance? For example, if the student scores 4.5 in reading on a standardized test but only reads with 75% accuracy in word recognition in the beginning fourth-grade basal reader used by the school, which is the best indication of how the student is achieving in reading? Typically, the best indicator is the student's daily classroom performance, although a student may appear to be achieving at a lower level in the regular class due to lack of effort or an inappropriate curriculum. Second, has the student's achievement pattern changed over time? Had the student previously been achieving at an acceptable level? Has the achievement, compared to that of peers, recently declined? If there has been a recent decline as reflected in results on criterion-referenced tests, norm-referenced tests, or even grades, there may be external factors beyond a learning disability that would account for the decline. How does the student's achievement pattern compare to that of classmates? If classmates exposed to the same instructional program have been successful achievers, the referred student would be considered more at risk for a learning disability.

Question 3: To what extent did the student's achievement improve in response to various *quantitative modifications* to the instructional program? Here the focus shifts to an evaluation of both the student's performance and an assessment of the mainstream environment (Bender 1988). As indicated earlier, a prereferral team of general educators can provide excellent information regarding instructional modifications in the regular class prior to referral. In the absence of a prereferral team, the regular educator on the multidisciplinary team would report on modifications that were initiated. First, to what extent did the student's achievement improve in response to the quantitative adjustments of giving the student work on a lower level (e.g., reading in the 3.1 basal reader rather than the 4.1 basal), giving the student more time to respond and complete work, providing more repetition on the material presented (instruction on four items about the main idea of a story instead of the one question presented in most commercial material), adjusting the pace of instruction (e.g., presenting just one new concept at a time to the group), and reducing the amount of material to be mastered at one time (e.g., having a spelling test over 5 new words rather than over 10)? Quantitative modifications would also include evaluating the effect of increasing the amount of academic learning time in areas in which achievement is low (Berliner 1988). If basic qualitative modifications are not enough to accommodate the student's learning problems, the student is more at risk for having a learning disability.

Question 4: To what extent did the student's achievement improve in response to providing instruction that was *motivating* and contingencies that were *reinforcing* (i.e., is the student's achievement problem based in not being able or not being willing to do a task—lack of effort, lack of persistence)? For example, problems perceived to be caused by the student's lack of attention but that occur primarily during the arithmetic class in which the student has difficulty may disappear during other subjects in which the student is more successful. The team will want to be especially aware of the extent to which providing an instructional program that is intrinsically motivating improves the student's achievement (Adelman and Taylor 1986). If the student's problems are not resolved by providing meaningful classwork and/or a contingency management program, the student is considered to be more at risk for having a learning disability.

Question 5: To what extent did the student's achievement improve when *setting demands* were modified? Setting demands would include the physical arrangement of the classroom (e.g., seating) and the degree and type of structure (e.g., how directions are given and work is monitored, amount of independent work required, size of instructional groups, and amount/type of peer interactions). The regular class teacher would be expected to provide much of this information, although the specialist in LD who observed the student working in the regular class frequently will have observed the student's response to instructional modifications, and the school psychologist may have noted the student's response to various task requirements during testing. If the student's achievement problems can be remediated through modifications of the setting demands, the student may not have a learning disability.

Question 6: To what extent does the student appear to need *individualized instruction*? Individualized instruction is typically direct instruction in which the goals and objectives of the regular class remain appropriate for the student but the method of presentation is supplemented to make it effective for a particular student. Individualizing instruction might include specific presentation modifications (e.g., modeling, cueing, giving individualized corrective feedback, and providing a mediator) and modifying the type of response (e.g., pointing, telling, drawing, or writing) to specifically meet the needs of the student. A student who requires individualized or small-group instruction, as opposed to the large-group presentation provided for general class peers, is more likely to be eligible for LD services.

Questions 7 and 8: To what extent does the student appear to need *alternative methods* and *alternative programs*? With alternative methods and programs, the ultimate goals of the general class instructional program remain intact, but the route for meeting those objects is altered. For example, the goal may still be to have the student master objectives in reading, but to master those objectives the student needs a synthetic phonics program rather than the traditional basal or whole language program as provided in the regular class. At this point the LD specialist and school psychologist, with the help of the regular class teacher, examine the learning characteristics of the individual student to identify how the particular responding patterns during the assessment correlate with classroom-based data. For example, is the type of difficulty a student had with the Similarities subtest of the WISC-R corroborated by evidence of comprehension problems involving word relationships in the reading text, and does this information indicate an underlying problem with categorizing and organizational skills? The student who needs either alternative methods or programs to meet the goals of general education is a likely candidate for placement in a program for students with LD.

Question 9: To what extent does the student appear to need help in *foundation skills* that are prerequisite for regular class success; for example, language therapy, physical or occupational therapy? This information is often presented by an SLP, physician, or physical therapist. A student who needs such prerequisite skills would probably be a candidate for a special education program.

Question 10: To what extent does the student appear to need *alternative goals*? Are the student's instructional needs such that many goals and objectives of the mainstream curriculum are no longer appropriate? For example, rather than learning how to diagram a sentence and interpret *Beowulf* in English class, does the student need to be able to fill out job application forms and read instruction manuals? Because many states require students to pass a basic competency test before being awarded a high school diploma, the skills assessed on the high school exit examination must be considered when examining the extent to which the general education goals are appropriate. Inputs from the regular educators, specialist in LD, parents, and the student are considered here.

The focus of these decision points is to determine whether a student's discrepancy between ability and achievement is due to a learning disability or to other factors, such as lack of opportunities to learn (Question 1), lack of instructional adjustments (Question 3), or lack of motivation (Question 4). While all students require instruction that provides adequate opportunities for learning and is motivating, appropriately structured, and at the appropriate level, most students whose achievement problems are due to a learning disability need instructional provisions beyond those typically available in general education classes (i.e., qualitative changes in the instructional program—questions 7, 8, and 9).

CLINICAL DECISION MAKING FOR PLACEMENT

For all practical purposes, the impact of the eligibility team decision on the placement team is to increase the number of options available for services to the student found to qualify for LD services. If the student is not eligible, the placement team (perhaps now called the "child study team") may still meet with parents and the student to discuss how to remediate the student's school problems.

The questions in Table 6.1 again provide a framework for decision making. When planning instructional services, who will provide them, and in what setting, the placement team generally works from deciding which goals are appropriate for the student (Question 10) down through other service and instructional options rather than beginning with Question 1 as did the eligibility team. Basic quantification factors (questions 1–3) are assumed to be part of any appropriate instructional program and probably do not need to be discussed if the

Table 6.2 Curriculum inventory for decision makers

Instructional Factors
  (From Table 6-1)

Mainstream Environment
  Teacher acceptance
  Teaching style
  Curricular alternatives
  Administrative support
  Scheduling flexibility

Parental Factors
Student Factors
  Student motivation
  Student age
  Expectations
  Home support

Special Education Environment
  Teacher training
  Program philosophy
  Caseload
  Administrative support

student is eligible for LD services. The most critical question for the placement or child study team to consider is the extent to which the planned instructional program will be intrinsically motivating and meaningful to the student—Question 4 (Adelman and Taylor 1986).

In addition to instructional factors, the placement team also considers the parent and student, mainstreaming, and special education factors listed in Table 6.2. Obviously, the desires of the parents and student are of paramount importance in developing the service plan. The student's age, for example, is typically an important consideration in making programming and placement decisions. A pull-out program might work well for a primary-age student but have serious social consequences for an adolescent. An assessment of the mainstream environment provides a profile of the type and extent of instructional modifications that are available outside of special classes (Bender 1988). Also, issues such as the amount of scheduling flexibility and administrative support by the principal are often important in determining the instructional plan for a student with learning problems. Other programming options for the student within the general education program, such as remedial reading and mathematics programs, cooperative learning opportunities, collaborative teaching, consultative services, or even modifications by the regular class teacher without intervention from the LD teacher, offer far broader options for a student eligible for LD services than does a special class. The placement committee will not only want to place the student in the least restrictive environment but also will use the least radical intervention that is appropriate (Adelman and Taylor 1986).

SUMMARY

The work of a multidisciplinary team, whether in judging if a student is eligible for services in a program for learning-disabled students or deciding on which placement and instructional services are needed, should ensure opportunities for all team members, especially the regular educator, to share information. The information used for decision making for both eligibility and placement must include data systematically drawn from the regular classroom and from attempts made there to modify the instruction for the student.

REFERENCES

Adelman, H. S., & Taylor, L. (1986). *An introduction to learning disabilities*. Glenview, IL: Scott, Foresman.

Algozzine, B., & Ysseldyke, J. E. (1981). Special education services for regular children: Better safe than sorry. *Exceptional Children, 48*, 238–243.

Algozzine, B., & Ysseldyke, J. E. (1986). The future of the LD field: Screening and diagnosis. *Journal of Learning Disabilities, 19*, 394–398.

Barton, J. (1983). Viewpoints on multidisciplinary teams in schools. *School Psychology Review, 12*(2), 186–189.

Bender, W. N. (1988). The other side of placement decisions: Assessment of the mainstream environment. *Remedial and Special Education, 9*(5), 28–33.

Berliner, D. C. (1988). The half-full glass: A review of research on teaching. In E. L. Meyem, G. A. Vergason, & R. J. Whelan (Eds.), *Effective instructional strategies for exceptional children*. (pp. 7–31). Denver, CO: Love.

Brey, N. M., Coleman, J. M., & Gotts, G. A. (1981). The interdisciplinary team: Challenges to effective functioning. *Teacher Education and Special Education, 4*(1), 31–49.

Dangel, H. L. (1988). Results of statewide LD needs assessment. In *SLD eligibility conference handbook* (pp. 1–8). Atlanta: Georgia Department of Education.

Dangel, H. L., & Ensminger, E. E. (1988). The use of a discrepancy formula with LD students. *Learning Disabilities Focus, 4*, 24–31.

Epps, S., McGue, M., & Ysseldyke, J. E. (1982). Interjudge agreement in classifying students as learning disabled. *Psychology in the Schools, 19*, 209–220.

Epps, S. Ysseldyke, J. E., & McGue, M. (1984). "I know one when I see one"—Differentiating LD from non LD students. *Learning Disabilities Quarterly, 7*, 89–101.

Federal Register (1977, Thursday, December 29) (52404–52407). Washington, DC: GPO.

Forness, S. R., Sinclair, E., & Gutherie, D. (1983). Learning disabilities discrepancy formulas: Their use in actual practice. *Learning Disabilities Quarterly, 6*, 107–114.

Fuchs, L. S., Fuchs, D., & Stecker, P. M. (1989). Effects on curriculum-based management on teacher's instructional planning. *Journal of Learning Disabilities, 22*, 51–59.

Gillespie, E. B., & Turnbull, A. P. (1983). It's my IEP! Involving students in the planning process. *Exceptional Children, 16*, 26–29.

Gilliam, J. E., & Coleman, M. C. (1981). Who influences IEP committee decisions. *Exceptional Children, 47*, 642–644.

Gordon, T. (1970). *Parent effectiveness training*. New York: Wyden.

Hendrickson, J. M., Ross, J. J., Mercer C. D., & Walker, P. (1988). The multidisciplinary team. *The Clearing House, 62*, 84–86.

Idol, L., Paulucci-Whitcomb, P., & Nevin, A. (1987). *Collaborative consultation*. Austin, TX: Pro-Ed.

Kroth, R. L. (1985). *Communicating with parents of exceptional children: Improving parent–teacher relationships*. Denver, CO: Love.

Lerner, J. (1988). *Learning disabilities: Theories, diagnosis, and teaching strategies* (5th ed.). Boston: Houghton Mifflin.

Lerner, J. W., & Cohen, S. (1981). Learning disabilities and the child care physician. In W. Cruickshank & A. Silver (Eds.), *Bridges to tomorrow* (vol. 2), (pp. 213–220). Syracuse, NY: Syracuse University Press.

Liberty, K. A., & Haring, N. G. (1990). Introduction to decision rule systems. *Remedial and Special Education, 11*(1), 32–41.

McLoughlin, J. A., & Lewis, R. B. (1986). *Assessing special students* (2nd ed.). Columbus, OH: Merrill.

Moore, K. J., Fifield, M. B., Spira, D. A., & Scarlato, M. (1989). Child study team decision making in special education: Improving the process. *Remedial and Special Education, 10*(4), 50–58.

Morsink, C. V., Thomas, C. C., & Correa, V. I. (1991). *Interactive teaming: Consultation and collaboration in special programs.* New York: Macmillan.

Pugach, M. (1982). Regular classroom teacher involvement in the development and utilization of IEPs. *Exceptional Children, 48*, 371–374.

Reynolds, C. R. (1984–1985). Critical measurement issues in learning disabilities. *Journal of Special Education, 18*, 451–475.

Ross, R. P. (1990). Consistency among school psychologists in evaluating discrepancy scores: A preliminary study. *Learning Disabilities Quarterly, 3*, 209–219.

Shea, T. M., & Bauer, A. M. (1991). *Parents and teachers of children with exceptionalities: A handbook for collaboration.* Boston: Allyn and Bacon.

Thurlow, M. L., & Ysseldyke, J. E. (1982). Instructional planning: Information collected by school psychologists vs. information considered useful by teachers. *Journal of School Psychology, 20*, 3–10.

Thurlow, M. L. Ysseldyke, J. E., & Casey, A. (1984). Teachers perception of criteria for identifying learning disabled students. *Psychology in the Schools, 21*, 349–355.

Vaughn, S., Bos, C. S., Harrell, J. E., & Lasky B. A. (1988). Parent participation in the initial placement/IEP conference ten years after mandated involvement. *Journal of Learning Disabilities, 21*, 82–89.

Ysseldyke, J. E. (1983). Current practices in making psychoeducational decisions about learning disabled students. *Journal of Learning Disabilities, 16*, 226–233.

Ysseldyke, J. E., Algozzine, B., & Epps, S. (1983). A logical and empirical analysis of current practices in classifying students as handicapped. *Exceptional Children, 50*, 160–166.

Ysseldyke, J. E., Algozzine, B., & Mitchell, J. (1982). Special education decision making: An analysis of current practices. *Personnel and Guidance Journal, 60*, 308–313.

PART III

Interventions for Learning-Disabled Students

This section begins with two chapters on general instructional practices. Both the behavioral model of instruction and the metacognitive instructional approaches have been successfully used with children and youth with LD. The behavioral instructional approaches have been the dominant instructional approach during the last 15 years within the field of special education generally. However, with the development of successful techniques emphasizing metacognitive instruction, a new array of effective instructional strategies has developed. These two models of instruction should be used in every class for children with LD in most of the behavioral and academic areas of concern. Further, a classroom for students with LD can easily incorporate numerous instructional strategies from each of these general models and utilize those strategies with different children as the needs arise.

The last five chapters of the text present the best practices in five specific areas of concern for children and youth with LD: language instruction, interventions for improving attention, social skills training, strategies for vocational training, and strategies for LD youth in a college environment. Research in each of these areas holds the promise that interventions that have recently been developed can alleviate many of the problems that students with LD manifest.

FACT SHEET ON INTERVENTIONS

- Most of the instructional practices commonly used with students with LD today are associated with the behavioral school of thought. Interventions such as behavioral contracts, token economies, level reward systems, and response cost systems are quite common in classes for students with LD.
- The emphasis on systematic behavioral instruction has resulted in increased use of instructional strategies that result in daily measures of achievement performance. Those measures of performance are then

graphed and used to determine the necessary adaptations in the educational program. Precision teaching, direct instruction, and time delay instructional strategies typically result in daily measures of performance.

- Metacognitive instructional practices represent a relatively recent development in the field. This concept can be traced to the early development of the advanced organizer concept.
- Numerous metacognitive instructional strategies are available to assist students with LD in particular types of tasks. Once the student learns a particular strategy, the student should be encouraged to use that strategy on every similar task by both the teachers at school and the parents during homework assignments.
- Visual imagery, story mapping, and self-questioning are examples of some common metacognitive strategies.
- Development of efficient language among students with LD is dependent upon lexical development, intentional usage, and communication management.
- Attention problems among students with LD are often noted. Three different interventions may be of use in alleviating these problems. These include behavioral treatments, metacognitive treatments, and drug treatments. Combination treatments are also very effective.
- Children with LD frequently have deficits in both social perception and in specific social skills. Numerous curricula have been developed to provide interventions for these deficits.
- The vocational outcomes for students with LD have not been as positive as professionals in the field had originally hoped. Therefore, scholars are recommending that an individualized transition plan be provided for each student with LD, to assist in the transition from secondary school to work. Also, more inclusion in vocational preparation courses is recommended for many students with LD.
- Numerous students with LD are entering postsecondary training in vocational schools or colleges. A series of assessments may help determine what the weaknesses of these students are, and provision of study skills classes, combined with a reduced course load, will often result in successful completion of college courses of study.

7

Behavioral Interventions

Cynthia O. Vail
Deborah J. Huntington

Behavioral technology provides a structure for determining behaviors in need of change, both social and academic, as well as a wide array of behavioral interventions empirically validated for individuals with learning disabilities (LD). Specifically, applied behavior analysis (ABA) focuses on changing socially significant behaviors that are operationally defined and observable. Through systematically manipulating environmental factors, targeted responses are changed, shaped, increased, or decreased. Direct observations and measurement provide means for documenting functional relationships between change in the target response and a specific behavioral intervention.

This chapter provides an overview of behavioral interventions and how they apply to individuals with LD. However, it is not intended to be a comprehensive review of ABA. Resources are available to provide a detailed account of ABA (Alberto and Troutman 1990; Cooper et al. 1987). The first section of the chapter focuses on general classroom management, while the second section discusses specific behavioral instructional techniques that have been found to be effective with individuals with LD.

Behavioral interventions are based on basic principles that have been demonstrated and empirically validated with both animal and human subjects. Behavioral responses can be altered by manipulating antecedent stimuli (e.g., environmental variables such as assigned academic task) or by manipulating the consequence that follows the behavioral response (e.g., teacher attention). The antecedent sets the occasion for a specific response to occur, while the consequence alters the probability that the behavior will increase or decrease in the future (Cooper et al. 1987). The first step in analyzing behavior is to conduct a functional analysis, whereby antecedent-response-consequence patterns are studied through direct observation. Decision models have been developed to systematically analyze the aberrant behavior of persons with severe disabilities (Gaylord-Ross 1980; Evans and Meyer 1985; Meyer and Evans 1989). The general flow of these models is to first assess whether the problem behavior is severe enough to warrant intervention. The next step is to determine ecological or curricular factors that may set the occasion for the behavior and consequences that may reinforce the unwanted response. This general approach is adapted in the following discussion of behavior management techniques for students with LD in classroom settings.

BEHAVIOR MANAGEMENT IN THE CLASSROOM

Students with LD may exhibit many challenging behavior problems in both school and home environments. Behaviors that seem to be most problematic for educators who teach students with LD usually include off-task behavior, noncompliance, problems in completing assignments, and inappropriate peer interactions. While these behaviors may seem overwhelming to some teachers, they can generally be managed through nonintrusive procedures such as providing a predictable, consistent environment and assigning academic tasks that are motivating, functional, and matched to the student's level of functioning. When problem behaviors persist despite a consistent classroom environment and well-matched curricular demands, more intrusive interventions may be needed. However, a number of questions must be answered.

1. Is the challenging behavior truly a problem when viewed in context of the behavior of other students?
2. Does it occur across settings and with different teachers, adults, or students?
3. Does it impede academic progress or social skill development?
4. Is the frequency, intensity, or duration of the behavior sufficient to warrant more intrusive intervention measures?

These questions can be answered through operationally defining the behavior and then systematically observing and measuring it through direct observation. It is important to observe the student in multiple settings to determine if the problem is context-specific. For example, talking out may only occur during math instruction. It is also vital to obtain measures for social comparison. Expectations and student behaviors may vary greatly from school to school and within various classrooms. Social validation measures can be obtained through collecting direct observation data on the behavior of interest as exhibited by three "typical students." For example, if the "typical students" talk out at a similar rate as the student with LD, then the target behavior is a normal level given the specific context.

If given these considerations the behavior is deemed problematic and medical explanations have been ruled out, more intrusive interventions may be warranted. It is essential that least intrusive interventions (e.g., linking rule following to teacher praise) are implemented and evaluated prior to using more intrusive interventions (e.g., withholding recess). In the next section, intervention options will be described, beginning with least intrusive measures, and moving to more intrusive yet educationally acceptable intervention options.

Consistent, Structured Environment

Many potential behavior problems can be prevented or minimized through providing a predictable, consistent, structured environment. It is unrealistic and unfair to expect students to maintain specific behavioral standards when the standards are unknown, unclear, or always changing. Behavioral expectations should be clearly stated through explicit classroom rules. Rules should be stated in a positive rather than negative manner. For example, "Raise your hand to speak," rather than, "Don't talk out." Although one could devise a list of 20 or more rules to cover potential behavior problems, rules should be kept to a minimum. Five rules or fewer seems to be a good rule of thumb. Finally, rules should be posted, taught, then reviewed frequently. Feedback provided by teachers in the form of specific praise for rule following is considered a best practice.

It is disappointing that research based on naturalistic observations of teacher–pupil interactions reveals that teachers are inclined to provide more negative than positive feedback to students (Strain et al. 1983; Thomas et al. 1978; White 1975). In addition, Strain and colleagues (1983) found that the general level of teacher feedback, both negative and positive, is remarkably low, and that positive feedback is often misplaced. For example, primary-grade teachers were noted to praise students as a group even when noncompliant students were among the group. It is likely that this praise provided inadvertent positive reinforcement for certain students' inappropriate behavior. In light of this research, teachers need to make a conscious effort to supply a high level of positive praise for student rule-following behavior. A four-to-one ratio of positive versus corrective is a good rule of thumb.

Students with LD often are characterized as being very disorganized. Specific environmental arrangement can facilitate student organization. First, teachers should provide predictable routines. For example, in a resource room, students might enter the room, pick up folders with daily work assignments from a predesignated area, then go to assigned seats to begin work. Students are informed of assigned times for working at computers, small-group instruction, and so forth as arranged in advance by the teacher. Advanced organizers are provided to ready students for changes in routines or schedules. Through structure, routines, and advanced organizers, misbehavior is often preempted. It must be recognized that, as with classroom rules, routines must be directly taught to the students prior to implementation.

Positive Consequence Environmental Interventions

For some students a predictable routine, enforced classroom rules, and consistent, contingent teacher praise for appropriate behavior are not enough to manage problem behavior. For these students a more intrusive intervention such as contingency contracting, specific level systems, or token economies may be necessary. These procedures represent special applications of general behavioral principles, specifically positive reinforcement and response cost. This section will highlight systems primarily based on positive reinforcement, in that response cost represents a more intrusive type of intervention and will be discussed in the following section.

Contingency Contracting

A stimulus or event that is administered contingently following a behavior is termed a *positive reinforcer,* if the future occurrence of the behavior increases. For example, if a student receives free reading time contingent upon completing a creative writing assignment at a certain level of accuracy, the likelihood that future completion of a creative writing assignment will increase if free reading time is a positive reinforcer for the student.

Reinforcers must be assessed individually for students (Ayllon and Azrin 1968). For example, free reading time may be a positive reinforcer for some individuals but not for others. Potential reinforcers may be determined through simply asking students what they prefer or observing which activities seem enjoyable. But the only way to determine whether a potential reinforcer will actually work for an individual student is to try it, then observe future behavior.

Another issue to consider when choosing a potential reinforcer is its level of intrusiveness. Ideally, reinforcers should be age-appropriate, natural, and context-appropriate. Providing time to work on a class enrichment project such as planting a tree for Arbor Day should be considered more context- and age-appropriate for a fourth-grade student than earning a brownie for exhibiting on-task behavior. Figure 7.1 illustrates a reinforcement hierarchy with food (a primary reinforcer) being the most intrusive yet often most potent reinforcer and grades being the least intrusive and frequently least potent reinforcer. Again, it must be recognized that reinforcers must be assessed individually.

Tokens or check marks often serve as interim reinforcers that are later exchanged for a back-up reinforcer. When using contingency contracting, token economics, and level systems, interim reinforcers are generally earned, accumulated, and then exchanged for back-up reinforcers.

A *contingency contract* is a written agreement that clearly specifies a contingent relationship between specific behaviors and access to a specified reward (Cooper et al. 1987; Schloss and Sedlak 1986). According to Cooper and colleagues (1987), a contingency contract is not merely a simple positive reinforcement contingency, but, rather, it represents a complex intervention package of related positive and negative reinforcement contingencies.

Contingency contracting involves mutual negotiation between the student and teacher regarding the amount of student behavior required to earn specific rewards. According to Kelley and Stokes (1982), contingency contracting provides students with some opportunities for self-management (i.e., setting and achieving goals). The contract includes the task (i.e., who, what, when, criteria), the reward (specifically stated), and a place to record the progress (which may serve as an interim reinforcer) toward the goal or reward. For example, a teacher and a student may stipulate that after each consecutive 5-day period that a student brings materials to class, he or she will receive 15 minutes of library time.

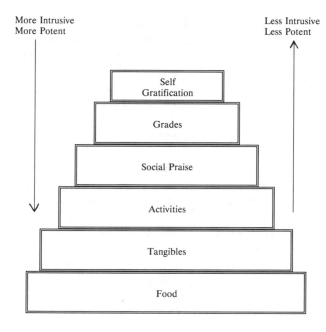

Figure 7.1
Reinforcement hierarchy.

Kelley and Stokes (1982) evaluated the effects of a student-teacher contracting system on the academic productivity of a group of disadvantaged high school students. The subjects attended a special program where they were paid for attendance. When the contingency contract was in place, students were paid according to an academic productivity and accuracy criterion that was negotiated between each student and the teacher. The researcher demonstrated through an ABA design that the level of academic productivity and accuracy dramatically increased for all students as a function of the contingency contracting system. Of course, considering that money was used as the reinforcer, these results are not surprising. As with all reinforcement systems, the challenge in contingency contracting is finding potent back-up reinforcers.

Token Economies
Token economies have been widely used as an effective behavior management technique with individuals in home, educational, and rehabilitation settings (Cooper et al. 1987; Kazdin 1982). A number of researchers have demonstrated the effectiveness of token economies for improving both academic and social behaviors of students with disabilities (McLaughlin and Malaby 1977; Pavchinski et al. 1989; Robinson et al. 1981). In general, behaviors to be reinforced, such as rule-following behaviors, are identified and defined. Then the token or interim reinforcer is selected (e.g., poker chips, star, check mark). Finally the back-up

reinforcers are determined. According to Kazdin (1982), token economies can be viewed as economic systems, in which "token-earning behaviors represent work output; the tokens represent income or wages; back-up events represent expenditures; and accumulated tokens can be viewed as savings" (p. 433). In light of this analogy, teachers must be cognizant of the relative effects of altering the rate of token delivery, cost of back-up reinforcers, and amount of tokens that can be accumulated in savings. The primary goal of motivating individuals to earn tokens by following rules can be maintained through adding potent, novel back-up reinforcers and by altering the rate of exchange.

Because token economies are intrusive, highly contrived systems to manage behavior, teachers should have a plan to withdraw the system yet maintain improved student behavior through less intrusive means. According to Cooper and colleagues (1987), this can be achieved through the following procedures. First, pair the token with descriptive verbal praise so that the verbal praise will acquire the reinforcing capability of the token. Next, the number of responses needed to earn tokens should be increased and the length or times per day the token economy is in effect should be decreased. The activities and privileges that serve as back-up reinforcers should reflect items that are in place in the natural mainstreamed classroom. Finally, the token itself should be gradually faded. For example, move from poker chips, to slips of paper, to tally marks, to tallies kept by the teacher and announced at the end of the day. Then the tokens should be faded completely.

Level Systems

Level systems provide a framework that employs aspects of token economies within a system that progresses from more to least intrusive. In general, level systems specifically list behavioral expectations, requirements and privileges for the student at each level, and standards for moving up or down the levels. Lower levels involve more teacher control and fewer behavioral privileges for the students than do higher levels. According to Bauer and colleagues (1986), the goal is self-management. As students move up through the levels, the behavioral expectations and privileges change, moving from external teacher control to internal self-management.

Mastropieri and Scruggs (1988) researched the effectiveness of a level system in a high school resource room for students with LD and/or behavioral disorders. Privileges linked to the low levels included allowing students to leave their seats without permission to sharpen pencils and to get water. As students moved up levels (contingent on appropriate behavior and accuracy of assignments), privileges were broadened to include allowing students to work independently in an adjacent room. In that research, students exhibited an increase in task completion and a decrease in disruptive and off-task behavior while the level system was in place. As illustrated through this study, as students demonstrated self control, teacher control was decreased.

Response Cost

Often token economies and level systems incorporate negative consequences or response cost procedures when students break rules or exhibit undesirable behaviors. The negative consequence usually entails the student losing previously earned tokens or moving down to a more restrictive level in a level system. Response cost is a form of punishment and should only be considered if less intrusive positive procedures are found ineffective in managing specific student behaviors. In general, research has revealed that in comparing response cost and reinforcement, both procedures are effective in curbing disruptive behavior with few differential effects (Iwata and Bailey 1974; Kaufman and O'Leary 1972). Therefore, it is recommended that when response cost is used, it should be paired with some type of reinforcement component (Cooper et al. 1987).

Schilling and Cuvo (1983) examined the effectiveness of a contingency-based lottery system on the behavior of tenth-grade students with LD and mild mental handicaps. Points were earned through coming to class prepared and remaining in assigned areas. Points were lost for talking out without permission. Points were accumulated and traded for lottery tickets, which, in turn, were backed up by tangible reinforcers such as record albums. Using a reversal design, the authors demonstrated that all three behaviors improved under the lottery condition.

Salend and Gordon (1987) evaluated the effectiveness of an interdependent group response cost contingency to reduce the talk-outs of students with LD and behavior disorders in an elementary-level resource room. A ribbon served as the discriminative stimulus and was displayed as long as no talk-outs occurred. When the ribbon was in place, the group received tokens every 2 minutes. If a talk-out occurred, the ribbon was removed for 1 minute and no tokens could be earned. The ribbon was replaced after 1 minute of no talk-outs and token earning resumed. Tokens were accumulated and traded in for group activities such as free time, popcorn parties, and the like. Through a reversal design the group contingency ribbon procedure proved to be an effective intervention in reducing student talk-outs.

Typically, when a token economy is structured around response cost alone, tokens are given to students at the beginning of a period and then taken away as rule infractions occur. While this type of procedure has been effective in managing the behavior of students with LD (Salend and Lamb 1986), it seems to focus more on rule infractions, rather than rule-following behaviors. Furthermore, students are more likely to perceive the system as punitive. Imagine working in a system where your salary is paid in advance but you are fined for missing deadlines. Contrast that with how you would feel if instead you were given a bonus for meeting deadlines.

Assertive discipline (Cantor 1976), a behavior change system that has been adopted wholesale by many school districts, is often practiced solely as a response cost system. Typically, when students break classroom rules, their names are written on the chalkboard and check marks are added for any additional rule infractions. Preset negative consequences such as loss of a privilege or a trip to see the principal are linked to the system. Because of the frequently punitive nature of its implementation and its lack of research base, assertive discipline has come under recent criticism (Evans et al. 1991; Gartrell 1987). It is disheartening that a system built around response cost, the most intrusive intervention described in this chapter, is used so widely in the mainstream with all students.

Summary

Applied behavior analysis provides effective, empirically validated interventions for managing classroom behaviors of students with LD. While it may be tempting to implement an intrusive intervention such as a response cost procedure as a first attempt to modify a student's behavior, it is not in the best interest of the student. As stated earlier, it is essential that less intrusive interventions be tried first because they are often effective, more ethical, and more likely to generalize to other situations and contexts.

Primary factors to consider when analyzing student behavior are specific teaching methods and curricular content. If an appropriate curriculum–student match is not made, problem behaviors often occur. The second half of this chapter will provide a discussion of systematic instructional methods and curricula found to be effective for students with LD.

SYSTEMATIC INSTRUCTION

A number of systematic instructional techniques have been validated through empirical studies. The techniques to be discussed in this section include precision teaching, direct instruction, and errorless learning.

Precision Teaching

The successful planning and management of instruction are based on sound decision making. Data-based decisions have been found to result in improvement in student achievement (Fuchs and Fuchs 1986), and student progress, when data are monitored on a regular basis, and provide a base from which individualized instruction programs can be developed empirically. Using data-based instruction procedures, long-term goals are selected, measurement systems are designed that correspond to those curricular goals, student progress is routinely monitored toward the goals using the management system, the data base is used to evaluate the effectiveness of the educational program, and instruction can be modified as needed to ensure goal attainment (Fuchs et al. 1987).

Making valid and reliable decisions from the actual raw data is extremely difficult. However, when data are displayed visually, the relationships of the data are more immediately apparent, especially when many performance scores are obtained for each of several students. Graphs are the major tools for organizing, storing, interpreting, and communicating the results of ABA (Cooper et al. 1987).

Graphs enable teachers to inspect and compare many data points without having to sort through pages of tabularized data and raw performance scores. The two basic types of graphs are equal interval graphs and proportional change graphs, which include logarithmic scales. When these two types of graphs are combined, the result is a semi-logarithmic chart in which one axis contains equal intervals and the other is scaled proportionally (Cooper et al. 1987).

A semi-logarithmic chart is the basis for the extension of cumulative response recording (Skinner 1976) to standard celeration charting, a practice known as *precision teaching*. In precision teaching a semi-logarithmic graph is referred to as a "standard celeration chart" because the logarithmic scale and other aspects of the chart are standardized. Use of a standardized scale and format helps teachers avoid the potential misinterpretations that may result from using many different formats and permits them to make consistent and reliable interpretations of instructional effectiveness.

A standard celeration chart displays learning (celeration or number per minute per week) on standard slopes for educational decision making (Lindsley 1991). Preferably the frequencies of correct and incorrect responses of each subject are recorded daily. The more frequently assessments are made, the more often decisions can be made about the effectiveness of instruction. A minimum of three data points (resulting from three assessments) is required to indicate a pattern of learning (West et al. 1990). For example, in Figure 7.2, Lisa's academic performance was assessed five times per week during three weeks, four times per week during three weeks, and three times per week during two weeks. Although it was not always possible for data to be recorded on a daily basis, these samples were sufficient for inclusion in ascertaining changes in academic performance.

Change in academic performance can be measured in terms of the number of responses per minute per week. In this context the change from week to week is referred to as "celeration." Celeration or rate times ($\times$) celeration represents scores that are increasing in value, while deceleration, or rate divided by ($\div$) celeration means that scores are declining in value. More specifically, the most representative score from the five scores in the first week is either multiplied or divided to obtain the most representative score in the second week. For example, in the graph for Lisa (Figure 7.2) it can be seen that the median of the scores in Week 1 was 20 correct responses per minute and the median of the scores in Week 11 was 25 correct responses per minute. The celeration score was 1.25, or 25% improvement, because 20 responses $\times$ 1.25 = 25 responses.

After academic performance has been charted for several weeks, a pattern on the semi-logarithmic chart can be observed. The value of the slope of the line that best fits the distribution of values plotted on the logarithmic scale is considered an indication of learning. The steeper the slope, the faster the learning is; the flatter the slope, the slower the learning is (West et al. 1990). For example, inspection of Lisa's chart indicates a steady increase in correct responses, or acceleration targets, as well as a steady decrease in errors, or deceleration points.

Inspection of the semi-logarithmic chart to note the value of the slope of the line is followed by an adjustment in instruction. A given instructional strategy is

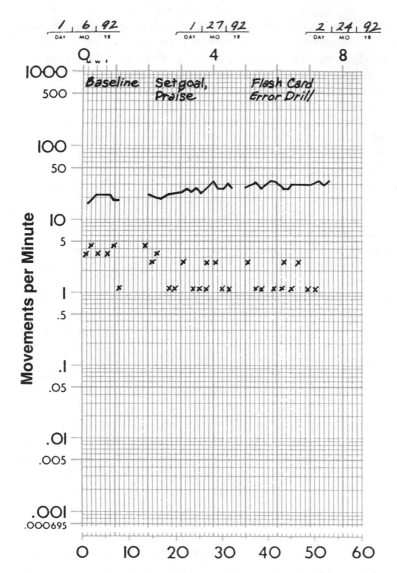

Figure 7.2 Standard behavior chart of the number of sight vocabulary words that Lisa read within one minute.

presumed to be effective if the learning slopes are steeper in the desired direction when the strategy is used than when the strategy is not used. When a learning slope is nearly flat or is going in the wrong direction, different teaching strategies are employed. For example, although Lisa (Figure 7.2) made steady progress when the instructional strategies of goal setting and praise for improvement were utilized, she did not reach the aim until instruction was changed to include flash card error drills. Thus, decisions to change instruction are made for each student separately; each student has an individualized instructional program based on his or her own rate of learning. As a result, the effects of any new teaching strategy are soon reflected in the rate of a student's response (West et al. 1990). More detailed information concerning the techniques, timing, and charting of precision teaching and its application with students with LD is given in several different publications (Downs and Morin 1990; Koorland et al. 1990; Lindsley 1990a, b; Peterson et al. 1990).

Any method or instructional approach can be used with precision teaching. For example, the direct instruction procedures, discussed below, have been combined with precision teaching quite effectively (Maloney and Humphrey 1982). The curricular change decisions, fluency aims, and 1-minute practice sessions from precision teaching readily link with the materials of direct instruction.

Direct Instruction

For students to learn, both the curriculum materials and teacher presentations of the materials must be clear and unambiguous. *Direct instruction* is a complex way of looking at all aspects of instruction, including classroom organization and management, the quality of teacher–student interaction, the design of instructional materials, and the nature of inservice teacher training (Gersten et al. 1987). Students with LD who are taught using direct instruction significantly outperform students with LD who are instructed using more indirect methods (Englert 1984; Leinhardt et al. 1981).

Direct instruction differs from other behavioral education approaches in its degree of emphasis on the antecedent stimuli (Kinder and Carnine 1991). In direct instruction, specific antecedent stimuli that are emphasized include the precise nature of teacher wording, examples, and how teachers present new material to students. The control of environmental variables in a teaching situation is dependent upon "faultless communication" (Engelmann and Carnine 1982). Instructional materials and teachers' delivery must be clear and unambiguous for faultless communication to take place (Kinder and Carnine 1991). Consequently, many direct instruction materials provide "scripts" for teachers to use during the instructional process.

Direct Instruction Procedures

Faultless communication can be developed through four principles common to all direct instruction materials: (1) explicit teaching of rules and strategies, (2) example selection, (3) example sequencing, and (4) covertization (Kinder and Carnine 1991). In the introductory stages of instruction, every step in applying rules and in problem solving is explicitly taught. Rather than simply stating a rule or strategy, the teacher overtly demonstrates each of the steps in applying a rule or strategy with precise explanations. Afterwards, students are provided with a carefully sequenced series of examples and are guided through the steps in applying the rule or strategy. The examples used are carefully selected to have only one attribute in common and a variety of irrelevant attributes to make the common attribute salient (Carnine 1991). The sequence includes instances when the rule is applied as well as when it is not. In addition, nonexamples, those similar in all but the critical quality, are used to aid in discrimination. The overt steps are faded in successive instruction. The number of leading questions is reduced so that the students' strategies become more covert. Students eventually can apply strategies silently and independently (Kinder and Carnine 1991).

One important aspect of direct instruction procedures is the emphasis on teacher behavior. Rosenshine (1983) investigated teacher behaviors that are correlated with enhanced academic performance of students (Rosenshine 1983; Rosenshine and Stevens 1984). Although Rosenshine's research was conducted in regular classrooms and often included low-income students, his model of instructional procedures has also been validated with students with LD (Englert 1984; Leinhardt et al. 1981). Rosenshine and Stevens (1984) found that students show higher academic achievement when teachers follow a consistent pattern of demonstration, guided practice, and feedback.

Since the early work by Rosenshine, other researchers have investigated the effects of teacher behavior on student achievement (Englert 1984; Gersten et al. 1982; Stallings 1980). Gersten and colleagues (1982) named four teaching skills as being most critical in differentiating a high-achieving teacher from a low-achieving teacher. They identified these critical teaching skills as (1) correcting student errors immediately, (2) maintaining a student success rate of at least 85%, (3) pacing lessons at a brisk tempo, and (4) following the teaching format in a direct instruction teacher's manual. These basic findings have been replicated with a larger sample (Gersten et al. 1986). Englert (1984) found that the effectiveness of direct instruction with students with LD was related to a brisker lesson pace, a higher accuracy rate, and the use of prompting rather than telling the students the correct answers. Leinhardt and colleagues (1981) found that the effectiveness of reading instruction for students with LD varied in terms of teacher instructional behavior, teacher affective behaviors, and instructional pacing.

Direct Instruction Curriculum

Some aspects of direct instruction are related to procedures, while others are associated more closely with curriculum. A structured, repetitive approach to teaching has been found to be effective for introducing new concepts. Beck and colleagues (1982) found that average-ability students needed 16 to 22 presentations of a new concept before they learned and remembered the definition. However, this degree of structure is not found in many of the teaching materials that are commonly available. A recent computer analysis found that, in the five most widely adopted basal series, only 26 words were targeted for review more than a dozen times. Most new words were introduced once and never reviewed.

If average-ability students need approximately 20 presentations to learn a new concept, it follows that students with LD may require additional presentations. Thus, the teacher is faced with the task of designing a curriculum that incorporates daily review, weekly review, monthly review, and quarterly review of materials presented previously, as well as the presentation of any new concepts or skills materials at least 20 times each.

As illustrated above, effective instruction is quite demanding, both in terms of the amount of teaching and its intensity. The critical features of direct instruction can be incorporated into commercially prepared or teacher-designed materials or through the use of computer-assisted instruction or videodiscs.

A number of commercially prepared materials are available that include all the critical elements of direct instruction. A classic example is the Direct Instruction Systems for Teaching Arithmetic and Reading (DISTAR) developed by Engelmann and Bruner in 1969. Updated revised editions are available for the initial teaching of reading, math, language, and spelling. In addition, separate remedial materials are available for decoding, comprehension, math, and spelling.

Efficacy of Direct Instruction

The original DISTAR materials have been empirically validated for the U.S. Office of Education by Stanford Research Institute (Stebbins et al. 1977). This longitudinal evaluation looked at the impact of eight instructional models on low-income students in the primary grades. Stebbins and his associates found that the direct instruction approach had a beneficial effect on the achievement of low-income students who participated for a full four years (kindergarten through third grade).

Although this study included some students with disabilities, they had not been identified as such. Several years later, researchers reanalyzed the data to look for implications that might relate to special education. Gersten and colleagues (1984) looked at the yearly achievement profiles of low-income minority children who entered the program with IQs of 70 or below on the Slosson Intelligence Test and those with IQs of 71 to 90. Students with IQs of 71 to 90 as well as those in the higher-IQ blocks demonstrated a one-year growth for each year in school in mathematics and even higher scores in reading.

Other research supports the effectiveness of commercially prepared direct instruction materials (Gettinger 1982; Lloyd 1980; Polloway et al. 1986). For example, Stein and Goldman (1980) compared the academic achievement of children with LD in primary school (ages 6 to 8) who received a full year of reading instruction in either the DISTAR reading program or the Palo Alto Reading Program, two phonetically based primary reading programs. Since random assignment to groups was not possible, students were pretested with the Peabody Individual Achievement Test (PIAT) reading recognition and comprehension subtests and intelligence tests to ensure that the groups demonstrated no significant differences prior to instruction. The mean gain for students using DISTAR was 15 months (over a 9-month period) as compared with a 7-month gain for students using Palo Alto.

White (1988) examined the effect of direct instruction on the achievement of special education students through a meta-analysis of 25 studies, approximately half of which were conference reports, ERIC reports, or unpublished manuscripts. Of the total number of studies used in the meta-analysis, 15 were experimental studies and 10 used quasi-experimental procedures. Nearly half examined direct instruction reading. Students with mild disabilities were subjects in 21 of the studies. White determined the effect size for each dependent measure and produced the effect sizes across all measures in the study. He also computed the proportion of measures that significantly favored the experimental (direct instruction) or comparison groups. The results showed that no measure in any of the studies significantly favored the comparison group and over half of the measures significantly favored the direct instruction groups. There was no significant difference in the mean effect size between studies with students with mild disabilities and studies with students with moderate to severe disabilities, demonstrating effectiveness across a range of ability levels. The data also showed that direct instruction was effective for a wide range of grades, elementary through secondary.

While earlier research investigated the effects of direct instruction on basic academic skills involving lower-level thinking, current research is focused on determining how these strategies apply to the teaching of complex cognitive skills such as the comprehension of literature, math problem solving, and law (Carnine 1989). Clear, detailed strategies have been developed and empirically field-tested to teach students to draw conclusions from basal passages (Carnine et al. 1982), to solve math problems (Cawley 1985; Cawley and Miller 1986; Darch et al. 1984), and to learn basic legal concepts (Fielding et al. 1983), and their research has demonstrated the efficacy of direct instruction in each of these areas.

Wilson and Sindelar (1991) investigated the use of direct instruction in math word problems with 62 elementary students with LD from nine elementary schools. Students were assigned to one of three instructional groups: strategy-plus-sequence, strategy-only, and sequence-only. The strategy-only group received direct teaching in strategies for translating word problems into equations. In the sequence-only group, word problems were presented in sequence according to type and difficulty. Students in the strategy-plus-sequence group, as well as those in the strategy-only group, scored significantly higher than did students in the sequence-only group.

Hofmeister and colleagues (1989) recently investigated the effectiveness of direct instruction in teaching chemistry to high school students with LD. Included in the instruction were concepts such as bonding, equilibrium, energy of activation, atomic structure, and organic compounds. The posttest scores of students with LD did not differ significantly from those of a control group of students in an advanced placement chemistry course.

Computer-Assisted Direct Instruction

In addition to the use of commercially prepared and teacher-designed materials, the critical features of direct instruction can also be presented through the use of well-designed computer-assisted instruction and videodisc instruction. *Computer-assisted instruction* (CAI) refers to software packages that attempt to teach new academic skills or review existing skills. Harrod and Ruggles (1983) describe six function areas in which CAI contributes to the education of students with LD. These areas are (1) drill and practice, (2) tutorial efforts, (3) instructional games, (4) simulation, (5) problem solving, and (6) demonstration and mini-programming for CAI.

The majority of CAI programs used in both elementary and secondary special education programs nationwide provide drill and practice (Becker 1986; Russell 1986). Programs are now available that provide initial instruction in basic skills. CAI has been successfully used for initial instruction in basic reading and mathematics skills with elementary students with LD (Trifiletti et al. 1987; Jones et al. 1987).

Computer-assisted instructional materials, just like any other instructional resource, need to be carefully evaluated for use by students with LD. Specific factors that should be included in such an evaluation include clear, concise teachable steps; explicit wording of directions and instructions; and adequate review of concepts or skills. In other words, CAI programs should meet the standards of other direct instruction materials (Vargas 1986).

One way that instruction can become more interactive with the learner's needs is through artificial intelligence programs (Hofmeister and Thorkildsen 1987). These programs adjust instruction to fit the needs of an individual learner. According to Smith (1991), key functions of artificial intelligence CAI programs include:

- Analyze student success rates to determine which presentation style to use for further teaching.
- Analyze whether the student uses an acceptable method to reach the answer, and, if not, provide more tutoring.
- Regulate the number of items presented based on the student's past learning rate.
- Analyze the nature of the errors and correct only serious misperceptions.
- Analyze the type of information that the student most often responds to correctly and present more of it.
- Interpret the words and intent of what the student has typed.

Collins and colleagues (1987) used an artificial intelligence program to teach adolescents with LD to draw syllogistic conclusions and critique arguments. Direct instruction principles were incorporated into the CAI programs. One student learned step-by-step procedures for constructing and criticizing arguments. Individualized feedback related student errors to previously taught rules. Each item a student missed was presented later in the lesson until the student answered the item correctly. Process feedback led to high scores on the post-test as well as a transfer test. Results strongly supported the use of CAI programs based on direct instruction procedures.

The same reasoning-skills program was later used by Collins and Carnine (1988) to compare the performance of high school students with LD, general education high school students, and college students in an introductory logic class. Following intervention, students with LD performed as well as their general education peers and the logic students on a test of argument construction. Based on this and other studies, we may conclude that research validates the use of CAI based on direct instruction with students with LD (Grossen and Carnine 1990; Hearne et al. 1988; Horton et al. 1988; Johnson et al. 1987; Mather 1988; Kelley et al. 1987).

Errorless Procedures

Successful teachers correct student errors immediately and maintain a student success rate at a level of 85% (Browder et al. 1981; Kowry and Browder 1986; Schuster et al. 1988). Some researchers have investigated obtaining a higher level of success, and this research has come to be known as *errorless learning*. Some errorless learning strategies that were originally used with students with moderate to severe handicaps have recently been successfully applied to students with LD (Kinney et al. 1988; Stevens and Schuster 1987; Wolery et al. 1991). These procedures are based on the assumption that learning will be more rapid and efficient if the teaching situation can be arranged to prevent errors.

Even when teaching includes all elements of instructional design and effective teaching practices are utilized, some students with LD will continue to make errors and have a slow rate of acquisition. However, stimulus control can be established by indirect assistance such as teacher manipulation of materials and by direct assistance such as extrastimulus prompts (Bailey and Wolery 1984), and this will reduce the occurrence of errors. Examples of ways that stimulus control can be established by indirect assistance include stimulus shaping, stimulus fading, and response shaping.

Stimulus/Response Variation

In stimulus shaping and stimulus fading, changes are made in the stimuli being presented to the student and, as a result, there is a change in stimulus control. In *stimulus shaping* the critical characteristics of the stimulus (those characteristics being taught) are changed as training progresses. In *stimulus fading* the irrelevant characteristics are gradually changed. For example, if stimulus shaping were used to teach Sue to read the word "car," instruction would begin with a small drawing of a car, would progress to the letters *c-a-r* above a pair of wheels, and would end with the word "car" (Bailey and Wolery 1984).

Stimulus fading takes many forms and may include variation of many different dimensions of the stimulus. Some aspect of the stimulus is manipulated to cue the child to the correct response. For example, to enhance the discrimination of the word "should" from the word "show," the word card for "should" could be placed closer to Sue or the word "should" could be written in Sue's favorite color.

To ensure that the student is responding to the correct characteristic of the stimulus, the incorporated cue (e.g., color and distance) is gradually removed (Bailey and Wolery 1984). For example, the card for "show" could be gradually moved closer to the card for "should" until they are equal distances from Sue. The color could be removed gradually, shade by shade, until both words are presented on white cards. If Sue continues to respond correctly, then there has been a shift in stimulus control. She has shifted from responding to irrelevant characteristics (distance and color) to relevant characteristics of the stimulus (sight word recognition).

Response shaping differs from stimulus shaping in that successive approximations of the target behavior are reinforced. During the initial phases of instruction the teacher might reinforce a response that is considerably inferior to the target behavior. Thereafter, closer approximations of the target behavior are gradually required before reinforcement is given (Bailey and Wolery 1984). For example, in teaching Sue the meaning of "whale," you may initially accept "lives in water." Approximations may include different levels of complexity and accuracy such as a fish, a big fish, a mammal, and so on.

Extrastimulus Prompts

One of the most powerful ways that a student can be supported in instruction is in the provision of *extrastimulus prompts*. Extrastimulus prompts should be sufficient to produce the desired behavior so that the behavior can be followed by reinforcement. Types of extrastimulus prompts include verbal directions, modeling, and physical guidance. Verbal directions can be used as a supplementary prompt to elicit responses. Verbal prompts can be one word, several words, or even a paragraph in length. *Verbal directions* are used routinely in the classroom setting. Using the regrouping example, Sandra could be told, "Add 9 and 3. The answer is 12. Write down the 2 and then carry the 1 to the tens column." A second extrastimulus prompt, *modeling,* involves demonstrating the desired behavior so that it can be imitated. Modeling prompts are slightly more intrusive than verbal prompts because the teacher must demonstrate the correct response. For example, Sandra could be given directions for regrouping and an example on a printed card that she could refer to as she completes her work. The third type of response prompt, *physical guidance,* involves bodily assisting a student through an action. Physical guidance is the most intrusive of the three response prompts mentioned in that it requires the teacher to be directly involved with the student. For example, Sandra is learning to boot the computer. Although she has already received verbal directions and the teacher has modeled the behavior, she is still having difficulty sequencing the actions. Using physical guidance, the teacher may place her hands on top of Sandra's and move her hands through the steps of booting the computer.

In some cases it is more efficient to combine prompts. For example, some students may need both auditory and visual prompting to elicit the correct response. Sandra may need to hear a one-word prompt as well as read the directions and observe the example on the card before she can proceed in regrouping. Therefore, whatever prompt is sufficient to elicit a correct response for a particular student in a particular situation is utilized. There is mounting evidence that providing prompts prior to students' responses decreases the probability of errors and increases the probability of error-free learning. Direct assistance in the form of an extra stimulus prompt ensures that learning will be errorless (Ault et al. 1989).

Extrastimulus prompts should be sufficient to produce the desired behavior, so that the behavior can be followed by reinforcement (Bailey and Wolery 1984). The prompt sufficient for a particular child in a particular situation is called a "controlling prompt." The prompt guarantees that the student will complete the correct response. Types of extrastimulus prompts include verbal cues, gestures, models, partial physical prompts, and full physical prompts. It is important to use the least intrusive prompt needed to obtain instructional control.

In order for the student to learn to complete a task independently, prompts must be faded. This can be accomplished through eliminating extrastimulus prompts for some of the trials. Another method of fading is to decrease the force of the prompt. In an example given above, Sandra will eventually remember to add numbers that have been recognized when she has been given a gestural prompt. The teacher can fade the prompt by raising her hand but not completely making the plus. Eventually it will only be necessary for the teacher to begin to raise her hand to elicit the desired behavior.

Time Delay Procedures

Time delay is an errorless learning method that uses extrastimulus prompts and systematically fades them through delaying prompt delivery. Time delay was introduced by Touchette (1971), who taught three students with severe intellectual disabilities a form discrimination task. It has been used to teach a variety of academic tasks to students with mild disabilities, including students with LD (Alig-Cybriwsky et al. 1990; Kinney et al. 1987; Schuster and Griffin 1990; Stevens and Schuster 1988). Student errors are minimized when using the time delay method because the prompt is consistently provided when the student does not respond independently. This procedure provides consistent opportunities for students to receive reinforcement for all correct responses (both independent and prompted).

The time delay procedure is an instructional strategy in which increasing amounts of time are inserted between the task direction and the controlling prompt. A *task direction* is a statement that tells the student to do the target behavior. A *controlling prompt* is a level of teacher assistance that ensures that the student will perform correctly (Gast et al. 1988).

Initially the controlling prompt is presented immediately after the task direction. These trials are called zero-second delay trials. When students respond correctly to zero-second trials, they are reinforced. If they do not respond correctly, the teacher provides a planned consequent event and determines whether the prompt controls the students' behavior. After several zero-second delay trials, the teacher systematically increases the amount of time the students have to respond correctly to the task directions before the controlling prompt is presented (Gast et al. 1988).

The objective of the time delay procedure is to teach students to respond correctly to the task direction without a prompt and to wait for the teacher's assistance when they are unsure of the correct response. After the teacher begins to delay the prompt, students respond correctly before the prompt or after it. In either case, reinforcement is provided. When a student responds incorrectly before or after the prompt or fails to respond after a prompt, the teacher either ignores the response or provides some other consequent event. According to this procedure, students have "learned" a behavior only when they respond correctly to the task direction before the anticipated prompt is given (Gast et al. 1988).

Researchers have used time delay in teaching academic skills to individual students with LD (Winterling 1990; Wolery et al. 1991). Schuster and colleagues (1990) used a 5-second time delay procedure to teach word definitions to three fifth-grade resource students, two of whom were students with LD. All students learned the 10 targeted definitions within eight to nine sessions. Students maintained a correct level of responding 6, 10, and 14 weeks after training and, in addition, generalized the newly acquired information across two skills not directly trained, reading the targeted word and providing the correct verbal label after hearing the targeted definition.

Wolery and colleagues (1991) investigated the effectiveness of a constant time delay procedure in teaching health and social studies facts to a group of four adolescents, two of whom had been diagnosed as learning-disabled and two of whom had been diagnosed as behaviorally disordered. Students acquired 64 facts with few errors. Results indicated that the time delay procedure was reliable and effective.

SUMMARY

In conclusion, ABA provides a framework for meeting the individual needs, both social and academic, of students with LD. Practitioners can use procedures discussed in this chapter to adapt both learning environments and instruction, based on individual student needs, and then to assess the effectiveness of the adaptations through systematic data collection. Through data-based decisions, teachers can ensure progress for many students with LD.

REFERENCES

Alberto, P. A., & Troutman, A. C. (1990). *Applied behavior analysis for teachers* (3rd ed.). Columbus, OH: Merrill.

Alig-Cybriwsky, C., Wolery, M., & Gast, D. L. (1990). Use of a constant time delay procedure in teaching preschoolers in a group format. *Journal of Early Intervention, 14,* 99–116.

Ault, M. J., Wolery, M., Doyle, P. M., & Gast, D. L. (1989). Review of comparative studies in the instruction of students with moderate and severe handicaps. *Exceptional Children, 55,* 346–356.

Ayllon, T., & Azrin, N. H. (1968). Reinforcer sampling: A technique for increasing the behavior of mental patients. *Journal of Applied Behavior Analysis, 1,* 13–20.

Bailey, D. M., & Wolery, M. (1984). *Teaching infants and preschoolers with handicaps.* Columbus, OH: Merrill.

Bauer, A. M., Shea, T. M., & Keppler, R. (1986). Level systems: A framework for the individualization of behavior management. *Behavioral Disorders, 12,* 28–35.

Beck, I. L., Perfetti, C. A., & McKeown, M. G. (1982). Effects of long term vocabulary instruction on lexical access and reading comprehension. *Journal of Educational Psychology, 74,* 506–521.

Becker, H. (1986). *Instructional uses of school computers.* Issue 1. Baltimore, MD: The Johns Hopkins University Center for Social Organization of Schools.

Browder, P. M., Morris, W. W., & Snell, M. E. (1981). Using time delay to teach manual signs to a severely retarded student. *Education and Training of the Mentally Retarded, 16,* 252–258.

Cantor, L. (1976). *Assertive discipline: A take charge approach for today's educator.* Los Angeles: Lee Cantor and Associates.

Carnine, D. (1989). Teaching complex content to learning disabled students: The role of technology. *Exceptional Children, 55,* 524–533.

Carnine, D. (1991). Curricular interventions for teaching higher order thinking to all students: Introduction to the special series. *Journal of Learning Disabilities, 24,* 261–269.

Carnine, D. W., Kameenui, E. J., & Woofson, N. (1982). Training of textual dimensions related to text based inferences. *Journal of Reading Behavior, 44,* 335–340.

Cawley, J. F. (Ed.). (1985). *Secondary school mathematics for the learning disabled.* Rockville, MD: Aspen Systems.

Cawley, J. F., & Miller, J. H., (1986). Selected views on metacognition: Arithmetic problem solving, and learning disabilities. *Learning Disabilities Focus, 2*(1), 36–48.

Collins, M., & Carnine, D. (1988). Evaluating the field test revision process by comparing two versions of a reasoning skills CAI program. *Journal of Learning Disabilities, 21,* 375–379.

Collins, M., Carnine, D., & Gersten, R., (1987). Elaborated corrected feedback and the acquisition of reasoning skills: A study of computer-assisted instruction. *Exceptional Children, 54,* 254–262.

Cooper, J. O., Heron, T. E., & Heward, W. L. (1987). *Applied behavioral analysis.* Columbus, OH: Merrill.

Darch, C., Carnine, D., & Gersten, R. (1984). Explicit strategy instruction in mathematical problem solving. *Journal of Educational Research, 77,* 350–359.

Downs, J., & Morin, S. (1990). Improving reading fluency. *Teaching Exceptional Children, 22,* 28–31.

Engelmann, S., & Bruner, E. C. (1988). *Reading Mastery.* Chicago: Science Research Associates.

Engelmann, S., & Carnine, D. W. (1982). *Theory of instruction.* New York: Irvington.

Englert, C. S. (1984). Effective direct instruction practices in special education settings. *Remedial and Special Education, 5*(2), 38–47.

Espin, C. A., & Deno, S. L. (1984). The effects of modeling and prompting feedback strategies on sight word reading of student labeled learning disabled. *Education and Treatment of Children, 12,* 219–231.

Evans, I. M., & Meyer, L. H. (1985). *An educative approach to behavior problems: A practical decision model for interventions with severely handicapped learners.* Baltimore, MD: Brookes.

Evans, W. H., Evans, S. S., Gable, R. A., & Kehlhem, M. A. (1991). Assertive discipline and behavioral disorders: Is this a marriage made in heaven? *Beyond Behavior, 2,* 13–16.

Fielding, G., Kameenui, E., & Gersten, R. (1983). A comparison of inquiry and direct instruction approaches toward teaching legal concepts and applications to secondary students. *Journal of Educational Research, 76,* 287–293.

Fuchs, L., & Fuchs, D. (1986). Effects of systematic formative evaluation: A meta-analysis. *Exceptional Children, 53*, 199–208.

Fuchs, L., Fuchs, D., Hamlett, O. L., & Hasselbring, T. (1987). Using computers with curriculum-based monitoring: Effects of teacher efficiency and satisfaction. *Journal of Special Education Technology, 8* (4), 14–27.

Gartrell, D. (1987). Assertive discipline: Unhealthy for children and other living things. *Young Children, 12*(2), 10–11.

Gast, D. L., Wolery, M., Ault, M. J., Doyle, P. M., & Alig, C. (1988). How to use time delay: Comparison of instructional strategies project. Lexington: Department of Special Education, University of Kentucky.

Gaylord-Ross, R. (1980). A decision model for the treatment of aberrant behavior in applied settings. In W. Sailor, B. Wilcox, & L. Brown (Eds.), *Methods of instruction for severely handicapped students* (pp. 135–158). Baltimore, MD: Brookes.

Gerber, M. M. (1986). Generalization of spelling strategies by L.D. students as a result of contingent imitation/modeling and mastery criteria. *Journal of Learning Disabilities, 19*, 530–537.

Gersten, R., Becker, W., Heiry, T., & White, W. A. T. (1984). Entry IQ and yearly academic growth of children in direct instruction. *Educational Evaluation and Policy Analysis, 6*, 109–121.

Gersten, R., Carnine, D., & Williams, P. (1982). Measuring implementation of a structured educational model in an urban school district: An observational approach. *Educational Evaluation & Policy Analysis, 4*, 67–79.

Gersten, R., Carnine, D., & Woodward, J. (1987). Direct instruction: The third decade. *Remedial and Special Education, 6*, 48–56.

Gersten, R., Carnine, D. W., Zoreb, L., & Cronin, D. (1986). A multifaceted study of change in seven inner city schools. *Elementary School Journal, 86*, 257–276.

Gettinger, M. (1982). Improving classroom behaviors and achievement of learning disabled children using direct instruction. *School Psychology Review, 11*, 329–336.

Grossen, B., & Carnine, D. (1990). Diagramming a logical strategy: Effects in difficult problem types and transfer. *Learning Disabilities Quarterly, 13*, 168–182.

Harrod, N., & Ruggles, M. (1983). Computer assisted instruction: An educational tool. *Focus on Exceptional Children, 16*, 1–8.

Hearne, J. D., Poplin, M. S., Schoeneman, C., & O'Shaughnessy, E. (1988). Computer aptitude: An investigation of differences among junior high students with learning disabilities and their nonlearning disabled peers. *Journal of Learning Disabilities, 21*, 489–492.

Hofmeister, A., Engelmann, S., & Carnine, D. (1989). Developing and validating science education videodiscs. *Journal of Research in Science Teaching, 26*, 665–677.

Hofmeister, A., & Thorkildsen, R. (1987). Interactive videodisc and exceptional individuals. In J. Lindsey (Ed.), *Computers and exceptional individuals.* Columbus, OH: Merrill.

Horton, S. V., Lovitt, T. C., & Slocum, T. (1988). Teaching geography to high school students with academic deficits: Effects of a computerized tutorial. *Learning Disability Quarterly, 11*, 371–379.

Iwata, B. A., & Bailey, J. S. (1974). Reward versus cost token systems: An analysis of the effects on students and teacher. *Journal of Applied Behavior Analysis, 7*, 567–576.

Johnson, G., Gersten, R., & Carnine, D. (1987). Effects of instructional design variables on vocabulary acquisition of LD students: A study on computer assisted instruction. *Journal of Learning Disabilities, 20*, 206–213.

Jones, K. M., Torgesen, J. K., & Sexton, M. H. (1987). Using computer guided practice to increase decoding fluency in learning disabled children: A study using the Hunt and Hunt I program. *Journal of Learning Disabilities, 20*, 122–128.

Kail, R. (1984). *The development of memory in children.* New York: Freeman.

Kaufman, K. F., & O'Leary, K. D. (1972). Reward, cost, and self-evaluation procedures for disruptive adolescents in a psychiatric hospital school. *Journal of Applied Behavior Analysis, 5*, 293–309.

Kazdin, A. E. (1982). The token economy: A decade later. *Journal of Applied Behavior Analysis, 15*, 431–445.

Kelley, M. L., & Stokes, T. F. (1982). Contingency contracting with disadvantaged youth: Improving classroom performance. *Journal of Applied Behavior Analysis, 15*, 447–454.

Kelly, B., Carnine, D., Gersten, R., & Grossen, B. (1987). The effectiveness of videodisc instruction in teaching fractions to learning disabled and remedial high school students. *Journal of Special Education Technology, 8*(2), 5–17.

Kinder, D., & Carnine, D. (1991). Direct instruction: What it is and what it is becoming. *Journal of Behavioral Education, 1*, 193–213.

Kinney, P., Stevens, K. B., & Schuster, J. W. (1987). Effects of a constant time delay procedure on the written spelling performance of a learning disabled student. *Learning Disability Quarterly, 10*, 9–16.

Kinney, P. G., Stevens, K. B., & Schuster, J. W. (1988). The effects of CAI and time delay: A systematic program for teaching spelling. *Journal of Special Education Technology, 9*, 61–72.

Koorland, M. A., Keel, M. C., & Ueberhorst, P. (1990). Setting aims for precision teaching. *Teaching Exceptional Children, 22*(3), 64–68.

Kowry, M., & Browder, D. M. (1986). The use of delay to teach sight words by peer tutors classified as moderately mentally retarded. *Education and Training of the Mentally Retarded, 21*, 252–258.

Leinhardt, G., Zigmond, N., & Cooley, W. W. (1981). Reading instruction and its effects. *American Educational Research Journal, 18*, 343–366.

Lindsley, O. R. (1971). Direct measurement and prognosis of retarded behavior. *Journal of Education, 147*, 62–81.

Lindsley, O. R. (1990a). Our aims, discoveries, failures, and problem. *Journal of Precision Teaching, 7*(2), 7–17.

Lindsley, O. R. (1990b). Precision teaching. By teachers for children. *Teaching Exceptional Children, 22*(3), 10–15.

Lindsley, O. R. (1991). Precision teaching's unique legacy from B. F. Skinner. *Journal of Behavioral Education, 1*, 253–266.

Lloyd, J., Cullinan, D., Heins, E., & Epstein, M. (1980). Direct instruction: Effects on oral and written language comprehension. *Learning Disability Quarterly, 3*(4), 70–76.

Maloney, M., & Humphrey, J. E. (1982). The Quinte Learning Center: A successful venture in behavioral education, an interview with Michael Maloney. *The Behavioral Educator, 4*(1), 1–3.

Mastropierei, M. A., & Scruggs, T. E. (1988). A level system for managing problem behaviors in a high school resource program. *Behavioral Disorders, 13*, 202–208.

Mather, N. (1988). Computer assisted instruction. In C. S. Bos & S. Vaughn (Eds.), *Strategies for teaching students with learning and behavior problems*. Boston: Allyn and Bacon.

McLaughlin, T. F., & Malaby, J. E. (1977). The comparative effects of token-reinforcement with and without a response cost contingency with special education children. *Educational Research Quarterly, 2*, 34–41.

Meyer, L. A. (1984). Long term academic effects of the direct instruction project follow through program. *Elementary School Journal, 84*, 380–394.

Meyer, L. H., & Evans, I. M. (1989). *Non-aversive intervention for behavior problems: A manual for home and community*. Baltimore, MD: Brookes.

Pavchinski, P., Evans, J. H., & Bostow, D. E. (1989). Increasing word recognition and math ability in a severely learning-disabled student with token reinforcers. *Psychology in the Schools, 26*, 397–410.

Peterson, S. K., Scott, J., & Sroka, K. (1990). Using the language experience approach with precision teaching. *Teaching Exceptional Children, 22,* 28–31.

Polloway, E. A., Epstein, M. H., Polloway, C. H., Patton, J. R., & Ball, D. W. (1986). Corrective reading program: An analysis of effectiveness with learning disabled and mentally retarded students. *Remedial and Special Education, 7*(4), 41–47.

Reith, H. J., & Frick, T. (1982). *An analysis of academic learning time of mildly handicapped students in special eduction service delivery systems. Initial report on classroom process variables.* Bloomington: Center for Innovation in Teaching the Handicapped, Indiana University.

Robinson, P. W., Newby, T. J., & Ganzell, S. L. (1981). A token system for a class of underachieving hyperactive children. *Journal of Applied Behavior Analysis, 14,* 307–315.

Rosenshine, B. (1983). Teaching functions in instructional programs. *Elementary School Journal, 83,* 335–352.

Rosenshine, B., & Stevens, R. (1984). Classroom instruction in reading. In D. O. Pearson (Ed.), *Handbook of research in teaching.* New York: Longman.

Russell, T. J. (1986). But what are they learning? The dilemma of using microcomputers in special education. *Learning Disability Quarterly, 9,* 100–104.

Salend, S. J., & Gordon, B. D. (1987). A group-oriented timeout ribbon procedure. *Behavior Disorders, 12,* 131–137.

Salend, S. J., & Lamb, E. A. (1986). Effectiveness of a group-managed interdependent contingency system. *Learning Disability Quarterly, 9,* 268–273.

Schilling, D., & Cuvo, A. J. (1983). The effects of a contingency-based lottery on the behavior of a special education class. *Education and Training of the Mentally Retarded, 18,* 52–58.

Schloss, P. J., & Sedlak, R. A. (1986). *Instructional methods for students with learning and behavior problems.* Boston: Allyn and Bacon.

Schoenfeld, A. H., & Herrmann, D. J. (1982). Problem perception and knowledge structure in expert and novice mathematical problem solvers. *Journal of Experimental Psychology: Learning, Memory, and Cognition, 8,* 484–494.

Schuster, J. W., Gast, D. L. Wolery, M., & Guiltinan, S. (1988). The effectiveness of a constant time-delay procedure to teach chained responses to adolescents with mental retardation. *Journal of Applied Behavior Analysis, 21,* 169–178.

Schuster, J. W., & Griffen, A. K. (1990). Using time delay with task analyses. *Teaching Exceptional Children, 22*(4), 49–53.

Schuster, J. W., Stevens, K. B., & Doak, P. K. (1990). Using constant time delay to teach word definitions. *Journal of Special Education, 24*(3), 306–318.

Silver, E. A. (1981). Recall of mathematical problem information: Solving related problems. *Journal for Research in Mathematics Education, 12,* 54–64.

Skinner, B. F. (1976). Farewell, my lovely! *Journal of Experimental Analysis of Behavior, 25,* 218.

Smith. C. R. (1991). *Learning disabilities: The interaction of learner, task, and setting* (2nd ed.). Boston: Allyn and Bacon.

Stallings, J. (1980). Allocated academic learning time revisited, or beyond time on task. *Educational Researcher, 9,* 11–16.

Stebbins, L., St. Pierre, R. G., Proper, E. L., Anderson, R. B., & Cerva, T. R. (1977). *Education as experimentation: A planned variation model* (vol. 4, A–D). Cambridge, MA: Abt Associates.

Stein, C., & Goldman, J. (1980). Beginning reading instruction for children with minimal brain dysfunction. *Journal of Learning Disabilities, 13,* 219–222.

Stevens, K. B., & Schuster, J. W. (1987). Effects of a constant time delay procedure on the learning disabled student. *Learning Disability Quarterly, 10,* 9–16.

Stevens, K. B., & Schuster, J. W. (1988). Time delay: Systematic instruction for academic tasks. *Remedial and Special Education, 9*(5), 16–21.

Strain, P. S., Lambert, D. L., Kerr, M. M., Stagg, V., & Lenkner, D. A. (1983). Naturalistic assessment of children's compliance to teacher's requests and consequences for compliance. *Journal of Applied Behavior Analysis, 16*, 243–249.

Thomas, J. D., Presland, I. E., Grant, M. D., & Glynn, T. L. (1978). Natural rates of teacher approval and disapproval in grade-7 classrooms. *Journal of Applied Behavior Analysis, 11*, 91–94.

Touchette, P. (1971). Transfer of stimulus control: Measuring the movement of transfer. *Journal of Experimental Analysis of Behavior, 15*, 347–354.

Trifiletti, J. J., Frith, G. H., & Armstrong, S. (1987). Microcomputers versus resource rooms for LD students: A preliminary investigation of the effects on math skills. *Learning Disability Quarterly, 7*, 69–76.

Van Horn, R. (1987). Laser videodisc in education: Endless possibilities. *Phi Delta Kappan, 68*, 696–700.

Vargas, J. (1986). Instructional design flaws in computer assisted instruction. *Phi Delta Kappan, 67*, 738–744.

West, R. P., Young, K. R., & Spooner, F. (1990). Precision teaching, an introduction. *Teaching Exceptional Children, 22*(3), 4–9.

White, M. A. (1975). Natural rates of teacher approval and disapproval in the classroom. *Journal of Applied Behavior Analysis, 8*, 367–372.

White, O. R. (1985). Precision teaching—Precision learning. *Exceptional Children, 52*, 522–524.

White, O. R., & Haring, N. G. (1980). *Exceptional teaching* (2nd ed.). Columbus, OH: Merrill.

White, W. A. T. (1988). A meta-analysis of the effects of direct instruction in special education. *Education and Treatment of Children, 11*, 364–374.

Wilson, C. L., & Sindelar, P. T. (1991). Direct instruction in math word problems: Students with learning disabilities. *Exceptional Child, 57*, 512–519.

Winterling, V. (1990). The effects of constant time delay, practice in writing or spelling, and reinforcement on sight word recognition in a small group. *Journal of Special Education, 24*, 101–116.

Wolery, M., Cybriwsky, C. A., Gast, D. L., & Boyle-Gast, K. (1991). Use of constant time delay and attentional responses with adolescents. *Exceptional Children, 57*, 462–473.

8

Metacognitive Strategies

Kristin S. Scott

The use of metacognitive strategies such as organizers and summarizing is not new, but research in this area is fairly recent and appears promising. Metacognitive strategies have been found to improve performance in reading (Billingsley and Wildman 1988; Tregaskes and Daines 1989; Wong et al. 1986), content area subjects (Haller et al. 1988; Wong et al. 1986), writing, (Ellis and Lenz 1987), and mathematics (Forrest 1981). Metacognitive strategies have been used to improve the academic performance of many students with learning disabilities (LD).

This chapter begins with a model and definition of metacognition, including the theory behind the use of metacognitive strategies, and discussion of the impact of metacognition on the field of LD. Next, research in the area of metacognition is examined in relation to characteristics of successful versus unsuccessful learners. Guidelines for teaching metacognitive strategies are detailed. Then, early theoretical applications of metacognition are examined, including use of advance organizers and the SQ3R method. The later part of the chapter is devoted to examining numerous current metacognition strategies, including mnemonics, visual imagery, self-questioning, mapping, reciprocal teaching, and learning strategies.

THE METACOGNITION MODEL

The term *metacognition* refers to "one's knowledge concerning one's own cognitive processes and products of anything related to them" (Flavell 1976, p. 232)—in other words, knowing what you know and how you know it. Two types of knowledge or activities are included in Flavell's definition: knowledge about cognition and regulation of cognition (Baker and Brown 1984). *Knowledge about cognition* refers to self-awareness of one's own cognitive processes, or awareness of how you think. It also deals with knowing one's cognitive strengths and knowing the relationship between the learning situation and the learner. *Regulation of cognition*, or self-regulation, puts this knowledge into action. The learner actively uses self-regulation to monitor and solve a problem. Activities included in the regulation of cognition are planning, checking, monitoring, testing, revising, and evaluating (Brown 1980). The two aspects of metacognition are crucially important to successful learning.

177

Groteluschen and colleagues (1990) have extended and expanded upon the definition of metacognition to develop a metacognitive model that includes three major components. This model incorporates specific strategy knowledge, executive processes, and general strategy knowledge. The first component, *specific strategy knowledge,* deals with knowledge and understanding of the various strategies that might be used to solve a given problem. The second component, *executive processes,* involves making decisions as to which strategy to employ in a given situation. It also involves monitoring the effectiveness of the strategies and making alternative decisions when necessary. These functions are regulation functions. The *general strategy knowledge* component is the understanding that employing a strategy takes effort and that choosing the correct strategy can lead to improved performance. This component deals with the motivational or attributional aspect of metacognition.

Groteluschen and colleagues (1990) assert that the three components—specific strategy knowledge, executive processes, and general strategy knowledge—interact with each other to promote strategy generalization, as illustrated in Figure 8.1. This model focuses on the purposeful use of a strategy to achieve improved performance.

Metacognition and Learning Disabilities

How important is metacognition to the field of LD? Before addressing this question, we will examine the *strategy-deficit model* of LD, which suggests that children with LD have a difficult time accessing and manipulating knowledge unless they are explicitly instructed to employ certain strategies. Children with LD are often viewed as inefficient learners who have poor or few strategies for solving academic problems. This production deficiency leads to an inability to reach their academic potential (Swanson 1989). The strategy-deficit theory holds that students with LD have problems choosing and using metacognitive strategies to solve problems.

Within the strategy-deficit viewpoint, metacognitive theory has relevance to both research and instruction in the field of LD. If a student with LD is viewed as a maladaptive learner, or one who does not actively participate in his/her learning through the use of strategies, then it follows that the student is having difficulty in some area of metacognition.

Wong (1987) stated that the field of LD has been significantly affected by metacognitive research in three major ways. First, there is an impact on the view of reading problems of individuals with LD. Research in metacognition has found that poor readers (and readers with LD) differ from skilled readers in that they tend to equate reading with decoding, they do not monitor their comprehension while reading, and they demonstrate a lack of effective strategies for reading comprehension (Wong 1987). Second, awareness of metacognition has influenced teaching practices in LD. Research in this area has shown that students with LD demonstrate strategy deficiencies, and thus metacognitive training has been promoted in LD classes (Wong 1987). Finally, metacognitive research has

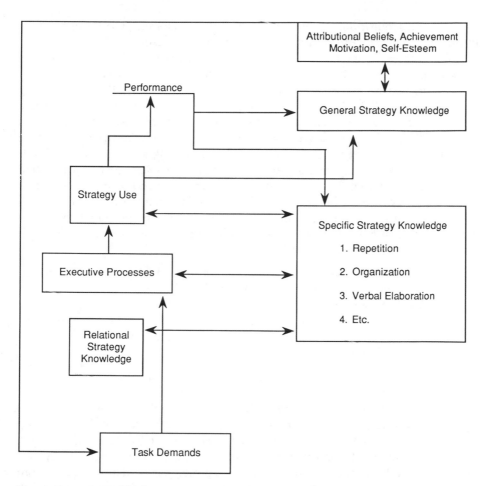

Figure 8.1 A model of metacognition. (From "General Problem-solving Skills: Relations Between Metacognition and Strategic Processing" by J.G. Borkowski, M.T. Estrada, M. Milstead, and C.A. Hale, 1989, *Learning Disability Quarterly,* *12,* 57–70. Reprinted by permission.)

had an impact on teacher awareness and professional interests (Wong 1987). Teachers are becoming increasingly aware and interested in the area of metacognitive strategies through the research literature. Metacognitive research in the field of LD has brought the theoretical aspects of metacognition closer to the practical aspects of using metacognitive strategies in the classroom.

Early Metacognitive Strategies

The adage "Give me a fish, and I can eat for a day—teach me to fish, and I can eat for a lifetime" epitomizes the philosophy of *early metacognitive strategies.* These strategies are defined as "techniques, principles, or rules that will facilitate the acquisition, manipulation, integration, storage, and retrieval of information across situations and settings" (Alley and Deshler 1979, p. 13).

Early research and use of metacognitive strategies are reflected in Ausubel's work in the area of cognitive structure. Ausubel published his first assertions on advance organizers in 1960 and explained his idea of meaningful verbal learning in 1963 (Searls 1983). According to Ausubel (1963), the *advance organizer* is a strategy that prepares the learner in advance to complete a task. This method is used to "bridge the gap between what the learner already knows and what he needs to know before he can meaningfully learn the task at hand." Examples of advance organizers could include general questions a teacher asks that are related to the story or a visual display to assist the student prior to reading. The teacher introduces the organizer before giving the material to be learned. While Ausubel did not specifically define what an advance organizer is, he proposed characteristics a text must have in order to be considered an advance organizer. The advance organizer must (Searls 1983):

1. Be more inclusive, abstract, and general than the learning material
2. Take into account preexisting knowledge of the learner
3. Connect ideas already learned with ideas to be learned
4. Be expository in nature when the learner has little prior knowledge
5. Be comparative when the material can be related to the learner's preexisting knowledge

This concept is one early form of metacognitive instruction, and many teachers in classes for students with LD use advance organizers.

A second metacognitive strategy that has been applied for over 40 years is *SQ3R* (Jacobwitz 1988). This approach, supported by information processing theory, is used to facilitate reading comprehension. It involves five steps: Survey, Question, Read, Recite, and Review (thus SQ3R). The learner sequentially performs each step with the text to be read. This strategy is perhaps the basis from which many other metacognitive strategies were developed. For example, S-RUN, a variation of SQ3R, is also used for improving reading comprehension (Bailey 1988). Both the advance organizer and SQ3R are strategies that have continually been used in the field over the years and have been influential in the development of other strategies.

GUIDELINES FOR USING METACOGNITIVE STRATEGIES
The Learner

When using metacognitive strategies, the teacher should be aware of different learning characteristics between efficient and inefficient learners. Many students with LD fall into the latter group. Some learners seem to come "equipped with strategies" to help them succeed in school; others, including many students with LD, do not possess or are not able to use strategies appropriately. Successful learners and strategy users know about and use strategies to facilitate and monitor their learning, and they can describe strategies they use to aid in their learning. They use a variety of strategies to accomplish a task (Pressley et al. 1989). Poor learners, on the other hand, often appear to be unaware of strategies they could use.

Successful strategy users are also active learners; they relate materials they have learned, they ask questions, and they determine main ideas. Poor learners are considered passive learners, often failing to evaluate and monitor their learning (Tei and Stewart 1984). Because students with LD are often poor strategy users, instruction in the use of strategies is important, and the teacher should keep these learner characteristics in mind.

The Teacher

The teacher of students with LD plays a major role in the teaching of metacognitive strategies. The teacher is the learning strategist, assessing and teaching strategies that the students need to succeed academically. The teacher of students with LD is often also responsible for working with and training other teachers in the school (Alley and Deshler 1979).

It is not sufficient to hand a student a piece of paper with a strategy on it, quickly explain it, and expect the student to be able to know how and when to use it. Teaching strategies to students with LD must be carefully planned and include guided and independent practice, as well as opportunities for generalization.

Palincsar and Ransom (1988) suggest the following way to teach strategies to students. When beginning instruction of metacognitive strategies, the questions "what," "why," and "where" should be answered. This lets the students know what the strategy is that is being taught, reasons why it is being taught, and situations in which the strategy could be used. The teacher might discuss the value and usefulness of the strategy. For example, if teaching a proofreading strategy, the teacher might point out how the strategy could help students carefully examine their school work, personal letters, and even job applications for errors, which in turn might earn the students a good grade or even a job.

Next, the teacher would determine the current ability level of each student with the strategy. The teacher may ask each student to write a short paragraph and proofread it for errors. Then the teacher would begin instruction by relating the steps used in employing the strategy. To determine the steps, the teacher might think about how she or he would complete the task, or a strategy may already be developed for implementation. Next, the teacher would model the strategy and how it is actually used. For example, the teacher might project a paragraph on the overhead to show and "think out loud" the steps used to proofread the text.

Once the strategy has been modeled for the students, the teacher should allow the students to memorize and practice the strategy. This is called *guided practice* and should be considered a team effort. The teacher gives each student the help he or she needs to execute the task, but no more. After guided practice, the students are given opportunities to practice the strategy independently. The teacher should given them feedback about their progress using the strategy. At this stage, maintenance and generalization of the strategy are programmed by providing the students with a variety of settings and situations in which to utilize the strategy. Throughout the strategy instruction, the teacher should be involving the students in the monitoring of their success of selecting and applying the strategies. These general guidelines can be used to teach a range of metacognitive strategies to students with LD.

COMPREHENSIVE METACOGNITIVE INSTRUCTIONAL MODELS
Reciprocal Teaching

Allowing the child to "play the role of teacher" is the basic idea behind *reciprocal teaching*. This is a comprehensive metacognitive instructional model because children effectively learn to govern their own learning endeavors by teaching the skills to others. This method involves the adult teacher assigning a student to be the teacher and "teach" a segment of the text to the small group. The members in the group each read the text silently; then the assigned "teacher" discusses that portion of the text with the group (Keller and Hallahan 1987). As the students begin to become more experienced teachers, they are given greater responsibility.

Reciprocal teaching can be thought of as a process of interactive dialogue among the members of the group (Palincsar and Brown 1984). Four theoretical elements are embodied in the strategy of reciprocal teaching (Moore 1988). *Scaffolding*, the most important element, is the support the teacher gives to the student or "novice" via dialogue that is modeled. The second element discussed by Moore (1988) is the *fading* of the teacher's or expert's role in modeling. Fading allows the students to take more responsibility for their own learning. The third element, *active involvement* in learning, is achieved by allowing the student to take the role of the teacher. *Feedback* is the final essential element of reciprocal teaching. It entails giving the student information as to the efficiency of his or her strategy use, as well as the value of the strategy.

Research in Reciprocal Teaching

While reciprocal teaching is most often considered a strategy to improve reading comprehension, it has also been used to teach the deaf prereading skills (Andrews 1985) and to teach listening skills to young primary children (Palincsar 1986). Research in the area of reciprocal teaching has shown it to be effective in improving comprehension scores; improving ability to summarize, question, clarify, and predict; enabling children to be active learners; and improving daily comprehension test and classroom measures of comprehension scores. These improvements have been found to maintain for up to six months, and regular classroom teachers have also been effective in using reciprocal teaching (Farstrup 1986).

In a study conducted by Palincsar and Brown (1984), seventh-graders who were at least two years behind in comprehension were assigned to one of four groups: reciprocal teaching, locating information, daily assessment, and control group. Students in the reciprocal teaching group were instructed using the reciprocal teaching strategy. Effects on comprehension, as well as on maintenance and generalization of the different approaches, were evaluated. Results showed that the reciprocal teaching group demonstrated significant gains in daily comprehension, while the other groups only made marginal gains. Positive results were also evidenced in maintenance and generalization of the reciprocal teaching approach. During maintenance phase the group obtained 80% correct on comprehension scores. Finally, reciprocal teaching positively affected the comprehension in social studies and science classes.

Instruction in Reciprocal Teaching

Reciprocal teaching is usually conducted in groups of four to seven, but it can be conducted one on one or in larger groups. According to Brown, six students to one teacher is optimum (Farstrup 1986). The adult teacher assigns a student to be the "teacher," who is responsible for a particular segment of text. The group silently reads that portion of the text, after which the assigned teacher leads a discussion on the segment. The discussion leader (1) summarizes or reviews what was read, (2) clarifies any questions or problems, (3) asks questions about the text, and (4) predicts what will happen next in the text (Farstrup 1986; Keller and Hallahan 1987). Throughout the session the adult teacher provides the students with guidance and feedback on their performance. When initially introducing reciprocal teaching to the students, it is important for the adult teacher to model the teacher role, including each of the four responsibilities. Students should be provided opportunities to practice these strategies.

Effective reciprocal teaching, according to Brown, is based on seven principles of instruction (Farstrup 1986). The first principle is the *cooperative learning environment.* The cooperative learning environment enables the students to achieve the goal of making sure that each member of the group understands the segment of text discussed. *Strategies,* including summarizing, questioning, clarifying, and predicting, are the second essential component. The third principle is that these skills or strategies are always *practiced in* the *context* of studying, not in isolation. Next, reciprocal teaching concentrates on *understanding both the content and the strategies* being used. The fifth principle deals with the *adult teacher modeling* the strategies and comprehension activities. *Personal feedback* is also essential so that the students are encouraged to continue their efforts and make progress. Finally, the responsibility for the activities should be placed with the students as soon as possible, thus allowing for *fading* of teacher assistance.

Learning Strategies Curriculum

Numerous strategies named with summarizing acronyms have been developed (e.g., Idol-Maestas 1985; Lenz and Hughes 1990; Schumaker et al. 1982); however, this section will focus on a set of strategies called the *Learning Strate-*

Table 8.1   Learning Strategies Curriculum

Acquisition	Storage	Expression and Demonstration of Competence
Word identification	First-letter mnemonics	Sentences
Paraphrasing	Paired associates	Paragraphs
Self-questioning	Listening and notetaking	Themes
Visual imagery		Test taking
MULTIPASS		Error monitoring
SOS		Assignment completion
Interpreting visual aids		

(From *Learning Strategies Curriculum: The Word Identification Strategy* by B. Lenz, J. Schumaker, D. Deshler, and V. Beals, 1984, by The University of Kansas, Reprinted by permission.)

gies *Curriculum*. These strategies were developed by the University of Kansas Institute for Research in Learning Disabilities to promote academic and social skills that are important for functioning effectively in school (Pressley, Symone, et al. 1989). Strategies addressed by these learning strategies include rehearsal strategies, transformational strategies, organizational strategies, mnemonic strategies, monitoring strategies, and motivational strategies. A wide range of skills are taught in the Learning Strategies Curriculum; the skills are broken down into three strands: acquisition, storage, and expression and demonstration of competence (see Table 8.1). This approach was designed to teach students how to learn rather than to teach specific content information (Deshler and Schumaker 1986).

Research in Learning Strategies

Research investigating the use of learning strategies has shown these strategies to be effective (Lenz and Hughes 1990; Schumaker et al. 1982). Research on two strategies, MULTIPASS and DISSECT, will be examined here. MULTIPASS is a complex strategy used for improving reading comprehension by enabling students to obtain information from text chapters. In an early study, Schumaker and colleagues (1982) taught adolescents with LD to use the MULTIPASS strategy. Instruction involved description of the strategy steps, modeling of the strategy, and practice using the strategy with ability-level and grade-level materials. The learning strategies all contain the same sequence of instructional steps. Table 8.2 shows the MULTIPASS strategy steps taught to the students. Results of the investigation demonstrated that the students learned the MULTIPASS strategy, were able to generalize it to grade-level materials, and improved grades on tests covering the text material. These results indicate that the MULTIPASS strategy was effective in improving reading comprehension.

second strategy, the DISSECT strategy, was investigated for its effective-
improving the word-identification skills of adolescents with LD. The
gy-specific steps for DISSECT can be seen in Table 8.3. In this investiga-
(Lenz and Hughes 1990), students were taught the DISSECT strategy using

Table 8.2 Learning Strategies Curriculum: A textbook reading strategy—MULTIPASS

Survey the chapter using *TISOPT*
    T itle read and paraphrased
    I ntroduction read verbatim and paraphrased
    S ummary read verbatim and paraphrased
    P ictures examined
    T able of contents examined

Size up the information in the chapter using *IQ-WHO*
    I llustrations interpreted
    Q uestions at the end of the chapter read and paraphrased
    W ords in italics defined
    H eadings for each—do *RASPN*
        R ead a heading
        A sk self a question based on heading topic
        S can for the answer
        P ut answer in own words
        N ote important information
    O ther cues that textbook employs are identified and used

Sort Out what has been learned from what needs to be learned using *RAMS*
    R ead the question
    A nswer the question if known
    M ark the question to indicate status
    S EARCH for the answer
        S elect a single heading
        E xamine the content carefully
        A nswer question if possible
        R epeat under another heading if needed
        C heck with someone if still not found
        H assle questions clarified with teacher

(From "A Component Analysis of Effective Learning Strategies" by E. Ellis and B. Lenz, 1987, *Learning Disabilities Focus*, 2, 94–107. Reprinted by permission.)

an eight-step instructional plan. A multiple baseline design across subjects was used to evaluate the effectiveness of the strategy. Results of the study demonstrated that the DISSECT strategy was effective in reducing the number of oral reading errors. However, the word-identification training affected student performance on reading comprehension measures differently.

Instruction in Learning Strategies

Instruction in the use of all learning strategies involves the same eight-step sequence; only the strategy-specific steps vary across the strategies. The steps used to teach a learning strategy are listed and described below (Lenz et al. 1984):

1. *Pretest and Obtain Commitment to Learn.* During this step the students are tested to determine current level of functioning on the particular skill dealt

Table 8.3 Learning Strategies Curriculum: Word identification strategy—DISSECT

D	iscover the context
I	solate the prefix
S	eparate the suffix
S	ay the stem
E	xamine the stem
C	heck with someone
T	ry the dictionary

(From *Learning Strategies Curriculum: The Word Identification Strategy* by B. Lenz, J. Schumaker, D. Deshler, and V. Beals, 1984, by The University of Kansas. Reprinted by permission.)

with by the strategy. The students are informed of their strengths and weaknesses, and a commitment to learn the strategy is obtained from the students.

2. *Describe.* The describe step involves the teacher explaining the strategy to the students. Advantages of using the strategy, when to use the strategy, and the steps of the strategy are all described.

3. *Model.* In this step the teacher models the strategy to the students by "thinking aloud" during each step of the strategy.

4. *Verbal Rehearsal.* During the verbal rehearsal step, the students learn to name the strategy steps to automaticity through "rapid fire" practice.

5. *Controlled Practice and Feedback.* This step involves the students actually practicing the strategy using controlled or ability-level materials. The students receive feedback on their use of the strategy to allow them to improve their performance.

6. *Grade-Appropriate Practice and Feedback.* During this step the students practice the strategy with grade-level materials. This step is seen as the real test of the students' ability to use the strategy. As with step 5, the students receive feedback on their performance and use of the strategy.

7. *Posttest and Obtain Commitment to Generalize.* The students are given a posttest to determine their level of functioning on the skill after receiving training with the strategy. A commitment to learn to generalize the strategy is also obtained.

8. *Generalization.* The last, and perhaps most important, step involves teaching the students to generalize the strategy to new materials and situations. Three phases make up the generalization step: orientation phase, activation phase, and maintenance phase. The students are instructed in the various situations in which the strategy can be used (orientation), are given practice in utilizing the strategy in these new situations (activation), and checked periodically to determine if the strategy has maintained (maintenance).

The Learning Strategies Curriculum utilizes a systematic and sequential set of procedures to teach the strategies. The consistency within the instructional procedures make it easier for students with LD to learn additional learning strategies because they know what to expect.

SPECIFIC METACOGNITIVE STRATEGIES
Visual Imagery

Visual imagery is a strategy by which learners conjure up a visual picture of what they are to learn—a story setting, word pair, or math problem. It is "internalized seeing" (Forrest 1981). This strategy can be used for remembering phone numbers, shopping lists, math formulas, chess moves, people's faces, word pairs, stories, spelling words, and text (Forrest 1981). Visual imagery involves two aspects of memory: visual recognition and visual recall.

Research in Visual Imagery

Research in the area of visual imagery has shown it to be effective with students with LD (Chan et al. 1990; Clark et al. 1984; Ferro and Pressley 1991; Rose et al. 1983). Clark and colleagues (1984) examined both visual imagery and self-questioning as strategies to improve comprehension of written material. Students using the visual imagery strategy were instructed to read a passage and then create a visual image of the passage to aid in the memory of the text. The students were then measured in comprehension of the passage they read. Within a multiple baseline design across strategies, the results demonstrated improvements in comprehension in both reading-ability material and grade-level material with the visual imagery approach. The researchers also noted that total instructional time was only five to seven hours.

The effects of visual imagery and verbal rehearsal as mnemonic aids for children with LD were investigated by Rose and colleagues (1983). Children were randomly assigned to one of three groups: visual imagery instruction, verbal rehearsal instruction, or unaided instruction on reading comprehension. The group receiving visual imagery instruction was asked to pause after reading a few sentences to make a picture or movie of what they had just read. Children in the verbal rehearsal group were taught to pause after reading a few sentences and talk to themselves aloud about what they just read. The unaided group, on the other hand, received no instruction other than to read the story carefully to remember as much as they could. Results of this investigation demonstrated that the group of students who received visual imagery instruction or verbal rehearsal performed better on the measure of comprehension than did the unaided group. As is evidenced from the literature, visual imagery has been shown to be an effective metacognitive strategy with students with LD.

Instruction in Visual Imagery

Because visual imagery relies on visualization ability, the strategy may not be useful for everyone. Poor visual imagers may not be able to effectively use visual imagery as a memory device; therefore, it is important to assess this ability before attempting to teach the visual imagery strategy. Forrest (1981) described a method for determining visual ability that involved asking the child to conjure up a specific image (e.g., friend's face). If he or she is able to do this, then the child is asked to shift the image by changing its color or content. If the child is found

Table 8.4   Visual imagery strategy: RIDER

R ead	Read the first sentence.
I mage	Try to make an image—a picture in your mind.
D escribe	Describe your image.
	If you cannot make an image, explain why you cannot and go on to the next sentence.
	If you can make an image, decide if it is the same as an old image, the old image changed slightly, or a completely new image.
	If you have an image, describe it.
E valuate	Evaluate your image for completeness.
	Check to make certain your image includes as much of the sentence content as possible. If content is missing, adjust your image and continue.
	If your image is complete, then continue.
R epeat	Read the next sentence and repeat steps 1 through 4.

(From "Visual Imagery and Self-questioning: Strategies to Improve Comprehension of Written Material" by F. Clark, D. Deshler, J. Schumaker, G. Alley, and M. Warner, 1984, *Journal of Learning Disabilities, 17,* 145–149. Copyright 1984 by PRO-ED, Inc. Reprinted by permission.)

to possess visualization ability, then he or she can be taught to utilize visual imagery as a metacognitive strategy.

When teaching visual imagery as a strategy, several points need to be considered. First, the strategy must be *taught;* while this may seem obvious, it must be remembered that children may not simply be able to "get a picture in their mind" just by being instructed to do so. Second, teach the strategy using materials that facilitate visual imaging; do not ask students to employ the visual imagery strategy on a passage that does not lend itself to imagery. Third, the strategy should be taught explicitly and step by step. Clark and colleagues (1984) have designed a step-by-step procedure for utilizing visual imagery as a strategy (see Table 8.4). Fourth, be sure to teach the learner when it is appropriate to use this strategy, as some passages do not lend themselves to visual imagery. This will aid in generalization of the strategy. Visual imagery can be a beneficial strategy for students with LD when taught within these guidelines.

Story Mapping

The strategy of story mapping is used to improve reading comprehension. A *story map* is a type of pictorial map that helps the learner to organize information from a story or text. Story mapping is based on the *schema theory,* which asserts that the relationship between a person's knowledge structures, or schemata, and the reading material determines the degree of comprehension (Idol and Croll 1987). Schemata can be built upon by helping the reader to become more aware of the relationship between the schemata and the reading material. This can be accomplished through the use of story mapping (Idol and Croll 1987). An example of a story map can be seen in Figure 8.2.

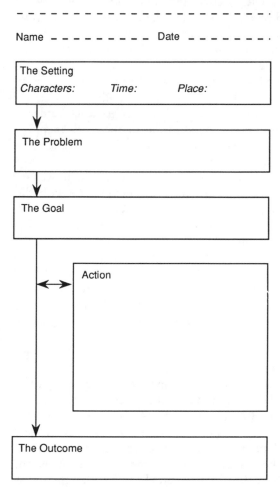

My Story Map

- .

Name - - - - - - - - Date - - - - - - - .

The Setting
Characters:　　*Time:*　　*Place:*

The Problem

The Goal

Action

The Outcome

Figure 8.2　Components of the story map. (From "Group Story Mapping: A Comprehension Strategy for Both Skilled and Unskilled Readers" by L. Idol, 1987, *Journal of Learning Disabilities, 20,* 196–205. Copyright 1987 by PRO-ED, Inc. Reprinted by permission.)

Research in Story Mapping

The use of story mapping has been found to be effective in improving the reading comprehension of students with mild handicaps (Fowler and Davis 1985; Idol 1987; Idol and Croll 1987). Torgesen and Licht (1983) assert that graphic representations make reading materials more accessible to students with LD. Often texts have poor structure, and story mapping facilitates the structuring of these texts for student comprehension.

A study that supports the use of story mapping was conducted by Idol and Croll (1987). These authors examined the reading comprehension of five elementary students with mild handicaps using a multiple-baseline ABA design. The primary dependent measure was a set of 10 comprehension questions. During baseline condition, students read a story and were then asked comprehension questions by the teacher. The intervention condition was made up of a model phase and a lead phase. The model phase consisted of the teacher modeling how to use the story map as the student came to relevant parts in reading the story. In the lead phase the student read the story and completed the story map. At the end of each session the teacher asked the student a set of comprehension questions. Results indicated that four of the five students demonstrated gains in comprehension on daily reading lessons from the baseline condition to the intervention condition. Also, the four students who reached mastery level were able to maintain their improvement. However, generalization of the story mapping strategy was not as successful; only two students showed improvement in generalization.

The *story frame approach,* similar to the story mapping approach, was investigated by Fowler and Davis (1985). These authors examined its use with two students with mild disabilities. Using the story frame approach involves the student filling in information about the story while reading it. This information might include the story problem, the sequence of events, how the problem was solved, and how the story ends. Results of this investigation demonstrated significant gains in comprehension from baseline to intervention conditions for both students. While this study involved only two students, their improvements are noteworthy. Story mapping has been shown to be effective in improving daily comprehension scores, though further investigation must be conducted regarding generalization of this strategy.

Instruction in Story Mapping

When teaching a student how to use story mapping to increase reading comprehension, the teacher should begin by modeling the procedure. The teacher should explain the story map (Figure 8.2), its components (the setting, the problem, the goal, action, and the outcome), and how it is used. After the child and teacher have read the story or text, the teacher completes each part of the story map, explaining to the student the reasoning behind the answers. After the teacher has modeled the entire process for the student, she or he may then wish to show the student how to retell the story from the story map. The student then practices story mapping with additional stories or texts by first reading the material and then filling in the story map. The teacher should have the student retell the story using the story map. The completed story map should successfully organize and structure the text so that the student will be better able to answer comprehension questions relating to the story.

Several points need to be remembered when teaching students the story mapping strategy. First, the teacher needs to be certain that each component of the story map is understood by the student and that the student can given an example of the type of information to be placed in each part. Second, the teacher must be sure to provide a proper process model for the student and allow for sufficient guided practice opportunities. Third, the how, when, and why of the strategy must be explained so that the student understands when it is proper to use story mapping, specifically how to execute the strategy, and that story mapping helps the student to organize and understand what he or she has read, thus improving comprehension.

Self-Questioning

Self-questioning is a strategy used to improve reading comprehension. It is based upon the self-regulation aspects of metacognition (Keller and Hallahan 1987) and allows readers to become independent in their understanding of the text (Swicegood and Parsons 1989). With this strategy, students are taught to generate questions about the text being read to facilitate comprehension of the text. This metacognitive intervention has been found to be effective in helping students with LD learn to recall main ideas, recall explicit and implicit sentences in text, monitor comprehension, and utilize previous knowledge to assist in comprehension (Wong 1985b). The self-questioning approach utilizes self-talk instruction to encourage active learning on the part of the student (Swicegood and Parsons 1989).

Research in Self-Questioning

Research in the area of self-questioning and students with LD has been somewhat positive. Findings have shown self-questioning and variations of self-questioning to be beneficial in improving reading comprehension (Billingsley and Wildman 1988; Graves and Levin 1989; Griffey et al. 1988; Wong 1985b; Wong and Jones 1982; Wong et al. 1986). For example, Wong and colleagues (1986) found that a self-questioning summarization strategy was effective in improving retention of social studies material, was generalizable to science, and that students with LD were able to modify the strategy to best fit their needs. When compared to a traditional approach and the keyword method (discussed later in this chapter), the self-questioning monitoring strategy was determined to be more effective than the other approaches (Graves and Levin 1989).

Wong and Jones (1982) conducted a study on the effects of self-questioning training in students with LD and normally achieving students on comprehension performance. In this study, eighth- and ninth-grade students with LD were randomly assigned to either a control group or the self-questioning training group. The training group received a five-step training session in which students learned to monitor their understanding of texts. Findings demonstrated that the training facilitated comprehension performance, enhanced awareness of important parts of the text, and increased ability to develop good questions about the text.

Billingsley and Wildman (1988) examined the influence of self-questioning and a variation of self-questioning on comprehension monitoring of adolescents with LD. In this study, students were assigned to one of three groups: control group, self-questioning only group, and self-questioning plus structure overview. The self-questioning only group was told to think of questions they would like to ask about the topic prior to reading the passage. The self-questioning plus structured overview group had the opportunity to ask questions prior to reading but also was given a framework of main ideas of the passage. Results from this study indicated that the group receiving self-questioning plus structure overview instruction performed significantly better than the other two groups. These results suggest that some type of prereading activity or advance organizer, in addition to self-questioning training, may be most beneficial. It should also be pointed out that the self-questioning strategy described in this study differed somewhat from the traditional self-questioning technique in that students were encouraged to ask questions only before reading the passage, rather than during the passage. The questions the students asked, therefore, may not have related directly to the actual passage topic.

Instruction in Self-Questioning

Wong (1985) proposed that the most effective self-questioning training includes direct instruction in planning and monitoring one's behavior, as well as performance on the task. Students must be made aware of the questioning process used to facilitate reading comprehension (Swicegood and Parsons 1989). The self-questioning strategy can be seen as showing the students what the teacher does when developing questions for a test and explaining to them that this method will facilitate their studying.

As with other strategies, the teacher models the process. During the direct instruction of the self-questioning strategy, several steps should be modeled (Wong and Jones 1982):

1. Ask "Why are you studying the text?" (To be able to answer questions later).
2. Locate and underline the main ideas in the text.
3. Develop questions about the main ideas.
4. Learn the answers to the questions.
5. Look back at the questions and answers to see how the new questions provide more new information.

In addition, the learner needs to be aware of the types of questions to ask prior to reading the passage, while reading the passage, and after reading the passage (Tei and Stewart 1984). Examples of these types of questions are given in Table 8.5.

Several considerations need to be kept in mind when teaching self-questioning to students with LD. First, self-questioning itself may vary in its goal, from problem solving to processing a passage (Wong 1985b); the goal should be considered when determining how instruction will be conducted. Second, students' prior knowledge may curtail or enhance their ability to develop relevant questions (thus facilitating comprehension), depending on the amount of relevant information they possess on the topic. Finally, the presence of explicit written instruction or direct instruction will lead to more successful self-questioning strategy usage than instruction that is not as structured (Wong 1985b). The teacher who attends to these considerations will be able to better develop a successful self-questioning training program (see Table 8.6).

Table 8.5 Self-Questioning

Question to Ask Prior to Reading:
How does the author convey the information?
What concepts are introduced?
How are the concepts related to each other?
How is the material organized?
Can I follow the organization?

Questions to Ask While Reading:
Did I understand the main ideas in the section?
How are the ideas in this section related to the previous section?
Did the author introduce a new concept in this section?
Can I make a connection between all concepts presented?

Questions to Ask After Reading:
Do I understand everything I have read?
Can I give a brief summary of what I have read?
Can I outline the chapter?
Can I list the main points of the text?
How much of this information is new and how much did I already know?

(Adapted from Tei and Stewart [1984].)

The Mnemonic Keyword Method

Mnemonic strategies are used to improve memory for information; the *keyword method* is a type of mnemonic strategy. This method "combines visual and auditory cues to provide a direct link between the 'asked' stimulus and the 'asked for' response" (McLoone et al. 1986, p. 45). The keyword method has three components: (1) the *recoding* component, which transform the term to be learned into a similar sounding, familiar "keyword"; (2) the *relating* component, in which an interactive picture of the keyword and the term to be learned is formed; and (3) the *retrieving* component, used as a recall strategy (Keller and Hallahan 1987). With the keyword method the teacher provides the students with a keyword for the word to be learned and a picture of the keyword interacting with the response word (McLoone et al. 1986). After learning the strategy, students may enjoy picking out keywords themselves and devising memorable pictures. This mnemonic method has been found to be effective in teaching English vocabulary, Italian vocabulary, attributes of North American minerals, attributes of prehistoric reptiles, reasons dinosaurs are extinct, and U.S. history (Pressley et al. 1989).

Research in the Mnemonic Keyword Method

Mnemonic strategies, the keyword method in particular, have been found to be quite beneficial in memory enhancement (Mastropieri and Mushinski-Fulk 1990; Mastropieri and Scruggs 1988; Mastropieri et al. 1985; McLoone et al. 1986; Pressley et al. 1982). Research has shown that using the keyword method

Table 8.6   Types of Question–Answer Relationships: A self-questioning technique*

Right There:
    These are questions that can be answered directly from the story. They are usually literal questions and can be answered from one or two sentences in the story.

Think and Search:
    Think and search questions are questions to which the answers can be found in the text, but the answer must be pulled together from several places in the text.

Author and You:
    These questions require the reader to use prior knowledge to make inferences and draw conclusions to develop answers.

On Your Own:
    On-your-own questions involve the reader in using his or her own experiences to answer the question. The questions cannot be answered from the text.

*The Question–Answer Relationships (QAR) method, developed by Raphael (1982), is used to aid in comprehension of stories and texts.

improves students' performance on immediate and delayed recall, students enjoy using the method, teachers enjoy using the strategy, teachers believe students are more motivated when using the strategy, and students participate more in instruction under mnemonic conditions (Mastropieri and Mushinski-Fulk 1990). In addition, when compared to self-questioning monitoring, the keyword method was found to be more effective for remembering main ideas (Graves and Levin 1989).

A study conducted by McLoone and colleagues (1986) compared the effects of mnemonic instruction (the keyword method) to direct rehearsal instruction on vocabulary acquisition of seventh- and eighth-grade students with LD. Students were randomly assigned to either the mnemonic instruction group or the direct rehearsal group; each group participated in a training task and a transfer task. The training task involved the instructor training the students to learn vocabulary words using the group-specific strategy. In the transfer task, students received training in how to use the strategy independently. Results demonstrated that students receiving the mnemonic instruction (keyword method) significantly outperformed the other group in both the training task and the transfer task.

While much of the research in mnemonic instruction deals with vocabulary acquisition, Mastropieri and Scruggs (1988) examined the effects of this strategy on the learning of U.S. history material. Junior high students with LD from four classrooms were instructed by their teachers using the mnemonic method (the keyword method) and the traditional textbook method. Each chapter was designated to be taught using one of the approaches. The order of the types of instruction was counterbalanced so that each class had a different treatment order. Students were tested at the end of each chapter, as well as with a cumulative test.

In the mnemonic approach the teacher identified the important information and then provided the students with the strategy to aid in their recall of the information. In the traditional method the teacher simply identified the important information. Results revealed that students learned more content using the mnemonic approach and performed better on the chapter tests and cumulative test. In addition, teachers and students rated the mnemonic approach more favorably than the traditional approach. The authors did note, however, that the students failed to transfer the strategy and use it independently, indicating that strategy generalization must be trained. Most of the research findings support the use of mnemonic strategies, such as the keyword method, for enhancing memory; however, it must be remembered that transfer of the strategy does not occur automatically.

Instruction in the Mnemonic Keyword Method

When instructing students in using the keyword method, the three components mentioned earlier—recoding, relating, retrieving—(Keller and Hallahan 1987) must be included. First the teacher should instruct the students in the meaning and function of a keyword: A *keyword* is a word that sounds like the word to be learned and is familiar and easily pictured. When the student understands the function of a keyword, an example is in order. The student is given a word to learn and its meaning. For example, the Italian word "testa" means head. A keyword that sounds similar to "testa" is "test," which can be easily pictured. The teacher then shows or has the students imagine an interacting picture of the word meaning and the keyword. In Figure 8.3, the picture shows a test (keyword, which sounds like "testa") sitting on a head (meaning). The teacher then instructs the students to remember the picture of the test on the head (McLoone et al. 1986).

To retrieve the information using the recall strategy, the students are taught to remember the keyword, remember the image, and retrieve the information to be remembered from the interactive picture (Keller and Hallahan 1987). The instruction session might be implemented as described by McLoone and colleagues (1986): The teacher presents a card with a vocabulary word, keyword, definition, and interactive picture. She or he then explains, "The keyword for (word) is (keyword), and (word) means (meaning). Remember this picture of (interactive picture). Remember this picture of what? ... And (word) means what? ... " Important considerations when using mnemonic strategies include reinforcing for recalling the information, feedback to strategy use (McLoone et al. 1986), sufficient modeling and explanation of the strategy, and training in generalization of strategy use.

SUMMARY

This chapter has examined metacognition and how it relates to students with LD. A definition and model of metacognition were provided as a framework for theory and research. Characteristics of good strategy learners were discussed

TESTA (TEST)   HEAD

Figure 8.3 Mnemonic keyword method representation of "testa" = head. (From "Memory Strategy Instruction and Training with Learning Disabled Adolescents" by B. McLoone, T. Scruggs, M. Mastropieri, and S. Zucker, 1986, *Learning Disabilities Research, 2,* 45–53. Reprinted by permission.)

in relation to how they use strategies, when they use strategies, and how they monitor strategy use. In addition, guidelines for teaching metacognitive strategies were detailed. Next, the impact of metacognition on the field of LD was described.

The latter part of the chapter focused on specific strategy approaches. Strategies including reciprocal teaching, visual imagery, self-questioning, keyword method and story mapping. Strategies summarized by acronyms (learning strategies) were also described. Research on the effectiveness of each strategy was discussed, and guidelines for teaching each strategy were given.

REFERENCES

Alley, G., & Deshler, D. (1979). *Teaching the learning disabled adolescent: Strategies and methods.* Denver, CO: Love.

Andrews, J. (1985). *Deaf children's acquisition of pre-reading skills using the reciprocal teaching procedure.* (Tech. Rep. No. 350). Urbana: University of Illinois, Center for the Study of Reading.

Ausubel, D. (1963). *The psychology of meaningful verbal learning.* New York: Grune & Stratton.

Bailey, N. S. (1988). S-RUN: Beyond SQ3R. *Journal of Reading, 32,* 170–171.

Baker, L., & Brown, A. (1984). Metacognitive skills of reading. In D. P. Pearson (Ed.), *Handbook on research in reading.* New York: Longman.

Billingsley, B. S., & Wildman, T. M. (1988). The effects of prereading activities on the comprehension of learning disabled adolescents. *Learning Disabilities Research, 4,* 36–44.

Bos, C. S. (1983). Comprehensive monitoring. *The Pointer, 27,* 22–27.

Brown, A. L. (1980). Metacognitive development and reading. In R. J. Spiro, B. Bruce, & W. F. Brewer (Eds.), *Theoretical issues in reading comprehension.* Hillsdale, NJ: Erlbaum.

Chan, L. K., Cole, P. G., & Morris, J. N. (1990). Effects of instruction in the use of a visual-imagery strategy on the reading-comprehension competence of disabled and average readers. *Learning Disabilities Quarterly, 13,* 2–11.

Clark, F. L., Deshler, D. D., Schumaker, J. B., Alley, G. R., & Warner, M. M. (1984). Visual imagery and self-questioning: Strategies to improve comprehension of written material. *Journal of Learning Disabilities, 17,* 145–149.

Deshler, D. D., & Schumaker, J. B. (1986). Learning strategies: An instructional alternative for low-achieving adolescents. *Exceptional Children, 52*, 583–590.

Ellis, E. S., & Lenz, B. K. (1987). A component analysis of effective learning strategies. *Learning Disabilities Focus, 2*, 94–107.

Ellis, E. S., & Lenz, B. K. (1990). Techniques for mediating content-area learning: Issues and research. *Focus on Exceptional Children, 22*, 1–16.

Farstrup, A. E. (1986). 1985 IRA award winning research. *Reading Teacher, 39*, 692–696.

Ferro, S. C., & Pressley, M. G. (1991). Imagery generation by learning disabled and average-achieving 11- to 13-year-olds. *Learning Disability Quarterly, 14*, 231–239.

Flavell, J. H. (1976). Metacognitive aspects of problem solving. In L. B. Resnick (Ed.), *The nature of intelligence*. Hillsdale, NJ: Erlbaum.

Forrest, E. B. (1981). Visual imagery as an information processing strategy. *Journal of Learning Disabilities, 14*, 584–586.

Fowler, G. L., & Davis, M. (1985). The story frame approach: A tool for improving reading comprehension of EMR children. *Teaching Exceptional Children, 17*, 296–298.

Graves, A. W., & Levin, J. R. (1989). Comparison of monitoring and mnemonic text-processing strategies in learning disabled students. *Learning Disability Quarterly, 12*, 232–236.

Griffey, Q. L., Zigmond, N., & Leinhardt, G. (1988). The effects of self-questioning and story structure training on the reading comprehension of poor readers. *Learning Disabilities Research, 4*, 45–51.

Groteluschen, A. K., Borkowski, J. G., & Hale, K. (1990). Strategy instruction is often insufficient: Addressing interdependency of executive and attributional processes. In T. E. Scruggs & B. Y. L. Wong (Eds.), *Intervention research in learning disabilities* (pp. 81–101). New York: Springer-Verlag.

Haller, E. P., Child, D. A., & Walberg, H. J. (1988). Can comprehension be taught? A quantitative synthesis of "metacognitive" studies. *Educational Researcher, 17*, 5–8.

Idol, L. (1987). Group story mapping: A comprehension strategy for both skilled and unskilled readers. *Journal of Learning Disabilities, 20*, 196–205.

Idol, L., & Croll, V. J. (1987). Story-mapping training as a means of improving reading comprehension. *Learning Disability Quarterly, 10*, 214–229.

Idol-Maestas. L. (1985). Getting ready to read: Guided probing for poor comprehenders. *Learning Disability Quarterly, 8*, 243–252.

Jacobwitz, T. (1988). Using theory to modify practice: An illustration with SQ3R. *Journal of Reading, 32*, 126–131.

Keller, C. E., & Hallahan, D. P. (1987). *Learning disabilities: Issues and instructional intervention*. Washington, DC: National Education Association.

Lenz, B. K., & Hughes, C. A. (1990). A word identification strategy for adolescents with learning disabilities. *Journal of Learning Disabilities, 23*, 149–158.

Lenz, B. K., Schumaker, J. B., Deshler, D. D., & Beals, V. L. (1984). *Learning strategies curriculum: The word identification strategy*. Lawrence: The University of Kansas.

Lewis, R. B. (1983). Learning disabilities and reading: Instructional recommendations from current research. *Exceptional Children, 50*, 230–240.

Mastropieri, M. A., & Mushinski-Fulk, B. J. (1990). Enhancing academic performance with mnemonic instruction. In T. E. Scruggs & B. Y. L. Wong (Eds.). *Intervention research in learning disabilities* (pp. 102–121). New York: Springer-Verlag.

Mastropieri, M. A., & Scruggs, T. E. (1988). Increasing content area learning of learning disabled students: Research implementation. *Learning Disabilities Research, 4*, 17–25.

Mastropieri, M. A., Scruggs, T. E., Levin, J. R., Gaffney, J., & McLoone, B. (1985). Mnemonic vocabulary instruction for learning disabled students. *Learning Disability Quarterly, 8*, 57–63.

McLoone, B., Scruggs, T. E., Mastropieri, M. A., & Zucker, S. F. (1986). Memory strategy instruction and training with learning disabled adolescents. *Learning Disabilities Research, 2*, 45–53.

Moore, P. J. (1988). Reciprocal teaching and reading comprehension: A review. *Journal of Research in Reading, 11*, 3–14.

Palincsar, A. (1986). Metacognitive strategy instruction. *Exceptional Children, 53,* 118–124.

Palincsar, A., & Brown, A. (1984). Reciprocal teaching of comprehension fostering and monitoring activities. *Cognition and Instruction, 1,* 117–175.

Palincsar, A., & Ransom, K. (1988). From the mystery spot to the thoughtful spot: The instruction of metacognitive strategies. *The Reading Teacher, 41,* 784–789.

Pressley, M., Borkowski, J. G., & O'Sullivan, J. (1985). Children's metamemory and the teaching of memory strategies. In D. L. Forrest-Pressley, G. E. MacKinnon, & T. G. Waller (Eds), *Metacognition, cognition, and human performance: Vol. 1. Theoretical perspectives* (pp. 111–153). New York: Academic Press.

Pressley, M., Levin, J. R., & Delaney, H. D. (1982). The mnemonic keyword method. *Review of Educational Research, 52,* 61–91.

Pressley, M., Scruggs, T. E., & Mastropieri, M. A. (1989). Memory strategy research in learning disabilities: Present and future directions. *Learning Disabilities Research, 4,* 68–77.

Pressley, M., Symone, S., Snyder, B. L., & Cariglia-Bull, T. (1989). Strategy instruction research comes of age. *Learning Disability Quarterly, 12,* 16–30.

Raphael, T. E. (1982). Question-answering strategies for children. *Reading Teacher, 36,* 186–190.

Rose, M. C., Cundick, B. P., Higbee, K. L. (1983). Verbal rehearsal and visual imagery: Mnemonic aids for learning-disabled children. *Journal of Learning Disabilities, 16,* 352–354.

Schumaker, J. B., Deshler, D. D., Alley, G. R., Warner, M. M., & Denton, P. H. (1982). MULTIPASS: A learning strategy for improving reading comprehension. *Learning Disability Quarterly, 5,* 295–304.

Searls, E. F. (1983). An advance organize is . . . all or none of the above. *Reading Horizons, 23,* 242–248.

Simmonds, E., Luchow, J. D., Kaminsky, S., & Cottone, V. (1989). Applying cognitive learning strategies in the classroom: A collaborative training institute. *Learning Disabilities Focus, 4,* 96–105.

Swanson, H. L. (1989). Strategy instruction: Overview of principles and procedures for effective use. *Learning Disability Quarterly, 12,* 3–13.

Swicegood, P. R., & Parsons, J. L. (1989). Better questions and answers equal success. *Teaching Exceptional Children, 21,* 4–8.

Tei, E., & Stewart, O. (1984). Effective studying from text: Applying metacognitive strategies. *Forum for Reading, 16,* 46–55.

Torgesen, J. K., & Licht, B. G. (1983). The learning disabled child as an inactive learner: Retrospect and prospects. In J. D. McKinney & L. Feagans (Eds.), *Current topics in learning disabilities* (pp. 184–197). Norwood, NJ: Ablex.

Tregaskes, M. R., & Daines, D. (1989). Effects of metacognitive strategies on reading comprehension. *Reading Research and Instruction, 29,* 52–60.

Wong, B. Y. L. (1985a). Metacognition and learning disabilities. In D. L. Forrest-Pressley, G. E. MacKinnon, & T. G. Waller (Eds.), *Metacognition, cognition, and human performance: Vol. 2. Instructional practices* (pp. 137–180). New York: Academic Press.

Wong, B. Y. L. (1985b). Self-questioning instructional research: A review. *Review of Educational Research, 55,* 227–268.

Wong, B. Y. L. (1987). How do the results on metacognitive research impact on the learning disabled individual? *Learning Disability Quarterly, 10,* 189–195.

Wong, B. Y. L., & Jones, W. (1982). Increasing metacomprehension in learning disabled and normally achieving students through self-questioning training. *Learning Disability Quarterly, 5,* 228–239.

Wong, B. Y. L., Wong, R., Perry, N., & Sawatsky, D. (1986). The efficacy of a self-questioning summarization strategy for use by underachievers and learning disabled adolescents in social studies. *Learning Disabilities Focus, 2,* 20–35.

9

Building a Pragmatic Language

Carol Weller

The process of building language in students with learning disabilities (LD) is similar to the process of building a house. If you've ever built a house, the analogies presented here will mean a great deal to you. If you're dreaming about building one—or even if you don't have such dreams—the analogies presented here should give you a concrete foundation that you can use to teach language skills to students with learning disabilities.

Building a house and building language require organizational processes that evolve and develop over time. From their earliest beginnings until they reach sophistication, language and houses require organized thinking to manage desired outcomes and affect social situations. Applied to language the process is called communication. Internal thought processes are *cognition;* external processes are *pragmatic language* (Bender and Golden 1988; Feagans 1983; Snyder 1982). Because language exists for the comprehension, formulation, and transmission of meaning, cognition and pragmatic language conjoin to manage social discourse (Oller 1989).

Three constructs must be addressed when considering the process of building language. These are: (1) *lexical development,* which provides the foundation for using sounds, words, meanings, and grammar; (2) *intentional usage,* which defines the purpose of language in social, situational, and communicative contexts; and (3) *communication management,* which dictates the flexibility and adaptivity with which the language is used. This chapter will describe these constructs and present examples of instructional practices that can be used to teach students with learning disabilities.

LEXICAL DEVELOPMENT

Lexical development is to social discourse as engineering is to building construction. Both begin with the acquisition of forms that evolve into networks that develop into patterns that interrelate to bring coherence to the environment. In the early years, students learn linguistic forms. These forms provide the footing for communication and include: sound formation (phonology), word formation morphology, word meaning (semantics), and sentence formation (syntax). As students acquire and enlarge their use of these forms, they develop lexical networks that can be used in communication (Nippold 1988). These networks harden to become structures used repeatedly in communication. Vocabulary networks organize classes of words including nouns, adverbs, descriptors, connectors, and verbs. Syntactic networks organize components of sentence building such as phrases, clauses, interrogatives, and declaratives. These networks mature into communication patterns that interconnect and provide essential fields of relationship that are used to solve problems.

Lexical development and building construction are analogous in the sequence used to develop ideas for houses and that used to teach language. In house building, rank beginners look at houses without seeing features. As they mature, they directly observe floor plans and study pictures of houses they like. In early language, preschoolers acquire language without knowing that others' communication is stimulating their learning. At about second-grade level, they begin to profit from direct instruction in lexical learning of linguistic forms in isolation (Nippold 1988). As lexical learning progresses, direct instruction is minimized and students are taught a scholarly method of using abstractions and contextual clues to develop networks of word classes based on meaning of unfamiliar words (Miller and Gildea 1987). In house building, this stage equates to getting a feeling for houses while driving through attractive neighborhoods and attending parade-of-homes tours.

At about the 4th-grade level, written language becomes the major contributor to lexicons and, as a result, students who read widely develop better vocabulary and syntactical networks (Nelson 1977; Oller 1979). Likewise, persons building their home avidly read relevant books, catalogs, and brochures. By the 12-grade level, most students have developed a sophisticated lexicon that includes words that are cultural, historical, scientific, technological, and political. In addition, they have developed an organized syntactic pattern where semantically related words become associated closely as synonyms, antonyms, and by shade of meaning (Dale and Eichholz 1960). By this level, home builders deal with equivalent external factors of terrain, climate, and potential for natural disaster. Like users of language, they integrate many factors—in this case probabilities, contingencies, consequences, and Murphy's law—into their lexicon.

The development of this lexicon is important in that it provides the foundation for pragmatic usage and rule making (Bates 1976; Blank et al. 1979; Spekman 1981). According to Gibbs and Cooper (1989), the prevalence of phonological, morphological, semantic, and syntactical problems among 8- to 12-year-old students with learning disabilities may reach as high as 90.5%. This prevalence is significant and indicates that teaching linguistic forms and networks to students with learning disabilities is an important consideration for instruction.

FORMS AND NETWORKS

In building construction, forms include foundations, frames, and systems for heating and cooling. Although they undergird a house, these forms are not sufficient by themselves. In lexical development, forms include phonology and

Table 9.1 Similarities among modes of communication

Characteristics*	Terms		
	Linguistics	Reading	Writing
Sounds	Phonology	Phonics	Letters
Words	Morphology	Decoding	Spelling
Meaning	Semantics	Comprehension	Vocabulary
Word order	Syntax	Grammar	Sentence Structure
Melody and rhythm	Prosody	Inflection	Flow
Social	Pragmatics	Application	Style

*Both understanding and use.
From Catts, 1992.

morphology. *Phonology* is the study of sound formation (phonemes) and is related to both speech and language. *Morphology* is the study of word formation (morphemes) and involves the understanding and use of words and word classes (e.g., pronouns, verbs, adverbs, connectives) as well as manipulating words in plural, possessive, and reflexive forms. Morphemic combining with affixes and production of compounds words also is involved. Phonology and morphology undergird language but are not the sum of an integrated communication system (Norris and Damico 1990). They are important to pragmatic language when poor discrimination of sounds, miscues in oral expression, or use of incorrect word structures either interfere with social communication or identify a student negatively (Bates 1976). In addition, these components of lexical development contribute to reading and written expression (Cummins 1983; Semel and Wiig 1975; Wiig et al. 1977).

In building construction, forms are incorporated into networks that are nonstructural (e.g., zones, cooking layouts, private versus public spaces) or structural (e.g., entryways, rooflines, exteriors, bedrooms). In lexicons, forms also develop into nonstructural and structural networks. *Nonstructural networks* are those that are abstract and include the use of vocabulary and word meaning (*semantics*) as well as paralinguistic features. *Structural networks* are those that are linear and include sentence order, word usage, and grammar (*syntax*). Students with insufficient lexical forms and networks have difficulty expressing, reading, and writing words that are not understood in their oral repertories (Magee and Newcomer 1978; Oller 1979; Semel and Wiig 1975). The similarities within and between the forms and networks of these modes of communication are presented in Table 9.1. Examples of problems students with learning disabilities encounter in understanding and using networks are described in the sections that follow.

Semantics

Difficulties understanding and using semantics have been purported to be a significant contributor to the communication problems of students with learning disabilities (Wiig et al. 1981). Semantics involves word meaning, and students with problems in semantics usually have a less than total ability to understand others or to express themselves (Semel and Wiig 1975; Wiig et al. 1977). Vocabulary may be limited, the shade of meaning between words such as "warm" and "tepid" may be misunderstood; the meaning of abstract words such as "justice" or "mercy" may be unclear; and confusion of duals may be evidenced (e.g., expecting to see blocks or steel girders rather than cards when hearing the word "bridge"). Other problems that may be present include:

1. Confusion with complex actions or movements associated with verbs such as "evading," "harnessing," or "twisting"
2. Misinterpretation of qualitative adjectives and adverbs such as "fast," "quickly," "distant," "infinite"
3. Confusion with temporal prepositional phrases such as "around 5 o'clock" or "after a while"
4. Miscommunication of adverbial qualifiers such as "never," "rarely," "seldom" and "perhaps," "definitely," "probably"
5. Problems with demonstrative pronouns such as "this," "that," "these," and "those" or "who," "whom," "which," and "that"
6. Misunderstanding of differences in connotation and denotation of given words
7. Misinterpretation of inferred negative statements such as "You really don't think this house is pretty, do you?"

Paralinguistics

Paralinguistics is the study of the artifacts of semantic communication (Prutting and Kirchner 1987). These artifacts include nonverbal features such as proximity of speaker to listener (e.g., too close or too distant); appearance and demeanor that relate to communication (e.g., dress, use of cosmetics, bathing); and kinesic use of the body, eye gaze, facial expression, and hand and arm movement that is inappropriate or mismatched to the semantic content of a communication (Minskoff 1980a,b). In addition, they include vocal features such as inappropriate laughter, pitch, tempo, loudness, pause, intelligibility, fluency, vocal quality, vocal intensity, and prosody (the musical intonation of speech). According to Lapadat (1991), deficiencies in understanding these cues when given by others and using them in personal lexicons constitute a significant difficulty for students with learning disabilities.

Syntax

Syntax is the structural arrangement of words in the appropriate orders that form the grammar of sentences. Like semantics, the understanding and use of syntax has been purported to be a major problem among students with LD (Wiig and Semel 1980). Lack of understanding of syntactical networks leads to confusion in the communication of humor, determination of courses of action, and logical reasoning. Difficulties in these areas mark students as shallow, boring, and socially impotent in conversations with their peers.

The syntax of English requires students to understand and use basic sentence types; understand and initiate sentence that are statements, questions, or commands; and to integrate appropriate phrases and clauses into these types (Wiig and Semel 1980). Syntax also requires adjusting sentence order to fit changes in tense, person, or voice by using inflection, intonation, and recombining (Vogel 1983). Syntactical difficulties are evidenced by:

1. Confusion with tenses in statements such as "He should have been ready sooner" or "I will have brought it by then"
2. Misinterpretation of nuance that gives a word such as "no" meanings of "yes," "maybe," "talk me into it," and "positively not!"
3. Confusion with negations in sentences such as "Is it not true, I do not know what to say to you?"
4. Misinterpretation of passive relationships such as "The kids are to be brought by their parents"
5. Confusion with sequences of events in if/then sentences, compound commands, and multiple actions, such as "If you wash your hands, you can have a snack, but you'll have to finish the yard work first"
6. Misinterpretation of statements of exception implying unanimity from statements such as "Everyone except Bob and Cliff was in favor of the motion"

PATTERNS

To ready a building for construction, architectural engineers draw plans and blueprints. According to a resource for residential and commercial design, *A Pattern Language* (Alexander et al. 1977), these plans are derived from patterns that move to create and embellish the structure. The sequence of the patterns is a summary of the forms and networks used and at the same time is an index to the pattern itself. Carrying the analogy to the process of social discourse, students consciously must recognize that patterns of communication can be drawn and developed from isolated lexical forms as well as semantic and syntactical networks (Cazden 1972). This recognition is referred to as *metalinguistic awareness* and allows speakers to construct patterns of language that will be useful tools for engineering communications (Menyuk 1983).

To prepare these patterns, students must identify forms and networks that should be used in the communicative tasks and then select those that will be most useful for meeting an objective or context. Students must formulate hypotheses about the effects and outcomes of these forms and networks on the communication of a pattern. Finally, after employing the pattern strategically in social discourse, they must use outcome and efficacy as evaluative measures to confirm, reject, or modify patterns as well as the methods used to select forms and networks (Wiig 1990).

To teach patterns of lexical usage to students with learning disabilities, both oral and written forms of language should be employed. According to Dreyfus and Dreyfus (1986), levels of competence using these patterns are progressive and move gradually toward expertise. Wiig (1985, 1989, 1990) described teaching strategies that assist students with this progression. These levels begin with basic training to develop awareness of patterns, concepts, and scripts; extend to pragmatic applications of the patterns in fairly simple communicative tasks; extend to patterns that employ more complex semantic features and figurative expressions; and culminate with independent application of acquired knowledge.

The use of lexical patterns in pragmatic communications with strangers, friends, family, superiors, teachers, and peers is more complex than merely the acquisition of the patterns themselves (Bender and Golden 1988; Feagans 1983; Prutting and Kirchner 1987). Therefore, the majority of methods and strategies for teaching lexical patterns employ a simultaneous presentation of both oral and written patterns to teach communication, reading, and written expression (Snyder 1982). Examples of teaching practices that have been used to teach patterns are described in Table 9.2.

INTENTIONAL LANGUAGE

If the analogy of building construction is extended to describe intention, design and architecture rather than engineering and building assume the preeminent role. A need is presented in the environment; a context in which change can be accomplished is initiated; and a response is formulated, evaluated, modified, and restated. Intention sets the tone for the exterior of the house as well as what is within and makes a statement about the individual who will call it home (Alexander et al. 1977).

Initiators of conversation, like persons who work with professional designers and architects to build their home, communicate needs, desires, requirements, and perceived outcomes for the event. They formulate a wish-list of requirements, acknowledge limitations on the amount of resources they intend to invest, and take a practical look at what they want versus what they need. During this process they enter a partnership for engaging in discourse about a topic, acknowledge the level of trust they have in their partners, and determine the extent to which they will display openness and tolerate compromise. In essence, they stipulate the parameters of the communication environment within which they and the respondent will operate.

Appropriate communication results in functional, purposeful, and pragmatic communication of intention from one person to another (Spekman and Roth 1988). If all goes well, interactions between them lead to agreement and a mutually satisfactory response. If conflicts of intention arise and persist, a poorly planned and poorly constructed conversation results. The knowledge base and personal characteristics of both speaker and listener dictate the context of the discourse, the manner in which change will be negotiated, and the outcome that will be accomplished. Both partners articulate their individuality and intentions for

Table 9.2 Teaching practices for patterns

Cueing: For word retrieval—Phonetic cues (beginning sounds or syllables of words); rhyming cues (*red, bed, head* to produce *lead*); and phonetic placement cues (a tongue extension to elicit the *th* in *thus*). Associative meaning cues (antonyms, synonyms); categories to which the word belongs; associated words (*knife* to elicit *fork*); and serial cuing (*June & July,* to elicit *August*).

Pattern completion: For teaching context—Temporal relationships ("Breakfast comes before _____"), inclusion or exclusion statements ("I like all _____" and "I do not like all _____"), cause and effect relationships ("I took an umbrella because it was _____").

Word association: For elaboration and word finding—Free association (naming as many things as can be thought of in one minute); naming opposites; naming synonyms; naming semantic categories (apple = fruit, shoes = footwear); naming locations (garage = truck, car, bus); naming action relationships (bake = cake, bread, cookies); analogies ("a person has hair, a fish has _____").

Rapid naming: Timed activities to speed recall—Classes or categories of names (students in class); actions (everything that can be done in one day); environmental locations (stores in the town); feelings (things that are liked a lot).

Cloze tasks: For context—Written or oral paragraphs with concept words omitted; familiar stories with missing parts. Note: Nouns are easier to cloze than other parts of speech and should be used first. Other parts of speech (adjectives and adverbs) should be clozed later.

Confrontation naming: For semantic reference and relationship—Naming unrelated objects, events, and attributes (e.g., three things that are big and two that are little; one thing that is living and four that are dead; things related to sports and farming that are not red or blue).

Elaboration of detail: For organizing conversational material—Direct questions about familiar objects; descriptions elicited by indirect questions ("Tell me more about it"); event sequences elicited by films or television shows); word associations with detail ("What do a cat and a Halloween costume of the devil have in common?").

Flexible meanings: For understanding and using multiple meanings—Forming sentences that incorporate more than one meaning of a word ("I wore my glasses to pick out some dinner glasses"); using a word as different parts of speech ("After the telephone rang, I decided to telephone Ray").

Role Playing: For pragmatic usage—Practicing time and place for humor; sentences that express sadness; appropriate laughter; serious sentences; telling stories with emotion; reading with interpretative feelings.

---

the event and leave their respective marks and signatures upon it. Throughout the partnership they use cues from visual, auditory, kinesthetic, tactile, gustatory, and olfactory senses; linguistic patterns and lexicons that have been learned; and continual awareness of audience (Prutting 1982; Spekman 1984). Whether an intention is conveyed orally, in writing, or by body language, knowledge of lexical patterns and communication codes is essential. These components are described in the sections that follow.

Knowledge of Lexical Patterns

The linguistic and paralinguistic forms, networks, and lexical patterns discussed in the first section of this chapter are comparable to the foundation and framing that support the intention of the exterior and interior of a house. Although lexical patterns represent only a small portion of intentional language (Bender and Golden 1988; Feagans 1983), they are vital for supporting intention (Spekman and Roth 1988). Halliday (1975) proposed that intentional communication depends primarily on the semantic forms used in functional lexicons. According to this author, intentions are conveyed from acquisitory forms such as: (1) heuristic requests to gain information ("tell me about"), (2) instrumental demands to acquire something ("I want"), and (3) regulatory commands for action by others ("follow my directions"). Also included are forms that signify intention to open communication such as: (1) informative intentions that provide facts and knowledge to others ("let me tell you about"), (2) interactional intentions that draw audiences into the communication process ("you and I"), (3) personal intentions that share information about oneself ("I believe"), and (4) imaginative and creative intentions that expand the realm of communication beyond the present situation ("what if").

Boucher (1984) used Halliday's (1975) intentional semantic forms to investigate statements made by students with and without learning disabilities. The results indicated that students with learning disabilities used the more immature semantic forms of imagination, information, and regulation than did their non–learning-disabled counterparts. In addition, use of these forms in interactions with peers and adults often was inappropriate or unjustified. Other authors (Shatz et al. 1980; Wiig 1990) agreed with these findings. Furthermore, they suggested that immature paralinguistic features of the lexicon (such as accompanying gestures, verbal qualifiers, and negations) are present with students with learning disabilities.

Communication Codes

When two or more individuals enter into conversation with each other, they make a tacit agreement to cooperate. Like an architect and client working together, they adopt a code that requires both parties to tell each other the truth, offer only information assumed to be relevant and informative, and request only that information that is necessary. This code uses mutual points of reference as points of departure and overcomes bounded rationalities of individual persons (i.e., "two heads are better than one").

Development of the code begins with presupposition. *Presupposition* refers to the information contained in a speaker's message that is not explicit but is shared in common between speaker and listener (Bates 1976; Spekman and Roth 1988). This information is basic and is accepted by two or more communicators without elaboration or definition. For example, architects and clients share a common understanding that bedrooms are places to sleep, patios are outside the enclosed structure of the house; kitchens have stoves, refrigerators, and other cooking accoutrements; and basements are below the main level of the house, and so forth. These terms are explicit in and of themselves and do not need definition or clarification. Communicators quote lines from current movies; state analogies that are integral to an international, national, or regional lexicon; recite proverbs that have universal meaning, and articulate catch phrases such as the one used parenthetically in the preceding paragraph to define bounded rationality. In each circumstance the extent of knowledge held by the other is assumed and is used as a short-hand communication of intention.

A code matures and becomes more meaningful and expressive when communicators personalize vocabularies to fit specific needs. Terms such as "soffit," "load-bearing walls," "gambrel roofs," and "tongue-and-groove construction" are defined for clients by architects. In turn, clients communicate their concept of libraries versus dens, contemporary versus traditional plans, and sprawling versus confined spaces. Likewise, conversational partners define terms and constructs that are meaningful to them without presupposing that the partner will understand the meaning unequivocally.

To reach the level of maturity required in a conversational code, communicators take the perspective of their partner and employ appropriate linguistic and paralinguistic patterns to share and infer information between them (Bates 1976; Spekman and Roth 1988). They discuss, arbitrate, compromise, and evaluate the effect of the code on one another. As codes become formalized between communicators, a mutuality of intention is achieved and parameters that engender trust, alleviate discomfort, and mediate discourse develop. At this juncture, codes reduce frustration, fear, rejection, and pain that is anticipated or has been experienced in previous discourses with other partners.

Several researchers have suggested that intentions of conversational codes are determined by the goal of the utterance rather than by the lexicon used to communicate it (Austin 1962; Cooper 1982; Nelson 1988; Nystrand 1982; Searle 1969; Steinman 1982). Inherent in this assumption is the notion that effectiveness of a communication code between partners is dependent on the integration of intention into it. According to Nelson (1988), these intentions would include the following:

1. *Organization:* Intention to organize content into a logical, sequential order giving proper attention to advance organizers and appropriate breaks for listener responses

2. *Information:* Intention to provide listeners with the proper amount of information about the topic being discussed—not too much and not too little

3. *Formality:* Intention to respond to questions and conversational topics with the amount of seriousness, humor, or flippancy required by the situation and circumstance

4. *Illocution:* Intention to use the correct word, most expressive word, and most situationally appropriate word to convey actual meaning and denotation

5. *Transparency:* Intention to convey feelings, connotative meaning, implications, and content in a manner that is sufficiently clear for listener to understand the position of the speaker

6. *Relevancy:* Intention to provide the listener with important information about the topic being discussed without digressive, tangential, or inconsequential information

7. *Accuracy:* Intention to present factual, objective information to explain an opinion or support a position—avoidance of falsehood and conjecture

8. *Perlocution:* Intention to persuade listeners to accept the communicator's point of view on a topic

9. *Opaqueness:* Intention to provide ambivalent or misleading information to listener that is usually employed to conceal personal shortcomings, lack of knowledge, or misunderstandings of situational demands

Studies of intentional language usage by students with learning disabilities have yielded information about several of these components. Wong and Wong (1980) found that students with learning disabilities possess a reduced ability to take the perspective of the listener. Spekman (1981) found them to lack essential information required by listeners, and Snyder (1978) indicated that their utterances tended to be minimally informative. In a study by Lapadat (1991), data from 33 studies that had been conducted with 3- to 12-year-old children with learning disabilities and language disorders were subjected to meta-analytic review. Six pragmatic categories that included intentional components and conversational codes were analyzed. These categories were: (1) topic selection, maintenance, and change; (2) variation in communicative style between audiences; (3) variations in speech acts; (4) cohesive, specific, and accurate selection of lexical forms; (5) intelligibility, intensity, fluency, and quality of paralinguistic features such as prosody, kinesics, proxemics, body posture, gestures, eye gaze, and facial expression; and (6) initiation of turn taking with appropriate feedback to speakers, adjacency, contingency, pause time, and conciseness. The results of the analysis indicated that students with learning disabilities exhibited consistent difficulties in using sufficient cohesion to communicate intention as well as in selecting and using lexical forms. Failure in cohesion led to difficulties following the intention of conversations, which in turn led to misunderstandings, confusion, and incomplete discourse. The results also indicated that these students lacked the ability to respond appropriately to directives, initiate new directives, query one another about the purpose of directives, acknowledge comments, and redirect comments back to the speaker. However, they usually were able to take conversational turns and vary the style of speaking when communicating with different types of conversational partners.

COMMUNICATION MANAGEMENT

At this stage of the analogy between building houses and building language, the materials (lexical forms and networks) are ready, the blueprints (lexical patterns) are drawn, and the partnership, code, and intention to build have been communicated. But the way these components will be consolidated to produce one final elegant and meaningful outcome depends on the management skills of the individual who serves as the general contractor. Let us assume that students who independently manage language are general contractors who manage their present knowledge base, new information, and the subcontractors who are their audience and communication partners.

According to persons who have managed the building of their own homes, the more they learn before beginning the task, the more skillful and insightful they become. They systematically evaluate the efficacy of all forms and networks they have available, judge the abilities of plans to meet specific needs, and articulate and modify their intentions based on realistic priorities and expectations. At this point, they become wary consumers who judge the strengths and weaknesses of the subcontractors with whom they will associate. They may even conduct surprise inspections of these persons to ascertain if the work they produce is of high quality. Most importantly, they use every management technique in their cognitive repertory to make decisions about what to select, what to deselect, and what to change. Once these decisions are reached, these persons take the plunge and build their house. With as much information in hand as possible, they successfully manage the enormous number of details and subtleties that must be considered, acted upon, scrutinized, and evaluated to achieve coherence and consistency.

Applying this analogy to pragmatic language, the triarchic theory of human intelligence by Sternberg (1985) provides a paradigm for the discussion of communication management. According to Sternberg (1986, 1987), the interaction of three factors within this paradigm—componential, experiential, and contextual—interrelate to serve as the foundation upon which human communication rests.

Componential

In Sternberg's (1985) theory, three components would be required to manage pragmatic language: knowledge-acquisition, metacomponents, and performance components. The first of these, *knowledge-acquisition,* is used to acquire new information and relies on the use of systematic processes of selective encoding (information sifting), selective information combining (forming integrated plausible wholes), and selective comparison (relating newly acquired information to information acquired in the past). To return to the general contractor analogy, the first order of business is to research mechanisms to accumulate information in a systematic and comprehensive manner. Just as independent general contractors search building codes for specifications about stress tolerance of roofs, drainage, and foundations, independent communicators study the situations and circumstances in which the language is to be used. Once comprehensive data bases are available, they associate the information they have obtained with information they already know, determine which information is relevant and should be kept, and discard the rest.

The second component, *metacomponents,* comprises thinking processes that are used to plan, monitor, and make decisions (Sternberg 1985). The primary function of these processes is deciding what the problem is and what needs to be solved. In language, as in home building, problem identification and solution require persons to take the time to sit back and imagine how they would like a situation to turn out. If they are building a home, they imagine what they want it to look like, how it can accommodate their needs, and how they want it to make them feel. If they are building a conversation, they imagine how they would like others to respond, what they would like to accomplish through the discourse, and how they will feel about themselves when it is concluded. In both situations, individuals recognize and address the problems that stand in their way and block them from getting where they want to end up.

Performance components are thinking processes that execute tasks (Sternberg 1985). Conversational performance components rely on discourse in the same way that house-building performance components rely on building the house or portions of it. In home building, differential performance components are required to complete the foundation, the plumbing, the house frame, and the landscaping. In pragmatic language, differential components also are required. These include variations in physical settings (e.g., home, classroom, community), variations among communicative partners (e.g., peers, parents, younger and older children, bus drivers, salespersons, other community service employees); and variations dictated in multiple audiences and contexts (Spekman and Roth 1988).

Componential deficiencies of students with learning disabilities such as narrative skills, shared knowledge, memory, turn taking, and social cognition have received substantial research attention in recent years (Brinton and Fujiki 1984; Bryan et al. 1981; Feagans 1933; Mathinos 1988; Schiffrin 1985; Torgesen 1980; Wilson et al. 1984). As a result, several instructional approaches have been suggested as appropriate for teaching strategies that develop componential skills required in communication. These include direct instruction of mnemonic devices for the rapid acquisition of problem-solving rules and facts (Lakoff and Johnson 1980); acquisition of logical questioning strategies through modeling and role playing (Wiig and Semel 1980); experiential training of schema usable in narratives and discourse (Lahey 1988; Stubbs 1983); learning by abduction (Pierce

1957) where learners use observations, facts, and background knowledge to arrive at sets of hypothetical assertions; learning higher-order thinking strategies of sameness through analogical and logical reasoning (Grossen 1991; Grossen and Carnine 1990); and executive strategy training (Ellis et al. 1989; Meichenbaum 1977), where learners focus on a problem situation, analyze the problem's critical features; generate steps to solve the problem, and monitor the effectiveness of the strategic solution. Each approach deals with one component of the communicative process, but none addresses the total body of skills needed for synthesis and organization of language as a whole.

Two instructional practices that are comprehensive approaches are whole language (Goodman and Goodman 1981) and instrumental enrichment (Feuerstein 1980). *Whole language* is an approach through which students learn language as an integrated process of speaking, reading, and writing (Norris and Damico 1990). Whole language prohibits attention to these curricula in isolation (Chaney 1990). As a result, students avoid fragmentation of the components of language that are described in Figure 9.1 and become competent in all levels of structure, meaning, and use of the lexicon.

Rather than a method of teaching, whole language is a dynamic attitude brought to communication to build cognitive themes in repeatable contexts (Goodman 1986, 1989; Goodman et al. 1987). Creating stories and reading children's literature are methods used initially to develop themes for knowledge acquisition and foster their use in pragmatic performance over time (Norris and Damico 1990). These themes embrace the principles of componential processes because they employ natural language to mediate and manage pragmatic discourse. It is this mediation of language and the dynamic nature of the instruction that reveals the similarity of whole language and instrumental enrichment (Feuerstein 1980).

Instrumental enrichment (IE) was designed to teach the organization of cognitive processes required to manage thought processes rather than to teach language per se (Feuerstein 1980). However, it provides a cognitive map by which language can be instructed. This map describes seven parameters by which all mental actions can be analyzed, categorized, and ordered (Sternberg 1985). Table 9.3 presents a description of these parameters. According to several researchers (Borkowski and Konarski 1981; Bradley 1983; Silverman and Waksman 1988), increasing students' abilities in these parameters generically modifies and corrects deficient cognitive functions.

Unlike whole language (Goodman and Goodman 1981), which focuses on the totality of information and language processing without suggesting specific lessons, IE consists of tasks called "instruments" that focus on one deficit of cognitive functioning at a time (Delclos et al. 1984). Typical instruments introduce a lesson, require a period of independent work with it, and conclude with a discussion of the work completed. The cognitive and language skills required in this latter step are mediated by the teacher to help students formulate general principles learned while completing the instrument. To mediate, teachers

Table 9.3 Cognitive map of instrumental enrichment

CONTENT	Mental acts are described according to subject matter and analyzed according to the content in which they are operating.
OPERATIONS	Operations are internalized, organized, and coordinated sets of action through which information derived from external and internal sources is elaborated and extended.
MODALITY	Modality describes the variety and combinations of languages (pictorial, figurative, symbolic, numerical, & verbal) in which mental actions may be expressed.
PHASE	Phase consists of the interconnection of input, elaboration, and output as they relate to information processing and related cognitive functions.
COMPLEXITY	Level of complexity relates to the quality and quantity of information needed to manage a mental act.
ABSTRACTION	Level of abstraction describes the distance (e.g., space or time) between a given mental act and the event or object on which it operates.
EFFICIENCY	Level of efficiency defines the rapidity with which a problem can be solved with mastery and precision.

create an awareness of the cognitive relationships that have been performed and how these relationships generalize beyond the immediacy of the situation (Falik and Feuerstein 1990). To achieve this, teachers take contents of learning sequences, group them by discrete features, and frame them within a context that relates to students' past and future needs (Tzuriel and Ernst 1990).

Instrumental enrichment has been used primarily to teach cognitive processes to students with mental retardation. However, its goals also are congruent with the cognitive management needs of students with learning disabilities. These goals include:

1. Using content-free situations to correct deficit cognitive functions
2. Teaching specific concepts, operations, and vocabulary for solving cognitive problems
3. Developing an intrinsic need for adequate cognitive functioning and spontaneous use of operational thinking, forming appropriate thinking habits, and crystallizing schema
4. Producing insight and understanding of one's own thought processes, particularly those that produce success and are responsible for failure
5. Producing motivation intrinsic to tasks by programming reinforcement from a social context
6. Changing the orientation of individuals from that of passive recipient to active generator of information (Feuerstein et al. 1981).

Research that examines the efficacy of adopting these goals for teaching pragmatics to students with learning disabilities is needed.

Experiential

Sternberg's triarchic theory (1985) purports that two experiential factors are involved in intelligence: (1) ability to deal with novel tasks and situational demands and (2) automatization of information processing. An excellent example of a novel task and its automatization into the information-processing strategies of an individual is a scenario that might be encountered during the initial stages of house building. Persons desiring to build their house are reading books. They find that they should be making choices about parging. For them, this task is novel. They read on to find that parging means covering the exterior of the house, but they must decide on the type of covering that will give them appropriate R and U values. Presented with this second novel task, they investigate to learn that R is the ability of insulating materials to resist the passage of heat and cold out of the house; U the ability of the outsulating materials to resist infiltration. They go through several more learning steps and finally decide on extruded outsulation. Through the process of making the decision they have automatized at least a dozen novel tasks to reach a pragmatic conclusion.

Automatization is considered an indication of maturity. Mature general contractors, like mature users of language, employ sophisticated cognitive management strategies to arrive at solutions to problems while they are engaged with the problem itself. Experienced contractors do not calculate every operation they will perform, because they realize that they will not make errors that cannot be corrected later. As a result, they are relaxed, smooth, and fluid in their approach to construction. Novice contractors, on the other hand, tend to be panic stricken. They agonize over details to such a degree that their overattention causes mistakes that cannot be corrected (Alexander et al. 1977). Because they do not fit details into a whole, they cannot control the plan. Beauty, symmetry, and subtlety are destroyed and, instead of their taking control over details, the details take control over them.

Wiig (1990) provided a similar description of the difference in communication management between mature and novice communicators. Despite interactive constraints, mature speakers organize information into wholes that take into account stored schema from similar interactions; formulate hypotheses about likely outcomes; and prepare themselves to monitor, revise, and repair communications during the conversation itself. Because of their experiences with social discourse, they are fluid and flexible speakers who respond to variables in the conversational environment without being overwhelmed by explicit details. Novice communicators, on the other hand, must be taught thinking processes that enable them to handle equivalent situations and demands with equal flexibility. Researchers such as Feuerstein and colleagues (1981) agree with this concept of maturity and purport that the relationship between newly acquired and practiced skills directly influences the facile use of communication.

Several authors have suggested instructional practices that can be used to improve the ability to automatize novel tasks. Wiig and Semel (1980) suggested modeling modifications to the communication environment to increase flexible pragmatic usage. Word defining and vocabulary lists were suggested, as was instruction in shades of word meaning. For example, instead of saying "The farmer cuts wheat," the teacher would say, "The farmer harvests wheat." Modeling also is suggested to teach oral analogies, synonyms, similes, metaphors, and allegories; outcome of literal and figurative speech (e.g., what would happen, and what would not happen if a person was "light as a feather"); endings of unfinished stories; use of proverbs that illustrate points; and descriptions of imaginary persons. Teachers and students were encouraged to use creativity to produce stories that were both probable and improbable, serious and humorous. When improbable, students were instructed to describe the humor. Unscrambling scrambled events, interpreting abstractions, justifying assumptions, and clarifying multiple and imprecise meanings also were suggested.

Goodman (1989) postulated that modeling experiential examples are less effective than mediating the totality of spoken and written language. Spekman and Roth (1988) contended that all environmental manipulations are less appropriate than direct instruction strategies. Communication situations employing imitation, expansion, prompting, successive approximation, and reinforcement, such as those described in Table 9.2 have been suggested. Research has indicated that direct instruction procedures (discussed in a later chapter) are appropriate for acquiring skills to identify novel language tasks, because they present structures in repetitive patterns, use rhythmic phrasing, accentuate patterns, give numerous examples, ask numerous questions, and prevent incorrect responding (Gersten et al. 1986; Tarver 1986). However, other research has indicated that the value of direct instruction is limited for generalizing these skills to other language situations once the novel skill has been acquired (Weller 1979).

Feuerstein (1980) asserted that systematic mediation rather than direct instruction is required to increase students' abilities to automatize novel information in communicative environments and suggested the use of an IE instrument called "the trial." This instrument modifies deficient processes of verbal input, elaboration, and output. Using the instrument, students take the roles of judge, defendant, prosecutor, and jury members and simulate discourse required for each. Teachers mediate and focus on input problems of quality and quantity of information students gather while attempting to reach a solution. If students' perceptions are too blurred, sweeping, impulsive, or unsystematic, teachers intercede with stimuli that possess affective, value-oriented, and motivational significance (Tzuriel and Ernst 1990). Teachers mediate students' paralinguistic gestures that indicate curiosity; request further information; indicate surprise, disagreement, or pleasure; and cue or clarify thinking processes. A one-sentence example of these pragmatic features and meanings that would be mediated are presented in Table 9.4.

Teachers also mediate problems of elaboration and output. They assist students to define the problem clearly, move toward appropriate responses, and separate relevant from nonrelevant cues. When concepts in students' cognitive repertoires are deficient, teachers mediate strategies of hypothetical thinking, organizational and planning behavior, and comparison of outcomes to reach a final solution. Once this solution is reached, output problems that interfere with the

Table 9.4 Pragmatic features for mediation

The effects of the simple sentence "I like you" can be used to teach pragmatic features. The following behaviors and effects should be role played and mediated.

Behaviors	Effects
With a smile; hand movements of reaching out; in close proximity; by a clean, well-attired person.	Substantiates and emphasizes the verbalization. Listener feels good.
With a smile of contempt; hand movements of reaching out; in close proximity to a dour, unkept, evil-looking person.	Amplifies the verbalization and listener feels threat, fear, and uneasiness.
With no smile, at a distance, with hands held to side.	Contradicts the verbalization and listener feels disbelief.
With a smile, said *very* slowly, *very* softly, in *very* close proximity by an appealing person.	Accentuates the verbalization, but listener feels compromised.

adequate communication of the solution to others are mediated. These include trial and error responding, impulsive or acting-out behaviors, blocking, egocentric modes of communication, lack of precision and accuracy in selecting responses to be communicated, and lack of verbalization tools for communicating.

Contextual

Sternberg (1985) defined contextual components as the "purposive adaptation to, and selection and shaping of, real-world environments relevant to one's life" (p. 45). These mental processes have been related to the construct of adaptive behavior by numerous researchers (Achenbach and Edelbrock 1983; Adams 1984; Bruininks et al. 1984; Greenspan 1981; McKinney and Feagans 1983; Reshly 1982). Encompassing the total rubric of adaptive behavior, these mental activities have been purported to be critical for self-management by students with learning disabilities (Kolligian and Sternberg 1987). In addition, they have been identified as critical for the effective use of social coping, production, pragmatic language, and communicative relationships with others (Bender and Golden 1988; Weller and Strawser 1981).

Sternberg (1988) considered adapting, selecting, and shaping somewhat hierarchical in the way most persons solve problems. Using the analogy of houses, the first option persons typically choose is to adapt themselves to the house in which they live. They change their lifestyles to accommodate the house and do not alter the home they have available. If this option is unsatisfactory, they use selection. They deselect their current residence, sell it, and choose a new one. Because different houses are available on the market at all times, they typically select from houses that already exist. If this option is unsatisfactory, they shape a new house by either remodeling the one in which they live or building a new one. If they choose the latter option, they must prepare themselves to adapt to circumstances and events they never expected nor anticipated.

When students with learning disabilities enter into conversations with others, they, like homebuilders, must adapt to situations that are minimally defined and potentially uncertain. They must realize that, although conversations require forethought and gradual building, many decisions cannot be made in advance. Although there are rigid circumstances from which deviation is not usual (e.g., social nicety scripts in communications), the majority of discourse uses decisions made during the communicative process (Spekman and Roth 1988). As pieces of new information are added to the conversational framework, these must be integrated with existing information to form cohesive wholes.

Students with learning disabilities must recognize that, like the styles or brands of materials and products that are available for building construction, there is no single set of behaviors that always must be used to achieve a conversational end. Choices must be made and students must attend to both verbal and nonverbal communications of others; transfer information from one situation to another; be assertive, submissive, tactful, or blunt as circumstances dictate; choose the word or words that convey their feelings, ideas, and emotions; respond to and show a sense of humor; and be an on-task speaker rather than scattered and rambling (Weller and Strawser 1981). They also must use different nonverbal speaking distances, body movements, gestures, postures, and facial expressions to achieve their goals. Because nonverbal behaviors contribute significantly to adaptivity and often are more meaningful and powerful than their verbal counterparts, appropriate variations that communicate thoughts and intentions are essential to manipulate and control social environments (Weller and Strawser 1987).

Increasing adaptive language abilities depends on frequent use of communication acts. A recent study by Mathinos (1991) revealed that students with learning disabilities possessed the skills to produce adaptive pragmatic utterances but chose to limit their conversational engagement with peers to a point where these utterances were not needed. Unlike persons building a home who bring an architect a picture or photograph of the staircase they want because they cannot describe it in sufficient detail, these students refuse to cope with the level of adaptation required in language. Because they do not persist with the exploration of all avenues of communication before they deselect, adaptive behaviors related to conversational production, interactional relationships, and social maturity are impaired (Weller 1980).

Spekman and Roth (1988) suggested that direct instruction of rule-making strategies be used to improve the adaptiveness of pragmatic language. Rules for regular pragmatic situations were introduced first and followed by those for variant situations. Other researchers have suggested modeling effective conversation either in person or from audio/video tapes, rehearsing scripts, role playing, and cooperative learning (Bryan et al. 1981; Donahue and Bryan 1983; Johnson and

Johnson 1982; Hazel et al. 1982; Sarason 1976). Weller and Strawser (1981) also suggested that modeling, role playing, and scripts be used to increase adaptive language, but they added charades and mime to incorporate paralinguistic features. These authors suggested ways that students could be instructed to mediate their own adaptivity, instruct themselves in the sequence of behaviors required in specific situations, discuss cause and effect relationships between situations and outcomes, and verbalize feelings they could have in certain situations. Developing lists of adaptive responses, weighing the advantages and disadvantages of using each, and setting time limits in which to use them were suggested. Teachers were instructed to verbalize feelings that they or students might have in situations that required adaptation. These suppositions were discussed with the students.

CONCLUSION

When people build a house, they go through a process called "closing in." After they have used their cognitive abilities, experiences, adaptivity, and communicative codes to express their intentions and put the forms, networks, and patterns in place, they fill the holes. At this stage the holes include not only missing embellishments of furniture, paint, wallpaper, art work, and floor coverings, but also any substand construction elements. Without this closing in, the house is incomplete, it does not look like other houses, and the owners feel uncomfortable.

Likewise, the closing in of this chapter delineates those aspects of research that are substandard or missing. For example, research deals with many practices for teaching lexical development but few that teach intention. Students have problems establishing presuppositions and communication codes, but there is little information about how to teach these skills. There are gaps in the practices used to teach componential, experiential, and contextual language despite our rather substantial knowledge of the problems students have in these areas. Of these areas, practices that move students from naive to mature communicators and those that teach pragmatic adaptation are most deficient. But perhaps the most critical practices that are missing are those that embellish language to sophisticated levels. To learn this, students with learning disabilities need instruction in more than just the basics of pragmatic language. Just as few persons would build a boxlike house without windows, doors, or something of interest on the facade and with monochromatic square rooms in the interior, few speakers would attempt to communicate without embellishment. Although it is beyond the scope of this chapter to solve this critical need, some of the embellishments that are needed are outlined in the section that follows.

Action-Reaction

Action-reaction skills are used in bargaining. When a home builder receives quotes from desperate plumbing companies that have not worked all winter and does not make an immediate response, the companies may respond to the delay with lower, competitive bids. Likewise, when students with learning disabilities are faced with making quick decisions about uncertain situations, they can use action-reaction to their advantage. Teaching action-reaction does not involve instructing the strategy, but observing, practicing, and evaluating *timing*. Videotapes and training programs for salespersons may be helpful.

Level of Emotion

Level of emotion is a pragmatic skill that is used in two ways. First, it involves identifying the intensity felt about a situation to determine whether or not to deselect or select it. If persons care intensely about something (color of carpet, brand of furniture) they should exhaust all avenues to obtain it. They should prepare sequential plans and conversation scripts that will get it for them. If they care little, they should not work so hard. Second, level of emotion is a useful strategy for situations where persons feel slighted, cheated, or betrayed. In these circumstances they systematically and purposefully build a conversation from calm discussion to righteous indignation. Because the strategy is purely manipulative and does not actually involve any emotional feelings, it can be used in circumstances that involve unmet timelines, obligations, and promises.

Circumstantial Priorities

When people building a home want to impress friends, neighbors, and enemies, they make sure that their home is slightly superior to those of others. They take painstaking care to make sure they are expressing the precise intention they want to convey and ask advice from persons they want to impress or aspire to emulate. Likewise, if students with learning disabilities choose to improve their language toward a more superior usage, they emulate peers who are more fluent than they and ask advice from them. To accomplish this, teachers should instruct students about how to develop and use assessment tools that identify communication strengths of others and ways to solicit advice from persons they admire.

However, teachers should realize that neither they nor their students always want to impress others. Sometimes they want to self-deprecate themselves just enough to make another person feel superior. To learn this communicative adaptation, students should assess the communication of peers to whom their discourse is superior and practice conversations that are a bit less fluent than their normal style.

Nonverbal Embellishments

Many houses that are of poor quality look good. Unless buyers are looking for stress cracks in the foundation, underneath the drywall at the insulation, and at the truss-joists in the basement, they see a facade that is acceptable to them. In the long run they may be disappointed with the construction, but they seldom give up their first impression that the house was superior.

It is this tendency of human behavior that works in favor of students with learning disabilities. Teaching students to present themselves using complex forms of paralinguistics that amplify, contradict, accentuate, or substitute for verbalizations (e.g., gestures, facial expressions, postures) as well as less complex nonverbal forms (e.g., deodorant, mouthwash, general appearance, manner of dress, cut and style of hair) is in order. When these skills are mastered, students, like prefabricated houses, look better. On the surface these nonverbal embellishments may appear to have little to do with communication, but attitudes of teachers, principals, and persons in the community attest to their importance to communication.

Terminating Conversations

Perhaps one of the most difficult adaptive skills to teach a person is knowing when to stop. When you build a house, when should you stop making changes, spending money, and making embellishments? Likewise, when should students stop talking (or authors stop writing)? Maybe the best strategy is to teach students (and encourage authors) to leave a few questions unanswered and a bit to the imagination.

REFERENCES

Achenbach, T. M., & Edelbrock, C. (1983). *Manual for the Child Behavior Checklist and Revised Child Behavior Profile.* Burlington: University of Vermont.

Adams, G. L. (1984). *Comprehensive test of adaptive behavior.* Columbus, OH: Merrill.

Alexander, C., Ishikawa, S., & Silverstein, M. (1977). *A pattern language.* New York: Oxford University Press.

Austin, T. T. (1962). *How to do things with words.* Cambridge, MA: Harvard University Press.

Bates, E. (1976). *Language and context: The acquisition of pragmatics.* New York: Academic Press.

Bender, W. N., & Golden, L. B. (1988). Adaptive behavior of learning disabled and nonlearning disabled children. *Learning Disability Quarterly, 11,* 55–61.

Blank, M., Gessner, M., & Esposito, A. (1979). Language without communication: A case study. *Journal of Child Language, 6,* 329–352.

Borkowski, J. G., & Konarski, E. A. (1981). Educational implications of efforts to train intelligence. *Journal of Special Education, 15*(2) [Special Issue].

Boucher, C. R. (1984). Pragmatics: The verbal language of learning disabled and nonlearning disabled boys. *Learning Disability Quarterly, 7,* 271–286.

Bradley, T. B. (1983). Remediation of cognitive deficits: A critical appraisal of the Feuerstein model. *Journal of Mental Deficiency Research, 27,* 79–92.

Brinton, B., & Fujiki, M. (1984). Development of topic manipulation skills in discourse. *Journal of Speech and Hearing Research, 27,* 350–358.

Bruininks, R. H., Woodcock, R. W., Weatherman, R. F., & Hill, B. K. (1984). *Scales of independent behavior.* Allen, TX: DLM Teaching Resources.

Bryan, T., Donahue, M., & Pearl, R. (1981). Learning disabled children's peer interactions during a small-group problem-solving task. *Learning Disability Quarterly, 4,* 13–22.

Bryan, T., Donahue, M., Pearl, R., & Strum, C. (1981). Learning disabled children's conversational skills: The "TV Talk Show." *Learning Disability Quarterly, 4,* 250–259.

Cazden, C. (1972). *Child language and education.* New York: Holt, Rinehart & Winston.

Chaney, C. (1990). Evaluating the whole language approach to language arts: The pros and cons. *Language, Speech, and Hearing Services in Schools, 21,* 244–249.

Cooper, M. M. (1982). Context as vehicle: Implicature in writing. In M. Nystrand (Ed.), *What writers know: The language, process, and structure of written discourse* (pp. 106–129). New York: Academic Press.

Cummins, J. P. (1983). Language proficiency and academic achievement. In J. W. Oller, Jr. (Ed.), *Issues in language testing research* (pp. 108–130). Rowley, MA: Newbury House.

Dale, E., & Eichholz, G. (1960). *Children's knowledge of words: Interim report.* Columbus: Bureau of Educational Research and Service, Ohio State University.

Delclos, V. R., Bransford, J. D., & Haywood, H. C. (1984, March/April). Program for teaching thinking: Instrumental enrichment. *Childhood Education,* pp. 256–259.

Donahue, M., & Bryan, T. (1983). Conversational skills and modeling in learning disabled children. *Journal of Applied Psycholinguistics, 4,* 251–278.

Dreyfus, H., & Dreyfus, S. E. (1986). *Mind over machine.* New York: Macmillan.

Ellis, E. S., Deshler, D. D., & Schumaker, J. B. (1989). Teaching adolescents with learning disabilities to generate and use task-specific strategies. *Journal of Learning Disabilities, 22,* 108–119.

Falik, L. H., & Feuerstein, R. (1990). Structural cognitive modifiability: A new cognitive perspective for counseling and psychotherapy. *International Journal of Cognitive Education and Mediated Learning, 1,*(2), 143–150.

Feagans, L. (1983). Discourse processes in learning disabled children. In J. D. Mckinney & L. Feagans (Eds.), *Current topics in learning disabilities* (vol. 1) (pp. 87–115). Norwood, NJ: Ablex.

Feuerstein, R. (1980). *Instrumental enrichment: An intervention program for cognitive modifiability.* Baltimore, MD: University Park Press.

Feuerstein, R., Miller, R., Hoffman, M. B., Rand, Y., Mintzker, Y., & Jensen, M. R. (1981). Cognitive modifiability in adolescents: Cognitive structure and the effects of intervention. *Journal of Special Education, 15*(2), 267–287.

Gersten, R., Woodward, J., & Darch, C. (1986). Direct instruction: A research-based approach to curriculum design and teaching. *Exceptional Children, 53*(1), 17–31.

Gibbs, D. P., & Cooper, E. B. (1989). Prevalence of communication disorders in students with learning disabilities. *Journal of Learning Disabilities, 22,* 60–63.

Goodman, K. (1986). *What's whole in whole language?* Portsmouth, NH: Heinemann.

Goodman, K. (1989). Research in whole language. *Elementary School Journal, 90,* 207–221.

Goodman, K., & Goodman, Y. (1981). *A whole language comprehension-centered view of reading development.* Occasional Paper no. 1. Tucson: Program in Language and Literacy, University of Arizona.

Goodman, K., Smith, E. B., Meredith, R., & Goodman, Y. (1987). *Language and thinking in school.* New York: Owen.

Goodman, Y. (1989). Roots of the whole-language movement. *Elementary School Journal, 90,* 113–127.

Greenspan, S. (1981). Social competence and handicapped individuals: Practical implications of a proposed model. In B. K. Keogh (Ed.), *Advances in special education* (vol. 3) (pp. 41–81). Greenwich, CT: JAI Press.

Grossen, B. (1991). The fundamental skills of higher order thinking. *Journal of Learning Disabilities, 24,* 343–353.

Grossen, B., & Carnine, D. (1990). Diagramming a logic strategy: Effects on more difficult problem types and transfer. *Learning Disability Quarterly, 13,* 168–182.

Halliday, M. A. K. (1975). Learning how to mean. In E. Lenneberg & E. Lenneberg (Eds.), *Foundations of language development: A multidisciplinary approach* (vol. 1) (pp. 239–265). New York: Academic Press.

Hazel, J. S., Schumaker, J. B., Sherman, J. A., & Sheldon-Wildgen, J. (1982). Application of a group training program in social skills and problem solving skills to learning disabled and non-learning disabled youth. *Learning Disability Quarterly, 5,* 398–408.

Johnson, R. T., & Johnson, D. W. (1982). Effects of cooperative and competitive learning experiences on interpersonal attraction between handicapped and nonhandicapped students. *Journal of Social Psychology, 16,* 211–219.

Kolligian, J., Jr., & Sternberg, R. J. (1987). Intelligence, information processing, and specific learning disabilities: A triarchic synthesis. *Journal of Learning Disabilities, 20,* 8–17.

Lahey, M. (1988). *Language disorders and language development.* New York: Prentice-Hall.

Lakoff, G., & Johnson, M. (1980). *Metaphors we live by.* Chicago: University of Chicago Press.

Lapadat, J. C. (1991). Pragmatic language skills of students with language and/or learning disabilities: A quantitative synthesis. *Journal of Learning Disabilities, 24,* 147–158.

Magee, P. A., & Newcomer, P. L. (1978). The relationship between oral language skills and academic achievement of learning disabled children. *Learning Disability Quarterly, 1,* 63–67.

Mathinos, D. A. (1988). Communicative competence of children with learning disabilities. *Journal of Learning Disabilities, 21,* 437–443.

Mathinos, D. A. (1991). Conversational engagement of children with learning disabilities. *Journal of Learning Disabilities, 24,* 439–445.

McKinney, J. D., & Feagans, L. (1983). Adaptive classroom behavior of learning disabled students. *Journal of Learning Disabilities, 16,* 360–367.

Meichenbaum, D. (1977). *Cognitive behavior modification: An integrative approach.* New York: Plenum Books.

Menyuk, P. (1983). Language development and reading. In T. M. Gallagher & C. A. Prutting (Eds.), *Pragmatic assessment and intervention issues in language disorders* (pp. 151–170). San Diego, CA: College Hill Press.

Miller, G. A., & Gildea, P. M. (1987). How children learn words. *Scientific American, 257,* 94–99.

Minskoff, E. H. (1980a). Teaching approach for developing nonverbal communication skills in students with social perception deficits: Part 1. The basic approach and body language cues. *Journal of Learning Disabilities, 13,* 9–15.

Minskoff, E. H. (1980b). Teaching approach for developing nonverbal communication skills in students with social perception deficits: Part 2. Proxemic, vocalic, and artifactual cues. *Journal of Learning Disabilities, 13,* 34–39.

Nelson, N. W. (1988). Reading and writing. In M. A. Nippold (Ed.), *Later language development* (pp. 97–125). Boston: College-Hill Press.

Nelson, K. (1977). The syntagmatic-paradigmatic shift revisited: A review of research and theory. *Psychological Bulletin, 84,* 93–116.

Nippold, M. A. (1988). The literate lexicon. In M. A. Nippold (Ed.), *Later language development* (pp. 29–47). Boston: College Hill Press.

Norris, J. A., & Damico, J. S. (1990). Whole language in theory and practice: Implications for language intervention. *Language, Speech, and Hearing Services in Schools, 21,* 212–220.

Nystrand, M. (1982). The structure of textual space. In M. Nystrand (Ed.), *What writers know: The language, process, and structure of written discourse* (pp. 75–86). New York: Academic Press.

Oller, J. W., Jr. (1979). *Language tests at school: A pragmatic approach.* London: Longman.

Oller, J. W., Jr. (1989). Conclusions toward a rational pragmatism. In J. W. Oller, Jr. (Ed.), *Language and experience: Classic pragmatism.* (pp. 223–250). New York: University Press of America.

Pierce, C. S. (1957). *Essays in the philosophy of science.* New York: Liberal Arts Press.

Prutting, C. A. (1982). Pragmatics of social competence. *Journal of Speech and Hearing Disorders, 47,* 123–134.

Prutting, C. A., & Kirchner, D. M. (1987). A clinical appraisal of the pragmatic aspects of language. *Journal of Speech and Hearing Disorders, 52,* 105–119.

Reshly, D. J. (1982). Assessing mild mental retardation: The influence of adaptive behavior, sociocultural status, and prospects for nonbiased assessment. In C. R. Reynolds & T. B. Gutkin (Eds.), *The handbook of school psychology.* New York: Wiley.

Sarason, I. G. (1976). A modeling and information processing approach to delinquency and aggression. In E. Ribes-Inesta & A. Bandura (Eds.), *Analysis of delinquency and aggression.* Hillsdale, NJ: Erlbaum.

Schiffrin, D. (1985). Conversational coherence: The role of "well." *Language, 61,* 1–38.

Searle, J. R. (1969). *Speech arts: An essay in the philosophy of language.* Cambridge, England: Cambridge University Press.

Semel, E. M., & Wiig, E. H. (1975). Comprehension of syntactic structures and critical verbal elements by children with learning disabilities. *Journal of Learning Disabilities, 8,* 53–58.

Shatz, M., Shulman, M., & Bernstein, D. (1980). The responses of language disordered children to indirect directives in varying contexts. *Applied Psycholinguistics, 1,* 295–306.

Silverman, H., & Waksman, M. (1988). Feuerstein's instrumental enrichment elicitation of cognitive interaction in the classroom. *Canadian Journal of Special Education, 4*(2), 133–150.

Snyder, L. S. (1978). Communicative and cognitive abilities and disabilities in the sensorimotor period. *Merrill-Palmer Quarterly, 24,* 161–180.

Snyder, L. S. (1982). Have we prepared the learning disordered child for school? In K. G. Butler & G. P. Wallach (Eds.), *Language disorders and learning disabilities.* Rockville, MD: Aspen.

Spekman, N. (1981). Dyadic verbal communication abilities of learning disabled and normally achieved fourth and fifth grade boys. *Learning Disability Quarterly, 4,* 193–201.

Spekman, N. J. (1984). Learning-disabled students and language use: Discourse and narrative skills. *Learning Disabilities, 3*(9), 103–115.

Spekman, N. J., & Roth, F. P. (1988). An intervention framework for learning disabled students with communication disorders. *Learning Disability Quarterly, 11,* 248–256.

Steinman, M. (1982). Speech-act theory and writing. In M. Nystrand (Ed.), *What writers know: The language, process, and structure of written discourse* (pp. 291–323). New York: Academic Press.

Sternberg, R. J. (1985). *Beyond IQ: A triarchic theory of human intelligence.* Cambridge: Cambridge University Press.

Sternberg, R. J. (1986). *Intelligence applied: Understanding and increasing your intellectual skills.* San Diego, CA: Harcourt Brace Jovanovich.

Sternberg, R. J. (1987). Most vocabulary is learned from context. In M. G. McKeown & M. E. Curtis (Eds.), *The nature of vocabulary acquisition* (pp. 89–105). Hillsdale, NJ: Erlbaum.

Sternberg, R. J. (1988). *The triarchic mind: A new theory of human intelligence.* New York: Penguin Books.

Stubbs, M. (1983). *Discourse analysis: The sociolinguistic analysis of natural language.* Chicago: University of Chicago Press.

Tarver, S. G. (1986). Cognitive behavior modification, direct instruction, and holistic approaches in the education of students with learning disabilities. *Journal of Learning Disabilities, 19,* 368–375.

Torgesen, J. (1980). Conceptual and educational implications of the usage of efficient task strategies by learning disabled children. *Journal of Learning Disabilities, 13,* 364–371.

Tzuriel, D., & Ernst, H. (1990). Mediated learning experience and cognitive modifiability: Testing the effects of distal and proximal factors by structural equation model. *International Journal of Cognitive Education and Mediated Learning, 1*(2), 119–142.

Vogel, S. A. (1983). A qualitative analysis of morphological ability in learning disabled and achieving children. *Journal of Learning Disabilities, 16,* 416–420.

Weller, C. (1979). The effect of two language training approaches on syntactical skills of language-deviant children. *Journal of Learning Disabilities, 12,* 470–479.

Weller, C. (1980). Discrepancy and severity in the learning disabled: A consolidated perspective. *Learning Disability Quarterly, 3,* 84–90.

Weller, C., & Strawser, S. (1981). *Weller-Strawser scales of adaptive behavior.* Novato, CA: Academic Therapy Publications.

Weller, C., & Strawser, S. (1987). Adaptive behavior of subtypes of learning disabled individuals. *Journal of Special Education, 21*(1), 101–115.

Wiig, E. H. (1985). *Words, expression, and contexts: A figurative language program.* San Antonio, TX: The Psychological Corporation.

Wiig, E. H. (1989). *Steps to language competence: Developing metalinguistic strategies.* San Antonio, TX: The Psychological Corporation.

Wiig, E. H. (1990). Linguistic transitions and learning disabilities: A strategic learning perspective. *Learning Disability Quarterly, 13,* 128–140.

Wiig, E. H., Lapointe, C., & Semel, E. M. (1977). Relationships among language processing and production abilities of learning disabled adolescents. *Journal of Learning Disabilities, 9,* 292–299.

Wiig, E. H., & Semel, E. M. (1980). *Intervention for the learning disabled.* Columbus, OH: Merrill.

Wiig, E. H., Semel, E. M., & Abele, E. (1981). Perception and interpretation of ambiguous sentences by learning disabled twelve year olds. *Learning Disability Quarterly, 4,* 3–12.

Wilson, T., Wiemann, J., & Zimmerman, D. (1984). Models for turn-taking in conversational interaction. *Journal of Language and Social Psychology, 15,* 159–183.

Wong, B. Y. L., & Wong, R. (1980). Role-taking skills in normally achieving and learning disabled children. *Learning Disability Quarterly, 3,* 11–18.

10

Interventions for Attention Problems

Deborah J. Huntington
William N. Bender

Attention problems among students with learning disabilities (LD) are apparently quite common (Lerner and Lerner 1991; Shaywitz 1987; Silver 1990). Numerous teachers report attention problems among students with LD, and researchers have looked fairly extensively among these students (see Shaywitz and Shaywitz [1988] and Silver [1990] for reviews).

The concern with attention problems among this population reflects a larger concern about attention problems that may be associated with various disabilities. In this broader context, a body of literature has developed on attention deficit disorder, which may be manifested in several different disabilities.

ATTENTION DEFICIT DISORDER
Definition and Prevalence

Attention deficit disorder (ADD) refers to the limited ability of some individuals to come to attention, focus on attending, or sustain attention. Examples of behaviors associated with this disorder include difficulty in organizing work, difficulty in concentrating, failure to complete tasks, and extreme overactivity. The American Psychiatric Association (1987) estimates that 3% to 5% of school-age children may have significant problems with ADD, both with and without hyperactivity.

According to the *Diagnostic and Statistical Manual of Mental Disorders, Third Edition (DSM III) (American Psychiatric Association* 1980), ADD can occur with hyperactivity (ADD/H) or without (ADD/WO). Although the *DSM III-R* (1987) utilizes an undifferentiated rating scale, the *DSM IV,* soon to be published, is expected to return to the previous classification system found in *DSM III* (Goodyear and Hynd in press). The classification system includes the three characteristics of attending, hyperactivity, and impulsivity. Students are diagnosed in terms meeting the criteria of symptoms of any two of these three characteristics. In addition, a diagnosis of ADD includes the requirements that the onset of the condition occurs prior to age 7 and exists over an extended period of time, at least six months.

227

Related Conditions

Evidence supports the existence of significant overlaps between ADDs, LD, and conduct disorders. Although ADD is often associated with LD (Silver, 1990), it frequently exists concurrently with other disabilities, such as behavior disorders. Thus, it is important to explore the relationship between ADD and these related conditions as well as to distinguish clearly among the associated terminology.

Attention Deficit Disorder and Learning Disabilities

Presently the exact relationship between LD and ADD is unclear (Silver 1990). A major problem in defining the relationship between LD and ADD is the inconsistent criteria used to diagnose both disorders. Each is presumed to result from a neurological disorder. In a learning disability, the basic psychological processes involved in academic functioning are impacted. However, in ADD at least two of three characteristics must be manifested: hyperactivity (deficits in controlling motor activity level), attentional (deficits in coming to attention, focusing attention, and sustaining attention), and/or impulsivity (lack of reflecting before acting) (Shaywitz and Shaywitz 1988; Silver 1990).

Estimates of the co-occurrence of ADD and LD vary considerably. The Interagency Committee on Learning Disabilities (Shaywitz 1987) estimates that the number of students whose LD are accompanied by hyperactivity and attention deficits vary from 5% to 25%. The most common estimates range from 15% to 20% (Silver 1990). Conversely, a large percentage of hyperactive children are also diagnosed as learning-disabled. Among students diagnosed as hyperactive, 30% to 40% have special educational needs (Epstein et al. 1991; Frick and Lahey 1991).

Attention Deficit Disorder and Conduct Disorders

Empirical evidence suggests that a hyperactive child is more prone to verbal and physical aggression than other children and these behavioral characteristics are typically associated with conduct disorders or emotional disturbance (Abikoff et al. 1977). Between 30% and 90% of students diagnosed with ADD/H have significant conduct problems (Frick and Lahey 1991). It is speculated that impulsivity manifests itself in lowered levels of self-control, which may predispose these youngsters to develop conduct disorders (Coleman 1992). For example, Lambert and her colleagues (Lambert 1988; Lambert et al. 1987) have conducted longitudinal studies that substantiate the risk of ADD/H children for developing conduct disorders as well as having problems with juvenile authorities.

As indicated previously, there are three distinguishing characteristics of ADD: attention, hyperactivity, and impulsivity. For a diagnosis of ADD, only two of these three characteristics must be manifested. Each of these three conditions will be described, with particular emphasis given to attention.

Attention

Parents and teachers have long complained that children with LD do not pay attention (Bender 1992; Lerner and Lerner 1991). Also, research supports the suggestion that these children have difficulty with attention (Bender 1985; Copeland and Wisniewski 1981; Swanson 1983). Behaviors associated with attentional difficulties are clearly delineated in *DSM-III* (1980). They include difficulty with turn taking, difficulty following through with directions, difficulty sustaining attention to task or play activities, not seeming to be listening to what is being said, and losing things necessary for tasks or activities.

Measures of these attentional behaviors are often confounded with memory and other types of cognitive demands (Krupski 1986). Although the completion of any task requires attention, very few tasks can be considered to be pure measures of attention. Thus, any cognitive task, such as those routinely undertaken in a school day, involves a number of psychological processes, including attention.

Most clinical research to date on the attentional problems of students with LD has focused on only two aspects of attention, sustained attention and selective attention (Coleman 1992; Krupski 1986; Nuechterlein 1983). A discussion of the clinical measurement of sustained attention and selective attention will be followed by a presentation of observational measures of attention in the classroom.

Sustained Attention

Sustained attention refers to the degree to which attention is maintained over time. A sustained attention research approach often employed has been to compare the performance of students with LD with the performance of normally achieving students on one or more attention-demanding tasks. Commonly used tasks involve vigilance or reaction time and the physiological correlates of reaction-time performance.

In a vigilance task the student is required to monitor a continuous stream of stimuli for an extended period of time to detect infrequent and unpredictable designated signals. For example, a student may be asked to detect changes in the brightness of a light or the loudness of a tone. One potential confounding effect in the measurement of vigilance is intelligence. If a task is cognitively demanding, measurement may reflect both vigilance and IQ. Consequently, only research using vigilance tasks involving minimal cognitive demands is described here.

Research on vigilance tasks indicates that students with disabilities almost always perform more poorly on vigilance tasks than do nondisabled students (Krupski 1986). Further, children with LD and children with ADD have been found to make more errors of omission than matched groups of nondisabled peers (Danier et al. 1981; Goldberg and Konstantareas 1981; Michael et al. 1981; Nuechterlein 1983; Rugel et al. 1978; Swanson 1980, 1983). The results of preliminary studies show that commission error data, like other vigilance measures, do not distinguish among nonhyperactive subgroups of students with LD and students with ADD/H; both groups performed similarly at a level significantly below that of matched normally achieving control groups (Nuechterlein 1983; Swanson 1983).

Another measure used to study sustained attention in children with LD is the reaction-time task. In this task a warning signal is given followed by a reaction signal. The student's job is to press a button or release a key as quickly as possible when the reaction signal occurs. As with vigilance, slower and/or more variable reaction times can be interpreted as a reflection of problems with sustained attention. Slower and/or more variable reaction time performance has been reported for students with LD and students with ADD/H (Cohen and Douglas 1972; Firestone and Douglas 1975; Rugel and Rosenthal 1974; Stroufe et al. 1973).

Physiological activity is often recorded simultaneously during reaction-time tasks. The degree of heart beat deceleration or skin conductance that occurs at the reaction signal can be interpreted as an index of preparedness or attention (Krupski 1975). The heart beat deceleration and skin resistance studies consistently provide evidence for problems of sustained attention among students with LD and students with ADD (Cohen and Douglas 1972; Firestone and Douglas 1975; Rugel and Rosenthal 1974; Stroufe et al. 1973; Zahn et al. 1975). Thus, evidence supports the contention that the sustained attention difficulties of students with LD can be demonstrated in each of these three areas.

Selective Attention

Another aspect of attention that has been associated with students with LD is selective attention. We are constantly immersed in a sea of information available to us through our senses. At any given moment we focus on only a small portion of the information. *Selective attention* refers to the ability to identify important stimuli and important aspects of a stimulus and disregard other stimuli in the environment (Alabisco 1972; Ross 1976). Two experimental paradigms recurrently used to study selective attention in students with LD and ADD/H are incidental learning and distractibility.

In one of the first studies of selective attention, Hagen (1967) compared the ability of a student to intentionally remember certain objects, the central task, to the ability to remember other objects incidentally. For example, if Susie was involved in the task of matching numerals and while doing so she overheard the teacher instructing other students in sequencing the days of the week, she may later recall the central task, matching numerals, as well as the incidental task, naming the days of the week in sequence. Although the incidental learning paradigm (Hagen 1967) was introduced as a measure of selective attention, its relevance has been questioned by researchers working more recently (Copeland and Wisniewski 1981; Krupski 1986). The incidental learning paradigm has been found to more closely measure memory than attention processes.

The other paradigm used to study selective attention is the distractibility paradigm. *Distractibility* can be defined as differential deterioration in task performance of experimental and control groups in a distraction as opposed to a no-distraction condition (Krupski 1986). Distractors can be categorized as distal, proximal, and embedded.

Distal distractors are those that occur some distance from the task at hand and are easily distinguishable from the task. Examples of distal distractors include the playing of "white noise," recordings of background classroom noise, intermittent chimes, or intermittent flashing of lights on the ceiling and walls (Browning 1967; Kirchner 1976; Nobler and Nobler 1975; Sykes et al. 1971). Results of experiments employing distal distractors are consistent: Students with LD and students with ADD are no more distractible under these conditions than are nondisabled control children (Kirchner 1976; Nobler and Nobler 1975; Sykes et al. 1971).

Proximal distractors, like distal distractors, are easily distinguishable from the task at hand but, unlike distal distractors, are in close proximity to the task. For example, photographs or pictures in reading texts may divert poor readers. Preliminary studies indicate that students with LD and students with ADD/H have greater difficulty than nondisabled students completing tasks under a proximal distraction condition (Radosh and Gittelman 1981; Samuels 1967).

A final category of distractors is *embedded* distractors, or distractors contained within the task at hand. For example, a student could be asked to sort all cards that include the color blue from all cards that do not. For this task, embedded distractors may include all other colors. Although no differential group effects were found in studies that employed embedded color, a variety of other visual and auditory embedded distractors had a greater effect on the performance of students with LD and students with ADD/H than on the performance of normal control groups (Blackwell et al. 1983; Laskey and Tobin 1973; Zentall and Shaw 1980).

These research-based measures of sustained and selective attention are typically operationalized in the public schools in terms of observational measures of attention in the classroom. It is critical for the practitioner and the researcher to examine attention in terms of actual behaviors exhibited in the typical public school classroom. Only within the classroom setting is it possible to compare and contrast the school behaviors of students with LD with the school behaviors of normally achieving classmates. Students with LD have been found to spend less time on task than their normally achieving peers (McKinney and Feagans 1983). Therefore, direct observation of a student in a particular learning situation is essential for accurate assessment and instruction (Abikoff et al. 1980; Bender 1992; Cooper et al. 1987).

Classroom attention can be measured through taking a frequency count of on-task behaviors or by calculating the percentage of time during which a student attends to a task (Bender 1992). Also referred to as *engaged time* or *attention span*, time on task is considerably lower for students with LD when compared with nondisabled students. Many researchers indicate that nondisabled students spend 60% to 85% of their time on task, while students with LD spend only 30% to 60% of their time on task (Bender 1985; Bryan and Wheeler 1972; McKinney and Feagans 1983; McKinney et al. 1982).

For example, McKinney and colleagues (1982) compared the task orientation of 22 pairs of students with LD and normally achieving students who had been matched by classroom, gender, race, and age. All students attended either the second or fourth grade. Observational data were collected by four observers over a period of four months during the second half of the school year. The results indicated that students with LD exhibited less on-task behavior than normally achieving children in the same classroom.

In summary, students with LD and students with ADD/H perform similarly on tasks purported to measure attention processes. In terms of sustained attention, both groups performed poorly relative to normal control groups on tasks measuring vigilance, reaction time, and physiological activity (Firestone and Douglas 1975; Michael et al. 1981; Rugel and Rosenthal 1974; Swanson 1980, 1983; Zahn et al. 1975). In terms of selective attention, neither experimental group had difficulty in studies where distal distractors were employed (Kirchner 1976; Nobler and Nobler 1975). Both students with LD and students with ADD performed poorly relative to normal control groups on tasks employing proximal and particular types of embedded distractors (Radosh and Gittelman 1981; Samuels 1967; Zentall and Shaw 1980). Finally, research in the classroom suggests that students with LD demonstrate higher levels of off-task behavior on school tasks (Bryan and Wheeler 1972; McKinney and Feagans 1983; McKinney et al. 1982).

Hyperactivity

Young children with *hyperactivity* exhibit excessive motor activity and are often described as being on the go or as running like a motor that has only one speed—fast. *DSM III-R* criteria referring to hyperactivity include fidgeting, difficulty remaining in seat, and talking excessively. Other classroom behaviors illustrative of hyperactivity include constant leg shaking when seated, pencil tapping, frequent pencil sharpening, and difficulty keeping hands to self. Older hyperactive children may be described as being extremely restless and fidgety with a tendency to talk too much in class. It is this quality of overactivity that distinguishes hyperactivity from ordinary overactivity in that hyperactivity tends to be haphazard and poorly organized (Lerner 1988).

Impulsivity

Impulsivity refers to the tendency to act without thinking. *DSM III-R* criteria referring to impulsivity include blurting out answers, shifting from one uncompleted task to another, difficulty with turn taking, and interrupting others. Impulsive children can be characterized as fast decision makers who make many errors, jump to conclusions, and guess wildly (Lerner 1988).

Although impulsivity has implications for task completion, its most detrimental effect may be in interpersonal relationships (Abikoff et al. 1980; Vincent et al. 1981). Intrusiveness of verbal interactions such as interrupting or otherwise intruding when socially inappropriate is a trait that has been found to discriminate hyperactive children from nonhyperactive children (Abikoff et al. 1980).

Other researchers have found that ADD/H children demonstrate intrusive behavior at higher rates and with greater intensity than nonhyperactive children (Vincent et al. 1981).

Academic Performance

A notable percentage of ADD children (23%–30%) do not achieve academically at a level commensurate with their age and intellectual ability (Epstein et al. 1991; Frick and Lahey 1991; Shaywitz and Shaywitz 1991). It is speculated that the basic behaviors of hyperactivity, impulsivity, and attention problems interact to produce academic problems (Weiss and Hechtman 1986). Substantiated academic problems of ADD/H students include failing grades (Barkley 1988) and underachievement despite intellectual potential (Coleman 1992).

ASSESSMENT OF ATTENTIONAL PROBLEMS

Attention deficit disorder is a diagnosis that requires a multimethod behavioral assessment. This assessment is undertaken for the purpose of making appropriate administrative decisions about eligibility for services and to facilitate linkages with other professionals and agencies as appropriate (Schaughency and Rothlind 1991). In addition to academic assessment, a school-based assessment of ADD should include multiple measures such as teacher rating scales; sociometric measures; and direct observation in both structured situations, such as classrooms, as well as unstructured situations, such as on the playground or in the lunchroom (Atkins and Pelham 1991; Schaughency and Rothlind 1991). Assessment is presented in greater detail in chapters 4 and 5 of this text.

Teacher Rating Scales

Teacher rating scales are the most common method of collecting information about attentional difficulties (Lerner and Lerner 1991). These measures can be used to obtain an overall picture of the child's functioning in the classroom, to identify social competency strengths and weaknesses, and to pinpoint specific characteristics associated with attentional problems. For students with LD it is advisable to begin with a measure of adaptive behavior (Leigh 1987; McKinney and Feagans 1983; Weller 1980; Weller and Strawser 1981).

Adaptive behavior refers to how well an individual can adjust to the roles he or she assumes in diverse settings. It includes assessment of the degree to which the individual meets the standards of personal independence and responsibility expected of his or her age and cultural group in both academic and nonacademic situations (Smith 1991). In an early review of the characteristics that make up adaptive behavior, McKinney and Feagans (1983) identified task-oriented behaviors, disruptive behaviors, hyperactive behaviors, and interaction with peers and adults as problem areas for students with LD. Weller and Strawser (1981) added one additional component, pragmatic language. Within the school setting the major adaptive issue is the degree to which students with LD can adapt to demands placed upon them in the mainstream.

Student attention behaviors in mainstream classes can also be assessed through more traditional behavior ratings such as the Behavior Problem Checklist (Quay and Peterson 1983) or the Child Behavior Checklist-Teacher Report Form (Achenbach and Edelbrook 1986). Both of these scales have been used extensively for screening school-related behavior problems and have strong normative and psychometric properties (Atkins and Pelham 1991).

In addition to these teacher ratings, a thorough assessment should also include one of the teacher rating measures designed specifically to evaluate hyperactivity in the classroom, such as the IOWA-Conners Rating Scale (Looney and Milich 1982) or the Swanson, Nolan, and Pelham Rating Scale (see Atkins and Pelham [1991] for details). The Iowa-Conners consists of 10 items derived from the Conners Teacher Rating Scale, 5 of which are designed to measure inattention/overactivity and 5 of which measure aggression. Another measure, the Swanson, Nolan, and Pelham, describes core symptoms of overactivity, inattention, and impulsivity, as well as peer-related aggression. Both the Iowa-Conners and the Swanson, Nolan, and Pelham have been found to have a high correlation to other measures of ADD, but a low correlation to objective measures of aggression (Atkins and Milich 1988; Atkins et al. 1988).

In summary, classroom rating scales can be easily obtained, require little time for administration, and are cost-effective for general assessment of attention and behavior problems. However, teacher rating scales have the disadvantage of subjectivity. Teacher ratings have been found to be more subjective than direct observation in that they require inference on the part of the teacher (Lerner and Lerner 1991).

Peer Evaluation

Students with attentional difficulties often have problems in social relations (Pelham and Milich 1984). Therefore, it is important to determine the degree to which students with disabilities are accepted by normally achieving students in extracurricular activities as well as in the classroom (Bender 1992). The two types of sociometric measures most often utilized in the schools are peer nominations and the roster rating.

In *peer nominations,* students are asked to nominate a predetermined number of peers (usually three) as students whom they like most and students whom they like least. Often separate ratings are obtained for work and play (Atkins and Pelham 1991). Tabulation of these results for an entire class results in the classification of children as "popular" (high positive, low negative), "rejected" (low positive, high negative), and "neglected" (low positive, low negative). Raw scores may then be converted to within-classroom standardized scores. Test-retest reliability, concurrent validity with teacher ratings, and predictive value tend to be high (Johnston et al. 1988).

A useful measure that can be derived from peer nominations is mutual positive nominations, or *reciprocal friends*. Reciprocal friends is determined by denoting friends selected by each student and then correlating these preferences. Such information is valuable for assessing social skills. For example, Howes (1988) demonstrated that rejected children with reciprocal friends had easier entries into playgrounds than rejected children without reciprocal friends.

A disadvantage of peer nominations is that no description is made of the behaviors that lead to popularity, neglect, or rejection (Atkins and Pelham 1991). In contrast, a *roster rating* is designed to generate this type of data on every member of the class. In a roster rating every student in the class rates every other student in the class (Bender et al. 1984; LaGreca and Stone 1990; Sabournie et al. 1990). Each student is given an item-by-item matrix with items appearing in one axis and names of students in the other. Each student rates each other student by placing an X in the box corresponding to items descriptive of the ratee. The score for each student is the percentage of peers nominating that child on each item. For example, a student may be asked to rate all of his or her classmates on attending behaviors.

Sociometric measures such as peer ratings or roster ratings are readily obtained, require little time for administration, and are cost-effective. These measures provide information not available from other sources that is valuable for individual teachers in planning instruction for their classes as well as for professionals who are developing an individualized instructional plan for one particular student (Bender 1992).

Observation

Pertinent information can also be obtained through *direct observation* of attention behaviors by resource teachers or by other educational specialists such as guidance counselors, psychologists, or school administrators. Resource teachers are the professionals most often involved in direct observation, both in their own classrooms and in mainstream classrooms. A resource teacher can easily record data on students while instructing a class in one of two ways, an anecdotal notebook or an event record. An *anecdotal notebook* is kept by the teacher for recording brief notes about particular children as events occur. At the end of a school day it is extremely difficult to reconstruct and record only a few of thousands of interactions that have taken place that day. In contrast, recording the date, time, and one or two phrases to describe a behavior can easily be done, especially when a notebook is readily available for this purpose.

Another observational tool is *event recording*. Using event recording, a check is made on an index card each time a targeted behavior such as out-of-seat behavior is observed during a specified duration of time (usually a class period). After several observations, data obtained from event recording may be transformed into a graphic format.

As mentioned previously, the student should be observed in a variety of settings including classroom(s), lunchroom, and during play or recess. The resource teacher most often conducts such observations for relatively short periods of time, probably no more than 10 to 20 minutes. (For a thorough discussion of these observational procedures, refer to Cooper et al. [1987] or Tawney and Gast [1984].)

Direct observation methods have documented differences between children both with and without ADD on objective measures of classroom behaviors (Abikoff et al. 1980). When compared with teacher ratings, direct observation methods have been found to be a more objective appraisal of behavior. Clearly defined measures minimize the possibility of inference on the part of the observer (Lerner and Lerner 1991). A disadvantage to the widespread use of direct observations is its cost for general assessment purposes.

In summary, when used concurrently, multiple classroom measures provide an accurate assessment of attentional difficulties (Atkins and Pelham 1991). Teacher ratings, peer ratings, and direct observation each assess independent aspects of students' attending behavior.

INTERVENTIONS FOR ATTENTION PROBLEMS

Following assessment, a course of action for intervention is devised. Generally, treatment for students with LD and a secondary diagnosis of ADD should begin with behavioral interventions, followed by cognitive-behavioral approaches and medically based interventions.

Behavioral Interventions

Applied behavioral analysis focuses on changing socially significant behaviors that have been observed and operationally defined (Cooper et al. 1987; Johnson and Pennypacker 1980; Tawney and Gast 1984; Vail and Huntington 1993). Environmental factors are systematically manipulated to increase, decrease, change, or shape targeted responses.

For example, Rosenbaum and colleagues (1975) used individual contingencies to manage several different behavior problems associated with hyperactivity in the classroom. Participants in the study included 10 boys age 8 through 12. A target behavior was chosen for each of the students in the individual contingency program. Staying in the seat or completing work were typical target behaviors. At the end of each hour the teacher distributed reward cards to each student who had met the criteria of his target behavior. At the end of the day, reward cards were exchanged for a primary reinforcer, candy. This individual contingency program ran for four weeks. Results demonstrated that the program was effective. Reinforcement was phased out. Four weeks later, follow-up observations were made. Students were found to maintain their improvements in behavior.

Consider how behavioral interventions could be designed for a hypothetical student. David, a fourth-grader, is frequently out of his seat and fidgets often

David – Out-of-Seat Behavior, 3rd Period Language Arts	
10 - 3	卌 卌 II
10 - 4	卌 卌 卌
10 - 5	卌 卌
10 - 6	卌 卌 I
10 - 7	卌 卌 III

Figure 10.1 Event recording form for David's out-of-seat behavior.

while in his seat. Easily distracted by noises, David looks up each time a car passes on the street outside the school, when a pencil is sharpened, or when the hum of the furnace can be heard through the vent. Although David's math achievement is average, he has very limited verbal expression and struggles with reading and any type of written expression. His written products are so sloppy and carelessly done that his teachers have difficulty grading his work. The classroom teachers assume that David's academic difficulties are caused by his poor attitude and his limited time on task.

In designing a behavioral intervention the LD teacher would first prioritize individual needs and then select a target behavior. The LD teacher might select out-of-seat behavior as the first behavior to be targeted. The teacher then develops an operational definition for out-of-seat behavior. Out-of-seat behavior may have been defined as any time the buttocks were not in contact with the desk.

Direct observation would then be started. Baseline data could be recorded by the resource teacher using an event recording procedure. For example, the teacher may use an index card divided into five sections for recording, with one section allotted for each observation (see Figure 10.1). Each out-of-seat behavior observed during the 55-minute class period could be recorded by placing a tally mark in the appropriate section of the index card. This procedure should be repeated until a stable baseline is reached.

Assume that such a method was utilized in recording baseline data for David's out-of-seat behavior. Baseline data indicates that David is out of his seat an average of 12 times per class period. The teacher would then consider possible behavioral interventions for dealing with this out-of-seat behavior. Behavioral interventions should generally be attempted first because they are easy to initiate in the context of the classroom and do not require the intervention of other professionals.

Reinforcement of incompatible behavior was used with David to reduce the frequency of out-of-seat behavior. As it is not possible for David to be out of his seat and in his seat at the same time, he was reinforced for remaining in his seat.

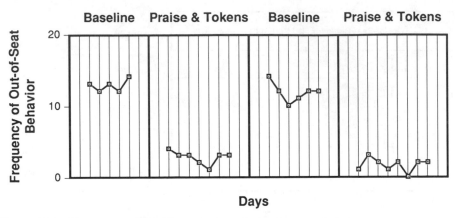

Figure 10.2 Frequency of David's out-of-seat behavior recorded during a 55-minute observation period in the classroom with behavioral intervention.

For every 3-minute period in which he did not leave his seat, he received 10 cents in the token economy, as well as verbal praise from his resource teacher. Again, the teacher used an index card to record the occurrence of out-of-seat behavior in each 3-minute interval during the class as well as to note reinforcement given for staying in his seat (see Figure 10.2). Thus, this type of intervention does not require a great deal of teacher involvement.

Results presented in Figure 10.2 indicate that during the next seven days, David reduced his out-of-seat behavior to an average of three times per class period. At his point the teacher questioned whether the change in behavior was due to the behavioral intervention or some other factor. To test this hypothesis, the behavioral intervention was withdrawn. David no longer received money in the token economy or verbal praise from the teacher for remaining in his seat. During the third phase of the intervention, David's out-of-seat behavior increased to the frequency level observed during the initial baseline phase. However, when the behavioral intervention was reinstated, David's out-of-seat behavior was again reduced to an average of three times per period. On-task behavior and productivity increased when David increased the amount of time he spent in his seat.

In summary, research supports the effectiveness of behavioral intervention for a variety of behaviors including attentional problems. Contingency contracting, peer-mediated interventions, token economies, time-out from positive reinforcement, and other reductive procedures based on reinforcement have all been successfully utilized to deal with problems with attention (Brown 1986; Cooper et al. 1987; Rosenbaum et al. 1975; Sindelar et al. 1982; Tawney and Gast 1984). Consequently, teachers who have noted attention problems among students with LD should utilize a behavioral intervention as the initial option of choice in the elimination of problems. Specific behavioral interventions are presented in detail in Chapter 7 of this text.

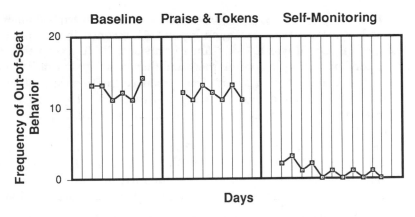

Figure 10.3 Frequency of David's out-of-seat behavior recorded during a 55-minute observation period in the classroom with self-monitoring.

Cognitive Behavioral Interventions

Cognitive behavioral instruction has been used for teaching students to act as their own behavior change agents. The strategy that seems most appropriate for intervention of attention behaviors is typically referred to as *self-monitoring* (Kendall and Braswell 1985; Meichenbaum 1977; Meichenbaum and Goodman 1971). Self-monitoring is the ability to repeatedly evaluate one's own behaviors in order to effect positive change in those behaviors (Rooney and Hallahan 1988). For example, Broden and colleagues (1971), in their classic study of self-monitoring, analyzed the effects of self-recording on the behavior of two eighth-grade students using an ABABCDA design. For example, the first student, Lisa, was observed by trained observers for 30 minutes per day throughout the study. Data from phase A (baseline) indicated that Lisa, on the average, exhibited appropriate attentional behaviors (e.g., facing the teacher, taking notes when appropriate) only 30% of the time. The B phases consisted of self-monitoring treatment phases in which Lisa was given a recording sheet with the printed directions to record her attending behaviors whenever she thought of it by marking a + when she was on task and a − when she was not. During phase C, self-recording was continued with the addition of the condition of praise by the teacher for good study habits. During phase D, self-recording was withdrawn and the praise was continued. The study was concluded with a return to baseline. Results demonstrated that these attention behaviors improved during treatment phases B, C, and D. Also, the frequency of these behaviors remained at relatively high levels when self-recording and praise were withdrawn.

An illustration of the principles of cognitive-behavioral intervention may be beneficial at this point. Let's return to David, the hypothetical student presented in the behavioral interventions section. Assume that the behavioral intervention was not successful and it was decided to initiate a cognitive-behavioral approach with David as shown in Figure 10.3.

For 11 days, David was given a cassette player with recorded bell tones that occurred at varying intervals averaging around 45 seconds in length. At the sound of the bell, David was to ask, "Am I in my seat?" He was instructed to check "yes" or "no" on his recording sheet and then return to the task at hand. During this 11-day intervention period, David reduced the frequency of his out-of-seat behavior to an average of two times per class period. The application of the cognitive-behavioral approach resulted in a considerable improvement in David's in-seat behavior.

In summary, self-monitoring has been successfully used among populations with disabilities, including those with LD (Broden et al. 1971; Hallahan et al. 1982; Rooney and Hallahan 1988). Research supports the effectiveness of self-monitoring for increasing on-task behaviors (see Hallahan and Sapona [1983] or Snider [1987] for reviews).

Medically Based Interventions

Medical science plays a major role in the area of ADD in the prescription of drugs to combat hyperactivity. If a student is hyperactive, he or she is more likely to have difficulty with learning. If educational remedies such as behavioral interventions and self-monitoring interventions have been tried and have not alleviated the problem, a drug intervention may be advised.

Types of Drug Interventions

Often the medication chosen for hyperactivity and attentional problems is one in the amphetamine family (Coons et al. 1987). The three stimulant medications most often prescribed for ADD are Cylert, Ritalin, and Dexedrine (Levine 1987). These medications vary in terms of their initial effectiveness rate and duration of action. Although Ritalin and Dexedrine become effective in less than half an hour, Cylert takes up to four weeks. Cylert is taken once a day and its effects are long-lasting. In contrast, the duration of action for Ritalin and Dexedrine is three to five hours. Therefore, it is necessary for a second dose of the medication to be administered at school. This may be problematic for school administration in terms of the security of the medication for the protection of other students as well as the provision of personnel to administer the medication to the student. An alternative is a time-release version of these medications; although the time-release version of Ritalin is called Ritalin, the time-release version of Dexedrine is called Spansule.

There is some concern about side effects of medication as well as possible abuse (Weiss and Hechtman 1986). An ideal medication controls hyperactivity, increases attention, and reduces impulsive and aggressive behaviors without inducing anorexia, drowsiness, insomnia, headaches, or other side effects (Forness and Kavale 1988; Levine 1987; Gadow 1986; Pelham 1986). Side effects are usually relatively minor and temporary and tend to diminish as tolerance develops, although effects vary from individual to individual (Levine 1987).

Medical Assessment

Clinical assessment procedures are used by pediatricians, pediatric neurologists, psychologists, and other specialists to diagnose ADD/H (Coleman 1992). These procedures may include but are not limited to measures of attention deficit, intelligence, achievement or visual-motor skills, assessment through use of an electroencephalogram, or pediatric-neurological evaluation.

The decision to prescribe medication should be based on these clinical findings, information provided by the parents, and, most importantly, on information provided by teachers. An attention deficit reaches its peak in a sit-down-all-day classroom situation (Safer and Allen 1976). For that reason, notes from anecdotal notebooks, observational recording forms, behavioral charts, and student work samples are critical to the decision-making process. Clearly, the less intrusive interventions should be attempted before initiation of a drug intervention. When the teacher can present data to indicate that one or more behavioral or cognitive-behavioral interventions has failed to result in improved attention, medical interventions may be considered.

A trial of medication is often a useful diagnostic tool to indicate the presence of a neurological abnormality. An atypical reaction to a medication such as Dexedrine or Ritalin can assist in making the diagnosis in that the use of such medication by a normal individual serves as an energizer. Therefore, a calming reaction to a stimulant medication serves as a diagnostic indicator of dysfunction in the central nervous system (Gadow 1986). However, not all hyperactive children are drug responders. Some researchers have found that 10% to 30% of hyperactive children become even worse on medication (Kinsbourne and Caplan 1979; Ross and Ross 1982).

Stimulant medications such as amphetamines have a more complex effect than the mere reduction of activity level. These drugs alter the quality of the student's activity and goal directedness. They can also have a significant effect on personality, mood, concentration, perception, and motor coordination. In addition, there are side effects associated with these medications. The teacher must be aware of the student's dosage and the type of medication prescribed in order to provide appropriate feedback in this regard. Since these effects are best observed by the teachers and parents, liaison of the medical personnel with the school and the family is necessary (Lerner 1988).

Thus, the teacher plays an important role in regulating the effectiveness of medical treatment. Daily data-based charts derived from event recording provide a visual representation of day-to-day performance and accurately portray changes in behavior that may require adjustments in medication. A chart such as the one found in Figure 10–3 should be provided to the physician on a regular basis. The physician utilizes such feedback in gauging the effectiveness of the medication and making appropriate modifications (Forness and Kavale 1988).

Efficacy of Drug Intervention

Numerous studies have shown that medically based interventions are effective in controlling problem behaviors in the classroom (Forness and Kavale 1988;

Silver 1987). Sixty percent to 90% of these students improve to varying degrees (Whalen and Henker 1976). Parent and teacher ratings, laboratory task performance, and direct observation have been utilized to document behavioral and attentional improvements.

Some research indicates that drug intervention improves academic classwork as well as behavior (Forness and Kavale 1988; Kavale 1982; Swanson et al. 1991). However, parents and teachers are often more interested in performance on standardized achievement tests, where the impact of drug interventions has been only modest. Further research is needed in which longitudinal designs are used to track children for a number of years to determine whether they think, learn, and socially function more effectively with medication, not whether they are quieter, more attentive, or productive in one particular situation (Kavale and Nye 1981).

Studies of the long-term effects of stimulant medications show no documented adverse consequences. Drug abuse has not been a problem for children who received stimulant medication for hyperactivity. In general, it appears that the long-term risks of medication are negligible (Levine 1987; Levy 1983).

For illustration, assume that our hypothetical student, David, has received behavioral intervention during the past month. Although there has been some improvement in the targeted behavior, David's in-seat behavior continued to vary significantly from that of his classmates.

The school multidisciplinary team conferred with David's parents regarding his high frequency of out-of-seat behaviors despite the rigorous application of behavioral interventions. The parents at that point chose to consult with their physician. After an initial examination, interviews with David's parents, and a review of all the assessment and intervention information from the school, the physician prescribed Ritalin for David.

As seen in Figure 10.4, during the baseline and praise and tokens phases, David was out of seat an average of 12 times per class period. However, when the change was made to a medically based intervention, out-of-seat behaviors dropped to an average of 2 occurrences per class period. David's teachers reported a significant change in attending behaviors, activity level, and permanent products. For example, work samples produced with and without the use of medication were compared. The handwriting, neatness, and accuracy varied so greatly that it was difficult to tell that the work had been completed by the same student.

Combined Approaches

Medication treatment by itself is seldom sufficient for dealing effectively with the total set of symptoms associated with attentional difficulties (Cherkes-Julkowski and Stolzengerg 1991). In the majority of cases, children do not take medication for attentional difficulties at home. As a result, the homework hour can be a particularly trying experience for all family members involved. Parents

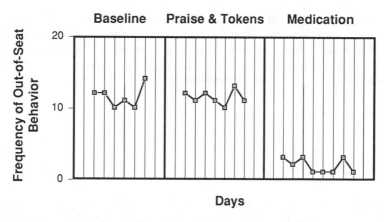

Figure 10.4 Frequency of David's out-of-seat behavior recorded during a 55-minute observation period in the classroom with Ritalin therapy.

also report that their children have difficulty sitting through a church service or functioning in some highly structured social situations (Silver 1987).

Empirical evidence supports the use of interventions that combine behavioral and medically based approaches (Abramowitz and O'Leary 1991; Pfiffner and Barkley 1990). As mentioned previously, behavioral approaches can be adapted to meet a child's needs in a variety of environments. A student may have a plan that combines several behavioral interventions to deal with different situations in the home such as homework, household chores, or bedtime. The approaches used at home may be similar or vary considerably from those employed in the school setting, depending on the needs of the individual student.

When researchers have studied impaired children with ADD/H, the results have been equivocal (Conrad et al. 1971; Richardson et al. 1988). However, none of the studies conducted during the past decade suggest that cognitive training enhances the beneficial effects of medication (Abikoff 1991).

In summary, behavioral and medically based interventions can be combined for different environments including school and home settings (Abramowitz and O'Leary 1991; Pfiffner and Barkley 1990). Further research is needed to investigate interventions that combine cognitive-behavioral and medically based approaches for students with LD and attentional difficulties.

SUMMARY

A considerable proportion of students with LD have a secondary diagnosis of ADD. Attention deficit disorder is characterized by impulsivity, hyperactivity, and attentional problems. Students with LD and ADD have been differentiated from normal control groups in terms of sustained attention, some types of distractibility, and task orientation. Assessment, which includes the components of teacher rating scales, peer evaluation, and direct observation, should be followed by behavioral intervention. This approach may later be supplemented by cognitive-behavioral and medically based interventions. Through these procedures the attention problems of most students with LD can be substantially controlled.

REFERENCES

Abikoff, H. (1991). Cognitive training in ADHD children: Less to it than meets the eye. *Journal of Learning Disabilities, 24,* 205–209.

Abikoff, H., Gittelman, R., & Klein, D. (1980). Classroom observation code for hyperactive children: A replication of validity. *Journal of Counseling and Clinical Psychology, 48,* 772–783.

Abikoff, H., Gittelman-Klein, R., & Klein, D. (1977). Validation of a classroom observation code for hyperactive children. *Journal of Consulting and Clinical Psychology, 45,* 772–783.

Abramowitz, A. J., & O'Leary, S. G. (1991). Behavior interventions for the classroom: Implications for students with ADHD. *School Psychology Review, 20,* 221–235.

Achenbach, T. M., & Edelbrook, C. (1986). Manual for the Teacher Report Form and teacher version of the Child Behavior Profile. Burlington: University of Vermont, Department of Psychiatry.

Alabisco, F. (1972). Inhibitory functions of attention in reducing hyperactive behavior. *American Journal of Mental Deficiency, 77,* 259–282.

American Psychiatric Association. (1980). *Diagnostic and statistical manual of mental disorders* (3rd ed.). Washington, DC: American Psychiatric Association.

American Psychiatric Association (1987). *Diagnostic and statistical manual of mental disorders* (3rd ed. rev.). Washington, DC: American Psychiatric Association.

Atkins, M. S., & Milich, R. (1988). The IOWA-Conners Teacher Rating Scale. In M. Hersen & A. Bellack (Eds.), *Dictionary of behavioral assessment techniques* (pp. 273–274). New York: Pergamon Press.

Atkins, M. S., & Pelham, W. E. (1991). School-based assessment of attention deficit-hyperactivity disorder. *Journal of Learning Disabilities, 24,* 197–204.

Atkins, M. S., Pelham, W. E., & Licht, M. H. (1988). The development and validation of objective classroom measures of conduct and attention deficit disorder. In R. J. Prinz (Ed.), *Advances in behavioral assessment of children and families* (vol. 4), (pp. 3–31). Greenwich, CT: JAI Press.

Barkley, R. A., (1977). A review of stimulant drug research with hyperactive children. *Journal of Child Psychology and Psychiatry, 18,* 137–165.

Barkley, R. A. (1988). Attention deficit disorder with hyperactivity. In E. J. Mash & L. G. Terdal (Eds.), Behavioral assessment of childhood disorders (2nd ed.), (pp. 69–105). New York: Guilford.

Bender, W. N. (1985). Differences between learning disabled and non-learning disabled children in temperament and behavior. *Learning Disability Quarterly, 8,* 11–18.

Bender, W. N. (1992). *Learning disabilities: Characteristics, identification, and teaching strategies.* Needham Heights, MA: Allyn and Bacon.

Bender, W. N., Wyne, M. D., Stuck, G. B., & Bailey, D. B. (1984). Relative peer status of learning disabled, educable mentally handicapped, low achieving, and normally achieving children. *Child Study Journal, 13*(4), 209–216.

Blackwell, S. L., McIntyre, C. W., & Murray, M. E. (1983). Information processed from brief visual displays by learning-disabled boys. *Child Development, 54,* 927–940.

Broden, M., Hall, R. V., & Mitts, B. (1971). The effect of self-recording on the classroom behavior of two eighth grade students. *Journal of Applied Behavioral Analysis, 4,* 191–199.

Brown, L. (1986). Assessing sociometric development. In D. D. Hammill (Ed.), *Assessing the abilities and instructional needs of students* (pp. 502–609). Austin, TX: Pro-Ed.

Browning, R. M. (1967). Effect of irrelevant peripheral visual stimuli on discrimination learning in minimally brain-damaged children. *Journal of Consulting Psychology, 31,* 371–376.

Bryan, T., & Wheeler, R. (1972). Perception of learning disabled children: The eye of the observer. *Journal of Learning Disabilities, 5,* 484–488.

Cherkes-Julkowski, M., & Stolzengerg, J. (1991). The learning disability of attention deficit disorder. *Learning Disabilities: A Multidisciplinary Journal, 21,*(1), 8–15.

Cohen, N. J., & Douglas, V. I. (1972). Characteristics of the orienting response in hyperactive and normal children. *Psychophysiology, 9,* 238–245.

Coleman, M. C. (1992). *Behavior disorders: Theory and practice* (2nd ed.). Boston: Allyn and Bacon.

Conrad, W. G., Dworkin, E. S., Shai, A., & Tobiessen, J. E. (1971). Effects of amphetamine therapy and prescriptive tutoring on the behavior and achievement of lower class hyperactive children. *Journal of Learning Disabilities, 4,* 45–53.

Coons, H. W., Klorman, R., & Borgstedt, A. D. (1987). Effects of methylphenidate on adolescents with a childhood history of attention deficit disorder. *Journal of the American Academy of Child and Adolescent Psychiatry, 26,* 368–374.

Cooper, J. O., Heron, T. E., & Heward, W. L. (1987). *Applied behavioral analysis.* Columbus, OH: Merrill.

Copeland, A. P., & Wisniewski, N. M. (1981). Learning disability and hyperactivity: Deficits in selective attention. *Journal of Experimental Child Psychology, 32,* 88–101.

Danier, K. B., Klorman, R., Salzman, L. F., Hess, D. W., Davidson, P. W., & Michael, R. L. (1981). Learning-disordered children's evoked potentials during sustained attention. *Journal of Abnormal Child Psychology, 9,* 79–94.

Epstein, M. A., Shaywitz, S. E., Shaywitz, B. A., & Woolston, J. L. (1991). The boundaries of attention deficit disorder. *Journal of Learning Disabilities, 24,* 78–86.

Firestone, P., & Douglas, V. (1975). The effects of reward and punishment on reaction times and autonomic activity in hyperactive and normal children. *Journal of Abnormal Child Psychology, 3,* 201–216.

Forness, S., & Kavale, K. (1988). Psychopharmological treatment: A note on classroom effects. *Journal of Learning Disabilities, 21*(3), 144–147.

Frick, P. J., & Lahey, B. B. (1991). Nature and characteristics of attention deficit hyperactivity disorder. *School Psychology Review, 20,* 163–173.

Fowler, S. A. (1986). Peer-monitoring and self-monitoring: Alternatives to traditional teacher management. *Exceptional Children, 52,* 573–581.

Gadow, K. (1986). *Children on medication* (vols. 1 and 2). San Diego, CA: College Hill Press.

Goldberg, J. O., & Konstantareas, M. M. (1981). Vigilance in hyperactive and normal children on a self-placed operant task. *Journal of Child Psychology and Psychiatry, 22,* 55–63.

Goodyear, P., & Hynd, G. W. (in press). Attention deficit disorder with (Add/H) and without (ADD/WO) hyperactivity: Behavioral and neuropsychological differentiation. *Psychological Bulletin.*

Gresham, F. M. (1981). Validity of social skills measures for assessing social competence in low status children: A multivariate investigation. *Developmental Psychology, 17,* 390–398.

Gresham, F. M., & Elliott, S. N. (1990). Social Skills Rating System manual. Circle Pines, MN: American Guidance Service.

Hagen, J. W. (1967). The effect of distraction on selective attention. *Child Development, 38,* 685–694.

Hallahan, D. P., Lloyd, J. W., Kosiewicz, M. M., Kauffman, J. M., & Graves, A. W. (1979). Self-monitoring of attention as a treatment for a learning disabled boy's off-task behavior. *Learning Disability Quarterly, 2,* 24–32.

Hallahan, D. P., Lloyd, J. W., & Stoller, L. (1982). *Improving attention with self-monitoring: A manual for teachers.* Charlottesville: University of Virginia Institute for Learning Disabilities.

Hallahan, D. P., & Sapona, R. (1983). Self-monitoring of attention with learning disabled children: Past research and current issues. *Journal of Learning Disabilities, 16,* 616–620.

Hamlett, K. W., Pelligrini, D. S., & Conners, C. K. (1987). An investigation of executive processes in the problem solving of attention deficit disorder-hyperactive children. *Journal of Pediatric Psychology, 12,* 227–240.

Howes, C. (1988). Peer interaction of young children. *Monographs of the Society for Research in Child Development, 53,* Serial No. 217.

Johnson, J. M., & Pennypacker, H. S. (1980). *Strategies and tactics for human behavioral research.* Hillsdale, NJ: Erlbaum.

Johnston, C., Pelham, W. E., Crawford, J., & Atkins, M. S. (1988). A psychometric study of positive and negative nominations and the Pupil Evaluation Inventory. *Journal of Abnormal Child Psychology, 16,* 617–626.

Kavale, K. (1982). Meta-analysis of the relationship between visual perceptual skills and reading achievement. *Journal of Learning Disabilities, 15,* 42–51.

Kavale, K., & Nye, C. (1981). Identification criteria for learning disabilities: A survey of the research literature. *Learning Disability Quarterly, 4*(4), 383–388.

Kendall P. C., & Braswell, L. (1985). *Cognitive behavioral therapy for impulsive children.* New York: Guilford.

Kibruz, C. S., Miller, S. R., & Morrow, L. W. (1985). Structured learning using self-monitoring to promote maintenance and generalization of social skills across settings for a behaviorally disordered adolescent. *Behavioral Disorders, 10,* 45–52.

Kinsbourne, M., & Caplan, P. (1979). *Children's learning and attention problems.* Boston: Little, Brown.

Kirchner, G. L. (1976). Differences in the vigilance performance of second grade males under four experimental conditions. *Journal of Educational Psychology, 68,* 696–701.

Krupski, A. (1975). Heart rate changes during a fixed reaction time task in normal and retarded adult males. *Psychophysiology, 16,* 262–267.

Krupski, A. (1986). Attention problems in youngsters with learning handicaps. In J. K. Torgesen & B. Y. Wong (Eds.), *Psychological and educational perspectives on learning disabilities.* (pp. 161–192). New York: Academic Press.

LaGreca, A. M., & Stone, W. L. (1990). LD status and achievement: Confounding variables in the study of children's social status, self-esteem, and behavioral functioning. *Journal of Learning Disabilities, 23*(8), 483–490.

Lambert, N. M. (1988). Adolescent outcomes for hyperactive children. *American Psychologist, 43,* 786–799.

Lambert, N. M., Sassone, D., Hartsough, C. S., & Sandoval, J. (1987). Persistence of hyperactivity symptoms from childhood to adolescence and associated outcomes. *American Journal of Orthopsychiatry, 57,* 22–32.

Laskey, E. Z., & Tobin, H. (1973). Linguistic and nonlinguistic competing message effects. *Journal of Learning Disabilities, 6*(4), 243–250.

Leigh, J. (1987). Adaptive behavior of children with learning disabilities. *Journal of Learning Disabilities, 20,* 557–562.

Lerner, J. (1988). *Learning disabilities: Theories, diagnosis, and teaching strategies* (5th ed.). Boston: Houghton Mifflin.

Lerner, J. W., & Lerner, S. R. (1991). Attention deficit disorder: Issues and questions. *Focus on Exceptional Children, 24*(3), 1–17.

Levine, M. (1987). *Developmental variation and learning disabilities.* Cambridge, MA: Educator's Publishing Service.

Levy, H. (1983). Developmental dyslexia: A pediatrician's perspective. *Schumpert Medical Quarterly, 1,* 200–207.

Lloyd, J. (1980). Academic instruction and cognitive behavior modification: The need for attack-strategy training. *Exceptional Education Quarterly, 1,* 53–63.

Looney, J., & Milich, R. (1982). Hyperactivity, inattention, and aggression in clinical practice. In M. Wolraich & D. K. Routh (Eds.), *Advances in behavioral pediatrics* (vol. 2) (pp. 113–137). Greenwich, CT.: JAI Press.

McBurnett, K., & Pfiffner, L. J. (1991). ADHD and LD. *Journal of Learning Disabilities, 24,* 258–259.

McKinney, J. D., & Feagans, L. (1983). Adaptive classroom behavior of learning disabled students. *Journal of Learning Disabilities, 16,* 360–367.

McKinney, J. D., McClure, S., & Feagans, L. (1982). Classroom behavior of learning disabled children. *Learning Disability Quarterly, 5,* 45–52.

Meichenbaum, D. (1977). *Cognitive-behavior modification: An integrative approach.* New York: Plenum Press.

Meichenbaum, D., & Goodman, J. (1969). The developmental control of operant motor responding by verbal operants. *Journal of Experimental Child Psychology, 7,* 553–565.

Meichenbaum, D., & Goodman, J. (1971). Training impulsive children to talk to themselves: A means of developing self control. *Journal of Abnormal Psychology, 77,* 115–126.

Michael, R. L., Klorman, R., Salzman, L. F., Borgstedt, A. D., & Dainer, K. B. (1981). Normalizing effects of methylphenidate on hyperactive children's vigilance performance and evoked potentials. *Psychophysiology, 18,* 665–677.

Nobler, L. W., & Nobler, E. H. (1975). Auditory discrimination of learning-disabled children in quiet and classroom noise. *Journal of Learning Disabilities, 8,*(100), 73–76.

Nuechterlein, K. H. (1983). Signal detection in vigilance tasks and behavioral attributes among offspring of schizophrenic mothers and among hyperactive children. *Journal of Abnormal Psychology, 92,* 4–28.

Pelham, W. (1986). The effects of psychostimulant drugs on learning and academic achievement in children with attention-deficit disorders and learning disabilities. In J. Torgesen & B. Wong (Eds.), *Psychological and educational perspectives on learning disabilities* (pp. 257–296). Orlando, FL: Academic.

Pelham, W. E., Atkins, M. S., & Murphy, H. A. (1981). Attention deficit disorder with and without hyperactivity: Definitional issues and correlates. In W. E. Pelham (Ed.), *DSM III category of attention deficit disorders: Rationale, operationalization and correlates.* Los Angeles: American Psychological Association.

Pelham, W. E., & Milich, R. (1984). Peer relations in children with hyperactivity/attention deficit disorder. *Journal of Learning Disabilities, 17,* 560–567.

Pfiffner, L. J., & Barkley, R. A. (1990). Classroom management methods. In R. A. Barkley (Ed.), *Attention deficit hyperactivity disorders: A handbook for diagnosis and treatment* (pp. 438–539). New York: Guilford Press.

Quay, H. C., & Peterson, D. (1983). *Manual for the Revised Behavior Problem Checklist.* Coral Gables, FL: Author.

Radosh, A., & Gittelman, R. (1981). The effect of appealing distractors on the performance of hyperactive children. *Journal of Abnormal Child Psychology, 9,* 179–189.

Richardson, E., Kupietz, S. S., Winsberg, B. G., Maitinsky, S., & Mendell, N. (1988). Effects of methylphenidate dosage in hyperactive reading disabled children: II. Reading achievement. *Journal of the American Academy of Child and Adolescent Psychiatry, 27,* 78–87.

Rosenbaum, A., O'Leary, K. D., & Jacob, R. G. (1975). Behavioral intervention with hyperactive children: Group consequences as a supplement to individual contingencies. *Behavior Therapy, 6,* 315–323.

Rooney, K. J., & Hallahan, D. P. (1988). The effects of self-monitoring on adult behavior and student independence. *Learning Disabilities Research, 3,* 88–93.

Ross, A. O. (1976). *Psychological aspects of learning disabilities and reading disorders.* New York: McGraw-Hill.

Ross, D. M., & Ross, S. A. (1982). *Hyperactivity: Current issues, research, theory.* New York: Wiley.

Rugel, R. P., Cheatam, D., & Mitchell, A. (1978). Body movement and inattention in learning-disabled and normal children. *Journal of Abnormal Child Psychology, 6,* 325–337.

Rugel, R. P., & Rosenthal, R. (1974). Skin conductance, reaction time, and observational ratings in learning disabled-children. *Journal of Abnormal Child Psychology, 2,* 183–192.

Sabournie, E. J., Kauffman, J. M., & Cullinan, D. A. (1990). Extended sociometric status of adolescents with mild handicaps: A cross-categorical perspective. *Exceptionality, 1,* 197–209.

Safer, D. J., & Allen, R. P. (1976). *Hyperactive children: Diagnosis and management.* Baltimore, MD: University Park Press.

Samuels, S. J. (1967). Attentional process in reading: The effect of pictures on reading responses. *Journal of Educational Psychology, 58,* 337–342.

Schaughency, E. A., & Rothlind, J. (1991). Assessment and classification of attention-deficit hyperactivity disorders. *School Psychology Review, 20,* 187–202.

Shaywitz, B. (1987). *Hyperactivity/attention deficit disorder. Learning disabilities: A report to the U.S. Congress.* Washington, DC: Interagency Committee on Learning Disabilities.

Shaywitz S., & Shaywitz, B. (1988). Attention deficit disorder: Current perspectives. In J. Kavanaugh & J. Truss (Eds.), *Learning disabilities: Proceedings of the national conference* (pp. 369–567). Parkston, MD: York Press.

Shaywitz, S., & Shaywitz, B. (1991). Introduction to the special series on attention deficit disorder. *Journal of Learning Disabilities, 24,* 68–71.

Silver, L. B. (1987). *Attention deficit disorders.* Booklet for parents. Summit, NJ: CIBA.

Silver, L. B. (1990). Attention deficit-hyperactivity disorder: Is it a learning disability or a related disorder? *Journal of Learning Disabilities, 23,* 394–397.

Sindelar, P. T., Housaker, M. S., & Jenkins, J. R. (1982). Response cost and reinforcement contingencies of managing behavior of distractible children in tutorial settings. *Learning Disabilities Quarterly, 5,* 3–13.

Smith, C. R. (1991). Learning disabilities: The interaction of learner, task, and setting (2nd ed.). Boston: Allyn and Bacon.

Snider, V. (1987). Use of self-monitoring of attention with LD students: Research and applications. *Learning Disability Quarterly, 10,* 139–151.

Stroufe, L. A., Sonies, B. C., West, W. D., & Wright, F. S. (1973). Anticipatory heart rate deceleration and reaction time in children with and without referral for learning disability. *Child Development, 44,* 267–273.

Swanson, H. L. (1980). Auditory and visual vigilance in normal and learning disabled readers. *Learning Disability Quarterly, 3,* 71–78.

Swanson, H. L. (1983). A developmental study of vigilance in learning-disabled and non-disabled children. *Journal of Abnormal Child Psychology, 11,* 415–429.

Swanson, J. M., Cantwell, D., Lerner, M., McBurnett, K., & Hanna, G. (1991). Effects of stimulant medication on learning in children with ADHD. *Journal of Learning Disabilities, 24,* 219–230.

Sykes, D. H., Douglas, V. I., Weiss, G., & Minde, K. K. (1971). Attention in hyperactive children and the effect of methylphenidate (Ritalin). *Journal of Child Psychology and Psychiatry, 12,* 129–139.

Tawney, J., & Gast, D. (1984). *Single subject research in special education.* Columbus, OH: Merrill.

Vail, C., & Huntington, D. (1993). Classroom behavioral interventions of students with learning disabilities. In W. N. Bender (Ed.), *Clinical approaches in learning disabilities: Best practices*. North Potomac, MD: Andover Medical Publications.

Vincent, J. P., Williams, B. J., Harris, G. E., & Duval, G. C. (1981). Classroom observation of hyperactive children: A multiple validation study. In K. D. Gadow & J. Looney (Eds.), *Psychological aspects of drug treatment for hyperactivity* (pp. 207–248). Boulder, CO: Westview Press.

Weiss, G., & Hechtman, L. T. (1986). *Hyperactive children grown-up: Empirical findings and theoretical considerations*. New York: Guilford Press.

Weller, C. (1980). Discrepancy and severity in the learning disabled: A consolidated perspective. *Learning Disability Quarterly, 3*, 84–90.

Weller, C., & Strawser, S. (1981). *Weller-Strawser scales of adaptive behavior for the learning disabled*. Novato, CA: Academic Therapy.

Whalen, C., & Henker, B. (1991). Social impact of stimulant treatment for hyperactive children. *Journal of Learning Disabilities, 24*, 231–241.

Zahn, T., Abate, F., Little, B., & Wender, P. (1975). Minimal brain dysfunction, stimulant drugs and autonomic nervous system activity. *Archives of General Psychiatry, 32*, 381–387.

Zentall, S. S., & Shaw, J. H. (1980). Effects of classroom noise on performance and activity of second-grade hyperactive and control children. *Journal of Educational Psychology, 72*, 830–840.

11

Social Skills Training: Why, Who, What, and How

Sharon Vaughn
Annette La Greca

Making and maintaining friendships is an integral part of development. Having friends, getting along with others, and being liked by peers is at least as important to youngsters as academic achievement and athletic prowess. The purpose of this chapter is to provide an introduction to the social functioning of students with learning disabilities (LD) and an overview of social skills interventions developed to assist youngsters who need help in friendship making, social problem solving, and social skills. The chapter is organized around four guiding questions: Why teach social skills? Who needs social skills training? What social skills need to be taught? How can we teach social skills?

WHY TEACH SOCIAL SKILLS?
Social Skills Problems

One reason social skills need to be taught is that many students with LD demonstrate social difficulties that interfere with their success in school and with their relationships with peers. Teachers (Vaughn et al. 1990), parents (McConaughy and Ritter 1986), and peers (e.g., Bruininks 1978; Bryan 1974, 1976; Gresham and Reschley 1986; Siperstein et al. 1978; Stone and La Greca 1990) recognize the social difficulties of students with LD.

Research on the social skills problems of students with LD was reviewed by members of the U.S. Interagency Committee on Learning Disabilities sponsored by the National Institute of Child Health and Human Development (NICHHD) (Kavanagh and Truss 1988). After extensive discussion the committee recommended to Congress a new definition of LD that includes *social skills* as one of the disorders manifested by individuals with LD. Based on empirical findings demonstrating that many students with LD have social difficulties, the U.S. Interagency Committee on Learning Disabilities proposed the following definition:

> Learning disabilities is a generic term that refers to a heterogeneous group of disorders manifested by significant difficulties in the

acquisition and use of listening, speaking, reading, writing, reasoning, or mathematical abilities, or of social skills. These disorders are intrinsic to the individual and presumed to be due to central nervous system dysfunction. Even though a learning disability may occur concomitantly with other handicapping conditions (e.g., sensory impairment, mental retardation, social and emotional disturbance), with socioenvironmental influences (e.g., cultural differences, insufficient or inappropriate instruction, psychogenic factors), and especially with attention deficit disorder, all of which may cause learning problems, a learning disability is not the direct results of those conditions or influences. (pp. 550–551)

This is the first definition that includes social skills as one of the potential difficulties associated with LD. Although this definition is yet to be adopted by the U.S. Department of Education, it is, nevertheless, an important statement about the role of social skills in defining learning disabilities.

Social Skills and Mainstreaming

A second reason social skills need to be taught is that students with LD are not learning social skills in mainstreamed classroom settings (Gresham and Reschly 1986; Vaughn 1985). One impetus for educating mildly handicapped students in the least restrictive environment was the presumption that the regular classroom would provide a social context for these students to acquire social skills from classmates and increase their range of friends. However, there is little reason to believe that this is occurring (Center and Wascom 1986; Vaughn 1985). Social skills are difficult to acquire and require systematic instruction. Merely placing students in the regular classroom as a means of improving their social functioning appears to be insufficient. The regular classroom may be a necessary context to observe and practice social skills, but such placement needs to be supplemented with appropriate instruction and intervention.

Social Alienation and Learning Disabilities

A third reason for increased interest in the social functioning of students with LD is the association between social alienation (an outcome of poor social functioning) and school dropout (Finn 1989). Students with LD are at higher risk for social alienation from teachers and classmates (Seidel and Vaughn 1991) and demonstrate higher school dropout rates than their non–learning-disabled classmates (Zigmond and Thornton 1985). Furthermore, these processes appear to be intertwined. When students with LD who dropped out of school were compared with students with LD who were school completers, the dropouts reported greater social alienation from both classmates and teachers than did the completers (Seidel and Vaughn 1991). The items that most significantly discriminated between school completers and dropouts were: "I thought of my teachers as friends," "Most of my teachers like me," "If I moved away, I would have missed my classmates," and "I looked forward to seeing my friends at school." School completers endorsed these items at a higher rate.

Students' social alienation is of particular interest because it is an excellent predictor of school dropout (Balswick and Balswick 1980; Finn 1989; Seidel and Vaughn 1991; Wheelock 1986). Furthermore, as our family and social structures change, schools are increasingly important as socialization agents (Callahan and Long 1983). Thus, students' feelings of being disengaged from their classmates and teachers increase the likelihood that they will drop out of school (Miller et al. 1987). The opposite side of social alienation is involvement, or affiliation (Finn 1989), and students with LD also demonstrate low involvement in school activities and low involvement in the learning process within the classroom (McIntosh et al. in progress). Many students with LD feel they are unimportant to their peers and teachers and that school is not a place where they are engaged or interested. Consequently it is not surprising that they also demonstrate low involvement in classroom and schoolwide activities.

Because social relations and feelings of inclusion are important to students' academic success, teachers have been encouraged to incorporate peer interactions into academic activities and to work with students for an extended period of time so that they can form personal relationships with classmates. Students' primary frame of reference is their peers and activities related to their peers (Strahan 1988). For many students, school seems meaningful primarily as a place to meet and keep up with the social activities related to friendships (Strahan 1988). Students with LD who feel alienated from teachers and peers may have insufficient reason to remain in school.

Low Social Status and Negative Outcomes

The fourth and perhaps most important reason social skills need to be taught is the persuasive evidence linking low social status with negative outcomes such as emotional maladjustment (Cowen et al. 1973; Roff 1963), criminality (Roff 1975; Roff et al. 1972), and school dropout (Kupersmidt 1983; Lambert 1972; Parker and Asher 1987). Furthermore, peers' perceptions of their classmates, especially *negative* perceptions, are relatively stable over time (Bryan 1976; Coie and Dodge, 1983; Howes 1990), so that social problems are likely to endure unless interventions are implemented.

In addition to the link between early peer relationship difficulties and later life problems, low peer acceptance is also associated with current emotional adjustment problems. Studies have shown that children who are disliked by their peers report significantly more social anxiety (La Greca 1989; La Greca et al. 1988) and loneliness (Asher and Wheeler 1985) than their more accepted classmates. Given these associations between peer relations and emotional adjustment, it seems imperative that interventions be developed and implemented to assist students in acquiring appropriate social skills to interact successfully with others and to reduce the negative consequences associated with low peer acceptance.

A number of studies have assessed the social status of students with LD (see, for review, Dudley-Marling and Edmiaston [1985]). With few exceptions (Prilliman 1981; Sabornie and Kauffman 1986), the majority of studies (e.g., Bryan 1974; Bryan and Bryan 1978; Bursuck 1983: Gresham and Reschly 1986; La Greca and Stone 1990; Siperstein et al. 1978; Stone and La Greca 1990) reveal that the peer acceptance of students with LD is lower than that of their non–learning-disabled classmates. Moreover, students with LD are disproportionately represented in negative social status classifications, such as rejected and neglected, and underrepresented in the positive social status classification of popular (Stone and La Greca 1990; Vaughn et al. 1990) (see Chapter 10). In sum, students with LD often are not well accepted by their classmates and are frequently rejected.

Despite these findings, it is important to note that many students with LD are accepted by their peers. Although a considerably higher proportion of students with LD than non–learning-disabled students are identified with low peer acceptance (approximately 50%) (Stone and La Greca 1990; Vaughn et al. 1991; Wiener et al. 1990), the remaining students with LD have adequate peer relationships and are not at risk for later problems. Ochoa and Palmer (1991) conducted a study that illustrates this point. They compared the peer acceptance of Hispanic students identified as learning-disabled with Hispanic non-LD classmates, finding that the Hispanic LD students received significantly lower peer ratings. Despite lower ratings of acceptance, half the Hispanic LD group attained at least average sociometric ratings, much like the results from studies with non-Hispanic students (Perlmutter et al. 1983; Sabornie and Kauffman 1986; Stone and La Greca 1990). The peer ratings of students with LD demonstrate considerable within-group variability, with many students experiencing satisfactory social status. However, sufficient numbers of students with LD exhibit extreme social difficulties that attention to these problems is a major clinical concern.

To date, most of the studies examining the social status and friendships of students with LD have been conducted in regular classroom settings. Less information is known about the friendship network of students outside the school setting. In one of the few studies in this area, Ackerman and Howes (1986) interviewed 28 students with LD regarding their "out of school" friendships. Interestingly, 20 of the 28 students with LD indicated that they had best friends, but only 5 (25%) indicated that the best friend was a schoolmate. The "after school" data on these students revealed that they participated in after-school activities and informal social activities with friends and generally led active social lives. Unfortunately, these students were enrolled in a private school rather than in a mainstreamed public school setting, which is more typical in the research literature. Thus, it is difficult to determine the extent to which social activities of these students may have been enhanced by a family network that is supportive of education and participation in extracurricular activities. The extent to which this active social life represents youngsters with LD as a whole needs to be determined.

In summary, this section of the chapter has elaborated on four reasons why it is important to teach social skills to students with LD. However, as discussed previously, not all students with LD demonstrate low peer acceptance or difficulties in social functioning. In the next section we will review several factors that are important to consider before identifying students for social interventions.

WHO NEEDS SOCIAL SKILLS TRAINING?

The social-emotional functioning of students with LD is quite heterogeneous (Fuerst et al. 1989). As previously stated, about half the students with LD demonstrate low peer acceptance, so it is unlikely that all students with LD would benefit from social skills training. Before we can adequately prescribe appropriate interventions for students with LD, we need to better understand the reasons underlying low peer acceptance of students with LD, which include poor academic achievement and behavior problems.

Achievement

Low achievement is a significant correlate of children's low social status (Dodge et al. 1982; Green et al. 1980; La Greca and Stone 1990). Since students with LD are by definition low performers academically, the extent to which they differ from low-achieving students in their peer acceptance needs to be determined.

Most of the initial studies that established the low peer acceptance of students with LD did not use a low-achieving contrast group. Recently, studies have attempted to discern the extent to which the peer acceptance of students with LD is distinct from other low achievers. In an examination of the peer acceptance of students prior to identification as learning-disabled, Vaughn and colleagues (1990) found that, as early as the second month in kindergarten, students with LD were less well accepted by their classmates and more frequently rejected than were average- or high-achieving students. There were no significant differences between the peer acceptance of students with LD and other low-achieving students, although students with LD were more frequently rejected by peers than were low-achieving students. A second prospective study followed students from kindergarten through third grade and reported that at no time did the peer acceptance scores of students with LD differ from those of low-achieving students (Vaughn et al. in press). While the sample size in this study was relatively small (10 LD; 10 low achievers) the findings are significant because they follow target students longitudinally and include different peer raters across grades.

When the peer relations of students with LD are contrasted with the low-achieving classmates, the findings have been somewhat equivocal. Several studies

have indicated that when achievement is controlled, there are few differences between LD and non-LD students on peer acceptance (Bender et al. 1984; Bursuck
1983; Oliva 1990). However, in the most comprehensive study to date, La Greca
and Stone (1990) matched a low-achieving (LA) group (n = 32) with an LD
group (n = 32) on sex, class, race, and reading achievement to examine social
status and peer ratings. A comparison group of average to high achievers (AA)
was also included. Their results indicated that students with LD received significantly lower ratings of peer acceptance and fewer positive friendship nominations than either the LA or AA groups. Surprisingly, the LA and AA groups did
not differ significantly. Results from a study by Bursuck (1989) provide support
for the La Greca and Stone findings that LD students can be differentiated from
LA students in terms of peer acceptance. Poor achievement alone cannot explain
the poor social status of youth with learning disabilities.

One of the interesting findings from the La Greca and Stone (1990) study
is that students with LD could not be differentiated from low-achieving students
on the basis of negative peer nominations. That is, LD students did not receive
significantly more "least liked" nominations than did low achievers. However,
LD students were more frequently identified as neglected (i.e., they received few
positive and few negative nominations from classmates). An important question
for future research is the extent to which the students with LD are known by their
classmates. Since students with LD were removed from the regular classroom for
several hours each day, usually during the academic time that involves group
work and social interaction, these students may not have been well known to
their classmates, thus explaining the frequency with which they were neglected.

Further research on how the social status of students with LD compares
with other low-achieving students is needed to ascertain the extent to which the
peer problems of students with LD are distinct from other low-achieving students. This issue is particularly relevant in light of the NICHD definition that
considers social skills as one of the deficits manifested by students with LD. Further research may reveal that social skills difficulties are common to the larger
subgroup of students who are low achieving and are not specific to students with
LD, or, alternatively that social skills deficits are overrepresented in a subgroup
of students with LD.

Behavior Problems

It is quite likely that some of the students who are poorly accepted by their
classmates demonstrate concomitant behavior problems (e.g., conduct disorders,
attention problems, aggression) that interfere with their social functioning. The
presence of behavior problems needs to be identified before implementing an intervention because the intervention should address the specific behavior problem.
For example, the type of social intervention developed for an extremely aggressive student who had no friends would be different than one developed for a shy,
anxious-withdrawn student who also had no friends.

Bender and Smith (1990) conducted a meta-analysis of 25 studies that compared the behaviors of students with and without LD. Five overall areas were evaluated: on-task behavior, off-task behavior, conduct disorders, distractibility, and shy/withdrawn behavior. Based on observational and teacher rating data, students with LD demonstrated significantly more behavior problems in all areas than non-LD students, with the effect size clustering around one standard deviation.

One caveat to these findings is that many of the studies have examined only boys. Thus, it is not apparent whether the same conclusions would apply to girls with LD. In view of this concern, the results of a recent study (Ritter 1989) examining the behavioral functioning of adolescent girls with LD is of particular importance. The 51 girls with LD who participated in the study demonstrated poor social competence and elevated behavior problems relative to nondisabled girls. Overall, students with LD demonstrate significant behavioral difficulties that have direct implications for their success in mainstreamed educational programs.

For the most part, students with LD are referred by their regular classroom teachers for evaluation and placement. Consequently, an important consideration for future research is the extent to which students who have serious learning problems coexisting with behavior problems are more likely to be referred for special services than students with serious learning problems alone. This issue is particularly pertinent to understanding existing research findings. For instance, the studies evaluated by Bender and Smith (1990) were conducted with school-identified populations and may therefore reflect a population of students with *combined* learning and behavior problems. Regardless, many students with LD display a range of behavioral difficulties from severely anxious and withdrawn to extreme conduct disorder. A complete educational program should consider both the behavior problems and serious learning problems of individuals with LD.

Of perhaps greater concern is the overlap between LD and attention deficit disorders. In one of the few studies that matched LD students with other low achievers (LA) and average to high achievers (AA) on the basis of sex, classroom, and ethnicity, La Greca and Stone (1990) found that the students with LD displayed significantly more attention problems, but not conduct problems or anxiety, than the AA students. Furthermore, the boys with LD were rated by teachers as having more attention problems than both the LA and AA boys, whereas the LD girls only differed from the average achievers in this area. Interestingly, girls with LD (but not boys) were reported to be significantly more anxious than either the LA or AA girls; in fact, the anxiety scores for the girls with LD were almost one standard deviation above the mean for the school population.

Consistent with these findings, in a prospective study examining the social functioning of students with LD prior to their identification as learning-disabled (Vaughn et al. 1990), students with LD differed from both the average-achieving and high-achieving groups in terms of anxiety withdrawal, psychotic behavior, and attention problems. Although their scores on anxiety withdrawal and psychotic behavior were in the average range, as early as kindergarten, LD students' scores on attention problems were one standard deviation above the norm.

In a study conducted by Lambert and Sandoval (1980), 40% of the elementary children with attention problems also met stringent criteria for the presence of a learning disability. Furthermore, several studies have examined students who demonstrate both LD and attention problems and found that these students evidence even more severe social and behavioral problems than do students with LD without attention problems (Bickett and Milich 1987; Breen and Barkley 1984; Flicek and Landau 1985). In view of findings that students with attention problems demonstrate substantial difficulties with peer relationships (Milich and Landau 1982), it is critical to evaluate the presence (or absence) of attention problems with children with LD prior to initiating social interventions.

Summary

Behavior problems and academic achievement are two important variables that influence how students are perceived by others as well as what type of social intervention is needed. Students with LD are an extraordinarily heterogeneous group, and the range in their social-emotional functioning reflects this heterogeneity. Some students with LD are accepted by peers and function extremely well both socially and emotionally. In fact, many of them describe social skills as one of their strengths. In contrast, there is a subgroup of students with LD who demonstrate behavior problems and difficulty getting along with peers and adults. These are the students who are likely to benefit from well-designed social interventions.

WHAT SOCIAL AREAS NEED TO BE TAUGHT?

Students with LD are as different from each other as they are from their non–learning-disabled peers. Thus, there is no single cluster of social behaviors that characterizes students with LD as a whole, nor is there a single social skill deficit that characterizes all students with LD. In this section of the chapter we will review several social areas that have been identified as particularly problematic for students with LD: social perception, communication, and social problem solving.

Social Perception

Social perception is the way we interpret behavior to better understand the thoughts and feelings of others (Reiff and Gerber 1990). Numerous studies have indicated that the social perception of students with LD is deficient (e.g., Axelrod 1982; Jackson et al. 1987; Reiff and Gerber 1990); however, others find that cognitive and/or attention factors account for at least some of the difference in the social perception of students with LD.

Stiliadis and Wiener (1989) compared the social perception of students with LD to that of average achievers. Results indicated that students with LD demonstrated lower peer acceptance and poorer social perception than the contrast group. These main effects were maintained even when IQ was used as a covariate to partial out group differences attributed to intelligence. Results also demonstrated significant relations between students' peer acceptance and their social perception, although social perception accounted for only a small part of the variance in peer acceptance of students with LD (Stiliadis and Wiener 1989).

Although several studies, such as the one by Stiliadis and Wiener (1989) suggest that students with LD display deficiencies in their social perception skills, different results have been obtained when potential attention differences between the students with learning disabilities and their nondisabled peers have been controlled. For example, Stone and La Greca (1984) compared boys with LD and nondisabled boys in their perceptions of nonverbal social stimuli, using the Profile of Nonverbal Sensitivity (PONS). To control for attentional differences between the two groups of boys, the students were reminded to attend to the task before each stimulus was presented and were given tokens for attending. Under these highly controlled conditions, no differences in nonverbal sensitivity were observed between the boys with and without LD. These findings suggest that boys with LD may not be deficient in terms of their social perception skills as much as in their attentional skills, as their social perception appears to be normal when they attend to the task at hand. Further research is necessary to clarify the role of attentional processes in the reputedly poor social perception of students with LD.

Communication

Many students with LD demonstrate communication difficulties that interfere with their social interactions. Vaughn and La Greca (1989) argue that the social difficulties of students with LD may be explained, in large part, by these difficulties.

Consistent with this viewpoint, students with LD have been found to be less likely to make adaptations in their communication to accommodate the listener (Bryan and Pflaum 1978; Soenksen et al. 1981). For example, most people adjust what they say, how they say it, and even their vocabulary to fit the needs of the listener. Evidence suggests that LD students do not make these accommodations. Knight-Arest (1984) conducted a study with normal-achieving students and students with LD in which they were asked to provide instructions for playing a game of checkers. The adult who was participating in the study pretended not to know how to play the game. On the whole, students with LD demonstrated significantly less effective communication skills than the other students. When the adult did not understand the message, students with LD were more likely to repeat the message without making any adjustments for the listener. In addition, students with LD talked more, provided less relevant information, were less responsive to the needs of the listener, and used more gestures and demonstrations.

Other studies have revealed that students with LD demonstrate an egocentric communication style in which they talk about themselves and infrequently consider the listener (Soenksen et al., 1981). Furthermore, comparisons of the verbal skills of children with LD and their nondisabled peers reveal the students with LD to be less assertive, less likely to disagree with others, less likely to argue their position, less likely to ask questions, and more likely to adopt a nondominant role (Bryan et al. 1981; Bryan, Donahue, et al. 1981). In addition, those students with poor social skills display much greater difficulty maintaining a social conversation than their more socially skilled and academically able peers (La Greca 1982, 1987). Across these various studies, a picture emerges that suggests students with LD have difficulty with the reciprocity and social responsiveness that are important to good verbal communication (La Greca 1987).

Although the communication characteristics of many students with LD are subtle and difficult to assess using traditional communication measures, their social partners are aware that their communication style is unresponsive. Such communication difficulties undoubtedly influence others' perceptions of the desirability of students with LD as social partners.

Social Problem Solving

Social problem solving is the ability to identify interpersonal problems, generate appropriate alternative solutions, evaluate the likely outcome of each alternative, and then implement the strategy that is most likely to be effective (Vaughn 1987). Students who are able to generate a range of alternatives to problem situations are more likely to be successful problem solvers. Perhaps of even greater importance, social problem-solving skills relate to behavioral adjustment (Shure and Spivack 1979, 1980).

In a study conducted with students from self-contained LD classrooms, their overall performance on measures of social problem solving was significantly lower than non-LD students, particularly on the number of alternative solutions generated to problem situations (Toro et al. 1990). Additional information on the problem-solving skills of students with LD is provided in a study conducted by Oliva and La Greca (1988). In this study, boys with and without LD were interviewed on the social goals and strategies they would use in four hypothetical problem situations with peers. Responses from the open-ended interview indicated that the goals of boys with LD were less sophisticated than those of non-LD students. However, when students were provided goals in a multiple-choice format, students with LD chose goals that were just as friendly and as sophisticated as their peers without LD. This suggests that students with LD can recognize appropriate solutions to social problems, but they have considerable difficulty *generating* solutions on their own. Consequently, efforts to promote positive social problem-solving skills may facilitate the social adjustment of youth with LD.

Summary

The social skills taught to students with LD who demonstrate difficulties in social functioning need to address the specific problems of the target child. However, this section discussed three common social areas that are problematic for students with LD: social perception, communication, and social problem solving. While many students with LD demonstrate difficulties with social perception, it is difficult to discern the extent to which their problems with attention may negatively influence their social perception. Communication difficulties appear to be the most pervasive and are demonstrated by an egocentric communication style, less assertive communication style, being less likely to ask questions, and being more likely to adopt a nondominant role. Social problem solving is frequently difficult for students with LD, who tend to avoid problems with others rather than systematically solve them.

HOW CAN WE TEACH SOCIAL SKILLS?

Both regular classroom teachers and special education teachers perceive students without LD as exhibiting significantly better social skills and behavior than students with LD (Baum et al. 1988; Center and Wascom 1986). Despite teachers' low perceptions of the social skills of students with LD, very few students receive the social interventions teachers feel they need.

There are several reasons why social skills are not being taught to students with LD who need them (see, for further explanation, Vaughn [1985, 1991]). First, and probably foremost, teachers feel they do not have sufficient knowledge about social development and social skills to provide an appropriate social intervention. Although teachers take coursework and field experiences that emphasize academic skills, they receive little or no instruction on teaching social skills. For this reason, teachers may feel uncomfortable providing social skills training. Second, many teachers feel that social skills are less important than academic skills. Given that students with LD have academic difficulties, teachers may be concerned that providing social intervention will take time away from their academic curricula.

In view of the importance of teaching social skills to students with LD who also have social difficulties, the last section of this chapter provides information on social skills intervention programs that have been developed and evaluated with students with LD.

Programs to Teach Social Skills

Several social skills intervention programs have been developed, implemented, and evaluated with special populations including students with LD. A number of other social intervention programs could be used with students with LD, but less empirical support for their use with this population is available.

Appendix A provides a listing of social skills interventions that have been developed. Many are available commercially, and this information is also provided in the appendix whenever available.

Mutual Interest Discovery and Contextualist-based Intervention

As stated previously, the type of social skills training needed by students depends on the nature of their social difficulties. Mutual interest discovery and contextualist-based intervention are two social skills interventions that are designed to produce different outcomes but could be taught simultaneously.

Mutual Interest Discovery Mutual interest discovery (Fox, 1989) is designed to increase the peer acceptance of students with LD by pairing them with students they do not know well in order to discover things they have in common. The rationale is that persons who have similar interests will be attracted to each other. Thus, the program provides structured opportunities for students to get to know each other better, which should increase their positive perceptions of each other. Specific procedures for mutual interest discovery involve pairing a student with LD with a well-accepted non–learning-disabled student from the same class. Students interact in semistructured activities directed by the teacher for approximately 40 minutes once each week. For example, students may interview each other on preassigned topics such as entertainment, hobbies, and sports. Following the interview, each person writes three items that they and their partner discovered they have in common about the topic discussed. The partners then keep a record (through written sentences and art activities) about their partner and themselves. Partners who participated in the mutual interest group demonstrated higher ratings of their partners over time than did partners in a control group.

While the mutual interest discovery intervention provides systematic opportunities for students to get to know each other, this intervention is only effective if it improves the peer acceptance of the target child. In cases where the target student demonstrates social skills deficiencies and poor interpersonal problem solving, increased exposure to a peer partner is unlikely to improve peer status.

Contextualist-based Intervention A contextualist perspective for increasing the social skills and peer acceptance of elementary students with LD has been developed and evaluated (Vaughn and Lancelotta 1990; Vaughn et al. 1988; Vaughn et al. 1991). This intervention model views social skills as an aspect of social competence that needs to be considered in the context of family, school, and other environmental factors. Teaching social skills without strongly considering the child's social context is unlikely to yield significant and long-lasting change in children's social behavior.

Implementing a contextualist intervention means including all significant aspects of the student's community. More specifically, significant members of the school setting (principal and teachers) are recruited to support the intervention. A schoolwide sociometric assessment is performed to identify popular students and students with LD who are not well accepted by peers (i.e., target students). Popular and target students are then paired to serve as the "social skills" trainers for their class and for the school as a whole. Students in the school are informed that the social skills trainers are selected through a lottery. They are announced to the school by the school principal. The social skills trainers are removed from the classroom by a research assistant two to three times each week, for approximately 30 minutes each session, to learn specific social skills strategies. The first social skills strategy the students learn is the FAST strategy.

- *Freeze!* Don't act too quickly. Stop and think, what is the problem?
- *Alternatives.* What are all my possible procedures for solving this problem?
- *Solution evaluation.* What are the likely consequences of each solution? What would happen next if I implement the selected alternative? Think about each alternative in the long run and short run.
- *Try it.* What do I need to do to implement the solution? If it doesn't work, what else can I try?

After students learn this strategy, they practice and rehearse with their own problems as well as problems suggested by other students in their classroom. Classmates' problems are written and placed in a problem-solving box. This provides an opportunity to record real-life problems at school and at home and to use the FAST strategy, as well as other strategies, to solve their social difficulties.

After social skills trainers have learned the FAST strategy, and rehearsed it with problems from the problem-solving box, they present the FAST strategy to the students in their class, with support from the researcher and classroom teacher. After teaching the FAST strategy to classmates, social skills trainers review and apply the FAST strategy with their classmates at least once a week. These reviews include large-group discussions and small-group problem-solving exercises using ideas from the problem-solving box. During the classroom activities, social skills trainers lead the class with support from the researcher and teacher.

Students with LD who have participated in the intervention received significantly more positive nominations at posttest than at pretest and received higher ratings of social skills from their teachers. One caveat, however, is that this intervention was less successful with students who demonstrate significant externalizing problems, such as aggressive and acting-out behaviors.

Cognitive-Behavioral Intervention

La Greca and colleagues (La Greca 1981; La Greca and Santogrossi 1980; La Greca et al. 1989) developed a program for teaching social skills to low-accepted elementary school students that has been adapted for students with LD (La Greca and Mesibov 1979, 1981). This program has typically been used in school settings and is based on a group treatment format (e.g., La Greca and Mesibov 1981; La Greca and Santogrossi 1980), although it can also be implemented with individual students (e.g., La Greca et al. 1989).

The content of the training program focuses on seven major skill areas: greeting others, positive affect, joining others, extending invitations, conversation, sharing, and providing positive feedback (e.g., complimenting others). These particular social skills, also referred to as "competence correlates," were based on extensive research that identified these social behaviors as important correlates of children's social competence. In addition to teaching positive skills for initiating and maintaining peer interactions, children are taught how to respond to "rejection experiences" from others, so that they don't become overly discouraged if their social interaction efforts are not well received.

Each of the main skill areas is divided into a series of components that facilitate teaching and learning the skills. For example, the components of conversation skills include:

- Maintaining eye contact (e.g., looking at the person most of the time when you are talking or listening)
- Asking questions, especially "open-ended" questions
- Sticking to the topic of conversation
- Taking turns in the conversations (e.g., intersperse questions with providing information about oneself)
- Sharing information about yourself (e.g., elaborate on responses to others' questions)
- Generating topics for conversation
- Developing good listening skills (e.g., maintain eye contact, ask relevant questions)

For each skill, training procedures include modeling, discussion, role playing, coaching, positive reinforcement, and extended "live" practice. First, skill trainers *model* the skill area and its components. For complex skills, such as conversation skills, more than one session may be necessary, to cover all the skill components. After modeling the skills, children are then encouraged to *discuss* the skill: What are the specific components? Why is this skill important? When is it appropriate or inappropriate to use this skill? How would other children feel if you used this skill? The main purpose of the discussion is to highlight children's awareness of their social behavior and its impact on others. Next, children practice the skills by *role playing* social situations with the trainer and with each other. Social situations are drawn from the children's actual social experiences, so that they can readily apply the skills in their interactions with peers. During the role playing, children are *coached* on their use of the skills (e.g., what they are doing right, what they need to improve) and are provided with *positive reinforcement* for their efforts. Children practice the social skills until they have mastered them. At the end of each session, children are given homework assignments to use the skills in *real life situations*. They discuss these assignments at length, so that they have a specific plan as to how they will complete the assignment. At the beginning of the following session, these assignments are reviewed, and additional coaching and positive feedback are provided.

This program has been used successfully with elementary school students (La Greca and Santogrossi 1980), and children with LD (La Greca and Mesibov 1981) and attention deficits (La Greca et al. 1989). In the authors' experience, students with LD and those with attention deficits may need extended practice until skill mastery is achieved. In addition, students who have concomitant problems with noncompliant or acting-out behavior appear to do best when the skill training is combined with a contingency management program to reduce problem behaviors (see La Greca et al. [1989]). Parental involvement in skills training is also recommended (La Greca et al. 1989).

A Social Skills Program for Adolescents (ASSET)

The ASSET program was developed to teach social skills and strategies to adolescents with LD who demonstrate difficulties in social functioning (Hazel et al. 1981). This social skills training program is extremely comprehensive and includes eight fundamental social skills: giving positive feedback, giving negative feedback, accepting negative feedback, resisting peer pressure, negotiation skills, personal problem solving, following directions, and conducting conversations.

Each of the social skills is further divided into several component skills. For example, the 12 social components that make up "Following Directions" are:

1. Face the person.
2. Keep eye contact.
3. Keep a neutral facial expression.
4. Use a normal voice tone.
5. Keep a straight posture.
6. Listen closely to the instruction so that you will know what to do and remember to give feedback with head nods and by saying "mmm-hmmm" and "yeah."
7. Acknowledge the instruction.
8. Ask for more information if you don't understand the instruction. "But I don't understand . . . "
9. Say that you will follow the instruction. "I'll do it . . . "
10. Follow the instruction.
11. Throughout, give polite, pleasant responses.
12. Do not argue with the person about the instruction: Go ahead and follow it and you can talk to the person later about problems.

The same nine-step teaching procedure is used to teach each social skill. Step 1 is to *review* previously learned skills and discuss and integrate homework assignments. Step 2 is to *explain* or describe the skill that is the focus of the lesson. Step 3 requires a *rationale* for learning the skill. This rationale should be a convincing statement about why the skill is necessary and should "hook" the students into wanting to learn the target skill. Step 4 provides an *example* of situations when the skill can be used. Examples are selected that relate directly to the students' experiences and interests. During step 5 the skills are *examined* using a skills sheet, which lists the subskills needed to effectively implement the target skill. Step 6 provides a *model* of the skill and subskills, through videotapes that can be purchased with the curriculum and/or by the social skills trainer. Opportunities for participating students to demonstrate and model specific skills are also provided. Step 7, *verbal rehearsal,* is a procedure for the students to learn the components of each skill. The students practice saying the skill components and play games and engage in activities that teach them the skills. Step 8, *behavioral rehearsal,* is when students demonstrate they can adequately perform each of the subskills and overall social skill that is the focus of the lesson. Step 9, *homework,* involves recording how and when to practice target skills outside of the training setting.

This intervention program has been used successfully with students with LD, incarcerated youth, and students with behavior problems. The program is particularly suited for adolescents and young adults.

The Structured Learning Curriculum

The Structured Learning Curriculum (Goldstein et al., 1980) was developed originally to teach appropriate social behaviors to adolescents. Structured learning consists of four components: modeling, role playing, feedback, and transfer of training. Each of these components is used to teach the specific skills needed. Two examples of structured learning skills used with adolescents are starting a conversation and negotiation. A breakdown of the steps that constitute each of these two skills follows.

Starting a Conversation:

1. Greet the other person.
2. Make small talk.
3. Decide if the other person is listening.
4. Bring up the main topic.

Negotiation:

1. Decide if you and the other person are having a difference of opinion.
2. Tell the other person what you think about the problem.
3. Ask the other person what he or she thinks about the problem.
4. Listen openly to his or her answer.
5. Think about why the other person might feel this way.
6. Suggest a compromise.

The Structured Learning Curriculum has been used extensively in school systems and mental health agencies. While not specifically developed and evaluated with students with LD, the program contains many elements that suggest it could be quite effective with those youngsters.

Summary

This last section of the chapter addressed how we can teach social skills to youngsters who have LD and social skills deficits. Although teachers frequently identify students with LD who demonstrate poor social skills and would benefit from social skills training, academic goals seem to supersede social goals and social skills training is rarely provided as part of students' instructional program. Most teachers do not feel comfortable teaching social skills, particularly without structured curricula, and so a number of social skills training programs were described. In addition, a list of materials is provided (see Appendix A at back of book).

CHAPTER SUMMARY

This chapter addressed four questions central to the social functioning of youngsters with LD: Why teach social skills? Who needs social skills training? What social skills need to be taught? How can we teach social skills?

Central to the notion of why we need to teach social skills are the negative outcomes associated with youngsters who have social skills difficulties, social-emotional problems, and/or low social acceptance. Considerable research accumulated over the past two decades indicates that students with LD demonstrate significantly more social-behavioral difficulties than do their non–learning-disabled peers and are generally poorly accepted by their peers. Their social difficulties include problems in communication, particularly subtle difficulties that interfere with their social communication; behavior problems, more specifically problems that relate to attention difficulties; and difficulties with interpersonal problem solving, particularly generating appropriate and relevant alternatives to solving social problems. Social skills interventions have been developed and evaluated with students with LD that elucidate social skills training components as well as suggestions for promoting peer interaction.

While a disproportionate number of youngsters with LD demonstrate social, behavioral, and peer relationship problems, by no means do all children and adolescents with LD have social problems, nor are students who have social problems necessarily homogeneous in their social functioning. For this reason it is important to identify which students could benefit from social skills interventions and to consider carefully, based on the type of social and behavioral problems demonstrated, the type of social intervention that would best meet each youngster's needs.

REFERENCES

Ackerman, D., & Howes, C. (1986). Sociometric status and after-school social activity of children with learning disabilities. *Journal of Learning Disabilities, 19*(7), 416–419.

Axelrod, L. (1982). Social perception in learning disabled adolescents. *Journal of Learning Disabilities, 15,* 610–613.

Balswick, J. K., & Balswick, J. (1980). Where have all the alienated students gone? *Adolescence, 15*(59), 691–697.

Baum, D. D., Duffelmeyer, F., & Geelan, M. (1988). Resource teacher perceptions of the prevalence of social dysfunction among students with learning disabilities. *Journal of Learning Disabilities, 21*(6), 380–381.

Bender, W. N., Bailey, D. B., Stuck, G. B., & Wyne, M. D. (1984). Relative peer status of learning disabled, educable mentally handicapped, low-achieving, and normal achieving children. *Child Study Journal, 13,* 209–216.

Bender, W. N., & Smith, J. K. (1990). Classroom behavior of children and adolescents with learning disabilities: A meta-analysis. *Journal of Learning Disabilities, 23,* 298–305.

Berndt, T. J. (1990, April). *Relations of friendships and peer acceptance to adolescents' self-evaluations.* Paper presented at the AERA, Boston.

Bickett, L. G., & Milich, R. (1987, April). *First impressions of learning disabled and attention deficit disordered boys.* Paper presented at the biennial meeting of the Society for Research in Child Development, Baltimore, MD.

Breen, M. J., & Barkley, R. A. (1984). Psychological adjustment in learning disabled, hyperactive, and hyperactive/learning for children. *Journal of Clinical Child Psychology, 13,* 232–236.

Bryan, T. H. (1974a). Peer popularity of learning disabled children. *Journal of Learning Disabilities, 7,* 261–268.

Bryan, T. H. (1974b). An observational analysis of classroom behaviors of children with learning disabilities. *Journal of Learning Disabilities, 7,* 26–34.

Bryan, T. H. (1976). Peer popularity of learning disabled children: A replication. *Journal of Learning Disabilities, 9,* 307–311.

Bryan, T. H., & Bryan, J. H. (1978). Social interactions of learning disabled children. *Learning Disability Quarterly, 1*(1), 33–38.

Bryan, T., & Pflaum, S. (1978). Social interactions of learning disabled children: A linguistic, social, and cognitive analysis. *Learning Disability Quarterly, 1,* 70–79.

Bryan, T., Donahue, M., & Pearl, R. (1981). Learning disabled children's peer interactions during a small-group problem-solving task. *Learning Disability Quarterly, 4,* 13–22.

Bryan, T., Donahue, M., Pearl, R., & Sturm, C. (1981). Learning disabled children's conversational skills: The "TV talk show." *Learning Disability Quarterly, 4,* 250–259.

Bursuck, W. (1983). Sociometric status, behavior ratings, and social knowledge of learning disabled and low achieving students. *Learning Disability Quarterly, 6,* 329–338.

Bursuck, W. (1989). A comparison of students with learning disabilities to low achieving and high achieving students on three dimensions of social competence. *Journal of Learning Disabilities, 22*(3), 188–194.

Callahan, R. C., & Long, V. O. (1983). Socialization and alienation: Perspectives on schooling. *The Clearing House, 56,* 418–420.

Center, D. B., & Wascom, A. M. (1986). Teachers perceptions of social behavior in learning disabled and socially normal children and youth. *Journal of Learning Disabilities, 19,* (7), 420–425.

Coie, J. D., & Dodge, K. A. (1983). Continuities and changes in children's social status: A five-year longitudinal study. *Merrill-Palmer Quarterly, 29,* 261–281.

Cowen, E. L., Pederson, A., Babijian, H., Izzo, L. D., & Trost, M. A. (1973). Long-term follow-up of early detected vulnerable children. *Journal of Consulting and Clinical Psychology, 41,* 438–446.

Dodge, K. A., Coie, J. D., & Brakke, N. P. (1982). Behavior patterns of socially rejected and neglected preadolescents: The role of social approach and aggression. *Journal of Abnormal Child Psychology, 10,* 389–410.

Dudley-Marling, C. C., & Edmiaston, R. (1985). Social status of learning disabled children and adolescents: A review. *Learning Disabilities Quarterly, 8,* 189–204.

Fertmann, C. I., & Chubb, N. H. (1990, April). *Evaluation of the effects of a personal empowerment program for adolescents.* Paper presented at the American Educational Research Association. Boston.

Finn, J. D. (1989). Withdrawing from school. *Review of Educational Research, 59,* 117–142.

Flicek, M., & Landau, S. (1985). Social status problems of learning disabled and hyper-active/learning disabled boys. *Journal of Clinical Child Psychology, 14,* 340–344.

Fox, C. L. (1989). Peer acceptance of learning disabled children in the regular classroom. *Exceptional Children, 56,* 50–59.

Fuerst, D. R., Fisk, J. L., & Rourke, B. P. (1989). Psychosocial functioning of learning-disabled children: Replicability of statistically derived subtypes. *Journal of Consulting and Clinical Psychology, 57,* 275–280.

Goldstein, A. P., Sprafkin, R. P., Gershaw, N. J., and Klein, P. (1980). *Skillstreaming the adolescent.* Champaign, IL: Research Press.

Green, K., Forehand, R., Beck, S., & Vosk, B. (1980). An assessment of the relationship among measures of children's social competence and children's academic achievement. *Child Development, 51,* 1149–1156.

Gresham, F. M., & Reschly, D. J. (1986). Social skills deficits and low peer acceptance of mainstreamed learning disabled children. *Learning Disability Quarterly, 9,* 23–32.

Hazel, J. S., Schumaker, J. B., Sherman, J. A., & Sheldon-Wildgen, J. (1981). *ASSET: A social skills program for adolescents.* Champaign, IL: Research Press.

Howes, C. (1990). Social status and friendship from kindergarten to third grade. *Journal of Applied Developmental Psychology, 11,* 321–330.

Jackson, S. C., Enright, R. D., & Murdock, J. Y. (1987). Social perception problems in learning disabled youth: Developmental lag versus perceptual deficit. *Journal of Learning Disabilities, 20,* 361–364.

Janke, R. W., & Lee, K. (1991). Social skills ratings of exceptional students. *Journal of Psychoeducational Assessment, 9,* 54–66.

Kavanagh, J. F., & Truss, T. J., Jr. (1988). *Learning Disabilities: Proceedings of the National Conference.* Parkton, MD: York Press.

Knight-Arest, I. (1984). Communicative effectiveness of learning disabled and normally achieving 10- to 13-year old boys. *Learning Disability Quarterly, 7,* 237–245.

Kupersmidt, J. B. (1983, April). Predicting delinquency and academic problems from childhood peer status. In J. D. Coie (Chair), *Strategies for identifying children at social risk: Longitudinal correlates and consequences.* Symposium conducted at the biennial meeting of the Society for Research in Child Development, Detroit, MI.

La Greca, A. M. (1981). Social skills training with elementary school students: A skills training manual. *JSAS Catalogue of Selected Documents in Psychology,* #2194.

La Greca, A. M. (1982, November). Issues in the assessment of social skills with learning disabled children. In S. Beck (Chair), *Children's social skills: Future directions.* Paper presented at annual meeting of the Association for the Advancement of Behavior Therapy, Los Angeles.

La Greca, A. M. (1987). Children with learning disabilities: Interpersonal skills and social competence. *Journal of Reading, Writing, and Learning Disabilities, 3,* 167–186.

La Greca, A. M. (1989, February). *Social Anxiety Scale for Children: Scale development and validation.* Miami, FL: Society for Research in Child and Adolescent Psychopathology.

La Greca, A. M. (1991, August). The development of social anxiety in children. In T. Ollendick (Chair), *Advances in children's anxiety disorders.* San Francisco: American Psychological Association.

La Greca, A. M., Dandes, S. K., Wick, P., Shaw, K., & Stone, W. L. (1988). The development of the Social Anxiety Scale for Children (SASC): Reliability and concurrent validity. *Journal of Clinical Child Psychology, 17,* 84–91.

La Greca, A. M., & Mesibov, G. B. (1979). Social skills intervention with learning disabled children: Selecting skills and implementing training. *Journal of Clinical Child Psychology, 8,* 234–241.

La Greca, A. M., & Mesibov, G. B. (1981). Facilitating interpersonal functioning with peers in learning disabled children. *Journal of Learning Disabilities, 14,* 197–199, 238.

La Greca, A. M., & Santogrossi, D. A. (1980). Social-skills training: A behavioral group approach. *Journal of Consulting and Clinical Psychology, 48,* 220–228.

La Greca, A. M., & Stone, W. L. (1990). LD status and achievement: Confounding variables in the study of children's social status, self-esteem, and behavioral functioning. *Journal of Learning Disabilities, 23*(8), 483–490.

La Greca, A. M., Stone, W. L., & Noriega-Garcia, A. (1989). Social skills intervention: A case of a learning disabled boy. In M. C. Roberts & C. E. Walker (Eds.), *Case studies in clinical child/pediatric psychology.* New York: Guilford Press.

Lambert, N. A. (1972). Intellectual and nonintellectual predictors of high school status. *Journal of Scholastic Psychology, 6,* 247–259.

Lambert, N. M., & Sandoval, J. (1980). The prevalence of learning disabilities in a sample of children considered hyperactive. *Journal of Abnormal Child Psychology, 8,* 35–80.

Mathinos, D. A. (1987, April). *Communicative abilities of disabled and nondisabled children.* Paper presented at the annual meeting of the Society for Research on Child Development, Baltimore, MD.

McConaughy, S. H., & Ritter, D. R. (1986). Social competence and behavioral problems of learning disabled boys ages 6–11. *Journal of Learning Disabilities, 19*(1), 39–45.

McIntosh, R., Vaughn, S., Schumm, J. S., & Haager, D. (in progress). Observations of classroom climate for students with learning disabilities in regular education classrooms.

Miller, S. E., Leinhardt, G., & Zigmond, N. (1987, April). *Experimental features of secondary schooling for high risk learning disability students.* Paper presented at AERA, Washington, DC.

Ochoa, S. H., & Palmer, D. J. (1991). A sociometric analysis of between-group differences and within-group status variability of Hispanic learning disabled and nonhandicapped pupils in academic and play contexts. *Learning Disability Quarterly, 14,* 208–218.

Oliva, A. H. (1990). *The social status of learning disabled children: An indepth analysis.* Unpublished doctoral dissertation, University of Miami, Coral Gables, FL.

Oliva, A. H., & La Greca, A. M. (1988). Children with learning disabilities: Social goals and strategies. *Journal of Learning Disabilities, 21*(5), 301–306.

Parker, J. G., & Asher, S. R. (1987). Peer relations and later personal adjustment: Are low-accepted children at risk? *Psychological Bulletin, 102,* 357–389.

Perlmutter, B. F., Crocker, J., Cordray, D., & Garstecki, D. (1983). Sociometric status and related personality characteristics of mainstreamed learning disabled adolescents. *Learning Disabilities Quarterly, 9,* 55–60.

Prillaman, D. (1981). Acceptance of learning disabled students in a mainstreamed environment: A failure to replicate. *Journal of Learning Disabilities, 14,* 344–352.

Reiff, H. B., & Gerber, P. J. (1990). Cognitive correlates of social perception in students with learning disabilities. *Journal of Learning Disabilities, 23*(4), 260–262.

Ritter, D. R. (1989). Social competence and problem behavior of adolescent girls with learning disabilities. *Journal of Learning Disabilities, 22*(7), 460–461.

Roff, M. (1963). Childhood social interactions and young adult psychosis. *Journal of Clinical Psychology, 19,* 152–157.

Roff, M. (1975). Juvenile delinquency in girls: A study of a recant sample. In R. D. Wirt, G. Winokur, & M. Roff (Eds.), *Life history research in psychopathology* (vol 4), (pp. 135–151). Minneapolis: University of Minnesota Press.

Roff, M., Sells, S. B., & Golden, M. M. (1972). *Social adjustment and personality development in children.* Minneapolis: University of Minnesota Press.

Sabornie, E. J., & Kauffman, J. M. (1986). Social acceptance of learning disabled adolescents. *Learning Disability Quarterly, 9,* 55–60.

Seidel, J. F., & Vaughn, S. (1991). Social alienation and the LD school dropout. *Learning Disabilities Research, 6*(3), 152–157.

Shure, M. B., & Spivack, G. (1979). Interpersonal cognitive problem solving and primary prevention: Programming for preschool and kindergarten children. *Journal of Clinical Child Psychology, 2,* 89–94.

Shure, M. B., & Spivack, G. (1980). Interpersonal problem solving as a mediator of behavioral adjustment in preschool and kindergarten children. *Journal of Applied Developmental Psychology, 1,* 29–44.

Siperstein, G. N., Bopp, M. J., & Bak, J. J. (1978). Social status of learning disabled children. *Journal of Learning Disabilities, 11,* 98–102.

Soenksen, P. S., Flagg, C. L., & Schmits, D. W. (1981). Social communication in learning disabled students: A pragmatic analysis. *Journal of Learning Disabilities, 14,* 283–286.

Stiliadis, K., & Wiener, J. (1989). Relationship between social perception and peer status in children with learning disabilities. *Journal of Learning Disabilities, 22*(10), 624–629.

Stone, W. L., & La Greca, A. M. (1984). Comprehension of nonverbal communication: A reexamination of the social competency of LD children. *Journal of Abnormal Child Psychology, 12,* 505–517.

Stone, W. L., & La Greca, A. M. (1990). The social status of children with learning disabilities: A reexamination. *Journal of Learning Disabilities, 23*(1), 32–37.

Strahan, D. (1988). Life on the margins: How academically at-risk early adolescents view themselves and school. *Journal of Early Adolescence, 8*(4), 373–390.

Toro, P. A., Weissberg, R. P., Guare, J., & Liebenstein, N. L. (1990). A comparison of children with and without learning disabilities on social problem-solving skill, school behavior, and family background. *Journal of Learning Disabilities, 23,* 115–120.

Ullmann, C. A. (1957). Teachers, peers, and tests as predictions of adjustment. *Journal of Educational Psychology, 48,* 257–267.

Vaughn, S. (1985). Why teach social skills to learning disabled students? *Journal of Learning Disabilities, 18,* 588–591.

Vaughn, S. R. (1987). TLC—Teaching, learning, and caring: Teaching interpersonal problem solving skills to emotionally disturbed adolescents. *Pointer, 31,* 25–30.

Vaughn, S. (1991). Social skills enhancement in students with learning disabilities. In B. Y. L. Wong (Ed.), *Learning about learning disabilities.* Orlando, FL: Academic Press.

Vaughn, S., Haager, D., Hogan, A., Kouzekanani, K. (in press). Self-concept and peer acceptance in students with learning disabilities: A four to five year prospective study. *Journal of Educational Psychology.*

Vaughn, S., & Hogan, A. (1990). Social competence and learning disabilities: A prospective study. In H. L. Swanson & B. K. Keogh (Eds.), *Learning disabilities: Theoretical and research issues* (pp. 175–191). Hillsdale, NJ: Erlbaum.

Vaughn, S., Hogan, A., Kouzekanani, K., & Shapiro, S. (1990). Peer acceptance, self-perceptions, and social skills of LD students prior to identification. *Journal of Educational Psychology, 82*(1), 101–106.

Vaughn, S. R., & La Greca, A. M. (1988). Teaching social skills to LD students. In K. A. Kavale (Ed.), *Learning disabilities: State of the art and practice.* San Diego, CA: College Hill Press.

Vaughn, S., & Lancelotta, G. X. (1990). Teaching interpersonal social skills to low accepted students: peer-pairing versus no peer-pairing. *Journal of School Psychology, 28*(3), 181–188.

Vaughn, S. R., Lancelotta, G. X., & Minnis, S. (1988). Social strategy training and peer involvement: Increasing peer acceptance of a female, LD student. *Learning Disabilities Focus, 4*(1), 32–37.

Vaughn, S., McIntosh, R., & Spencer-Rowe, J. (1991). Peer rejection is a stubborn thing: Increasing peer acceptance of rejected students with learning disabilities. *Learning Disabilities Research and Practice, 6*(2), 83–88.

Wheelock, A. (1986). *The way out: Student exclusion practices in Boston middle schools.* Boston: Massachusetts Advocacy Center.

Wiener, J., Harris, P. J., & Shirer, C. (1990). Achievement and social-behavioral correlates of peer status in LD children. *Learning Disability Quarterly, 13,* 114–127.

Zigmond, N., & Thorton, H. (1985). Follow up of postsecondary age learning disabled graduates and dropouts. *Learning Disabilities Research, 1*(1), 50–55.

12

Vocational and Independent Living Skills

Phillip J. McLaughlin
Margaret A. Martin

A learning disability does not disappear when the individual matures and is facing postschool transitions (Buchanan and Wolf 1986; Cohen 1984; Horn et al. 1983; Mick 1985). The school-to-community transition environment is critical to the maturational process into adulthood, and appropriate support and services are crucial to the individual after matriculating from the more "protective" school environment (Price and Johnson 1986). Although there is general agreement about the need for postsecondary support for individuals with learning disabilities (LD), little research exists for guiding those with LD in managing their transition from school to life in the community (Deshler et al. 1984; Sergent et al. 1988; C. Smith 1986; S. Smith 1986; Zetlin and Hosseini 1989).

This chapter presents information on postsecondary vocational and independent living strategies for students with LD. These students are faced with the options of higher education or vocational and job placement avenues (skills training, receiving career counseling, job preparation, and help in maintaining employment).

VOCATIONAL STRATEGIES

Vocational options and the development of job skills are often seen as a critical developmental link in the process of maturing toward adulthood for learning-disabled students (Bencomo and Schafer 1984; Brown 1984; Mori 1980). In general, maintaining a job is considered a rite of adult self-esteem and status (Fourqurean et al. 1991), yet many individuals with LD are unemployed (Smith 1988), even though a majority of those with a learning disability enter the work force after matriculation from high school (Bender 1992). Higher employment rates tend to be enjoyed by high school graduates than do those who exit high school prior to matriculation (Edgar 1988). While Horn and colleagues (1983) have found in a long-term study of learning-disabled individuals that vocational outcomes present a more encouraging outcome than academic or social/

emotional outcomes, Smith (1988) and Schalock (1986) suggest the level of vocational success is still below that of nonhandicapped individuals.

Required Services

It is important to recognize that a student who may require a number of services in a large and competitive academic program in higher education may be able to manage studies independently in an open enrollment, two-year college with a vocational-technical orientation (Shaw and McGuire 1987). However, little is available in the professional literature concerning effective academic strategies for a student with a learning disability in these settings. Institution selection procedures and study strategies that are effective for colleges and universities will be helpful in selecting an appropriate vocational or technical training program. These are described in the next chapter.

Gregory and colleagues (1986) suggest that the typically negative academic outcomes and more encouraging vocational outcomes for individuals with LD may be attributed to the types of jobs many of the individuals from this population accept. That is, a majority accept minimum wage positions that require little reading or math ability (Mithaug et al. 1985). These positions tend to be entry-level positions, with low salaries, minimal opportunity for advancement, and few, if any, benefits (Edgar 1988). With the scarcity of literature to guide development of secondary programs for meeting the needs of students with LD in planning for the transition from high school to adult life (Fourqurean et al. 1991), what can individuals with LD do to enhance their options for employment they will find satisfying?

Since 1981, when the Rehabilitation Services Administration added LD to its list of recognized disabilities, vocational rehabilitation has become more available to individuals with LD, and some vocational rehabilitation offices offer programs specifically for job seekers with LD. For an example of a program of this nature, see Frith (1984).

Individualized Transition Plan

By the time the student with LD is 16, his or her transition from school to independent living and employment should be addressed in an individualized education program (IEP). That part of the IEP is usually called a *transition plan*. It should focus on three major areas: vocational education programs; instruction in community-based environments; and paid, part-time employment (Langone 1990). The focus on transition from school to work should not overshadow all other curriculum components, but it should be an equal partner.

During the last two years of a student's program, his or her transition plan should emphasize moving from paid, part-time employment to a full-time job or to postsecondary vocational training. During this time the responsibility of the student's program begins to shift from school personnel to rehabilitation specialists in other community agencies.

Table 12.1 Sample transition goals

Vocational Education Program:
John will enroll in the small engine repair class. He will learn to service, maintain, and repair starting systems of wind-up type and electric type small engines.
Mr. Smith, a vocational education teacher, is responsible for this instruction. Ms. Jones, a special education resource room teacher, will help by providing related instruction in her class. The related instruction will include helping John with assigned textbook readings and monitoring workbook assignments.

Community-Based Instruction:
John will use the public transportation system to go to and from his part-time job. He will learn to use bus schedules to catch the correct bus to arrive at work on time. He will also practice correct conversational skills with the bus driver and fellow passengers. Ms. Jones is responsible for this instruction. The instructional activities will be carried out primarily in the community; i.e., at the bus stop and on the bus. This will require Ms. Jones to work outside the school building during a portion of the instructional day.

Paid, Part-Time Employment:
John will work from 3:00 until 6:00 P.M. on Mondays, Wednesdays, and Fridays at Sloan's Small Engine Repair. He will start by doing basic cleaning of engine parts and by stocking the parts department shelves. He will also practice appropriate social skills with coworkers.
John's work will be monitored by Mr. Smith and Ms. Jones. Both teachers have extended day contracts in order to provide on-the-job supervision.

Table 12.1 presents some sample transition goals for a 17-year-old student with a learning disability. The student, John, is a sophomore at a comprehensive high school. He first showed an interest in automotive/engine repair during some job exploration activities while in junior high school. John's vocational education goal is learning entry-level job skills. His community-based environment goal focuses on a job-related and independent-living skill. John's paid, part-time employment goal allows him to establish a work history while still in school.

John's transition plan will expand as he progresses through high school. Transition activities will be the major part of his high school curriculum during his junior and senior years. Depending on his specific skills, John should be able to move into competitive employment or be ready for advanced training at the local vocational-technical school.

The development of a transition plan requires special educators, vocational educators, and rehabilitation counselors to work together in consultation with the parents and the student to plan and implement an appropriate program. This collaboration among school and community agencies is necessary to ensure the student's successful transition to an appropriate postsecondary program (Neubert et al. 1989). Such collaborative efforts should expand in the 1990s and result in more learning-disabled students being prepared for postsecondary training, independent living, and employment.

Special Education and Vocational Education Courses

Mithaug and colleagues (1985) indicate the importance of special education and vocational education courses to postsecondary vocational and personal success. Hasazi and associates (1985) also found the number of vocational courses the students were enrolled in to be a major indicator of successful job performance after high school. A complete career counseling process is most helpful when initiated during junior high or middle school. The process is expanded during high school in order to plan for postsecondary transitions, thus allowing sufficient time and resources to provide optimal alternatives (Shaw and McGuire 1987).

Fourqurean and colleagues (1991) advocate that students with LD acquire optimal math skills and gain work experience while in secondary education. Schalock (1986) advocates job-search skills and community-based training of functional skills to ensure the success of the transition process. Establishing interagency funding agreements is also an important part of the process. Training in use of on-the-job tools has been cited as a main factor in postsecondary job success for students with a handicap (Okolo and Sitlington 1986). Repeatedly noted in the literature is the importance of family involvement and support of the student with a learning disability as a predictor variable associated with employment-related outcomes (for example, see Schalock [1986]).

Vocational Rehabilitation Counselor

A vocational rehabilitation counselor is of vital importance to the learning-disabled individual who is seeking employment (Price and Johnson 1986). For example, Brown (1984) suggests the counselor can serve as a liaison between the individual and employer in striving for effective and practical workplace accommodations. McKinney and West (1985) advocate providing employers with accurate information to dispel myths about LD. This is particularly relevant in light of the finding by Minskoff and colleagues (1987) that some employers held a more negative view of hiring an individual with a learning disability over other handicaps, and they lacked supervisory experience with this population. Bender (1992) highlights the fact that employers often are not aware or sensitive to the needs of workers with LD. For example, many employers are not aware of problems such as trouble understanding written instructions or difficulty in making friends with coworkers. For examples of other problems employees with LD have on the job and the help they can receive through state vocational rehabilitation offices, see Brown (1982a,b).

Price and Johnson (1986) provide a brief review of the literature and an annotated bibliography on vocational or job-related skill development and transition issues and theories. Job-search strategies, resumé building, learning the application process and how to complete application forms, effective interviewing skills, work ethics, and skills for maintaining employment are all important vocational strategies for learning-disabled individuals to learn.

Job Search Strategies

The vocational opportunities available to individuals with a high school education are limited. These limitations are increased if a person has a learning disability. Under any circumstances, getting a job is a time-consuming process. In searching for a job, careful planning and an ample time allowance for preparation are highly important to a successful search. The process can seem overwhelming at first, but by having the individual with a learning disability take one step at a time, a successful job search can be exciting and rewarding.

Personal Inventory

The first step in getting a job is taking a *personal inventory,* or a thorough self-evaluation. This process leads to a deeper and more objective understanding of personal interests, values, skills, and abilities. *Interests* are the activities one finds enjoyable. Almost any interest, such as cooking or carpentry, can lead one to a satisfying type of work. *Values* are priorities or factors that are important in a job. For example, some people enjoy a variety of job duties, such as office work where one may answer the phone, type letters, and greet clientele, while others prefer performing a regular task, such as assembly line work. For some people a regular schedule is important, and others prefer a more flexible schedule. It can be helpful to remember that job-related values may vary from personal values. For example, one may value listening to music yet not have music as a part of work.

Skills can be divided into two basic areas: technical and adaptive skills. *Technical skills* are essential to particular jobs and require special training. For example, carpentry, sewing, computing and hairstyling require technical skills. *Adaptive skills* are personal traits or characteristics that can be of value on and off the job. Such skills include time management, communication, and an ability to get along with others.

Other areas of self-knowledge to consider include special talents, such as singing, painting, or working with animals or younger children. Special achievements, such as leadership positions in clubs and organizations, developing a neighborhood babysitting service, or volunteer work, need to be highlighted. Hobbies and avocational interests are also important. For example, recreational and leisure-time activities can be listed. In beginning the job-search strategy early, these types of activities can be undertaken to gain experiences, build skills, enhance self-esteem and increase attractiveness to prospective employers. It will also be important to prospective employers to know if full-time or part-time work is sought, as well as temporary or permanent employment.

Job Matching

Once a deeper understanding of self and what one can offer an employer is developed, the next step is to match this self-knowledge with occupations and specific companies. This matching includes two steps: researching occupations, and talking to others. Researching occupations involves finding out what opportunities are available; obtaining job descriptions, employment figures and projections, and earning information; and ascertaining which occupations current levels of education and training are appropriate for and whether more training is required. More general types of information about certain jobs are important to research also. For example, the size and stability of the hiring company, general atmosphere, reputation, attitudes towards employees, and future opportunities are important to the matching process. The *Dictionary of Occupational Titles* (DOT) and the *Occupational Outlook Handbook* (OOH) are key resources for providing this information. Most libraries have these available. Also, look in the card catalogue under "Jobs," "Careers," "Occupations," and specific occupational titles at the library for more information. Books, such as *The Complete Job Search Handbook* (Figler 1981), should be available as additional resources. Also, government offices can be contacted for more information about occupations by looking under "Employment Agencies" and "Government Offices" in the telephone book.

Many schools and communities offer workshops to aid in this process of self-knowledge, and school counselors can assist in assessment through inventories and questionnaires, such as the Career Decision-Making System (CDM) (Harrington and O'Shea 1982), which also helps identify job areas to explore. Some schools offer computerized career intervention programs, such as SIGI+ (System of Interactive Guidance and Intervention-Plus) that will guide this process, and some computerized programs also match assessment results with specific career areas.

Prejob Interviewing

Once career awareness information has been gathered, the second part of this process begins. Prior to actual job interviewing, it is helpful to request from personnel directors, managers, or supervisors an *informational interview*. It is important to state that a job interview is not requested: rather, an opportunity to talk with someone employed in that field in order to gain a deeper understanding of the daily work and the requirements to meet the work is desired. These informal interviews need to be followed up with a note thanking the particular individual for his or her time and the information that was provided. Other individuals to contact for additional information include family friends involved in the field of interest, school counselors and teachers, and Division of Rehabilitation Service counselors.

The next step of the job search involves having the student develop a resumé as well as locating specific job openings. Networking with other teachers, counselors, parents, family friends, clergy, and community leaders is a way to locate job openings. Follow-up activities with high school graduates with LD can also provide helpful information. Check bulletin boards in post offices, libraries, personnel offices, schools, and government offices, such as local employment or human resources offices. Newspaper classified sections sometimes list possible job positions. The Division of Rehabilitation Services can be an excellent resource in the job search process if the LD specialist has done a good job of preparing the students and has "sold" their employability to the rehabilitation counselor.

Utilizing a combination of all of these contacts is a most effective strategy. However, remaining cognizant of fee policies of some employment agencies can help avoid costly placement fees. While eagerness is important, it is prudent to be wary of catchy or "get-rich-quick" advertisements. In fact, teaching students to read advertisements critically is an essential part of the high school curriculum. Another key point throughout the job-search process is teaching the students to view themselves from a prospective employer's position.

Resumé Building

The first step in developing a resumé is gaining self-knowledge. This process is addressed as part of the job-search strategy, but it is enhanced by reviewing accomplishments, skills, interests, qualifications, and so on at this point. The objective of a resumé is to sell oneself and to get a personal interview. Through stressing accomplishments and what one has to offer prospective employers, a resumé can serve as a valuable tool in one's absence.

Format

Choose a format and style most fitting for the desired, realistic presentation. Basic formats for resumés are: *functional,* which emphasizes skills instead of work or educational history; *chronological,* which presents employment history in reversed time order; or *mixed,* which combines the first two styles. Books on resumé writing can be located in career information centers and local libraries and present examples of different resumé formats.

Content

Whatever format is decided upon, the objective is to highlight skills, abilities, and experiences that sell oneself to the prospective employer. List areas of strengths first. (Be sure to place name, address, and telephone number(s) at the top of the page.) It is important to be aware of job objectives on a resumé; these optional statements tell prospective employers what one's short- and longer-range goals are. Objectives need to be realistic, be appropriate to the job, and demonstrate an awareness of the fit between one's background and the position. The statement should just be a short phrase. After the employment objectives, list educational and special training, employment and volunteer experiences, and a reference list.

Education and special training are significant to list. These accomplishments can be highlighted by listing them first. List the schools(s) attended, address, and projected or actual graduation date. List special classes and training to highlight skills.

Employment and experiences are listed next, in reverse chronological order. List the company worked for, then the address. Accuracy with employment dates is important; dates should include month and year from when work started to the ending date. Follow this information with an organized list of specific job duties and tasks from each position. Begin by listing every activity engaged in during the typical work period, then summarize these for the resumé in a list that concisely delineates responsibilities and skills the applicant has developed in each position. Limited volunteer experience, identified as such, can be listed under this category. If more extensive volunteer work is involved, a separate category can be included, again listing the organization, address, dates of experience, and duties involved.

The references on the reference list are people whom prospective employers can contact to inquire about work habits, interactional style, and confirmation of what is in the resumé. Good references include teachers, principals, counselors, professional family friends, clergy members, and others who know the applicant well. Make sure that each person has agreed to serve as a reference before submitting his or her name, and make sure that names, titles, address, and phone numbers are accurate.

Properties of an Effective Resumé
The most effective resumés are one-page; typewritten or produced on a word processor; honest; neat; concise; complete; readable; and perfect, in spelling, punctuation, and grammar. Many communities have professional services that will develop a resumé format for a fee. Otherwise, asking others to proofread a typewritten resumé can provide valuable feedback. Make extra copies for other application situations. For a basic outline, see the example resumé in Appendix B at the end of this book.

Application Process

First impressions are important during the application process. Key ingredients to making a positive first impression include following the instructions the employer gives for the application process (for example, "Applications accepted between 2–4 pm") and submitting neat and thoroughly completed forms. Introducing oneself and giving a concise statement of the purpose of the visit is the next step. Having a neat copy of a finished resumé, a note pad, and pen presents a picture of a potential employee who is serious about the position, allows the applicant to jot notes rather than rely on memory, and can help keep fidgeting to a minimum by having something to hold onto.

Form Completion
To ensure neatness, appropriateness, and completeness of application responses, ask if the application can be returned at a later time. If not, follow the directions on the application form precisely, copy pertinent information from the resumé, and remember to relax while filling out the form. Jotting down responses on the note pad before writing the responses onto the formal application form can allow an opportunity to check responses and can increase confidence. If the employer is agreeable to your returning the application form at a later time, ask

when the most convenient time to return the completed form is, and return it at that time. When allowed this opportunity, write out responses on a separate piece of paper, ask a reliable person to proofread the responses, and then carefully type in the responses on the actual form. Corrections can be neatly made with the use of correction tape or fluids.

When submitting the completed form at the agreed-upon time, appearance and impressions are again important. Thank the employer for the opportunity to fill out the application, and for consideration for the position. Let the prospective employer know that you look forward to hearing from him or her.

Employer Contact

If no contact has been made by the potential employer within a reasonable amount of time after the application acceptance closing date, a phone call to the prospective employer can be appropriate. First, identify oneself, explain that a completed application was submitted, and politely ask if the position has been filled. If someone else has been hired for the position, politely thank the individual for the opportunity to apply for the position. Remember, many applications are maintained in a revolving file! If a decision has not yet been made, ask if additional information would be helpful to their decision, if you have any available to provide. If not, let the individual know you are still interested in the position, thank the person for his or her time, and close by letting the individual know you look forward to hearing from him or her.

Job Interview Skills

The job interview can be one of the most crucial aspects in the hiring process. In the personal interview an applicant is offered the opportunity for personal contact, and to demonstrate to the future employer the ability to successfully do the work. It also gives the interviewee an opportunity to learn more about the employer and the position.

Preparation

Preparation is a key word for a successful job interview. Preparation encompasses the following areas: interview skills, critical impressions, appearance and dress, interpersonal skills, and follow-up.

Interview skills include such areas as knowing one's interest, values, or what is important in a job: previous experiences; abilities and skills; strengths and weaknesses; and short- and long-range goals. It is important to emphasize one's strengths, to avoid criticizing previous employers, and to practice job interview skills prior to the interview. Mock interviews (done though use of audiotaping, or preferably, video taping) are pretend interviews with someone role playing the prospective employer. This individual will ask questions typical of an interview, allowing the interviewee to rehearse responses before the actual interview. In reviewing the tape, one can evaluate voice tone, content of responses to questions asked, nonverbal behaviors, and other mannerisms. This type of interview is most effective if the "interviewee" is dressed as though the interview is the actual one.

First Impressions

First impressions are critical. Krannick (1982) found that impressions formed during the first few minutes of an interview typically do not change. Appearance and dress; being on time; how the receptionist is treated; nonverbal behaviors such as how one sits, walks, and shakes hands; and how one presents oneself verbally are all vital in creating a positive impression.

Appearance and dress are critical dimensions of managing your initial impressions on prospective employers. Research indicates that, when the evaluator has little information about a person, appearance makes the largest difference in impressions and drawing conclusions (Krannick 1982). General personal hygiene considerations are of utmost importance. For example, clean and neat hair, clothing that is not soiled or wrinkled, little or no perfume or shaving lotion, moderate use of cosmetics, and freshly polished shoes can help in making a positive first impression.

Follow-Up

Many employers respond well to follow-up after the actual job interview. For example, within a day or two after the interview, a thank-you note to the prospective employer can demonstrate enthusiasm about the job. Keep the note short and to the point, use active words and correct grammar and punctuation, and make sure to address the note to the individual who was the interviewer. If one has not heard from the prospective employer within a reasonable length of time, a polite phone inquiry about where the employer is in his or her decision-making process about hiring for the position may be appropriate.

Work Ethics and Maintaining Employment

Many problems in maintaining employment for individuals with LD result from a skills deficit in interpersonal interactions. For example, many individuals with LD have trouble with conversational interactions with peers and find it difficult to resolve conflicts. Specific training in developing interpersonal skills is necessary to avoid problems in the workplace (Okolo and Sitlington 1986). These skills should be addressed in the student's individualized transition plan.

The most important strategy for maintaining employment is to teach the learning-disabled student that he or she must work hard. Learning-disabled employees do not lose their jobs because of their disability; they lose their jobs because they cannot do the work satisfactorily or they do not get along with their coworkers.

Through the self-assessment completed during the job search strategy step, one can develop strategies to compensate for potential on-the-job problem areas. For example, if one experiences difficulty in controlling emotions when frustrations arise, counting slowly to 10 before responding can help alleviate outbursts that are later regretted.

VOCATIONAL CASE STUDIES
Harry: An Informal Approach

Harry was an 18-year-old high school senior with a learning disability in writing and math. He began looking for paid employment right before his high school graduation, as he had declined applying for college or for vocational-technical school training. Since he had decided early in high school not to pursue his educational options, he had paid little attention to the career development training offered in his high school program, although the program was appropriate for his needs.

On Saturday mornings, Harry would look in the classified section of his local newspaper for current job listings. However, he found only a few listings, as many employers had already hired summer help. Harry would put on his favorite blue jeans and head for the address of the first job listing. Often managers were not in on Saturday mornings or, at fast-food restaurants, were busy and could not meet with applicants.

Harry often had difficulty in filling out the application forms, as his writing was poor and sometimes he was unsure of what an application question was asking. He had no volunteer or previous work experience, so he left blank spaces on his application forms. He could typically only think of one or two references on the spot and was not sure about the address of one of his references.

When Harry did get a job interview, he tended to become nervous, failed to make eye contact with his interviewer, and offered an awkward handshake. His answers to questions of prospective employers tended to be obviously spontaneous. For example, one employer at a fast-food restaurant asked Harry why he was interested in the position. Harry responded, "I want to buy a car."

After one month of applying for positions from the Saturday morning paper, Harry had not yet been offered a position. He had applied for positions such as fry cook at a local fast-food restaurant, salesperson at a clothing store, and gas station attendant as well as positions he was unqualified for, such as record store manager (though he often listened to music).

Harry felt discouraged and resigned himself to the idea that nobody wanted to hire him because he has a learning disability. He ended up spending the summer without work, except for a few jobs mowing lawns for neighbors, and had no idea what his plans for fall would be.

Sally: A Formal Approach

Sally was a 19-year-old high school senior who was held back one year and had struggled though her schooling. She was enrolled in a strong secondary program, however, that began her career development and planning process early in her high school career. Through this process she attended a career development course. She was aware of her areas of strengths and weaknesses, as well as postsecondary options for those not opting for higher education. After her unsatisfying academic experience, Sally readily declined any further academic endeavors, and chose a vocational avenue.

Through her vocational education courses at her high school, she understood that she needed to enhance her experiences in order to be hired after high school graduation. Since Sally lacked the interpersonal skills and experience at this point to seek a regular part-time job, she volunteered at her local Young Women's Christian Association (YWCA) to help with the after-school programs offered there. She also accepted babysitting jobs in her neighborhood to increase her reference list and save money for new clothes for after high school. She also offered to help the sports coaches record times from athletic meets at her high school. These records were kept by several other time keepers who could check her accuracy. Not only did this endeavor increase the skills she had to list on her resumé; she also had practice in her math skills that she struggled with, and she found the timing activities a pleasurable avenue for refining her math skills.

The summer before her senior year of high school, Sally applied for a number of part-time jobs and was accepted for employment at a local fast-food chain restaurant for the summer. Sally graduated from high school with minimal grades, but she had worked to build her job-related skills. She had also worked hard to build a resumé highlighting the skills she had gained through her career development training, she had refined her interview skills, and she was well prepared to begin her postsecondary job search. Her resumé is displayed in Appendix B at the end of this book.

Since Sally had done extensive research into the matching of her self-assessment with occupations, she was able to discern positions she was eligible for. She had canvassed all possible avenues, such as the Division of Rehabilitation Services, family friends, bulletin boards, contacts with school teachers, and the newspaper, and she developed a list of prospective employers to submit applications to. She planned her strategy by developing a time line that included records of when applications were picked up, completed, and submitted; when employer contacts were made; when interviews occurred; and when thank-you notes were written and mailed.

When Sally requested job applications, she brought them to her home if allowed and typed in the information, as she often had difficulty discerning what the questions were asking; plus, her handwriting was illegible at times. She asked her parents and a high school teacher to proofread each application after she thoughtfully completed it. Again neatly dressed, she submitted each application with her resumé at an agreed-upon time and thanked each employer for the opportunity to take the application home to complete.

Sally received a number of invitations for interviews and was offered three different positions. She accepted a position with a small company as a full-time receptionist and began her new position after her high school graduation.

INDEPENDENT LIVING STRATEGIES

Little information is available about community and independent living for individuals with LD. However, many individuals with LD will be confronted with obstacles in becoming financially independent. This is especially true given the growing emphasis on the need to complete postsecondary training programs (Fourqurean et al. 1991). The social, emotional, and personal difficulties experienced by many adults with LD may affect their ability to adapt to life tasks (Bender 1992; Deshler et al. 1984). Evidence shared by adults with LD about their past educational experiences and current problems suggests that they lack preparation for competent functioning in the everyday world (Minskoff 1982). Activities such as shopping and meal preparation, money management, reading bus schedules, and other practical daily living activities can be problematic.

A paucity of information and research is available on the topic of transitional preparations for adolescents with LD. However, some research suggests that individuals with LD encounter difficulties in transitioning from school to independent community living. They are less satisfied with their jobs and hold jobs of lower social status than their peers without LD, are less satisfied with their social lives, tend to still be living with relatives, and tend to not actively pursue leisure time activities (Deshler et al. 1984). What follows are guidelines for daily living skills and social skills strategies for the individual with a learning disability.

Daily Living Skills

Daily living skills need to be taught in a functional, community-based approach. That is, basic skills must be taught directly and in the setting in which they will be used (Minskoff and Minskoff 1976). For example, *survival reading* should be taught. While providing motivation for general reading, survival reading provides success in reading words in the environment required for independent living skills. Depending upon the decoding skills of the individual, words such as "danger," "yield," "signature," "telephone" and "hospital" are important to independent living (Minskoff 1982). Practice activities, such as reading oven temperature settings, car odometers, and identifying and counting money, are also important to independent living (Minskoff 1982).

Daily living skills must be an integral part of the learning-disabled student's curriculum. This is true not only at the elementary level but also at the secondary level. In brief, mastery of daily living skills is just as important as mastery of academic skills.

Independent living training is also provided by Independent Living Centers that are funded by the Rehabilitation Services Administration. This postsecondary training is accessed through a rehabilitation counselor. Many learning-disabled individuals will need this type of postsecondary training, and it should be specified in their transition plan.

Social Skills

Due to a variety of reasons, including the fact that many individuals with LD are not incidental learners, some individuals have not learned to monitor social information that occurs during daily interactions. For example, which direction the sun rises and the fact that one side of a street has even numbers are typical bits of social information that allow most individuals to interact smoothly within society (Minskoff 1982). Additionally, many individuals with a learning disability are unable to intuitively perceive verbal and/or nonverbal social cues that signify appropriate responses (Shaw et al. 1987). The attitudes, emotions, and intentions communicated by others through nonverbal language such as body posture or facial expressions may be difficult for an individual with a learning disability to interpret (Smith 1991).

Many adolescents with LD have problem-solving abilities equivalent to those exhibited by juvenile delinquents (Schumaker et al. 1982). "Poor achievement," "lack of motivation," and "short attention span" are terms that frequently apply to both juvenile delinquents and young adults with LD. Other similarities include: low frustration tolerance, negative self-concept, and a general lower ability for social-cognitive problem solving (Smith 1991).

One way to overcome social skills problems is the direct teaching of generic cognitive skills. Cognitive skills such as problem solving, goal setting, relaxation techniques, and self-evaluation are important for dealing with social skills problems faced by individuals with LD (Deshler, et al. 1984). Not only should these skills aid in secondary-to-postsecondary transition, but they also prove useful during transitions that occur throughout the life span. In sum, social skills problems should be addressed in a learning-disabled student's IEP and transition plan.

Individuals with verbal social skills problems may need to learn to address communications on the basis of four factors: participants, topic, setting, and objective. When addressing participants, consideration of sex, authority, and age is important. For topic, the degree of formality is important, as is degree of sensitivity and seriousness. For setting, place and time are important, and for objective of a communicative exchange, focus on whether data or feelings are being exchanged (Minskoff 1982).

The most problematic social skill deficit may be social perception disabilities: an inability to recognize or identify the meaning of others' behavior, related to issues in understanding nonverbal communication (Johnson and Myklebust 1967; Minskoff 1982). Standing too close to others; misunderstanding facial expressions, postures, and gestures; inappropriate touching; misunderstanding of voice pitch, volume, or artifactual cues transmitted though cosmetics or clothing can lead to problems. Teaching discrimination, understanding, usage, and application is important to overcoming these social barriers. For example, learning to discriminate auditory and visual social cues in one's own as well as others' behaviors is important. How to express appropriate verbal and motor social cues can be taught next. Techniques such as behavior modification, coaching, cognitive behavior modification, cooperative projects, modeling, and managing behaviors though self-monitoring can be used to teach social skills (Bender 1992; Minskoff 1980a,b; Okolo and Sitlington 1986; Shaw and McGuire 1987).

INDEPENDENT LIVING CASE STUDIES
Joe: A Private Approach

Joe was a 19-year-old male who had struggled though his secondary education and who after high school matriculation declined options of furthering his education. Although his parents were quite wealthy, he intended to find employment. Even with his parents' prodding, he found himself avoiding all job-search strategies and ended up day after day watching television. He began to lose interest in the friends he had from high school, particularly since many had gone on to college or found jobs. Joe's parents became increasingly disturbed at his social isolation, as well as his immobility and other signs of depression. They contacted their local mental health center, a psychology clinic and LD center from a large state university, and developed a list of several LD specialists to contact. After consultation interviews with each of the specialists and therapists, Joe and his family decided upon Dr. Rogin, who had a private practice within driving distance. Dr. Rogin completed a formal assessment of Joe, then, based on the results of the assessment, behavioral observations, and an interview with Joe's parents, he and Joe developed a contract for specific goals Joe wished to attain. The three main areas of focus were social skills, employment opportunities, and independent living. Since Joe needed a great deal of remediation, particularly in the area of social skills, Dr. Rogin worked with him on a set of generic cognitive skills that would generalize over all of these areas. For example, problem-solving skills; goal-setting, goal-implementation, and goal-modification task behaviors; coping strategies; self-efficacy techniques; rational belief measures; cognitive restructuring techniques; and relaxation techniques were addressed.

Dr. Rogin had also administered a battery of career interests, values, skills, and aptitudes inventories to aid in teaching Joe the career planning process. Included in this process were the matching of viable job options for Joe, teaching of the decision-making process, development of a resumé, learning to fill out job applications appropriately, practice with interview skills, and role-playing rehearsal for potentially difficult employment situations (such as receiving criticism from an employer). Job-search strategies for employment within Joe's local community were developed, and Joe began seeking employment.

While social skills enhancement was addressed in all areas of Joe's work with Dr. Rogin, specific strategies were also employed. Through behavior modification and techniques of approximation, Joe began rehearsing new social behaviors and interactions in new social settings. They also developed a list of leisure time and recreational activities for Joe. Joe's parents worked with him to teach basic living adaptation skills, such as utilizing public transportation, basic meal planning and preparation, using a washer and dryer, and shopping.

Joe was hired in an entry-level position at a local chain restaurant that allowed for periodic pay raises and an optional insurance plan. He was able to save enough money after several months of employment to share an apartment with a coworker. Joe attends weekly growth group sessions, where he can monitor and enhance his social skills.

Lisa: A Social Services Approach

Lisa was a 27-year-old female who was recently divorced. She married after high school graduation and had no children. Lisa did not receive any further education and had a sporadic employment history. She typically kept an entry-level position for one to four months, then either quit out of frustration or was terminated by her employer for insufficient work quality. Since her divorce, she was faced with having to support herself financially. While Lisa was able to manage a home, except for money management, she had few marketable skills and limited experience in any occupational area.

Lisa was encouraged by a clergy member to contact the state Vocational Rehabilitation Service or Division of Vocational Rehabilitation and find out about available resources. Lisa called her local office and was informed that the process involved making an appointment, filling out an application for services, and receiving a medical examination that the state would provide for. Eligibility and services (which would be at no cost to her) would then be determined.

Lisa made an appointment to meet with a vocational rehabilitation counselor. They completed the necessary paperwork and Lisa received a medical examination. Lisa was then referred to a large state university evaluation laboratory for assessment for her learning disability. Included in the test battery were career interests; a neurological screening; visual-motor screening; intelligence level; and current academic levels of spelling, reading, arithmetic, and reading comprehension. Test and inventory results, as well as areas of identified strengths and weakness, and suggestions based on these results, were then sent to Lisa's vocational rehabilitation counselor. All of this was executed in a confidential manner.

Together Lisa and her counselor planned short and long-range academic vocational goals. Lisa's battery results suggested she had the aptitude and interest to attend a school of cosmetology. She enrolled in a nearby school and, after receiving her certification, found steady employment as a hairdresser and cosmetologist.

Lisa's area of greatest academic difficulty had been in mathematics and numerical reasoning. These difficulties were manifested on a daily basis in handling money; managing a household budget; balancing a checkbook; and, once employed, in charging customers for her services, making change, and bookkeeping. To compensate in her employment arena, Lisa's employer worked with her to make a chart of different service prices and for correct amounts of change when she is given certain amounts. Lisa's employer agreed to doublecheck her bookwork for her. Lisa found that writing checks rather than using cash worked best for larger sums of money (for example, clothing purchases, large grocery trips, rent, doctor/dentist visits). On a daily basis she doublechecked her checkbook balance, using a calculator. In handling cash, Lisa only carried small sums of money at a time and was aware of how much she kept with her. She double-checked the amounts she spent and any change she received. She kept all receipts and also on a daily basis, checked the amount she had left with the sums of the receipts on her calculator. For tax record keeping she utilized the services of a local tax accounting firm.

CONCLUSION

Critical to the maturational process into adulthood for an individual with a learning disability is the school-to-community transition environment. While appropriate support and services are of paramount importance when exiting the more "protective" secondary school environment (Price & Johnson 1986), little research exists for guiding those with LD in managing their transition from school to life in the community (Deshler et al. 1984; Sergent et al. 1988; C. Smith 1986; S. Smith 1986; Zetlin & Hosseini 1989).

Post-secondary vocational options and independent living strategies for students with LD are addressed in this chapter. Although vocational outcomes tend to present a more encouraging outcome than academic or social/emotional outcomes (Horn et al. 1983), Smith (1988) notes that many individuals with LD are unemployed. Gregory and colleagues (1986) attribute the more encouraging vocational option over academic pursuits to the types of jobs many of the individuals from this population accept. These jobs tend to be minimum wage, entry-level positions that offer few, if any, benefits, and minimal opportunities for advancement (Edgar 1988). Little research is available to guide development of secondary programs for meeting the needs of students with LD, but individuals can empower themselves through enhancing their options for satisfying employment.

Vocational rehabilitation has become more available to individuals with LD since 1981, when the Rehabilitation Services Administration added LD to its list of recognized disabilities. Some vocational rehabilitation offices offer programs specifically for job seekers with LD. To aid in full utilization of these services, the student's IEP should address the transition from school to independent living and employment shifts from part-time to full-time employment or post-secondary vocational training by the time a student is 16 years of age. This part of the IEP, called a *transition plan,* focuses on vocational education programs, instruction in community-based environments, and paid part-time employment (Langone 1990). During the last two years of a student's program, the responsibility of the student's program begins to shift from school personnel to rehabilitation specialists in other community agencies. Collaboration among special educators, vocational educators, rehabilitation counselors, parents, and the student is necessary to planning and implementing an appropriate program.

The career counseling process is most helpful when initiated by junior high or middle school, and should be expanded during high school in order to plan for post-secondary transitions to ensure sufficient time and resources to provide optimal alternatives (Shaw et al. 1987). Special education and vocational education courses are important to vocational and personal success as well (Mithaug et al. 1985). Other important variables to ensure success of the transition process include: acquisition of optimal math skills, work experience (Fourqurean et al. 1991), job-search skills and community-based training of functional skills (Schalock 1986), establishing interagency funding agreements, training in use of on-the-job tools (Okolo and Sitlington 1986), and the importance of family involvement and support (Schalock 1986).

A vocational rehabilitation counselor can be of vital importance to the student with LD who is seeking employment (Price and Johnson 1986). The counselor can serve as a liaison between the individual and employer in striving for effective and practical workplace accommodations (Brown 1984), as well as dispel myths about LD by providing employers with accurate information (McKinney and West 1985).

Job search strategies, résumé building, learning the application process and how to complete application forms, effective interviewing skills, work ethics, and skills for maintaining employment are all important vocational strategies. Job search strategies include taking a personal inventory, or a thorough self-evaluation; job matching, or matching self-knowledge with occupations and specific companies; and pre-job interviewing, or informational interviews. Résumé building involves gaining more in-depth self-knowledge, choosing a résumé format, focusing on content presentation (highlighting skills, abilities, and experiences that sell oneself), and learning about the properties of an effective résumé. The application process involves managing first impressions made on a prospective employer, neatness, appropriateness and completeness of application form responses, and making the appropriate contact with a prospective employer. Preparation, managing first impressions, and appropriate follow-up with the interviewer are key ingredients to a successful interview. Knowledge of work ethics and skills for maintaining employment can help prevent on-the-job difficulties and increase the likelihood of successful and satisfying employment experiences.

The social, emotional and personal difficulties experienced by many individuals with LD may affect their ability to adapt to life tasks (Bender 1992). Daily living skills taught in a functional, community-based manner (Minskoff and Minskoff 1976), such as survival reading (Minskoff 1982), are important to successful independent living. Learning daily living skills must be an integral component of the student's curriculum beginning at the elementary level and continuing through the secondary level, and should be specified in the transition plan.

Social skills are another important dimension of independent living strategies. Learning to appropriately perceive and respond to verbal and non-verbal social cues can be accomplished through the direct teaching of generic cognitive skills such as problem solving, goal-setting, relaxation techniques, and self-evaluation. These skills need to be addressed in a student's IEP and transition plan, and can prove useful in secondary to post-secondary transitions, as well as in transitions that occur throughout life.

Verbal-social-skills problems can be addressed on the basis of participants, topic, setting, and objective of the interaction. The most problematic social skill deficit may be social perception deficit (Johnson and Myklebust 1967; Minskoff 1982), but techniques such as behavior modification, coaching, cooperative projects, cognitive behavior modification, modeling and managing behaviors through self-monitoring can be used to teach social skills (Bender 1992; Minskoff 1980; Okolo and Sitlington 1986; Shaw and McGuire 1987).

Although the student with LD may face a difficult post-secondary school transition to working and independent living, many strategies are available to increase the likelihood of successful experiences. Planning, beginning as early as the elementary school years; collaborative efforts between school personnel, community agencies, parents and the student; independent living skills training; social skills training; knowledge of job search strategies; résumé building; awareness of the job application process and job interview skills; and polished work ethic skills all help to ensure that a student with LD can reach and enjoy his or her potential.

REFERENCES

Bencomo, A., & Schafer, M. (1984, April/May/June). Remediation and accommodation for clients with learning disabilities. *Journal of Rehabilitation*, [Special Issue]. pp. 64–67.

Bender, W. N. (1992). *Learning disabilities: Characteristics, identification and teaching strategies.* Boston: Allyn and Bacon.

Brown, D. (1982a). *Independent living and learning disabled adults.* Washington, DC: President's Committee on Employment of the Handicapped.

Brown, D. (1982b). *Rehabilitating learning disabled adults.* Washington, DC: President's Committee on Employment of the Handicapped.

Brown, D. (1984). Employment considerations for learning disabled adults. *Journal of Rehabilitation*, [Special Issue] pp. 74–77.

Buchanan, M., & Wolf, J. S. (1986). A comprehensive study of learning disabled adults. *Journal of Learning Disabilities, 19*, 34–38.

Cohen, J. (1984). The learning disabled university student: Signs and initial screening. *NASPA Journal, 21*(3), 22–30.

Deshler, D. D., Schumaker, J. B., Lenz, B. K., & Ellis, E. (1984). Academic and cognitive interventions for LD adolescents: Part II. *Journal of Learning Disabilities, 17*(3), 170–179.

Dictionary of Occupational Titles. (1982). Washington, DC: U.S. Government Printing Office.

Edgar, E. (1988). Employment as an outcome for mildly handicapped students: Current status and future directions. *Focus on Exceptional Children, 21*(1), 1–8.

Figler, H. (1981). *The complete job search handbook.* New York: Holt, Rinehart & Winston.

Fourqurean, J. M., Meisgeier, C., Swank, P. R., & Williams, R. E. (1991). Correlates of post-secondary employment outcomes for young adults with learning disabilities. *Journal of Learning Disabilities, 24*(7), 400–405.

Frith, G. H. (1984). Rehabilitating learning disabled clients: A model program for adolescents. *American Rehabilitation, 10*(2), 3–9.

Gregory, J. F., Shanahan, T., & Walberg, H. (1986). A profile of learning disabled twelfth-graders in regular classes. *Learning Disability Quarterly, 9*, 33–42.

Harrington, T. F., & O'Shea, A. J. (1982). *Career decision-making system.* Monterey, CA: Publishers Test Service.

Hasazi, S. B., Gordon, L. R., & Roe, C. A. (1985). Factors associated with the employment of handicapped youth exiting high school from 1979 to 1983. *Exceptional Children, 51,* 455–469.

Horn, W. F., O'Donnell, J. P., & Vitulano, L. A. (1983). Long-term follow-up studies of learning disabled persons. *Journal of Learning Disabilities, 9,* 542–554.

Johnson, D., & Myklebust, H. (1967). *Learning disabilities: Educational principles and practices.* New York: Grune & Stratton.

Krannick, C. R. (1982). *Interview for success.* Virginia Beach, VA: Impact.

Langone, J. (1990). *Teaching students with mild and moderate learning problems.* Boston: Allyn and Bacon.

McKinney, L. R., & West, C. (1985). *Extending horizons: Employers as partners.* Research and Development Series No. 257E. Columbus: Ohio State University. National Center for Research in Vocational Education. (ERIC Document Reproduction Document Service No. 260 241.)

Mick, L. B. (1985). Connecting links between secondary and post-secondary programs for learning-disabled persons. *Journal of College Student Personnel, 26*(5), 463–465.

Minskoff, E. H. (1980a). A teaching approach for developing non-verbal communication skills in students with social perception deficits. Part I. *Journal of Learning Disabilities, 13,* 118–124.

Minskoff, E. H. (1980b). A teaching approach for developing non-verbal communication skills in students with social perception deficits. Part II. *Journal of Learning Disabilities, 13,* 203–208.

Minskoff, E. H. (1982). Training LD students to cope with the everyday world. *Academic Therapy, 17*(3), 311–316.

Minskoff, E. H., & Minskoff, J. G. (1976). A unified program for remedial and compensatory teaching for children with process learning disabilities. *Journal of Learning Disabilities, 9,* 215–222.

Minskoff, E. H., Sautter, S. W., Hoffman, F. J., & Hawkes, R. (1987). Employer attitudes toward hiring the learning disabled. *Journal of Learning Disabilities, 20,* 53–57.

Mithaug, D. E., Horiuchi, C. N., & Fanning, P. N. (1985). A report on the Colorado statewide follow-up survey of special education students. *Exceptional Children, 51,* 397–404.

Mori, A. A. (1980). Career education for the learning disabled: Where are we now? *Learning Disability Quarterly, 3,* 91–101.

Neubert, D. A., Tilson, G. P. Jr., & Ianacone, R. N. (1989). Postsecondary transition needs and employment patterns of individuals with mild disabilities. *Exceptional Children, 55,* 494–500.

Occupational Outlook Handbook. Bureau of Labor Statistics, U.S. Department of Labor. Distributed by Associated Book Publishers, Inc., Scottsdale, AZ. Published annually.

Okolo, C. M., & Sitlington, P. (1986). The role of special education in LD adolescents' transition from school to work. *Learning Disability Quarterly, 9,* 141–155.

Price, L., & Johnson, K. E. (1986). The secondary to post-secondary transition process for learning disabled adolescents and adults: An annotated bibliography. (Report No. EC192125). Washington, DC: Department of Education. (ERIC Document Reproduction Service No. ED 280 224.)

Schalock, R. L. (1986). Employment outcomes from secondary school programs. *Remedial and Special Education, 5*(6), 37–39.

Schumaker, J. B., Hazel, J. S., Sherman, J. A., & Sheldon, J. (1982). Social skills performances of learning disabled, non-learning disabled, and delinquent adolescents. *Learning Disabled Quarterly, 5,* 388–397.

Sergent, M. T., Carter, R., Sedlacek, W. E., & Scales, W. R. (1988). A five-year analysis of disabled student services in higher education. *Journal of Postsecondary Education and Disability, 6,* 21–27.

Shaw, S. F., & McGuire (1987). *Preparing learning disabled high school students for post-secondary education.* Paper presented at the annual convention of the Council for Exceptional Children, Chicago. (ERIC Document Reproduction Service No. ED 285 316.)

Smith, C. (1986). The future of the LD field: Intervention approaches. *Journal of Learning Disabilities, 19*(8), 461–472.

Smith, J. O. (1988). Social and vocational problems of adults with learning disabilities: A review of the literature. *Learning Disabilities Focus, 4,* 46–58.

Smith, S. (1986, July 23). *College students with learning disabilities: Identification and teaching.* Paper presented at a faculty development program, New Brunswick, NJ: Rutgers University.

Zetlin, A. G., & Hosseini, A. (1989). Six postschool case studies of mildly learning handicapped young adults. *Exceptional Children, 55,* 405–411.

13

College-Level Instructional Interventions

Margaret A. Martin
Phillip J. McLaughlin

The transition between secondary and higher education environments can be difficult for the most capable of students, and the difficulty is exacerbated for individuals with a disability, who face a range of difficulties after their high school graduation (Fourqurean et al. 1991). For individuals with learning disabilities (LD), the transition may be especially difficult, since their disability is not typically visible and thus is often misunderstood or ignored. Traditional postsecondary options are frequently limited for the individual with LD, due to insufficient academic achievement or poor social functioning (Fourqurean et al. 1991).

However, given the right conditions and support, the option of higher education can be appropriate for the individual with LD. Favorable conditions include socioeconomic advantages and intelligence levels that allow for remediation of or compensation for the LD. While it is unclear which other factors are most influential to favorable outcomes, factors such as learning and/or emotional strengths, vocational and educational choices, and types of emotional support can all contribute to favorable outcomes of postsecondary education (Smith 1991). For example, Bruck (1985) reported that 80% of a group of learning-disabled young adults of middle socioeconomic status had graduated from high school, 58% entered college, 31% entered graduate school, and 11% were unemployed.

Rawson (1968) reported that 86% of 56 reading-disabled subjects in another study had graduated from college. Finucci and colleagues (1985) reported a follow-up study of learning-disabled graduates from a boarding school who were from a middle to high socioeconomic status. Thirty-eight percent of the graduates received some technical training or college. Fifty percent of the graduates completed a bachelor's degree, and approximately 8% also received a graduate degree. Only 6% did not complete high school.

While services for learning-disabled students are more available on college and university campuses than before (Phelps 1985; Sarns 1986), they are still minimal (Putnam 1984), and consistent guidelines for effective service delivery

295

are unclear (Keogh 1986; Mick 1985). This situation is exacerbated by the lack of understanding by the student with a learning disability of the new demands involved in higher education. This results in the student feeling buried by the rigor and pace of academic instruction (McGuire et al. 1991). Weinstein and colleagues (1988) note that many of these students lack the strategies and skills necessary for self-monitoring and managing their learning in a number of contexts.

While these findings may present a bleak picture for the student with a learning disability facing a college or university program, it is vital to adhere to a realistic approach in order to have a successful experience in higher education through use of services offered and compensatory strategies the student can employ. Barbaro (1982) acknowledges the devastation one can experience in failing in higher education yet highlights that prematurely discouraging a student with a learning disability away from higher education can diminish that person from realizing his or her potential.

REHABILITATION ACT OF 1973

An awareness of Section 504 of the Rehabilitation Act of 1973 (P.L. 93–112) will help a student with a learning disability select a college or university. Section 504 states: "No otherwise qualified handicapped individual in the United States shall solely by reason of handicap, be excluded from the participation in, be denied the benefits of, or be subjected to discrimination under any program or activity receiving federal financial assistance" (p. 49). Thus, an increase of college and university support services are being offered to students with LD (Mick 1985). The implications of this act are often manifest in the admissions procedures of many colleges and universities, as institutions receiving federal assistance are prohibited from soliciting information about the disabilities of college applicants (Guildroy 1981).

Schools also attempt to comply with Section 504 in their admissions testing. Many programs will accept nonstandardized testing procedures in their admissions decisions for students with disabilities (Gerber and Reiff 1985). Most university admissions tests allow for special testing accommodations with a letter at registration requesting such services, typically without initial documentation required. Special accommodations include extended test time, proximity seating, separate testing areas, extra rest time, and adjustments in physical conditions. Special materials include braille, audio cassette, large print, cassette recording with accompanying illustrative materials, large-print answer sheets, readers, and helpers to record or copy answers. In particular, the Scholastic Aptitude Test (SAT) and the Graduate Record Examination have made provisions to accommodate students with LD (Gerber and Reiff 1985). Markel and colleagues (1985) present more information about the SAT and students with LD.

A college's or university's commitment to working with students with LD is shown by the number and quality of support services offered. Administrative flexibility is of paramount importance in selecting a college or university. For example, specific modifications and accommodations that have been made for other students are an indication of the school's commitment to work with students with a disability. The number of inservice programs provided for faculty and staff addressing the needs of students with LD is another indication of commitment (Bender 1992). McGuire and Shaw (1987) suggest that the characteristics of the institutions under consideration, the specific characteristics of the support services available for students with LD, and the characteristics of the individual student should be important areas of consideration in the selection process.

Table 13.1 presents a list of questions to ask admissions officers prior to applying for admission. With answers to these questions, prospective students will be better equipped to make personal decisions regarding the institution that will best serve their individual academic, financial, psychosocial, and learning needs.

ASSESSMENT STRATEGIES

In order for postsecondary services to be successful in meeting the needs of learning-disabled students, this population must be clearly identified and diagnosed (Deshler et al. 1984; C. Smith 1986). Cohen (1984) advocates comprehensive neuropsychological diagnostic testing to identify the specific disability, psychological concerns that interact with the disability, and the student's strengths. Assessment of academic strengths and weaknesses is of particular importance in discerning the types and timing of courses to be enrolled in (Bender 1992). The psychosocial and psychoeducational assessment process can be an expensive endeavor, but many institutions offer free or fee-based services or accept assessments from high school. For information about required assessments and specific services, the prospective student should contact the institution's learning center, disabled student services, or counseling and testing centers.

After the assessment process the student with a learning disability should be more cognizant of strengths and areas of concern and equipped with other self-knowledge. Thus, career counseling is an important component of the higher education experience and should be introduced early in a student's academic career in order to ascertain realistic assessments of values, interests, skills, and capabilities. For a learning-disabled student, career counseling should cover decision-making skills, motivation evaluation, and career and self-exploration, and should include the development of a plan of action (Shaw and McGuire 1987).

Contacting the state Division of Rehabilitation Services office can be helpful in the selection of a college or university. Some offices provide assessment services and aid in locating sources of financial support for assessment and educational expenses.

ACADEMIC EFFECTIVENESS STRATEGIES
Preparing for Higher Education

Many strategies are available to enhance learning-disabled students' experiences in higher education. Before actually arriving on campus to begin a college

1. What is the level of campus awareness of LD? Are inservice meetings provided for college faculty and staff addressing the needs of students with LD? Do faculty and staff members support programmatic efforts? How? What institutional provisions are there for educating students without LD about students with LD?

2. How are services provided for students with LD different from services provided for underachieving and high-risk students? What differentiates the service approaches for these different student groups?

3. Are Writing Center, Reading Center, Counseling Services, Career Planning and Placement, Learning Assistance Center, Disabled Student Services, Study Skills Center and Tutoring services available? What is the cost of the services provided?

4. Can the student receive individual as well as group special instruction on (a) study skills; (b) personal concerns; (c) LD?

5. What type of campus networking and "liaisoning" exists for larger campuses that provide a wide range of support services to students? For example, will the Learning Center aid students in accessing the Reading Center, Counseling Center, or Career Center, and work with the student's academic advisor? For smaller institutions, is the approach to service provision for students with LD holistic, and are any specialists available to assist this student population?

6. Is a study skills, learning strategies, or academic effectiveness program available? If so, are note-taking and classroom strategies, concentration and study skills, test-taking strategies, text anxiety, time management, and paper writing covered?

7. Is there a summer training program, beyond orientation, for students with LD?

8. Is more than a basic or general tutorial program offered to students with LD? That is, are specialists in LD available for tutoring services? What are the costs?

9. What psychosocial institutional supports are available specifically for students with LD?

10. What type of counseling is provided for parents?

11. Can students enroll in fewer than the required number of courses each term without sacrificing full-time status, which may have implications for financial aid considerations, or residence hall space?

12. Are special admissions requirements available to students with LD? For example, nonstandardized admissions test scores, WAIS-R scores, school records and other forms of documentation of a learning disability, recent IEPs, letter of recommendations from high school LD specialists, personal interviews with the Director of Admissions or other directors of special service programs, parent interviews?

13. Are professors encouraged to design and develop course materials that include specific accommodations appropriate for students with LD?

14. Is an academic protection clause available, allowing students with LD to be exempt from academic probation?

Table 13.1 Questions to ask about college LD services (*continued*)

15.	Are special university courses offered where course content is the same as regular courses but with smaller student enrollment, extended course time, and more individual instruction?
16.	Is a bridging or linking precollege program available where students enroll during the last part of their high school in different types of activities and courses to aid in adaption to the adult college environment to foster interpersonal skills and enhance planning skills?
17.	What forms of assessment are available, and what are the costs? Is diagnostic testing used to develop an IEP for service provision?
18.	For student athletes with LD, are any easements of grade restrictions allowed, particularly if a scholarship is involved?
19.	What is the typical class size, particularly for general classes?
20.	Is flexibility allowed for graduation if a student with a learning disability cannot meet certain requirements such as a foreign language?
21.	Are modifications available for graduation if the state or Board of Regents requires a graduation examination?

or university program of study, students can utilize field trips to college campuses (Dalke and Franzene 1988), summer training opportunities for students with LD (Learning Disability and College Preparation 1989), presentations by college students with LD (Litt and McGuire 1988), and collaborative planning for transition (Seidenberg 1986).

Extensive precollege preparation while still involved in secondary education has been advocated (Dexter 1982). A remedial approach to both writing and reading skills during high school in anticipation of college and university level coursework may be necessary (see Price and Johnson [1986]). McGuire and colleagues (1991) advocate specific instruction in study skills, as many students with LD have, during their secondary education experience, received tutoring in course content to enhance success in mainstreamed classes, but not in learning or study strategies or in written expression. These authors' findings suggest that students with LD often experience an "organizational" deficit that continues into adulthood. Poor time management, unsystematic lecture notes, and struggles in writing organization, and examination preparation and taking may be symptoms of this deficit. Reading and writing skills and learning a new language, generally categorized under language-related processes, as well as mathematics-related processes, are common areas that may be problematic for students with LD studying at colleges or universities (Cohen 1984).

Acknowledging that one may be dealing with deficits is a key to addressing remedial and compensatory strategies for academic effectiveness. Instruction in learning strategies, writing skills, and self-advocacy skills training is important in remediating these areas (McGuire et al. 1991), as is learning how to acquire, organize, store, and retrieve information (Shaw et al. 1987). Many student with LD require assistance in time-management skills (C. Smith 1986; S. Smith 1986). Instruction to enhance comprehension (Palincsar and Brown 1984), process-oriented writing approaches (Bos 1988; Flower and Hayes 1981; Graham and Harris 1987, 1988), and learning to use the computer as a writing tool (Mac-Arthur 1988), are also helpful. Memory and listening skills improvement, vocabulary development, reading comprehension skills, library use, writing skills and paper-writing strategies, effective use of college textbooks, note-taking strategies, and test-taking preparation are important areas of skill development (Barbaro 1982), Markel and colleagues (1985) advocate development of test-taking skills, particularly with standardized examinations such as the American College Test (ACT) or SAT. For more about the educational characteristics of students with LD, see Johnston (1984).

Study Skills Strategies

A tutorial model assigns tutors to help students attain the competencies required in their college courses. Cost may range from no charge up to a considerable fee, depending on the source of the tutor (Mick 1985). The effectiveness of a tutorial program is contingent on the tutor's level of knowledge and skills, the intensity and quality of the support, and the student's commitment. The success of a compensatory strategies model depends on the diagnostic ability of the professional who decides which compensatory strategy the student requires. The strength of this model is in the individualized instruction the student receives. To learn about tutoring services, names of tutors, and help with compensatory strategies, contact the college's or university's learning center, student services office, disabled student office, study skills program, counseling center, or academic affairs office. Learning centers can play a vital role in the collegiate experience of the learning-disabled student (Nayman 1982).

In general, it seems a deeper understanding of metacognitive instructional procedures can be helpful to students with LD. That is, understanding the process of cognition, or, as Brown (1978) suggests, "knowing how to know" and grasping the different ways to approach a problem, can be a basic foundation for higher education coursework. For example, understanding that paraphrasing information from a college or university textbook can involve skills of serial learning as well as recall (McGuire et al. 1991) can make this academic task manageable.

Many students with LD experience difficulty in organization of assignments and scheduling (C. Smith 1986), and in reading college textbooks (Cohen 1988). Strategies that have been helpful include keeping a daily and weekly assignment schedule (Cohen 1988), as well as a term overview calendar that allows planning for papers, examinations, and projects. Reading assignments aloud and highlighting textbooks, or purchasing textbooks already highlighted have been helpful to some students (Cohen 1988), although caution is warranted in purchasing already highlighted books. A student will want to peruse the book to make sure it is in good shape and has not been haphazardly or overhighlighted.

Table 13.2 Academic effectiveness strategies

Students with LD can use a variety of strategies for enhancing their academic effectiveness, including:

- Obtain permission from professors to tape-record lectures.
- Use a reader in completing assigned text materials.
- Use tutoring assistance.
- Seek extended course time.
- Use a calendar for planning for term projects, for weekly assignments, quizzes, examinations, and other important deadlines.
- Request untimed tests.
- Take examinations and tests by means other than the written word.
- Use taped textbooks ("Talking Books").
- Use large print textbooks.
- Highlight important textbook material.
- Use the SQ3R method of study (Survey, Question, Read, Review, Recite).
- Ask a classmate to take notes for the student to copy later.
- Learn graphic skills, such as reading tables, charts, diagrams and maps.
- Use a calculator.
- Use computers and word-processing programs.
- Enroll in school part-time, or take reduced class loads.
- Plan an extended program of study (perhaps one extra year).
- Enroll in study skills course before entering college.
- Enroll in a summer diagnostic session.
- Take one to three summer credits of college work in preparation for the first fall session.
- Follow course and text objectives closely.
- Identify faculty and staff who are knowledgeable about LD.
- Request study guides from professors to follow.
- Learn strategies that enhance metacognitive understanding of course material.
- Learn to arrange study areas for maximum enhancement of on-task behavior.
- Enlist the services of the Counseling Center, Disabled Student Services, Tutorial, Study Skills, Writing Center, and Reading Center.

Specific strategies can be implemented for particular subjects. For example, in math classes, many students find consulting with the instructor or classmates to be helpful. However, in reading-oriented classes, many students find that self-study, such as highlighting, is more helpful. Using audiotaped textbooks and tape-recording lectures are other strategies. See Table 13.2 for a list of additional academic effectiveness strategies.

PSYCHOSOCIAL STRATEGIES

Counseling and psychological services can provide invaluable emotional support to students with LD, particularly since research with students with LD reflects problems with externally oriented attributional tendencies, diminished academic achievement and motivation, and learned helplessness (McGuire et al.

1991), as well as fear of failure, anxious and depressive concerns, or concentration difficulties (Cohen 1984). Separate from academic frustrations, many students with LD experience psychosocial deficits that can be more disruptive than their academic problems (Barbaro 1982; Cohen 1984). Cox (1977) calls for helping students with LD to establish a sense of self-confidence and self-worth, and research and practice literature highlights the need to address their emotional and social needs (Barbaro 1982). Dalke and Schmitt (1987) believe that effective college programs for students with LD provide some forum, such as weekly meetings for students to discuss problems and gain support. Many programs provide a trained facilitator for these meetings. For more about the psychological characteristics of students with LD, see Johnston (1984).

Perhaps one of the most appropriate models for addressing postsecondary transitions is one reflecting transition as a life-long adjustment process, as employed in the Netherlands and Denmark (Gerber 1984). While the Dutch and Danish differ in their systems, both highlight continual collaborative efforts among the different service providers working with students with LD over their lifetime. The National Joint Committee on Learning Disabilities (1983) also supports the need for increased sensitivity to individual differences in the development of students with LD, including a need for understanding the socio-emotional needs, and also for a focus on transition as a life-long process.

FIRST-YEAR DIFFICULTIES

The lack of preparation for college (Harris 1983) and a lack of career planning (Magruder 1982), as well as a lack of information by high school students, their parents, and school counselors about college and university support services for students with LD, all contribute to problems that may be encountered during a student's first year in higher education. Concern has been raised about a complacent attitude observed among disabled students in higher education (Sarns 1986). The importance of understanding the new demands required by higher education is paramount; often students with LD are emotionally unequipped for the pace and rigor, as well as the amount, of coursework demanded (McGuire et al. 1991).

To help ameliorate first-year difficulties, an awareness of the specific types of programs and support services offered by colleges and universities is important. While many institutions of higher education purport to have specialized services, it is important to ascertain the accessibility of the programs for students with LD. Table 13.1 provides a list of questions to use as a guide in investigating the resources available at different institutions.

Most students with LD have been provided with an individualized education plan and an individualized transition plan while in secondary education. However, these types of developmental plans may end after high school matriculation (Siperstein 1988). Thus, to help in minimizing transition problems during the first-year experience, the preparation of an individualized college plan (ICP) can be helpful. An ICP could include such areas as needs identification, accommodation strategies, coping skills, learning barriers, and an academic plan. Periodic reevaluation of the ICP is an important dimension of this process (Siperstein 1988).

Table 13.3 shows the academic plan section of an ICP for a 19-year-old male (Jerry) diagnosed with a learning disability in reading. Jerry recently graduated from public high school with passing grades. He received special assistance for his reading disability throughout his public education. The special assistance included services in a special education resource room and private tutoring at home. He has been accepted at a medium-size local university.

The high level of personal and academic responsibility assigned to students in higher education cannot be stressed enough. The individual student in higher education is held accountable for his or her own success. Persistence, tenacity, a high level of commitment, and a willingness to utilize available resources are all key ingredients for learning-disabled students in higher education. Pace (1984) acknowledges the importance of the elements that influence who goes to college and where but emphasizes that what counts most is what the student does once he or she arrives on campus.

CASE STUDIES
Ned: An Informal Approach

Ned was an 18-year-old male who was in the first part of his senior year of high school. He had been diagnosed as learning-disabled during his late elementary public education and had been in special education classes throughout middle and high school. He wanted to study art in college and could draw quite well. One of Ned's areas of strength was his motor coordination, and he also had good hand–eye coordination. However, his mathematical and reading levels of academic functioning created some concern for successful completion of college- or university-level coursework. He also experienced a high level of test anxiety, which resulted in even lower testing scores. Ned could be described as socially shy, yet adept in his social skills. He dated infrequently, and he had shared with his high school counselor concern about the quality of his social life on a college or university campus.

Ned and his parents, with the help of his special education teacher and school guidance counselor, completed in-depth investigations of a number of larger state universities as well as small, independent institutions. He was accepted at several different institutions. Ned's final decision was to attend a small college, although that particular college did not offer a formal, designated program for students with LD, nor did it have LD specialists on campus.

Ned had been attracted to this college from the first time he met with the director of admissions. Though the director was prohibited by law from inquiring about any disability Ned may have, Ned volunteered to her that he was a student with a learning disability. The director then encouraged Ned to request special accommodations during SAT testing. The director arranged for individual interviews with two faculty members from the Art Department (one who would serve

Table 13.3 Individualized college plan

Name: Jerry H.	Date: 04-19-93 Date of Graduation: Spring, 1998
Current Age: 19	D.O.B.: 03-09-74

ACADEMIC PLAN:

Career Counseling.
Jerry's values, interests, skills, and capabilities need to be assessed in relation to developing his academic course of study in relation to his career plan.
Beginning Date: Summer Orientation
Agencies Involved: University Career Development Center.
Contact Person: Career Counseling Specialist.

Summer Orientation Program.
Jerry is enrolled to attend the university's summer orientation session designed specifically for students with LD.
Beginning Date: July 1, 1993.
Sector Responsible: Admissions; Residential Life; Learning Disability Clinic.
Contact Person: Learning Disability Clinic Director; Director of Admissions; Director of Residential Life.

Academic Effectiveness Program.
Jerry is enrolled in the study skills program offered at the university. Time management, note taking and classroom strategies, term paper writing, textbook reading strategies, test-taking strategies, and test anxiety management skills are covered.
Beginning Date: First day of classes.
Sector Responsible: Learning Center
Contact Person: Learning Center Director

Computer Skills.
Jerry should continue with the computer class he has been enrolled in through Adult Education. He is enrolled for a 1-credit "Introduction to University Computing" course during orientation to familiarize him with university resources.
Beginning Date: July 1, 1993
Sector Responsible: Computer Services
Contact Person: Director of Computer Services Education

Library Skills.
Jerry's attendance at a Library Skills Orientation Seminar is included as part of his summer orientation.
Beginning Date: July 1, 1993
Sector Responsible: Library Services; Learning Disability Clinic
Contact Person: Director of Libraries; Learning Disability Clinic Director.

Academic Advising.
Jerry has been assigned to the English Department Chair for academic advising. The Chair has agreed to serve as Jerry's academic liaison for waiving course requirements if necessary, with university faculty for special classroom accommodations, and with the Learning Center to monitor Jerry's progress.
Beginning Date: Currently meeting regularly.
Contact Person: English Department Chair.

Table 13.3 Individualized college plan (*continued*)

Personal Counseling.	Jerry is currently meeting with the university Counseling Center Director, who has special training in LD. Through his counselor, he will receive social skills training, assertiveness training, and gain emotional support. Beginning Date: Currently meeting regularly. Contact Person: Counseling Center Director.
Financial Aid.	Jerry is currently meeting with the university's Director of Financial Aid and his rehabilitation counselor to arrange payment of fees, textbooks, housing, and special aids (tape recorder, tutorial assistance). Beginning Date: Currently meeting regularly. Contact Person: Rehabilitation Counselor; Director of Financial Aid.

as Ned's academic advisor), the department chair of the Math and Computer Sciences Department, and the Director of Counseling and Career Planning. Ned and his parents were impressed by the "liaisoning" that had occurred and felt encouraged by the willingness of the faculty and staff to accommodate Ned's special needs.

The Director of Counseling and Career Planning agreed to meet with Ned throughout the summer before fall session to address his test anxiety. Ned learned test-preparation and test-taking strategies and relaxation techniques and was able to face the fall quarter with a higher level of competence and confidence about college-level examinations. Ned and the director also addressed special classroom strategies (such as sitting close to the front of the classroom and away from doors and windows that may prove to be distracting), note-taking strategies (such as using a tape recorder and reviewing a friend's notes or reviewing the instructor's lecture outline), textbook reading (using the SQ3R method—highlighting, writing key words in the margins then covering up the text and reciting out loud the definition of the words or concepts [see Table 13.2]), paper-writing skills (using word processing applications, library skills, organizational strategies), and time management. Ned and the Director of Counseling and Career Planning also began Ned's career development process and addressed some of Ned's concerns about dating on a college campus. The director agreed to be a main contact person for Ned's parents and provided both Ned and his parents with her home phone number.

The Dean of Students agreed to provide resident hall programming to educate students about LD in general. The dean also agreed to work in conjunction with the Director of Counseling and Career Planning to provide in-service workshops for faculty and staff about the needs of special students. The faculty were requested by the college president to consider the needs of special learners in designing their course curricula.

Ned was assigned to the department chair of the Art Department as his academic advisor. In conjunction with the Vice-President of Academic Affairs, the department developed a program of study for Ned, allowing him to waive the foreign language requirement in exchange for more extensive coursework in computer skills. Also, in conjunction with the Counseling and Career Planning office and the Financial Aid office, peer tutors were identified who could proof-read Ned's written work and coach him through his required math courses. The tutors would be hired and compensated as work-study students. This approach not only provided Ned with peer interaction and fewer demands on faculty time: it provided the tutors with an opportunity for employment and teaching experience. Extended test times would be arranged as needed.

While certainly some faculty and staff were aware of Ned's learning disability, special accommodations were handled in a highly confidential manner, disclosing information only with Ned's signed permission for release of information. Students knew of Ned's learning disability only if he told them himself.

Ned enrolled for fewer than full-time credits each term. He struggled through some courses, but with an informal approach that was collaborative and holistic, Ned succeeded in earning his B.F.A. degree in five years. After matriculation, he was hired as a commercial artist in a small advertising firm.

Valerie: A Formal Approach

Valerie was an 18-year-old high school senior who wanted to be in management. Her career goals were unclear, but she felt she would enjoy working with people, since she experienced great difficulty in organizing her written work. Her mathematical aptitude was below average, yet with persistence she had been able to complete her high school work. Valerie had wanted to attend a large university for "as long as she could remember." Her parents were supportive of her wishes to enroll in college but were able to provide only partial financial support. With the aid of Valerie's high school guidance counselor and special education teacher, the state Division of Rehabilitation Services office was contacted. In conjunction with a local university's learning disabilities clinic, and the Rehabilitation Service's evaluation laboratory, a full assessment was completed. The results suggested that with appropriate support services, coupled with self-motivation and persistence, Valerie might be able to successfully complete a university's program of study.

In compliance with Section 504 of the Rehabilitation Act of 1973, Valerie was accepted for enrollment at a large state university, and her education was funded by the Division of Rehabilitation Services. Before applying to any of the large institutions she had desired to attend, Valerie had contacted each institution to determine the services offered. In conjunction with her parents, her Division of Rehabilitations Services counselor, and her high school counselor, she made her decision on the basis of the support services offered.

The university Valerie chose had a Learning Disabilities Clinic. This clinic offered diagnosis and assessment, as well as remediation, as a free service to students. She also learned of a Reading Center where specialists were available to assist her in her reading skills. A Writing Clinic provided special sessions for students with LD to address their special writing needs. Through Handicapped Services, Valerie was able to make provisions for taping lectures and accessing "Talking Textbooks" and large-print materials. Also through these services, Valerie met other students with LD and formed a social network with those facing similar learning situations. Valerie attended study skills programs presented through the various centers on campus and enlisted the aid of Tutoring Services in locating tutors for specific subjects she struggled with. Beginning her first year, Valerie maintained contact with a professional from the Career Planning and Placement Center to aid her in developing realistic and attainable career goals and a plan of action. She also attended weekly counseling sessions with a psychologist at the Counseling Center to address issues surrounding self-confidence, interpersonal interactions, conflict resolution, and stress management. Due to the rigor of her coursework demands, Valerie was able to attend growth groups only on a short-term basis.

Through collaborative campus efforts coordinated by the Director of Admissions with the Dean of Academic Affairs and Dean of Educational Services, Valerie's program of study was developed so that she would be enrolled for lighter course loads each term without sacrificing full-time status and was allowed a four and one-half year program of study, including summer school. Advanced foreign language course requirements were waived, but she was required to enroll in one term of foreign language on a pass/fail basis. While Valerie ended up failing a math class and two business classes and had to retake them, she was able to pass them the second time.

Valerie could not be involved in the extracurricular activities that so many university students enjoy because of her strenuous involvement with the support services available at her university. However, without these services she would not have been able to matriculate with her Bachelor's degree and land a position in small business management that will provide her with independent living and allow her to make the kinds of contributions in life she desired to make.

CONCLUSION

It is important to investigate the support services provided by colleges and universities. Repeatedly the literature raises concern about programming and training for higher education available at the secondary level to students with LD (for example, see Okolo and Sitlington [1986]). Early transitional planning—and the earlier the better—seems to be a recurring theme. For example, course waivers in secondary math and/or foreign language might disqualify a student from admission to some institutions of higher education (Shaw et al. 1987).

Research suggests that students with LD tend to reach their highest level of skill development during the secondary years (Shaw & McGuire 1987). Therefore, learning skills and strategies and metacognitive strategies need to be taught in secondary school, particularly in light of the level of personal responsibility expected of students in higher education. Psychosocial developmental issues are paramount, particularly when one considers the types of interpersonal interactions involved in higher education—for example, developing a relation-ship with a roommate and other peers, consulting with the Dean of Students and other program directors, and interacting with faculty.

Deciding on a college or university is an exciting process, but one that can seem overwhelming. It is suggested that one keep in mind the excitement of the process and the laudable accomplishment a student with a learning disability has attained in considering higher education as a postsecondary option.

Price and Johnson (1986) reviewed the literature addressing secondary ed-ucation and the learning-disabled student and postsecondary services and the learning-disabled adult. They also provide an annotated bibliography on second-ary to postsecondary transitions of students with LD. Johnston (1984) gives a brief overview of eight college programs designed to meet the needs of students with specific LD.

REFERENCES

Barbaro, F. (1982). The learning disabled college student: Some considerations in setting objectives. *Journal of Learning Disabilities, 15*(10), 599–603.

Bender, W. N. (1992). *Learning disabilities: Characteristics, identification and teaching strategies*. Boston: Allyn and Bacon.

Bos, C. S. (1988). Process-oriented writing: Instructional implications for mildly handi-capped students. *Exceptional Children, 54*, 521–527.

Brown, A. L. (1978). Knowing when, where and how to remember: A problem of meta-cognition. In R. Glasser (Ed.), Advances in instructional psychology (pp. 77–165). Hillsdale, N.J. Erlbaum.

Bruck, M. (1985). The adult functioning of children with specific learning disabilities: A follow-up study. In I. E. Siegel (Ed.), *Advances in applied developmental psychology* (vol. 1). Norwood, N.J.: Ablex.

Buchanan, M., & Wolf, J. S. (1986). A comprehensive study of learning disabled adults. *Journal of Learning Disabilities, 19*, 34–38.

Cohen, J. (1984). The learning disabled university student: Signs and initial screening. *NASPA Journal, 21*(3), 22–30.

Cohen, S. E. (1988). Coping strategies of university students with learning disabilities. *Journal of Learning Disabilities, 21*, 161–164.

Cox, S. (1977). The learning-disabled adult. *Academic Therapy, 13*(1), 79–86.

Dalke, C., & Franzene, J. (1988). Secondary-postsecondary collaboration: A model of shared responsibility. *Learning Disabilities Focus, 4*, 38–45.

Dalke, C., & Schmitt, S. (1987). Meeting the transition needs of college bound students with learning disabilities. *Journal of Learning Disabilities, 20*, 176–180.

Deshler, D. D., Schumaker, J. B., Lenz, B. K., & Ellis, E. (1984). Academic and cognitive interventions for LD adolescents: Part II. *Journal of Learning Disabilities, 17*(3), 170–179.

Dexter, B. L. (1982). Helping learning disabled students prepare for college. *Journal of Learning Disabilities, 15*(6), 344–346.

Finucci, J. M., Gottfredson, L. S., & Childs, B. (1985). A follow-up study of dyslexic boys. *Annals of Dyslexia, 35*, 117–136.

Flower, L., & Hayes, J. R. (1981). A cognitive process theory of writing. *College Com-position and Communications, 32*, 365–387.

Fourqurean, J. M., Meisgeier, C., Swank, P. R., & Williams, R. E. (1991). Correlates of post-secondary employment outcomes for young adults with learning disabilities. *Jour-nal of Learning Disabilities, 24*(7), 400–405.

Gerber, P. J. (1984). *A study of the school to work transition for learning disabled students and the learning disabled adult in society in the Netherlands and Denmark.* (Report No. GN: 22-P-59032/2-02). New Orleans, LA: World Rehabilitation Fund, University of New Orleans-Lakefront. (ERIC Document Reproduction Service No. Ed 258 382.)

Gerber, P. J., & Reiff, H. B. (1985). A growing issue for university admissions officers: The learning disabled applicant. *Journal of College Admissions, 109,* 9–13.

Graham, S., & Harris, K. R. (1987). Improving composition skills of inefficient learners with self-instructional strategy training. *Topics in Language Disorders, 7,* 66–77.

Graham, S., & Harris, D. R. (1988). Instructional recommendations for teaching writing to exceptional students. *Exceptional Children, 54,* 506–512.

Guildroy, J. (1981). The learning-disabled college applicant. *College Board Review, 120,* 17–30.

Harris, R. (1983). When the transcript is splattered with the milk of human kindness. *1983 Proceedings of the Association on Handicapped Student Services in Post-Secondary Education.* Detroit, MI: Wayne State University Press.

Horn, W. F., O'Donnell, J. P., & Vitulano, L. A. (1983). Long-term follow-up studies of learning disabled persons. *Journal of Learning Disabilities, 9,* 542–554.

Johnston, C. L. (1984). The learning disabled adolescent and young adult: An overview and critique of current practices. *Journal of Learning Disabilities, 17*(7), 386–391.

Keogh, B. K. (1986). Future of the LD field: Research and practice. *Journal of Learning Disabilities, 19*(8), 455–459.

Learning disability and college preparation. (1989, Spring). *Information from HEATH,* p. 2.

Litt, V., & McGuire, J. M. (1988, March). *Personal insights of college LD students.* Panel presentation at the annual state conference of the Association for Children and Adults with Learning Disabilities, Hartford, CT.

Lopez, M., & Clyde-Snyder, M. (1983). Higher education for the learning-disabled student. *NASPA Journal, 20*(4), 34–39.

MacArthur, C. A. (1988). The impact of computers on the writing process. *Exceptional Children, 54,* 536–542.

Magruder, S. (1982). A pre-college assessment center. *1982 Conference Proceedings of the Association on Handicapped Student Services in Post-Secondary Education.* Detroit, MI: Wayne State University Press.

Markel, G., Bizer, L., & Wilhelm, R. M. (1985). The LD adolescent and the SAT. *Academic Therapy, 20*(4), 397–409.

Mick, L. B. (1985). Connecting links between secondary and post-secondary programs for learning-disabled persons. *Journal of College Student Personnel, 26*(5), 463–465.

McGuire, J. M., Hall, D. & Litt, A. V. (1991). A field-based study of the direct service needs of college students with learning disabilities. *Journal of College Student Development, 32*(2), 101–108.

McGuire, J. M., & Shaw, S. F. (1987). A decision-making process for the college bound student: Matching learning, institution, and support program. *Learning Disability Quarterly, 10,* 106–111.

National Joint Committee on Learning Disabilities. (1983). *Learning disabilities: The needs of adults with learning disabilities.* A Position Paper of the National Joint Committee on Learning Disabilities. (ERIC Document Reproduction Service No. Ed 235 642.)

Nayman, A. L. (1982). College learning assistance services and the learning disabled college student. In M. R. Schmidt & H. Z. Sprandel, *New directions for student services: Helping the learning disabled student* (no. 18) (pp. 69–85). San Francisco: Jossey Bass.

Okolo, C. M., Sitlington, P. (1986). The role of special education in LD adolescents transition from school to work. *Learning Disability Quarterly, 9,* 141–155.

Pace, R. C. (1984). *Measuring the quality of college student experiences: An account of the development and use of the College Student Questionnaire.* Los Angeles: Higher Education Research Institute, UCLA Publication Services.

Palincsar, A. S., & Brown, A. L. (1984). Reciprocal teaching of comprehension-fostering and comprehension-monitoring activities. *Cognition and Instruction. I*, 117–175.

Phelps, M. (1985). *Compendium of project profiles.* Transition Institute at Champaign, IL.

Price, L., & Johnson, K. E. (1986). The secondary to post-secondary transition process for learning disabled adolescents and adults: An annotated bibliography (Report No. EC192125). Washington, DC: Department of Education. (ERIC Document Reproduction Service No. ED 280 224.)

Putnam, M. L. (1984). Post-secondary education for learning disabled students: A review of the literature. *Journal of College Student Personnel, 25*(1), 68–75.

Rawson, M. B. (1968). *Developmental language disability: Adult accomplishments of dyslexic boys.* Baltimore, MD: Johns Hopkins Press.

Rehabilitation Act of 1973. Section 504, 1973.

Sarns, J. (1986). Then was then: Now was now. *AHSSPE Bulletin, 4*(3), 80–83.

Seidenberg, P. L. (1986). *The high school/college connection: A guide for the transition of learning disabled students.* New York: Long Island University Transition Project. Document #8.

Sergent, M. T., Carter, R., Sedlacek, W. E., & Scales, W. R. (1988). A five-year analysis of disabled student services in higher education. *Journal of Postsecondary Education and Disability, 6*, 21–27.

Shaw, S. F., & McGuire, S. M. (1987). *Preparing learning disabled high school students for post-secondary education.* Chicago: Paper presented at the annual convention of the Council for Exceptional Children, (ERIC Document Reproduction Service No. ED 285 316.)

Siperstein, G. N. (1988). Students with learning disabilities in college: The need for a programmatic approach to critical transitions. *Journal of Learning Disabilities, 21*(7), 431–436.

Smith, C. (1986). The future of the LD field: Intervention approaches. *Journal of Learning Disabilities, 19*(8), 461–472.

Smith, C. R. (1991). *Learning Disabilities* (2nd ed.). Boston: Allyn and Bacon.

Smith, S. (1986, July 23). *College students with learning disabilities: Identification and teaching.* Paper presented at a faculty development program. New Brunswick, NJ: Rutgers University.

Weinstein, C. E., Zimmerman, S. A., & Palmer, D. R. (1988). Assessing learning strategies: The design and development of the LASSI. In C. Weinstein, E. Goetz, & P. Alexander (Eds.), *Learning and study strategies: Issues in assessment, instruction, and evaluation* (pp. 25–40). New York: Academic Press.

Zetlin, A. G., & Gosseini, A. (1989). Six postschool case studies of mildly learning handicapped young adults. *Exceptional Children, 55*, 405–411.

Appendix A

Social Skills Intervention Programs

PROGRAMS SPECIFICALLY GEARED TO SOCIAL SKILLS

Preschool/Primary

Title: Let's Be Social
Author: Social Integration Project, adapted by Linda Levine
Publisher: Communication Skills Builders,
    3830 E. Bellevue/P.O. Box 42050-E91,
    Tucson, Arizona 85733
Description: This program includes easy-to-use lesson plans that focus on language-based social skills for preschool at-risk children. The lesson plans are flexible enough to use with the entire class and to integrate handicapped students into classroom interactions. The kit includes a manual, illustrated social situation cards, two card puppets, and a storage box.

Title: Play Together, Grow Together: A Cooperative Curriculum for Teachers of Young Children
Authors: Don Adcock and Marilyn Segal
Publisher: Mailman Family Press
Description: This is a collection of 67 activities that focus on the early development of social skills, such as sharing, cooperating, playing in a group, and making friends.

Title: Taking Part: Introducing Social Skills to Children
Authors: Gwendolyn Cartledge and James Kleefeld
Publisher: AGS, American Guidance Service,
    4201 Woodland Road, P.O. Box 99
    Circle Pines, MN 55014-1796
Description: This program has 30 stimulating lessons, filled with activities that make it fun to learn and teach social skills. The six units address making conversation, expressing oneself, communicating nonverbally, co-operating with peers, playing with peers, and responding to aggression. It can be used with children from regular and special education classrooms

311

from preschool through grade 3. The materials include a manual, puppets, reinforcement puppet stickers, and skill posters.

Title: Taking Part: Introducing Social Skills to Young Children
Authors: Gwendolyn Cartledge and James Kleefield
Publisher: AGS, American Guidance Service
4201 Woodland Road, P.O. Box 99
Circle Pines, MN 55014-1796
Description: This is a preK–3 social skills curriculum linked directly to assessment. Through sociodramatic role play, stories, masks, and practice, young children learn the skills they need to get along with others both in the classroom and at home. This program can be used for regular and special education classrooms.

Elementary

Title: Social Decision-Making Skills: A Curriculum Guide for the Elementary Grades
Authors: M. J. Elias and J. F. Clabby
Publisher: Aspen, Rockville, Maryland
Description: This is a curriculum developed for elementary-age students that can be used in both regular and special education classes to teach decision making and interpersonal problem solving skills. It can also be used with middle and high school students and parents. The curriculum provides for two readiness areas and eight steps for social decision making and problem solving. The curriculum guide is also complete with sample worksheets, directions for how to teach students to role play, and many helpful "teaching tips."

Title: The Walker Social Skills Curriculum
The ACCEPTS Program: A Curriculum for Children's Effective Peer and Teacher Skills
Authors: Hill M. Walker, Scott McConnell, Deborah Holmes, Bonnie Todis, Jackie Walker, and Nancy Golden
Publisher: Pro-Ed
8700 Shoal Creek Boulevard
Austin, Texas 78758-6897
Description: ACCEPTS is a complete curriculum for teaching classroom and peer-to-peer social skills to handicapped and nonhandicapped children in grades K–6. The curriculum, designed for use by regular and special education teachers, teaches social skills as subject matter content. The program includes a nine-step instructional procedure, scripts that teach important social skills, and behavioral management procedures. An op-

tional color videotape demonstrates children using the classroom competencies and social skills in the ACCEPTS program.

Title: SSS: Social Skills Strategies
Authors: Nancy Gajewski and Patty Mayo
Publisher: Thinking Publications
1731 Westgate Road, P.O. Box 163
Eau Claire, WI 54702-0163
Description: Through structured activities, focused discussions, visualization tasks, and home assignments, youth learn 63 appropriate skills to sur-
vive socially and to perform better academically and vocationally too. This
has been useful for students who have language disorders, LD, behavioral
disturbances, or mild retardation.

Adolescents

Title: The Walker Social Skills Curriculum
The ACCESS Program: Adolescent Curriculum for Communication
and Effective Social Skills
Authors: Hill M. Walker, Bonnie Todis, Deborah Holmes, and Gary
Horton
Publisher: Pro-Ed
8700 Shoal Creek Boulevard
Austin, Texas 78758-6897
Description: ACCESS is a complete curriculum for teaching effective
social skills to students at middle and high school levels. The program
teaches peer-to-peer skills, skills for relating to adults, and self-management
skills. The ACCESS curriculum, which is designed for use by both regular
and special education teachers, can be taught in one-to-one, small-group, or
large-group instruction formats. ACCESS contains teaching scripts for 30
social skills; an eight-step instructional procedure; a student study guide;
and suggestions for grouping of students; as well as motivational, behavior
management, and generalization strategies.

Title: The Waksman Social Skills Curriculum: An Assertive Behavior Pro-
gram for Adolescents (3rd edition)
Authors: Steven Waksman, Cooki Landis Messmer, and Deborah Denney
Waksman
Publisher: Pro-Ed
8700 Shoal Creek Boulevard
Austin, Texas 78758-6897
Description: This is a complete program for teaching adolescents appro-
priate assertive behavior skills. The 9-week, 18-lesson format contains
specific instructions, activities, worksheets, and homework assignments.

Lessons include getting along with peers, teachers and family; expressing feelings appropriately; accepting criticism; problem solving; reducing tension and anger; communicating more effectively; and displaying assertive and self-confident behavior. The program can be used for handicapped and nonhandicapped students and is particularly helpful with children and adolescents who display behavior disorders, hyperactivity, and emotional problems.

Title: Scripting: Social Communication for Adolescents
Authors: Patty Mayo and Patti Waldo
Publisher: Thinking Publications
        1731 Westgate Road, P.O. Box 163
        Eau Claire, WI 54702-0163
Description: This provides young people with opportunities to practice valuable social skills through a script approach. Students assume the characters in each script as they dramatize situations presented. Scripts are provided for each of 53 social communication skills. Scripts are written at approximately a fifth-grade readability level, but even nonreaders can benefit from ideas presented in "Scripting."

Title: Social Skills for Daily Living
Senior Developers: Jean Bragg Schumaker, J. Stephen Hazel, and Colleen
        S. Pederson
Publisher: AGS, American Guidance Service
        4201 Woodland Road, P.O. Box 99
        Circle Pines, MN 55014-1796
Description: "Social Skills for Daily Living" has been suggested for special education students from ages 12 to 21 years. The program teaches 30 social skills that students need to function more effectively in the school and in the community. Each skill has been divided into different modules that follow an effective instructional sequence: awareness, practice, and application. The kit includes an instructor's manual, skills books, workbooks, comic books, practice cards, and Blackline Masters.

Title: Essential Social Skills
Publisher: EBSCO Curriculum Materials
        Division of EBSCO Industries, Inc., Box 11521
        Birmingham, Alabama 35202
Description: This program provides a variety of exercises and activities addressing social situations typically experienced by most teenagers; for example, dating, sex roles. It includes spirit duplicating masters.

Multi-Age

Title: Developing Social Acceptability

Publisher: Walker Educational Book Corp.
720 Fifth Avenue
New York, New York 10019

Description: This program has been designed for *parents* of children of all ages in special education. It is a training program for helping the handicapped child interact smoothly in the community. Emphasis is on personal health care and grooming and basic social skills. It includes a 208-page manual and 67 picture cards.

PROGRAMS SPECIFICALLY TARGETING FEELINGS AND SELF-ESTEEM

Preschool

Title: I Am, I Can, I Will: Mister Rogers Audiotapes, Books and Videotapes
Developed by: Mister Rogers and Family Communications, Inc.
Publisher: Pro-Ed
8700 Shoal Creek Boulevard
Austin, Texas 78758-6897

Description: The Mister Rogers materials reinforce students' positive self-images by encouraging them to explore what they can do and helping them to understand their feelings. These materials are ideal for teachers who work with preschool and primary grade children, and they can be used in regular or special education classes. The kit includes 15 audiotapes that help children understand their individual strengths and weaknesses and develop positive feelings about themselves and others; 5 books by Mister Rogers that contain stories, activities, and things to think about for very young children of all ability levels; and a series of videotapes designed to help teachers discuss and explore with young children their feelings and fears about shyness, being mad, feeling left out, happy, or sad, and much more.

Title: Have Fun with Your Feelings
Publisher: Childswork/Childsplay
Center For Applied Psychology—3rd Floor
441 N. 5th St.
Philadelphia, PA 19123

Description: This is a game to help children express feelings. Deck of 64 playing cards depicts 16 different emotions in four suits. It includes instructions for four games already familiar to most children: Concentration, Crazy Eights, Go Fish, and Rummy. Ages 4–10.

Elementary

Title: 9 to 19: Crucial Years for Self-Esteem in Children and Youth
Author: James Battle

Publisher: Academic Therapy Publications
20 Commercial Boulevard
Novato, CA 94949-6191
Description: Dr. Battle offers 110 strategies that have been documented in actual case reports to show how positive shifts in self-esteem can be induced in students and offspring. He offers concrete ways to identify the problems and what to do to correct them, both in the classroom and in the home.

Title: Seeds of Self-Esteem: An All-School Program
Authors: Robert B. Brooks, Jane Ward, and Gerard Pottebaum
Publisher: AGS, American Guidance Service
4201 Woodland Road, P.O. Box 99
Circle Pines, MN 55014-1796
Description: This inservice program has been designed for classroom teachers from K–12 to help cultivate a supportive classroom environment and to develop the self-esteem of students. Detailed descriptions of inservice ideas and strategies plus engaging anecdotal examples are provided. The kit includes two videotapes, a teacher's handbook, a journal, and posters.

Title: 200 ways to Enhance Self-concept in the Classroom
Publisher: Canfield and Wells, Prentice-Hall
Englewood Cliffs, NJ 07632
Description: This is a book with a variety of activities to enhance self-concept in the elementary school.

Title: Feelings
Developed by: ATC Publishing Corp., J.S. Latta, Inc.
P.O. Box 1795
Santa Monica, California 90406
Description: Primary to intermediate. Light-hearted stories help children understand and deal with feelings. Appropriate for children with learning problems. Each set consists of four color filmstrips with four cassettes. Set 1: Feelings—"Outside/Inside," "When I Grow Up," "I Am Many Different People," and "Stop Acting Like a Baby." Set 2: Feelings—"That's Not Fair," "Everybody's Afraid of Something," "G-r-r-r-r," and "But I Don't Know How."

Title: Understanding Your Fears
Developed by: Opportunities for Learning, Inc.
8950 Lurline Ave., Department 9AB
Chatsworth, CA 91311
Description: Filmstrips introduce the emotions of anger, fear, sadness, and happiness. Children learn ways of expressing these emotions and are encouraged to discuss their feelings.

Title: Get in Touch with Your Emotions
Produced by: Kimbo Educational Activities
P.O. Box 477
Long Branch, New Jersey 07740
Description: Grades 3 to 6. Color filmstrips help students become more aware of their emotions. Manual contains scripts and discussion questions. Titles include: "It's Natural to Be Angry or Afraid," "You Can Show Love and Affection," "Adjusting to Unhappiness," "The Brighter Side of Life." Set of four filmstrips, two cassettes, and a manual are included in the kit.

Adolescent

Title: Pouvant I: A Semester-Long Course in Self-Esteem for Middle and High School Students
Author: Frank Dane
Publisher: Pro-Ed
8700 Shoal Creek Boulevard
Austin, Texas 78758-6897
Description: This is a step-by-step classroom curriculum program for students from 12 to 18 years of age who are in regular or alternative classes. The activities are intended to help students improve their self-esteem, as well as their ability to introspect, to reflect, to communicate their thoughts and feelings, to interact cooperatively with others, and to make mature decisions. The manual is accompanied by an hour-long audiocassette tape that can be used for relaxing and imaging exercises.

Title: How to Cure Low Self-Esteem
Author: Raymond J. Maloney
Publisher: Academic Therapy Publications
20 Commercial Boulevard
Novato, CA 94949-6191
Description: This self-help book presents the results of workshops conducted with more than 10,000 people. It is loaded with practical, down-to-earth strategies that work. Key topics include risk taking, self-motivation, forgiving and forgetting the past, and goal setting.

PROGRAMS SPECIFICALLY TARGETING SOCIAL UNDERSTANDING OR SOCIAL PROBLEM SOLVING

Elementary age (and younger)

Title: DUSO-Revised: Developing Understanding of Self and Others
Authors: Don Dinkmeyer, Sr. and Don Dinkmeyer, Jr.

Publisher: AGS, American Guidance Service
4201 Woodland Road, P.O. Box 99
Circle Pines, MN 55014-1796

Description: This program has been suggested for regular and special education students from K–4. Duso the Dolphin helps children build self-esteem, social awareness, and problem-solving abilities through a variety of activities, songs, discussions, and stories. The kit includes a teacher's guide, story books, audiocassettes, activity cards, puppets, discussion pictures, charts, and a storage case.

Title: Think Aloud: Increasing Social and Cognitive Skills—A Problem-Solving Program for Children
Publisher: Research Press
Box 31773
Champaign, Illinois 61821

Description: Structured learning activities are designed to help elementary school children think through social situations and cope with various problems. Children are trained in problem-solving techniques and ways to use self-speech to direct social behavior. The program is divided into three levels: grades 1–2, grades 3–4, and grades 5–6.

Title: Learning to Care: Classroom Activities for Social and Affective Development
Publisher: Scott, Foresman and Company
1900 East Lake Avenue
Glenview, Illinois 60025

Description: This program consists of instructional activities designed to help elementary children (1) recognize and label various emotions, (2) assume and experience another's viewpoint, and (3) empathize with the experiences of others.

PROGRAMS SPECIFICALLY TARGETING PROBLEM BEHAVIORS

Elementary

Title: Making Friends
Developed by: BFA Educational Media
2211 Michigan Ave.,
P.O. Box 1795
Santa Monica, CA 90406

Description: Grades 4 to 6. Captioned filmstrips explore desirable personality and behavior traits. Designed as a unit in personal guidance with review frames and checklists for students to rate themselves. Titles include: "How Do You Rate at Home?" "How Do You Rate at School?", and "How Do You Rate with Your Friends?" Set of three filmstrips (captioned).

Appendix B:

Example Résumé

Sally Smith
100 Angela Lane
Anytown, GA 08888
(404) 123-4568

OBJECTIVE:
> To apply basic business and clerical skills training in a full-time, permanent position.

EDUCATION:
> Jennings High School, 128 Jennings Road, Anytown, GA 08888
>> Graduation date: May 1992
>> Special classes in: Basic Business Skills, Clerical Training, Interpersonal Skills, Home Economics.

EXPERIENCES:
> Uncle Joe's Burger Chain, 695 Shannon Lane, Anytown, GA 08888
>> May–August, 1991. SERVER.
>> Responsibilities included: Meeting and greeting customers; receiving and filling food orders; food preparation; clean up.
>
> Jennings High School, 128 Jennings Road, Anytown GA 08888
>> September, 1989–May 1991. Volunteer TIME-KEEPER.
>> Duties included: Accurate keeping of team members' performances; checking times with other time keepers; turning in completed time sheets under a time constraint.
>
> Young Women's Christian Association. 16 Christopher Street. Anytown, GA 08888
>> September–May, 1988–1991. Volunteer CHILD CARE WORKER.
>> Duties included: Receiving elementary-age students from transportation shuttle; providing after-school care; developed and presented four different after-school activities involving kitchen skills, manners, and careers.

REFERENCES: Provided upon request.

Index